MW00379553

The Real World Guide to Psychotherapy Practice

The Real World Guide to Psychotherapy Practice

EDITED BY

Alex N. Sabo and Leston Havens

Harvard University Press
Cambridge, Massachusetts, and London, England
2000

Library of Congress Cataloging-in-Publication Data

The real world guide to psychotherapy practice / edited by Alex N. Sabo and
      Leston Havens.
    p. cm.
  Includes bibliographical references and index.
  ISBN 0-674-00324-1 (alk. paper)
    1. Psychotherapy. 2. Psychotherapist and patient. 3. Managed mental health care.
    I. Sabo, Alex N., 1952-   II. Havens, Leston L.

RC480.5.R3655 2000
616.89—dc21   00-040975
Designed by Gwen Nefsky Frankfeldt

*To our families, who have supported us
and taught us so much*

Contents

Contributors

TODD GRISWOLD, M.D., is an Instructor in Psychiatry, Harvard Medical School at the Cambridge Hospital.

JAMES P. GUSTAFSON, M.D., is Professor of Psychiatry, University of Wisconsin Medical School. He is also the author of *The Complex Secret of Brief Psychotherapy, Self-Delight in a Harsh World, Brief Versus Long Psychotherapy, The Dilemmas of Brief Psychotherapy, The New Interpretation of Dreams,* and *A Guide to the Most Common Dynamics in Psychiatry.*

LESTON HAVENS, M.D., is Professor of Psychiatry, Harvard Medical School at the Cambridge Hospital. He is also the author of *Approaches to the Mind, Participant Observation, Making Contact, A Safe Place, Learning to be Human,* and *Coming to Life.*

CEDAR R. KOONS, L.I.C.S.W., is a Consulting Associate, Department of Psychiatry and Behavioral Sciences, Duke University Medical Center, a Consultant with Behavioral Technology Transfer Group, and is in private practice in Santa Fe, New Mexico.

ALFRED MARGULIES, M.D., is Associate Professor of Psychiatry, Harvard Medical School at the Cambridge Hospital and is Training and Supervising Analyst, Psychoanalytic Institute of New England, East. He is also the author of *The Empathic Imagination.*

EMILY NEWMAN, M.D., is Assistant Clinical Professor, Department of Psychiatry, University of California, San Francisco.

CAREN PLANK, M.A., L.M.H.C., L.M.F.T., is in private practice in Brooksville, Maine.

BLISS INUI RAND, M.D., is an Instructor in Psychiatry, Harvard Medical School at the Cambridge Hospital.

CLIVE J. ROBINS, PH.D., is Associate Clinical Professor of Psychiatry, Department of Psychiatry and Behavioral Sciences, Duke University Medical Center.

ALEX N. SABO, M.D., is Chairman of the Department of Psychiatry and Behavioral Sciences, Berkshire Medical Center; Director of Psychiatry for the Joint Venture with Mental Health and Substance Abuse Services of the Berkshires; Lecturer on Psychiatry, Harvard Medical School at the Cambridge Hospital; and Associate Professor of Clinical Psychiatry, University of Massachusetts Medical School.

DONALD SCHERLING, PSY.D., M.DIV., C.A.D.C., is Director of the McGee Unit Substance Abuse Treatment Program at Berkshire Medical Center.

JANNA MALAMUD SMITH, L.I.C.S.W., is a Lecturer on Psychology, Harvard Medical School at the Cambridge Hospital. She is also the author of *Private Matters: In Defense of the Personal Life.*

The Real World Guide to Psychotherapy Practice

Introduction: Psychotherapy at the Start of a New Century

Alex N. Sabo

The Value of Relationship

Twenty-five years ago Leston Havens identified the major schools of psychiatric thought—the biologic descriptive, the psychoanalytic, the interpersonal, and the existential—and argued that each had its place in a psychotherapist's tool chest.[1] Each therapist has a natural inclination toward a type of psychotherapy: understanding the structure and function of the mind, looking underneath the surface of symptoms and thoughts, looking at the interdependence of people in a social field, or "being with" a person struggling against isolation. Each therapist should recognize his or her own inclinations, learn the theory and techniques that elaborate them, but then develop skills in the other areas as well. People who present for psychotherapeutic help come with varied problems set in the context of very different life circumstances, and no single school of psychotherapy can serve them all. One type of psychotherapy may be appropriate now, while another fits the circumstances and the person's need at a later point. The principle of developing one's skills in diverse approaches and applying them to suit an individual's need is as sound today as it was then. An effective relationship is the vehicle through which a therapist intelligently makes this determination.

The hegemony of psychoanalysis a quarter-century ago and the relative affluence of the health care system at that time created a climate in which consumers of health care expected long-term psychotherapeutic treatments. Teaching programs often subsidized the long-term psychotherapies of those who could not pay. Typical psychotherapies involved relationships between patient and therapist that existed over several, if not many, years.

Psychotherapy has undergone radical change in the past few decades. Although private practice provides opportunities for therapists and patients who wish to practice as they choose, even those private practitioners who choose to accept insurance payments are becoming more highly regulated by managed care. Psychoanalysis and its assumptions have been extensively critiqued at the same time that many of its basic concepts have found their way into our cultural ethos.

The long-term therapeutic relationship is a casualty of today's health care. This stems from two reasons: first, managed care is organized to limit health care spending in general, and, with respect to behavioral health care, specifically to limit the number of psychotherapy sessions a person may receive. In many teaching programs, and in almost all community mental health centers and health maintenance organizations, utilization review committees scrutinize any case that exceeds eight sessions and certainly any case that requests "free care" or a sliding fee scale. Second, the scramble of managed care companies to close panels to new providers and the frequent acquisitions and mergers of health care plans often mean that people lose their therapists when their health care coverage changes. Therapists themselves move from institution to institution and from place to place searching for a better working environment, and these changes also lead to therapeutic disruptions. Taken as a whole, these developments make it difficult for a therapist and client (or patient) to develop a long-term therapeutic relationship.

Another current development is that cognitive-behavioral psychotherapies, with a sound research literature supporting their efficacy in several disorders, are bringing time-limited, practical, step-by-step approaches to their delivery. Despite the fact that they require a sound relationship to achieve their results, they are popular with the managed care industry both because of their efficacy and for the hope that they will provide a brief formula for success regardless of the practitioner providing the therapy. These treatments will be guided by manuals. One pill or one formula for "cognitive restructuring" can be delivered by "any willing provider" to the "covered life." Outcomes will be measured, and a continuing quality improvement program will accompany the delivery of the service. But will anyone attend to the unique qualities of the individual seeking help or to the particular circumstances of the person's life? Does the individual life survive, or do we structure a health care of psychosocial sameness?

Against this background, we assert in this book that an effective relationship is the essential first step toward ensuring quality in psychotherapy and pharmacotherapy. An individual psyche and the biochemistry that serves its function are always set in a complex social context and personal history. The relationship is the vehicle for understanding and respecting this complexity and for developing the most effective psychotherapy or pharmacotherapy. In the grander scheme, we also believe that attention to the quality of relationship ensures the survival of the individual, the carrier of human experience.

It is our belief that this approach will outlast the current impulses to conceptualize care for people with mental illness as "one size fits all." A medical director of one of the largest behavioral-health managed care companies recently remarked that any therapist who needs more than eight sessions to solve a mental health problem has "a seriously flawed method" of treating patients. He teaches his case reviewers to make this assumption when they scrutinize a case. We hope that managed care companies learn to support the value of a therapeutic relationship, whether brief, intermittent, or long-term.

A sound alliance established in a first session often makes a brief treatment possible. Attention to the quality of relationship proves "cost-effective" when the total consequences of not forming effective relationships are considered: misdiagnosis, doctor-shopping, downward spiral, poor compliance, litigation, and so on. In treating mental illnesses, diagnosis is highly dependent on the history and symptoms that a patient is able to explain. The quality of the relationship with the doctor or psychotherapist profoundly influences the quality of the information that the therapist uses to make the diagnosis. Mediocre or poor relationships lead healthier patients to search for better therapists and waste time in getting to the heart of the problem that brings them into treatment. The sicker patients do not have the capacity or the strength to find better therapists when the relationship is poor, and that leaves them exposed to less than optimal treatments. Some borderline patients, some with the stubbornness of a psychosis or a tendency to somatize, rapidly escalate into a stalemate or even a downward spiral when the relationship with the therapist settles into a comfortable pattern that brings out the worst in the person's pathological repertoire. Instead of solving the problem, an ineffective relationship accentuates the problem and makes the treatment more costly both in dollars and in terms of the patient's self-esteem.

Often, the patients with the most difficult illnesses—the severe depressions, some of the schizophrenias and bipolar illnesses, and some of the borderline cases—require medications and the most careful coordination of their care among a team of treaters. In these cases compliance with medications is highly dependent on the quality of the relationship with the therapist and/or doctor. Whether the treatment proceeds at all is dependent on trust in the relationship, and there will inevitably be times when the treatment is uncertain, and only trust in the relationship allows the patient and therapist to struggle through the confusion to a more secure place. Without an effective relationship, these treatments are certainly more costly and repetitive, and sometimes even result in death. Another consequence of poor relationship is litigation. When trust and respect are at the core of a therapeutic effort, it is rare for a patient to sue a doctor or therapist, even when things go wrong. Litigation is always costly in terms of time, money, and the well-being and emotional energy of the parties involved. Time spent ensuring quality of relationship at the onset of a therapeutic endeavor is time well spent.

How the Work Gets Done in a Rapidly Changing World

Psychotherapy works because of its capacity to rely on the chemistry of attachment and its influence on the symbol-forming capacity of the mind, that is, a person's ability to attach meaning and emotional energy to an insight, idea, or icon. Current economic incentives stress psychotherapies that favor the latter. Limiting costs by strictly limiting sessions often backfires because the cost of not supporting the development of a relationship is often far greater than the cost of supporting it. Sometimes a change in the meaning of a symbol will effect a lasting change, yet often it is the quality of an effective relationship that allows proper understanding of a symbol to unfold.

While psychiatrists often complain about the intrusions of managed care into clinical practice, social work is, perhaps, the discipline most entrusted with the fate of relationship in the practice of psychotherapy. Social workers represent the single largest group of clinicians practicing psychotherapy. By their sheer numbers, they bear the greatest pressure to keep psychotherapy brief and "cost-effective."

They are on the front lines of community mental health centers and HMOs, as well as private practice. They treat many of the most difficult clients and many clients who have the most adverse social circumstances. They are pushed both by managed care and by necessity to do brief cognitive-behavioral, solution-focused, and supportive psychotherapies—all this in the face of the very dire life circumstances of the people they treat. Thus social workers, perhaps more than any other discipline, feel the tension between using a brief treatment model and building a relationship with their clients that is sensitive to the complexity of the client's individual circumstances. Janna Smith's chapter in this volume, "Psychotherapy with People Stressed by Poverty" (Chapter 3), poignantly illustrates one therapist's effort to address such complexity. Forming effective relationships under difficult circumstances is central to the task of social workers on the front line and central to the focus of this book.

Clinical psychologists are the most under-appreciated of the professionals practicing psychotherapy today. After years of intensive studies involving the scientific basis of psychopathology and its treatment, they emerge from their clinical programs to face a world of diminished support. Academic appointments are scarce, reimbursements slim, insurance panels often closed, and the extensive loans needed to get through graduate school are coming due. Yet these therapists are often the best trained in cognitive-behavioral psychotherapy, interpersonal therapy, and solution-focused therapies, and they often have the clearest conceptual understanding of what it is that they are trying to do. Thus it is fitting that dialectical behavioral therapy, one of the most innovative psychotherapies to emerge over the past ten years, was developed by a clinical psychologist. Though the therapy is often explained in cognitive-behavioral terms, the quality of the relationship is shaped by the conceptualization of the problem and its treatment. In Chapter 10, Clive Robins and Cedar Koons explore the significance of relationship while skillfully applying the concepts of dialectical behavioral therapy. In Chapter 4, Donald Scherling, another clinical psychologist, describes the use of relationships to move a group of violent men toward the beginnings of respect and compassion for one another.

Even pharmacotherapies require that doctors form effective relationships with their patients. The medications themselves often take six to twelve weeks to work, and much healing can begin before that through the power of an effective relationship. The longer-term man-

agement of a difficult illness also requires an effective relationship to
share information and arrive at complex decisions regarding options
for treatment. Relationship actually affects the biochemistry of the
physiological processes that impact mental illnesses. Consider the antidepressant effects of the natural hormone oxytocin, or the opiate-mediated separation cry that is at the core of mammalian physiology.[2] "Good chemistry" is literally good chemistry.

Despite numerous studies that support the efficacy of psychotherapy and a national survey documenting consumers' satisfaction with
its benefits, there is a pervasive effort in the managed care industry to
seriously limit its use. Support is instead given to pharmacotherapies
both because they are effective and also because they will limit the expense of doctors spending time with patients. Recent legislation has
given nurses with master's degrees and appropriate certification the
privilege to prescribe medication in order to greatly increase the numbers of patients who receive psychotropic medication. Some hypothe-
size that in the future, psychiatrists will do no psychotherapy at all
and will become neuroscientific consultants with a distribution of one
per 25,000 "covered lives."[3]

This creates a dilemma for the psychiatrist today, if he or she understands the value of relationship in the healing process. We know
that the "placebo effect" is an important factor in pharmacological
interventions, and that the prescribing doctor achieves a good result,
in part, from the effect of a positive relationship and the patient's
hope that something salutary will come from it. We also know that
clinicians who form effective relationships with their patients produce
better outcomes. Will the psychiatrist as neuroscientist and consultant lose crucial information that derives from a good relationship
with the patient as well as the opportunity for healing that comes, in
part, from the relationship? This matter is not yet settled, but there
has already been dramatic change.

Over the past thirty years, the psychiatrist's dyadic role with patients has been greatly altered. Psychiatrists continue to evaluate and
sometimes manage cases, but the emphasis on psychotherapy has
shifted to an emphasis on evaluation, monitoring medications, and
managing risk. As a result of these changes, psychiatrists treat many
more patients who are also treated by other people. Most patients receive psychotherapy from social workers, nurses with master's degrees, or clinical psychologists. They may receive practical advice as
well as supportive psychotherapy from nurses or case managers with

bachelor's degrees. Substance abuse counselors and sponsors from AA and NA are sometimes involved as well. Beyond these professionals and self-helpers, a host of medical providers may be involved: primary care doctors, their nurses and support staff, and, if the patient has a specific chronic illness, his or her medical specialist, such as a neurologist, cardiologist, or rheumatologist. In addition, the greater access to medical information afforded by the Internet introduces another "player" in the clinical system. For those patients with Internet access and the wherewithal to use it, medical databases provide abundant information about illnesses and the various medications available to treat them. Thus, the relationship of doctor and patient is embedded in an increasingly complex caregiving system.

The expanded role of advanced practice nurses in prescribing medication illustrates the increasingly complex relationship among treaters and treated. In 1993, the Massachusetts State Legislature enacted Chapter 112, Section 80b, "An Act Relative to Expanding the Role of Nurses in the Delivery of Health Services," which, among other things, gave nurses with a master's degree in behavioral health (registered nurse, clinical specialist; RNCS) the right to prescribe psychotropic medications under the supervision of a psychiatrist. The psychiatrist and RNCS develop a scope of practice agreement that conforms to the state law, Department of Public Health, and Board of Registration in Nursing regulations. Managed care companies also produce "performance specifications" which address issues such as supervision and clinical situations that require consultation with the supervising psychiatrist. The RNCS uses the federal Drug Enforcement Administration and state controlled-substance registration numbers of the supervising psychiatrist as well as her own. The psychiatrist and RNCS are "equally responsible" for the care of the patient.

Using similar strategies, federal, state, business, and managed care industry efforts are aimed at keeping health expenditures down. The new business managers of health care put the goal simply: "lower cost per unit of service." One strategy involves limiting the time that doctors spend with patients. Laws like the Massachusetts Act (Chapter 112, Section 80b) described above encourage the more extensively trained and expensively educated physicians to interact with their patients through "physician extenders," less expensively trained and less expensive professionals who provide good care under the right circumstances. If taken to its extreme, this approach means that physicians eventually might never interact directly with their patients. "Extenders" might come to include computer software programs that would form cyber-relationships with patients and gather the data; the physician would deal with patients by reviewing computer-generated referrals and other reports from those who take the history and examine the patient. There is no doubt that medical practice is moving farther in this direction, and some good has already come from it. Still, thinking about how far it could go is unsettling. Should the physician "supervise" the care by never meeting the patient in person, but rather by talking with the direct provider and reviewing the data? Many of us already provide a number of such "curbside consults" each day, but these are for cases where we are not identified as the primary caregiver. We are not "equally responsible" for the care of the patients for whom we give these types of consultations. What does equal responsibility mean, if the physician has never met the patient?

Few physicians would ultimately subscribe to the extreme implications of this approach, and it is doubtful that consumers of health care would agree either. The use of the concept of "physician extender" to exclude the physician from having any in-person relationship with the patient doesn't work because there is art (as well as science) in the practice of medicine. The interview with the patient is a complex interactive process; different interviewers will get different data depending on how they interact with the patient. There is a science as well to the work, and one can examine how the interviewer affects the symptomatic data (what the patient explains about his condition) as well as how the patient feels (see also the comments on oxytocin and Substance P in Chapter 2). It is especially true in psychiatry, but also in other branches of medicine and surgery, that the relationship with the patient affects the quality of the data that the doctor gets from the patient, and it may actually affect the way the patient feels. The thesis of this book is that sound clinical practice involves building a sound relationship with the patient. How much relationship will work? How does one define good care under the right circumstances? The managed care organization overseeing behavioral health for Medicaid in Massachusetts currently requires the supervising doctor to see the patient at least once a year, and more frequently if the patient is suicidal, psychotic, or presenting a complex picture that is "beyond the scope of the RNCS practice." This performance standard attempts to answer our questions from a managed care company's point of view, but there is still a great deal of flexibility needed for this practice to evolve.

In my own clinical network, we have viewed the advent of the psychiatrist RNCS team with both enthusiasm and trepidation. We are enthusiastic about the quality of the nurses involved and their opportunity to develop a new set of skills and to practice in an advanced way. We hope that more patients will be seen in a timely manner. We have hired nurses in this role who have many years of experience doing psychotherapy or delivering other clinical care for patients and who have good skills in forming effective relationships. These skills make it more likely when a patient is becoming suicidal or psychotic that the nurses will experience the change in a way that leads to appropriate intervention and consultation. We have designed an ongoing psychopharmacology seminar attended by doctors and nurses which provides didactic material some of the time but mainly focuses on case presentation and discussion of the various approaches to clinical situations. The seminar is a forum for shared clinical experience and learning. It symbolizes a key element of effective relationship, whether between treater and patient or among treaters themselves: shared learning from experience.

Our trepidation about the new developments comes from two major areas: first, given the fact that most of the advanced practice nurses have significantly less psychopharmacological training than the doctors, are the RNCSs practicing beyond the scope of their expertise? Will this lead to serious adverse events? The supervising doctor is equally responsible, so just as most physicians worry a good deal about the difficult decisions they themselves make in a day, now there is worry about the decisions someone else is making. The doctor has responsibility with less control. Will the excellent clinical skills of the RNCSs and their experience in building effective relationships offset their less advanced training in psychopharmacology?

The second worry applies to the doctor's potential loss of direct relationship with patients. Will the advent of the RNCSs remove the doctor from any contact with his or her patients? The loss of the relationship may affect the patient's care *and* the health of the doctor. Good relationships make difficult work manageable. A busy chairman of a complex psychiatry department recently remarked that his eight hours of work per week seeing patients was "the only part of my job that keeps me sane." Relationship can have a healing quality, and it affects both parties.

Preliminary evidence from our experiment indicates a mostly positive outcome. Clinically shrewd to start with, the RNCSs we have enlisted do a very good job of handling more routine matters within the scope of their expertise, and they consult with the supervising psychiatrist when necessary. The doctor still sees plenty of patients, but has the opportunity to form a relationship with the patients (and sometimes their families) who have the more difficult problems. The doctor also has the opportunity to learn about the care of a larger number of patients than he or she normally would through review of the RNCS's work and discussions with her. In addition to extending outreach to a greater number of patients, the "physician extender" provides the opportunity to extend the psychiatrist's clinical experience and to extend his or her base of clinical support. The advantages of this system are thus a greater sense of professional connectedness, the regular input of another perspective on the work, a positive experience of support, and an opportunity to see more than one would if working alone.

This example illustrates the kinds of challenges to the role of relationship in healing posed by efforts to reduce health care costs. Such challenges call for deeper understanding of the various relationships that may lead to better outcomes for patients. In addition, we need a more complex understanding of the interaction of relationship with other dimensions of therapeutics.

The explosion of research in neuroscience is rapidly expanding our understanding of the functioning of the brain, and this research is used to support pharmacotherapies in place of psychotherapies. Yet this same research is also showing the powerful influence of the environment and individual learning on the actual structure and function of the brain. Relationship is a key element of psychotherapy and learning. Although pharmacological agents have been dramatically improved over the past twenty-five years, enlarging the scope of mental illness that is treatable, a shift away from psychotherapy is neither warranted by scientific data nor wanted by the consumers of health care. At the same time that there is an effort in the health care industry to limit psychotherapy, there are powerful cultural forces at work to expand its scope.

Psychotherapists may well constitute the fastest-growing profession in the United States.[4] They are called upon to replace diminished community supports, religious workers (themselves increasingly trained in psychotherapy), and more and more dispersed family members. Psychotherapists today address both our heightened expectations of life, in this country largely beyond food and shelter, and the breakdown of many conventional values. Our society confronts crises involving gender, longevity, race, changing family and work patterns, rapid social mobility within countries and across their boundaries, and a culture that encourages many addictions such as gambling and then must deal with the consequences. Choosing among values is a need to be addressed as much as symptom relief, while the recognition of psychological syndromes has expanded dramatically. Medications are widely prescribed, and the relief provided only increases the demand for a psychotherapy that deals with underlying problems. New legal requirements call upon psychological expertise, as in decisions about the termination of life or in Louisiana's two-tiered marriages: "covenant" marriages encourage the consultation of therapists and their use in the event of subsequent difficulties.[5] World-wide, a call goes out: "How do we determine and shape a life of our own?"— a central goal of psychotherapeutics, heard now from even the most ancient and settled cultures.

What are the essential elements of psychotherapy? The current scientific and economic environments encourage short-term and cognitive-behavioral psychotherapies, while considerable data suggest that common elements such as restoration of hope, an opportunity to practice new routines, and the quality of the psychotherapeutic relationship are important determinants of outcome. Consumers of psychotherapy report greater benefit and satisfaction from longer-term psychotherapies.[6] Perhaps the longer psychotherapies, no matter what their orientation, permit the development of a relationship between therapist and patient that is essential to psychotherapy's fullest benefit. Whether brief or longer-term, the therapeutic relationship is a key component of a successful psychotherapy. In this book, two of the more theoretical chapters (Clive Robins and Cedar Koons on dialectical behavior therapy, Chapter 10, and James Gustafson on brief therapy, Chapter 9) highlight the importance of psychological growth obtained through struggle with a dilemma. Does a strengthened self emerge from a person experiencing the tension of opposites? Carl Jung considered this tension fundamental to psychological development. The Romantic poet William Blake argued, "Without contraries there is no progression," and it may be that the relationship between therapist and patient serves as a container for the tension of opposites, the struggle with a dilemma, to stimulate growth. How does one go about building such a container? What tensions might it hold? How does courage develop in the context of relationship? Can we take the building of relationships for granted? We do not think so. People are complex and unique, and care must be taken from the start to see that the foundation is sound.

Leston Havens once remarked to me, "If I had the courage of my convictions, we would teach interviewing to residents in psychiatry by watching the Oprah Winfry Show." By this, he meant that Oprah's ability to "make conversation," to put people at ease, created a relaxed atmosphere in which something mutual and invigorating might occur between two people. We hope that the chapters in our book illustrate the details of mutuality and respect that are at the heart of creative human interaction, the art of psychotherapy.

Many of the contributors to this book at one time studied and practiced psychotherapy at the Cambridge Hospital, a teaching site of Harvard Medical School. This community-based program of psychiatric and substance abuse services for the people of Somerville and Cambridge, Massachusetts, has always emphasized the value of relationship in clinical work. It is an eclectic program where residents and interns are encouraged to discover for themselves what works and what doesn't. The services are available to all the people, rich or poor, acute or chronic, moderately or severely ill. The work is done in the community, close to the everyday experiences of the patients who are served. For the past six years, I have been fortunate to work with a group of clinicians and administrators in the Berkshires who share this vision of bringing services to patients in the community, regardless of the severity of their illness or ability to pay. At a time when psychotherapy is often reduced to algorithms and oversimplified by easy answers, we believe that the real-world, daily struggles of our patients give the work its dignity.

Part I of this book focuses on the essential elements of relationship. Chapter 1 addresses principles for building sound relationships, and Chapter 2 explores the role of relationship in psychopharmacological practice. Part II, "How the Work Gets Done," contains six chapters about difficult but common circumstances and the thinking of therapists who struggle with them. Part III, "Rethinking Psychotherapy," includes four theoretical chapters which address the way therapists integrate paradigms as they reconsider their work. The book also contains two commentaries and an epilogue. The commentaries are like river guides, placed at the beginning of Parts II and III to point out bends in the river or fast currents before they arrive. The epilogue speaks to the still unsolved problem of finding the person in the midst of our assumptions about health and illness. It is the editors' belief that our focus on relationship as well as on current trends will serve practitioners well as they navigate the rapids of change.

Notes

1. Havens, L. 1973. *Approaches to the Mind: Movement of the Psychiatric Schools from Sects Towards Science.* Boston: Little, Brown.
2. Sabo, A. N. 1996. "The Stress Response and the Separation Cry in Medical and Psychiatric Illness." *Berkshire Medical Journal,* 4(4):5–10.
3. Detre, T., and McDonald, M. C. 1997. "Managed Care and the Future of Psychiatry." *Archives of General Psychiatry,* 54:201–204.
4. Hacker, A. 1997. "The War Over the Family." *New York Review of Books,* 44 (19), December 4, 1997, p. 36.
5. Ibid.
6. Seligman, M. E. P. 1995. "The Effectiveness of Psychotherapy: The Consumer Reports Study." *American Psychologist,* 50:965–974.

I   The Relationship in Clinical Work

1 Forming Effective Relationships

Leston Havens

Prevailing practice is still modeled on the medical examination of dependable and cooperative patients through questions aimed at historical and contemporary details. Necessary as such an approach may seem in emergency situations, for general orientation, or to elicit symptoms and syndromes responsive to chemical agents, it assumes an objective and reliable informant. Psychiatric conditions, on the other hand, entail some measure of emotional, cognitive, volitional, or perceptual impingement on the integrity of the reporting person; hence the term *psych*iatric. Such problems are by definition hard to "get at," sometimes at the level of symptom-reporting and certainly beyond it. It is for this reason that practitioners are sought out.

It is for the same reason that forming effective relationships is difficult, just as it characteristically has been in the patients' personal and work lives. Special skills are needed but can be applied quickly and repeated in the course of other efforts, so that relatively little time is required.

What follows are, first, general principles for beginning the work; second, specific means to deal with common problems, for example, self-derogatory and dissembling trends; and, finally, the most frequent obstacles to carrying this difficult work through. The principal ways in which effective relationships can be thought to shape outcomes follow naturally from the ways in which specific obstacles have been overcome.

General Principles

With shy patients particularly, it is wise at first to seek common, unthreatening ground, which may require discussing the weather or other general interests. The best topics are those about which the patient can feel informed and confident because the idea is to meet initially as respectful people and only secondarily as therapist and mentally ill. Keep in mind that for many the therapist's decency and trustworthiness are not givens, and mental illness is a delicate subject.

There are three psychological analgesics that make possible an approach to painful subjects. The first and most important is protection of the patient's self-esteem. We can assume this is already endangered by the patient's being with us, so that significant relief follows from not threatening it more. If, in addition, we can raise the patient's self-esteem by respect and admiration, a path is cleared. We would do well to remember that the integrity of the persons before us, that is, their capacity to "hold it together" in order to inform us as well as to relate effectively, partly depends upon how they feel in our presence.

The second analgesic, some measure of understanding and accepting, depends upon a partial joining of perspectives. We all stare forth from individually shaped and genetically different nervous systems onto a world seen from this particular time and place by no one else. This means that understanding one another is difficult. To grasp a part of the patient's perspective relieves psychic pain by validating or revising that perspective and by providing a companion or ally to someone perhaps hitherto alone. By understanding and accepting is meant not only some intellectual grasp of the patient's predicament but an ability to see it from the other's point of view. We need to appreciate how perspectives can be painful: the situation may seem dangerous, hopeless, or humiliating, for example, because the patient has learned to pick out and emphasize threatening, despairing, or shaming possibilities. Such pain is relieved by being shared, that is, apportioned and divided with the sharer who then also experiences the pain, thereby validating it. ("No wonder you feel awful.") A painful perspective is relieved too by being seen afresh, in the light of happier possibilities, perhaps for actions not previously imagined. We also step inside the other's perspective so that any later movement outside that perspective will be better informed and accepted.

The third analgesic is provision of a future. A large number of patients come to us with little or no hope, even in this time of powerful chemicals; we flatter ourselves by thinking our presence is sufficient ground for belief in a viable future. It is therefore important to make allusion to a possible better life. This is best as only an allusion, since outright assurance will not yet be convincing, and it is easily appended to an empathic remark: "It seems hopeless to you *now.*"

These three analgesics facilitate honest and dependable reports. Without them defensive maneuvers (for example, outright lying) occur secondary to pain in the interview, distortions of perspective pass unnoticed and uncorrected, and the material elicited reflects only past or present experience without reference to possible changed circumstances.

Nothing destroys the development of an effective relationship more rapidly than the diagnostic, pathological ideas we communicate to patients. It is sad to assert this in the face of the great efforts that workers of all backgrounds make to increase their knowledge. It is equally true that our knowledge is necessary in predicting complications and dictating modes of action. Nevertheless, relatively untutored beginners often form the solidest and most supportive relationships. As a result, the experienced worker needs to recover some of the lightness and innocence with which he or she began.

In any case, there is no way to prevent therapists from developing ideas that the patient is sick or wrong, despite the chilling effects these ideas have on relationships. I recommend that such ideas be first seen as signs of the collision of the patient's and therapist's perspectives, that is, differences in the way each sees the world. A continued search can then be made to bridge the differences. For example, early in the first interview with a 25-year-old man, the interviewer felt the patient must be manic. The interviewer postponed this conclusion, however, to search for possible sources of the patient's excitement and agitation. It turned out that the patient had discovered his immediate boss was selling company secrets to a competitor. The patient was fearful of exposing the boss but eager to prevent the sale and perhaps take the boss's position. Hesitantly revealing this situation, and then hearing an appreciation of both the situation and his hopes, he became calmer and worked out a plan to inform higher company executives, which he carried through successfully. Over a three-year period, there were no further suggestions of mania. This incident can be seen as illustrating the value of placing the possibility of health before that of sickness, as in the legal presumption of innocence before guilt.

Even when the impression of pathology seems incontrovertible, as in bizarre delusional states, it is generally best to receive it hospitably rather than to correct or characterize it. This is done by taking the patient's side and looking for some justification of the patient's position. Our present knowledge of the causes of even extreme psychiatric states does not exclude situational and interpersonal factors; some believe, for example, that people may drive each other mad, as in folie à deux.

Many bizarre delusions appear to be, at least in part, efforts to explain puzzling situations and sensations, the illumination of which is often profitable. For example, some patients' ideas of influence by allegedly implanted electrodes seem related to the experience of being heavily under the influence of a dominant person who, in fact, does transmit strong ideas to the patient. A hospitable acceptance of such delusions avoids fruitless quarrels (together with repeated humiliation of the patient) and may establish a relationship strong enough to permit later, more objective review. Just as important, it signals to the patient that the worker has not prejudged him and has an open mind for unusual human experiences.

Not uncommonly an interviewer's rapid conclusion about the patient signals, instead, a rejecting or dehumanizing response that follows on the interviewer's being frightened or overwhelmed. Confronted by such feelings, which inevitably sweep over us in the course of the interview, we can protect ourselves best by an alert expectation of just this result. Indeed, the interviewer must not only anticipate unexpected feelings but welcome them as signs that the human process is engaged: we have met and are experiencing each other, however uncomfortably. It is not possible to stop such feelings. It *is* possible to learn from them.

For workers new to the intricacies of psychological treatment, this is lesson number one: keep alert to your felt responses to the patients. Lesson number two is the obverse: be alert to your emotional impact on the patients. Nothing so clearly identifies the experienced worker as the care with which the interviewer uses herself or himself, by which I mean the level of attention to untoward impacts on the patient and one's ability to offset them subtly and easily. "Gentleness" conveys part of this stance, but every worker must learn to blend into his or her spontaneous approach different elements that make good work with a wide range of personalities possible. I introduced this need before when I referred to the ready impingements on the integrity of their persons that psychiatric patients bring to the interview. For example, patients may unpredictably take offense or not be effective at protecting themselves or offer bait to depreciate them with: a full list comes near to describing the problems of the work as a whole. It is these difficulties that we must be prepared for, not with the expectation of preventing them, but in order to note them quickly and compensate.

If an impingement is habitual, we will not only become familiar with it, we will be positioned to "lean against it"—to begin the slow work of rendering it less habitual. In the next section I discuss the means by which such "leanings" can be effected. In the final section I address some common dilemmas presented by this task, including the problem of whether we alert the patient to what we are leaning against, and when, or whether we go on "leaning," with the goal of extinguishing the response.

Finally, what is needed throughout is the willingness not to pretend to know, that is, not to be confident of formulations in the face of material for which there are many formulations, while remaining confident of the process. This is the most difficult of all these recommendations because it asks that we go forward *without knowing,* trusting that the development of an effective relationship will both secure the patient for the work and move toward valid conclusions.

Specific Means for Common Problems

Many people deceive themselves; an undetermined number choose to deceive others. Clinical states themselves, such as depression, color strongly the material and relationships provided. These tendencies are so strong that routine interviewing protocols secure reliable findings across diagnostic groups, but in what sense are patients' self-descriptions *true?* In the absence of the independent, quantitative tests that correct clinical impressions in general medicine, the following means can be useful in providing valid data as well as effective relationships.

Some patients consistently *derogate themselves.* Many are at least mildly depressed, emphasizing any impression of defect or worthlessness we reflect and lengthening the lists of pathological findings and historical failures we record. These patients offer themselves up both as defective objects to be criticized and as people hopeless of any change. Reassurance may be quickly rejected and becomes increasingly difficult for therapists to mobilize. No wonder medications are reached for.

The first task is to overcome the contagious despair that soon grips both parties. It is a frequent paradox of clinical experience that the more therapists despair, the more patients are relieved, so that a despairing therapist can be a hopeful sign in suicidal cases. A further paradox is that self-criticism, so often a close cousin to self-derogation, may be evidence of that human reflectiveness and self-correction often seen in people of the highest intelligence. We should not be surprised to learn that great accomplishment is, perhaps regularly, a product of this merciless reflectiveness. We may find ourselves saying to the self-derogatory patients, later in the work, that the goal of treatment is to modify self-derogation and not to replace it with mindless self-satisfaction. I emphasize these points to offset the pessimism that so often overtakes therapists under these circumstances.

The goal is not, however, to replace pessimism with a thoughtless optimism for the therapist either. We need to keep in touch with the patient's despair, to experience it as fully as we can, *while remaining confident*. For a considerable time the patient's despair must be extended and excavated; we need even to reach beyond its limits until the other consistently calls us back to better news. Patients need to know that *we know* how fully the self-derogation has signaled deep-running doubts about their capacities and lovableness. Meanwhile, we are the carriers of hope. This will be most difficult for newcomers to the work, who have not yet experienced the success of the process. But even those long familiar with the problem of self-derogation will find the exact balance between sharing despair and remaining confident a daunting challenge.

Therapists' attitudes and postures, and sometimes their facial expressions, can carry the optimism while their words reach for despair. Above all one wants to be able to feel both, the bad news and the good. Sometimes it is useful to say, "Of course you can't believe things will be different. I wouldn't want you to pretend to. You'll only believe it when it happens!" The therapist, while carrying hope, must not prematurely shift it to the patient. Later there will be a transplantation of attitudes: the therapist's esteem moves into the space cleared by remembering and sharing the despair.

As a rule, something more has to happen. Human attitudes are so much a function of human circumstances that we must work toward changes in the latter too. In discussions of psychotherapy and psycho-therapeutic change, much has been made of patients' attitudes and too little of their circumstances. New attitudes are extraordinarily difficult to maintain in old circumstances, the latter having been slowly aggregated by interactions between old attitudes and the world. Our most inclusive goal is the creation of viable existences. To some extent the new patient must live in a new world, and until that is possible we cannot rest content with the outcomes. This is an important lesson for pharmacotherapeutics, too. Simply to alter patients' moods without being sure they can also change their circumstances is to risk interminable drug treatment, complications, and gradually lessening drug effects.

A second group of patients needs to be *left alone*. They seek treatment through a wide range of complaints, not believing they are in fact capable. For this group Freud's invention of a therapeutic method both holding the patient with the therapist and then forbidding much intervention constituted an exact solution. Therapeutic holding is necessary because such patients readily enlist other helping people, for instance medical personnel by means of bodily complaints, to continue their dependence. In some measure they can be encouraged and supported, but unless they are held, sometimes for the considerable period required to discover their independent selves, they will go elsewhere.

Recognizing these cases will remain a central problem until we have quantitative measures, such as brain mapping, for evaluating human capacities. In the meantime there are crude measures directed toward concepts of health: evidence of reflectiveness and self-correcting together with the patient's ability to convey robustness, emotional presence, or continuing integrity—all necessarily subjective judgments on our part.

Happily, many of these patients like to talk and value being listened to. It is as if they are trying themselves out, before venturing on a more independent existence; thus many are not difficult to hold in a relationship while doing little. The therapist's main problem is resisting the temptations to give advice, explain, or otherwise reinforce the patient's need for others. The attitude sought is one of quiet enthusiasm while riding out demands for help or alleged evidence of helplessness or threats of disaster, until the patients prove themselves to themselves. A teacher of mine replied to a patient demanding to know what he was doing under these circumstances, "I'm trying to keep out of your way." The teacher was implying: you will be able to do what you need to do if I don't undercut your independence. A non-infantilizing relationship is being built.

With a third group of patients, the search for an effective relationship has to overcome not self-derogating or dependent trends but *the wish to please or support therapists.* The integrity of the person is decentered by a habitual tipping toward the feared needs of the other. Done subtly, this may escape notice for long periods, particularly by means of a staged independence through which therapists are flattered or soothed.

The affective signal is an unusual sense of well-being in therapists: the work is going too well. Healthy human relationships are as a rule bumpy because the two separate perspectives have to correct and adjust to each other. Such well-being on the therapist's part is especially suspect, for he or she is getting not only a pleasant ride but a paid-up one! Look first for evidence of special efforts or cleverness on the patient's part. If discovered, do not depreciate these efforts. They generally represent *the best the person has learned how to do,* sometimes the sole source of the patient's security in the world. I have found that even such remarks as "I wish I could be as pleasant and helpful toward you as you are toward me" come across as jarring, I suspect because they seem sarcastic or ironic. More useful is spotting the same trend in the patient's dealings with others and pleading for justice in those relationships. Later the same plea can be brought into the treatment. The largest error is seeking compliance. Sudden efforts by the patient at "not pleasing" are almost certainly a response born out of fear rather than a sensible entitlement, and they only signal that the patient feels further endangered. A genuine freedom from needing to please must await increased security in relationships that is best achieved first in the treatment.

In dealing with women patients, it is important to locate the need to please at least partly in a culture that assigns this responsibility to women. Thus, further blaming the patient is lessened. It is also valuable to acknowledge that pleasing people is a priceless capacity when it is not undertaken habitually or compulsively or toward people whose ingratitude should be discouraged. As in almost all psychotherapeutic work, the discovery of family examples and pressures toward pleasing opens the way to fresh perspectives. Too often, however, this is done in such a way as to "blame" the family and then substitute a new person, the therapist, who is to be pleased. Throughout, it is best if the goal is not predominantly an intellectual one, that is, formulating the patient's plight in terms of past examples and pressures, but rather working out the treatment relationship so that the patient is liberated. The medium should carry the message.

Any effort to specify the language, postures, or personal style that will best carry these messages must backfire because individual therapist variables are so many and so critical that at most one can specify a general goal. One therapist conveys a great deal by a gesture or facial expression; another needs to talk; and since communication is a final common pathway of diverse, often conflicting messages, what needs to be emphasized, by one therapist or another, varies greatly. The schools of psychotherapy in many instances are individual styles writ large, often in fact what the originator had trouble doing and therefore felt needed emphasis, which may be exactly what another worker needs least of all. Shaw remarked: those who can, do; those who can't, teach.

A subgroup of pleasers work in very subtle ways, particularly if what pleases them to do, pleases us. One woman was accustomed to establishing herself by enabling men to act more effectively than they had hitherto, in causes she favored. The men were slow to see that these causes were not their own. Her first husband had died; her second was ill and exhausted. Eventually a therapeutic goal of enabling her to work on her own was established, but not before the therapist had almost left his profession and family to complete one of the patient's projects. The difficulty was in admiring the patient's extraordinary abilities rather than enjoying the powerful sense of accomplishment and reward she conveyed. Once again, close attention to the patient's strengths and abilities will sometimes expose processes not immediately apparent from disease concepts or conflict and defense analysis.

Another, less common group seems intent on *displeasing*. Some of these have begun by pleasing, often mightily, and then turned on us. I have long felt our work is so difficult and problematic that few complaints about it are altogether wrong, but especially if one has a plaintive companion at home or an overbearing boss at work, negative patients can be wearing. Two therapists I knew were unable to tolerate complaints during their children's adolescence, which reemphasizes the importance of local climate. Being well-paid helps, as does a temperament that enjoys challenges.

In dealing with critical patients I try to assume the patient has noted something foolish I am doing. Being conversant with many of my less pleasing features, I can recognize familiar complaints and acknowledge their justice. This usually clears the air. I try to keep in mind as well that the work suffers more from patients' concealing complaints than from airing them, so that a welcoming attitude, sometimes even toward virulent abuse by the patient, is appropriate. I have noticed, too, that when patients who have long concealed dissatisfaction begin to express it, the change is particularly trying, though we may have consciously sought it. This is partly due to a lack of straightforwardness in berating that is characteristic of people not altogether at home doing it.

The tendency to see all complaints as projections, for example in the light of transference or transference resistance, is problematic. Not only are such claims poorly received; they often seem defensive or self-serving. Again, we need to model the behavior we wish to encourage, in this instance an openness to different or unpleasant possibilities. Moreover, some element of projection is a feature of all human mentation, in the sense of putting between ourselves and the world a particular perspective. This concept is represented in Magritte's painting of a pipe under which he wrote: this is not a pipe. I am arguing for an acknowledgment of the incomplete, hypothetical, problematic nature of all our perspectives on one another. Of course this is the very ground of transference, one name for our unconscious hypotheses. We would do well to receive them aware of the extent to which our own responses reflect additional hypotheses.

This is not to contend that everything is reasonable or right. Much human pain arises from the very contentiousness, premature concluding, and closed-mindedness I am condemning in ourselves. Dealing effectively with contentious people is one of the great challenges of therapeutic work, rich with possibilities for assisting lives mired in hatred, isolation, or destructiveness. I emphasize these possibilities in order to bring cheerfulness to clinical situations that many times are approached with dread.

A 40-year-old man complained of his dissolving marriage and a career that had started well only to become unproductive. He showed a strong didactic bent, was unusually well-informed as well as discriminating, and had been to a number of therapists some of whom matched him in their capacity to find fault. From the first visit he invited a stimulating battle of wits. When this was not forthcoming from me, he ridiculed my lack of crisp formulations. I replied, "I don't seem to find them," to his apparent relief. Still, he continued to demand the insights and corrections that his situation appeared to him to require. I increasingly felt that his personal relationships were most familiar, almost comfortable, when they were insulting. I did not want to blame his mother and sister for starting this, though I suspected they had, lest it seem a formula; it was better for him to learn that my not correcting him was a sincere expression of the conviction that he deserved better. I could admire the precision and ingenuity of many of his complaints and the mental power that both lay behind the complaints and could gradually be moved into his newly successful work. Again, what I wanted to provide was a more livable relationship that he might carry into the world.

Still another group of patients are *preoccupied*. Whatever else they are discussing, their minds snap back to the preoccupations—a loss, a love object, a fear; the list is endless. Once these conditions were called monomanias, dipsomania for example, to categorize one of the most pervasive ills of humankind. Such patients are never fully present in any relationship, except with the preoccupation, so that the difficulties of making effective contact can seem insurmountable.

The first principle is not to oppose the patient's concern but to ally with it, in the sense of learning to experience the hold, the deep attraction the preoccupation has. One can observe the same principle at work in such established methods of treating preoccupations as Alcoholics Anonymous: the idea of wanting to drink is acknowledged, its pervasiveness is underscored, while the shared experience of addiction and danger is used to build relationships that control the addiction. Note that these are not non-judgmental relationships, but the judgments, often fiercely made, are *shared*. The point is, the most destructive preoccupations can generate convictions and then relationships in which the shared convictions master the preoccupations.

I have discussed already one of the commonest preoccupations, the conviction of being defective, in error, or inadequate, and measures that can be taken against it. Here too, an important goal is gaining a shared conviction. Easiest would be a shared conviction that the patient is indeed defective; I have observed many interminable therapeutic relationships based on that idea. Success depends on a very different idea, as I suggested earlier.

One preoccupation that is often unsettling to therapists is preoccupation with the therapist, as through expressions of love. The prevailing advice, to find out what such expressions mean, may encounter the patient's conviction that they mean just that, "I love you." This should not surprise us. The presence of an attentive and interested listener, the personal nature of the topics discussed, even a modicum of understanding are immensely appealing and, not uncommonly, unique events in the patient's experience. Freud referred to the "cure through love," by which he meant patients coming to love their therapists and then mobilizing past attachments with the result that these ties might be clarified and loosened. There was also the possibility of patients coming to life, that is, discovering through the treatment resources of feeling and capacities for making relationships that were previously attenuated or long dormant.

On being told "I love you," it is insensitive for the therapist to inquire what the other means, to refer to transference phenomena, or to ask for associations. Especially with shy people, who may have called up great courage to make the declaration, our reception should be gracious or at least respectful, for example by saying "Thank you." With patients who one fears are hopeful of consummating their devotion or otherwise transcending professional boundaries, it may be useful to say, "This is good news for the treatment. Now we can take those feelings and find someone out in the world with whom they can be enjoyed." Again, as with all these formulas, particular persons and circumstances forbid any literal application.

The therapist should keep in mind that there will be many other occasions on which transference explorations can be made. These will also be better tolerated if the patient's intimate feelings have been well received.

In long-term work, different responses to declarations of love are often necessary. Then the intensity of feelings may be so great and the patient's new experience of love and closeness so real that finding someone besides the therapist with whom the feeling could occur seems unimaginable. And this may be true for the therapist as well. I suspect that some violations of professional ethics are the result of just such experiences. I remind both patients and therapists that "in love" feelings are transient (generally of four to six months' duration), heavily dependent on limited contact, and most likely to flourish only in special circumstances, including being forbidden, and without known correlation with enduring love. Of course, reason under these circumstances may have little chance. Nevertheless, the reminders can be useful to therapists embarking on long-term work. And when both parties have not fallen victim to that attractive psychosis we call "being in love," one party may be able to preserve the therapeutic relationship by means of such reflections.

The Intricate Balances of Psychological Work

I have already mentioned the difficulties of balancing despair and confidence in work with self-derogatory patients. What follows are discussions of other tensions and dilemmas commonly encountered. For all their intricacies and the resulting inevitable failures, these problems give the work much of its dignity, challenge, and reward, raising it to a refined professional discipline requiring long experience and never fully mastered. The tensions and dilemmas also point to the ways in which effective relationships produce good outcomes.

Preserving both credulity and skepticism is central. The prevailing schools tend to give major emphasis to one or the other, for example, self-psychological practitioners emphasizing the first and interpretive workers sometimes the second. Neither approach serves well a broad range of cases. But how is one to preserve in the same mind both a full openness to the other's reports of experience and doubts about their validity? Nothing so challenges our mental resources. It is similar to the problem I referred to earlier, of proceeding without knowing, that is, hearing without concluding. I suppose the most familiar instance is of scientific work in general, by which hypotheses are at once accepted and tested, so that credulity is exercised in the presence of doubt. Many will protest that we cannot throw ourselves into the experience of the other, indeed deepen that awareness, while keeping some part of mental life apart. But that is just what is demanded. Surely its achievement will signal the elevation of psychotherapy to the ideals of science.

It is for this reason that I recommend beginners immerse themselves in the full range of the schools of psychotherapy. Let them gain an appreciation of all the major positions while avoiding sectarianism. What they lose in immediate confidence is more than offset by grasping the work as a whole, with less leaping to conclusions, more respect for the difficulties of psychological knowing, and an approach to the patient that is receptive of the unique. We can say that openness replaces credulity, a widening out of perspectives to many possibilities, while mere skepticism or compulsive doubting gives way to another openness, this time to surprise. By the latter I mean that clichés or established answers should be suspect in work that unavoidably entails one unique perspective meeting another. Established answers are useful—in fact, they are the basis of everything we do, having worked their way into our minds—but to experience their variety and contradictions, to look for fresh combinations, even to catch a glimpse of something only recognizable because it is different from what we have already in mind, constitutes a significant part of the field's excitement and usefulness.

There is another central paradox. We want to give the patients freedom—to speak, to explore the past, present, and future, to confront what may be terrifying. But how does one *give* freedom? Freud's answer was the "fundamental rule," the basic instruction of psychoanalysis, to "say whatever comes to mind." Here another paradox intervenes. The analytic patient is being *ordered* to be free; the medium once again undercuts the message. Instead we need to take positions *embodying* freedom, not prescribing it. Are we shocked by disagreements, can we confess we're wrong, are we free ourselves to think or speak unexpected thoughts? Above all, do we give ourselves and others freedom to feel? How censorious are the voices within us to the range of humanness?

Closely related are two needs: in Sabo's language, to "be with" and to "let be." Everyone needs the support of others. Can we give support *without constricting?* An element of blackmail subtly enters many helping gestures—kindness as a means of control. I feel in myself the often insidious growth of "knowing what's best" for the patient, a slight twisting of my bodily posture toward influencing or protecting. Moreover, I may be right; I may know better than the patient. The point is, to keep aware and sometimes to speak what we feel.

Possibly the most essential and trying decision in all of clinical practice is how much to respond to demands for help, understanding, even outright control. The patient cries out, "I'll die if you don't." "My suffering is too much." Are these statements true, or are they, for example, manipulations? I believe some patients commit suicide because we do too much rather than too little, thereby escalating their wants, confirming their helplessness, and promoting greater and eventually unmeetable demands. Often there is nothing to help us decide except our felt bodily response. Am I truly saddened or restless and uneasy? Do I feel, if only a little, twisted away from my integrity and toward actions that don't "feel right"? Often we hardly know but have to decide, meanwhile confronting what can mean life or death.

Note that while impingements on the patient's integrity comprise the varied ground of psychiatric practice, our own integrity is sorely tested as well. Are we seducible, irascible, overcompliant? How readily can we be twisted away from our real feelings? Sooner or later, every practitioner stumbles on his or her own Achilles' heel.

This is not to suggest that sincerity and honesty (except to ourselves) must always guide therapeutic action. Many clinical situations call for "good management," in Winnicott's phrase. We could also term this "counter-manipulation" because good management generally means bringing distorted relationships back into livable shape. For example, the displeasing, sometimes insulting patient I discussed could often be dealt with directly and sincerely. But there was much else that could not be so "up front," lest I return him to the exchanging of arguments and corrections with which he was so familiar. I therefore sometimes withdrew, diminishing my presence to signal that I didn't want to fight with him; I was also modeling what would later serve him well in his family. When he was particularly intrusive, I tried to stop listening altogether, so as not to be drawn into quarrels. As I remarked before, I would occasionally "play dead" in the sense of assuming a posture of helplessness in which I was incapable of being as clever as he hoped. He and I both knew this was an exaggeration, if possible, of my incompetence, telling him what I was not interested in doing. Such behaviors are close to the "leanings" to which we now return.

One of my own Achilles' heels is a stubborn reluctance to confront or interpret. The reader of this chapter is hereby warned that indirect means will generally get my vote. Early on I was influenced by the saying, "If you have to tell someone something, it's already too late." As a result, I am not so familiar with the steady tension that many workers feel between telling and not telling patients what we think is wrong. These workers have told me how trying this tension can be, even distracting from attention to the current flow. Often the seemingly perfect moment to speak has passed, so that we are now distracted by regret! With my non-interpretive ways it is easy for me to rationalize this outcome, noting that other chances will occur or that the interpretation was probably wrong or that the patient knows my little wisdom already. In this fashion I am content to go on attitudinally leaning against whatever I don't like, faintly disapproving, not reinforcing, hinting away. The triumphant moment occurs when the patients stop doing whatever it is for a moment or express repugnance for the old behavior on their own.

Many other therapists like to work in the open air, freely exchanging ideas with patients, correcting and recorrecting one another. But to me this is naïve; it plays into compliance and throws an intellectual cast over the whole enterprise. No doubt what I gain by avoiding these situations I lose in other ways.

I am very familiar with the tension springing from the last of the dilemmas I discuss, that between taking and giving responsibility. A great deal in the supervision and analytic training that I received spoke against taking responsibility, the goals being neutrality and an evenly hovering attention that only watches and comments. I came to see that this was necessary for those patients I mentioned earlier who are intent on moving responsibility to us. But many more are already too overwhelmed to take more upon themselves, so that the responsibility is simply ours. One wants to be able to feel that.

We should practice feeling the tension between doing more and doing less, between not abandoning patients who need more of us and not intruding on what must develop autonomously. First I look for moments when the patient seems impinged upon—not quite himself or herself, less than I have experienced them being. There occurs an immediate tension between acting against the impingement and not embarrassing the patient by calling attention to it. I take responsibility for surmounting the rough spot, at first by not noticing or by changing the subject until I sense what needs to be done. Perhaps the patient felt abandoned or humiliated. Commonly I start a dialogue with a possible critic internal to the patient prompting the feeling, "I have done something wrong." This verdict of the patient's critic is familiar and carries weight; I want to sound a different note. Throughout, my tension has been rising: I must speak up but must also "mind my own business" until I have found what works. I will know it works because the patient looks better and may report feeling good when with me. The relationship has been rescued.

What I take responsibility for is making the relationship effective. I have been asserting throughout that explaining what is wrong is not useful at least until there is a relationship strong enough to bear it, and being able to make the relationship work usually means that we have hit upon and offset much of what is wrong. I am also claiming that to make relationships effective, we need a range of action that includes all that the various schools have emphasized, whether sharing, managing, or explaining. We are each of us born into one school or another, being by temperament inclined to a particular emphasis, so that learning psychotherapy means expanding our repertoires to deal with the possibilities before us.

These attentions to therapists' dilemmas should not suggest any less attention to the patient's dilemmas. Engaging with the patient's struggles is a large part of forming effective relationships. This will be illustrated repeatedly in the chapters that follow and given systematic exposition in Chapter 9 by Gustafson. There is no more important path to profound engagement.

Psychotherapy encompasses a single brief contact, occasional or frequent visits, long-term intensive work, and a lifetime of many times interrupted visits. In this it is as varied as medical contacts directed at the body.

It also extends from giving a piece of advice or restraining from doing so, treating symptoms, through the resolution of conflicts or destructive habits and character, to the making of viable existences, sometimes from scratch.

It may also involve more than one patient, as in couples or group work, or other family members in family therapy.

It does not exclude other treatments, for example medications; oftentimes it requires them.

2 The Relational Aspects of Psychopharmacology

Alex N. Sabo and Bliss Inui Rand

Knowing and Not Knowing

The dialectic between knowing and not knowing is central to psychotherapeutic work, but its boundaries are even sharper in psychopharmacological work. The patient comes to us because we know. Yet our knowledge is transient and limited. What we know today will be radically different from what we know tomorrow. For instance, the leading cause of dementia praecox or schizophrenia at the beginning of the twentieth century was tertiary syphilis. With the advent of diagnostic tests and a novel treatment (penicillin), this infectious cause of psychotic symptoms has nearly been eliminated. In the 1960s we learned we could treat mania with lithium carbonate, a salt, in the 1970s with anticonvulsants, in the 1980s with calcium channel blockers. In the 1990s we learned that fish oil augments the effect of a mood stabilizer, and that all these medications may act by "anti-kindling and dampening effects on post-synaptic signal transduction."[1] Thirty years ago almost no one used valproic acid, an anticonvulsant prescribed for absence seizures, to manage acute mania. Today, we "load" an acutely manic patient with 20 mg/kg of valproic acid in the first 24 hours of treatment and often produce, with relatively few side effects, a remarkable calming and clearing of thought within several days. If the psychiatrist of the 1960s scoffed at the idea that antiepilectic drugs would rival lithium carbonate or that fish oil might find a place in the treatment of bipolar disorder, he would later miss the boat. Widely available computer databases accelerate the rate of change in prevailing practice, so that taking a respectful stance toward knowing and not knowing becomes more important than ever. This is certainly true at the conceptual level, but in psychopharmacology it is even more true at the relationship level with the individual patient.

Our respect for the tension between knowing and not knowing limits mistakes of arrogance. After listening carefully, we can reflect back to the patient: "You're not sleeping well, appetite is off, you feel down in the dumps but worse in the morning, and you're blaming yourself for many things going wrong. You've been crying at the drop of a hat, and you find yourself more irritable than usual. This shift in mood started about two months after your girlfriend broke up with you, and it's been dragging on for about three months now. You want some help, and there are several things that may help: psychotherapy and/or medication. Does one or the other or both have some appeal?"

We know that clinical trials of medications show response in some but not all patients. We know that pharmaceutical companies, racing to get FDA approval for their new medications, will carefully screen out the more complicated cases (those with comorbid substance abuse, personality problems, or medical illness—the very conditions so common in our actual clinical practice), and will usually test for only eight to twelve weeks (when newly activated protein synthesis and receptor density changes are seen, but before the central nervous system makes adaptations to those changes), with the result that we are usually treating people with more complex problems and for longer periods of time than those in whom the medications were originally tested. The scenario noted above more often runs like this: "You've had trouble sleeping and eating since you broke up with your girlfriend. People have rarely appreciated your intelligence, and if they have, they've been envious and done what they could to undermine you. Alcohol has been a reliable friend for many years, but it has led to its own difficulties. Your license was revoked after the second DWI, and now you're more stressed by having to take the bus. While the alcohol causes trouble, you also feel it helps you be more at ease in social situations, and you don't really want to give it up."

Our real patients are more difficult to treat than the patients tested in the early medication trials. This means that we must be humble at the outset. We balance our belief that we've made a good choice that is likely to help the patient (knowing) with our knowledge that our individual patient may either be in the majority group of patients who respond to the medication or in the minority group of patients who will not respond (not knowing). In the example just given, the medication effect may ameliorate the depressive symptoms and provide the margin for the patient to give up the alcohol or loosen his tendency to see others as not appreciating him or envious of his talents. On the other hand, either the patient's alcohol use or his tendency to see himself as victim may be more powerful than anything the medication can do. It is only by forming a respectful, understanding relationship with the patient that the psychiatrist can explore the various possibilities for treatment—psychotherapy, AA, or antidepressant medication—and work with the patient and perhaps another therapist while those possibilities are considered and tried.

The Relationship Itself

A good psychopharmacologist brings the best diagnostic and technical knowledge to bear. He also uses skill in developing an effective relationship with the patient. The goal of the initial evaluation is to come away with both a sense of the particular symptoms from which the patient seeks relief and a sense of the whole person in the context of his or her life circumstances. One of two patterns usually unfolds: patients who are more comfortable if you focus quickly on their chief complaint, and those who are more at ease by your first learning a bit about them as a person. With the former type, the person is eager to explain the symptoms from the outset, so the psychopharmacologist listens carefully to the symptoms, eliciting more detail and testing them against familiar syndromes. When this has been thoroughly done over the first 20 or 30 minutes, there comes a pause, when the doctor can ask the patient to shift gears and tell more about his life, whom he lives with, where he works, who is important in his current circumstances. This conveys concern for the whole person while adding valuable information regarding the situations that have an impact on the symptoms. The patient relaxes a bit at this point, and the quality of information that the doctor obtains improves. The trust is better and the subjective reports deeper.

The second pattern simply reverses the sequence. The patient appears tense about getting into the symptoms immediately, and it is more tactful to start the session with a declarative statement about the day's weather or an alliance-building comment like, "I hope the parking wasn't as bad today as usual." After the ice is broken, the doctor explains that before moving to specific symptoms, she would like to gain perspective on the person's life situation. The session then moves to a request for background about life circumstances, such as whom the patient lives with, daily activities, and significant others.

The goal is to put the patient at ease, to let him know what you're up to so the patient has a sense of control, and for the doctor to come away with a sense of the person and the person's life as well as specific syndromal information. If you are going to ask a patient to ingest a mind-altering substance with possibly significant side effects, you had better first develop a relationship that conveys your concern with him as a person.

Another facet of putting the patient at ease involves the psycho-pharmacologist's sensitivity to the meaning of medication for the patient. The patient may come with a sense of failure, regarding medication as a last resort after months or even years of work in therapy. Or he may come hoping for a quick fix or miracle cure, with little interest in the complex interaction between life circumstances and symptoms. Ideally, the doctor will be able to acknowledge the patient's perspective while at the same time offering a gentle reframing of the work as one approach to the relief of suffering. On one end of the spectrum, the psychiatrist could emphasize the synergy of psychotherapy and psychopharmacology, and at the other, the psychiatrist might want to highlight the empirical nature of the work, presenting our knowledge of the brain in realistic terms.

While working in a scientific mode, as an investigator trying to discover patterns likely to respond to a medication, the psychiatrist is also working psychologically, using techniques of healing to jump-start what the medication can do over time. The most important of these is the co-investigator process itself. An effective psychiatrist establishes a relationship of respect and mutuality. Through attentive listening and a thorough assessment of the medical and psychosocial context of the patient's symptoms, the psychiatrist reinforces the importance of the patient and her concerns. The psychiatrist explains that the process will require the patient to prioritize the symptoms to be addressed, and to pay close attention to the effects and side effects of the medication. The patient becomes a co-investigator. Once this role is established, the patient actually becomes stronger as a result of bringing important observations to bear on each session and on each decision that is made regarding the choice and dosage of medication. The back and forth, the give and take, the shared decision-making are push-ups of self-esteem that make the patient stronger with each encounter. While the authors of this chapter favor establishing the patient as a co-investigator whenever possible, we acknowledge that some patients do better if the doctor plays a more traditional role. Patients from cultures in which the doctor holds a great deal of status, for example, do better if the doctor assumes this role. The psychopharmacologist must be attuned to what works best for each individual patient.

In the previous chapter, Havens mentioned three "psychological analgesics": protection of the patient's self-esteem, some measure of understanding and accepting, and provision of a future. *These analgesics are as important for the psychopharmacologist as they are for the therapist.* Establishing the patient's role as a co-investigator does a great deal to protect the patient's self-esteem. Externalization has received a good deal of attention recently from "narrative" therapists working in the paradigm articulated by Michael White.[2] The technique refers to the strategy of helping a patient locate a problem outside of himself so as to avoid defensiveness and provide more opportunity for making constructive change. A recent example from the domestic front comes to mind. One of the authors (AS) had the occasion to manage a dinner for himself and six girls between the ages of 8 and 12. The house was becoming quite noisy, and the three 8-year-olds were getting out of control. He called aside the most spirited and wildly behaving among them and requested her help. He wondered if she had noticed how wildly the others were behaving and explained that we needed to settle the house before dinner. If he could count on her support to calm the others, he would be most appreciative. She immediately agreed, and within a short time order was restored. By externalizing the problem, he was able to elicit a creative solution from one who could produce a major impact on the disturbance. No shame was involved, and working collaboratively with her dinner host enhanced the girl's self-esteem. One might say she became a "co-investigator," an ally in achieving the objective of the evening. The clinical situation is different in that it brings two adults together. Yet, by identifying the "chemical imbalance," the psychopharmacologist effectively externalizes the problem, so that she and the patient are free to focus on that problem and not attribute any motivation or shame to the patient's behavior. In both examples, effective change occurs with a minimum of shame to one who could produce a major impact on the disturbance.

Psychopharmacological interventions, by their very nature, externalize the problem. The psychopharmacological approach posits a biological or chemical abnormality that leads to behavioral or mental symptoms. Since chemicals behave by their own sets of rules, the problem is seen as a chemical imbalance rather than moral weakness or defect of character. Many depressed people reflexively see themselves as bad. They show great relief when the doctor mentions how common it is for self-criticism, lack of energy, and irritability to be associated with imbalance of serotonin, dopamine, or norepinephrine. To the extent that the doctor believes this relative truth, the patient feels relieved, let off the hook, and less a focus of blame by his new acquaintance. This externalization opens the field for fresh observations and lightens the heavy load the patient has been bearing. The externalization is a way to administer the first of Havens's analgesics: protection of the patient's self-esteem.

If one follows this remark with options for restoring a proper balance of serotonin, dopamine, or norepinephrine, one begins, as Jerome Frank pointed out, the major work of psychotherapy: the restoration of hope. The patient may visibly respond to this hope, which can be seen by a shift of position, often a lifting up of the head or a raising of the shoulders. The patient literally appears lighter, more relaxed, brighter. If so, one can offer the medication now or later, if a trial of psychotherapy does not lift the depression in a month or two. If the patient is more severely depressed, the body posture will not change. It is better to stay affectively in tune with the patient, to acknowledge the depressed perspective. It is one which cannot see a future. As Havens mentioned in the first chapter, the use of an adverb might quietly open the future while the doctor bears with the patient's depressed viewpoint: "It would be difficult for you to see *now* how a medication could restore your sleep and appetite, even your old pleasure in going for a walk. I can see how you must doubt this, but I would like to offer medicine which I believe will help." If it doesn't help, the doctor has still established himself as a person who is attentive to the patient's perspective but who also sees the possibility of a better future. The doctor becomes a fellow passenger on the bus the patient is riding—a passenger who can listen, but who also has fresh ideas.

The closer the psychopharmacologist can come to being an informed fellow passenger on the bus, the better the relationship will be. In the words of the "relational" therapists, this stance "empowers" the patient. The patient's observations are seen to be at least as valuable as the psychopharmacologist's. The patient who uses the Internet to search medical databases can be encouraged to bring forward new data for the two to consider. Regardless of their Internet interest, patients will come up with many useful ideas, such as dosing at various times of day or titration of one drug's dose against another, that fine-tune the treatment beyond what is possible if the patient leaves the driving entirely to the doctor. While depression is often highly treatable with medication, at least 10% of patients with depression do not get better no matter what we do. In that case the psychopharmacologist has an especially important role as a fellow passenger, bearing with the patient during long years of significant suffering. He may also lift some of the burden from the patient who suffers from a refractory depression by accepting part of the blame for the failure of the treatment: "You have done all you can, you have a right to be frustrated with me. Here I am, the doctor, the one who's supposed to relieve your suffering as quickly as possible. [Long pause; watch the patient for an inclination to do something with this apology. It may lead to an expression of anger, a request for consultation, or a statement of camaraderie. Any of these can be helpful.] . . . We may have to take consolation in the small gains we have made and wait for this thing to burn itself out, or perhaps for a better treatment to come along." The psychopharmacologist makes an empathic statement. The important point is to notice where the patient takes it, and then to move forward when that is clearer.

There are other times, as with seriously suicidal patients, when the doctor must act more like the bus driver than a fellow passenger. These cases call for the doctor to "drive" the bus to the place of loved ones and other support people such as crisis worker and therapist. When the psychopharmacologist recognizes such a situation, she is often in a unique position to call a family meeting or a meeting with family and other significant treaters such as a therapist, AA sponsor, or crisis worker. The point of such a meeting is to explain the good news and the bad news, to enlarge the support network, and to share risk in a responsible way. The good news is that the patient does not have to die, and the people who care most about the patient are in the room together looking at what they can do to help prevent a suicide.

The bad news is that patients in these situations sometimes do kill themselves, and the patient's recent near-fatal attempt or carefully thought-out plan has made that risk clear. At best, such a meeting calls attention to a serious risk of the treatment before irreparable harm is done. More often than not, the meeting reduces the patient's isolation, a serious risk factor for suicide. It also lets members of the family and the treatment team know they can be open with the patient and with one another about their concerns. Sometimes this openness leads to better information about positive or negative effects of medication and treatable symptoms. Sometimes a decision to hospitalize the patient is appropriate. At a minimum, this approach allows those closest to the patient to meet the treaters so that if the patient does commit suicide, a relationship based on mobilizing support to prevent this existed prior to the patient's death. This intervention reduces the risks of suicide, severe psychological damage to family members, and malpractice litigation should the patient choose to kill himself. It is usually better if the psychopharmacologist can function like a fellow passenger and suggest that the patient himself call the meeting, but when the patient lacks the resources to do so, the psychopharmacologist should take the initiative just as an on-the-ball passenger would if the bus driver were suddenly stricken with a heart attack.

As we consider the relationship itself in this era of managed care and ever greater "productivity," one cannot overestimate the importance of spending adequate time with the patient at the first evaluation. Malpractice claims involving medication errors have risen sharply in the past several years, and patients are angry about the way their doctors rush them out of the room in order to meet the requirements of managed care's fifteen-minute medication check.[3] More and more patients are feeling like automobile parts on an assembly line, and if the psychopharmacologist takes the time to listen carefully to both the syndromal and the personal elements of the patient's story, much is accomplished toward developing a good relationship. This includes asking for permission to obtain pertinent past records as well as talking with current primary care doctors (for a tactful sharing of pertinent medical information) and with the therapist if this is a shared treatment. Spending time at the start is not over-indulgent. Forty-five to ninety focused minutes will usually do. More harried interactions at later points are often forgiven if the doctor has taken good care to give full attention at that first visit. With urgent situations or sometimes with an astute therapist's awareness that a patient's suffering should be relieved sooner rather than later, a psychopharmacologist may need to see a patient for a brief initial visit of fifteen to twenty minutes. The patient is grateful to have the immediate attention and much is done toward establishing a healthy alliance, but this briefer initial evaluation may not be sufficient to gather all the pertinent history, psychosocial context, and medical information. If this occurs, it is important to schedule a fuller follow-up visit as soon as possible. Since psychopharmacologists see many more patients than psychotherapists do, it is especially important to keep a record that will remind the clinician quickly of both the person as a person and the necessary clinical information. The record need not reveal much that is personal—and indeed, with the many parties who now have access to records, it should not reveal anything too personal— yet something as simple as the type of pet the patient has or an interest noted on that first visit quickly reorients the psychopharmacologist and conveys a positive connection at the next visit.

Dilemmas for the Psychopharmacologist

Several dilemmas present themselves regularly: first, should medication be prescribed at the outset, or should psychotherapy be given time to work first? If a therapist or a doctor is respectful, listens carefully, seems to grasp the problem, and conveys some degree of hope for approaching it, there is a good chance that the patient will feel significantly better after the first session. Will this improvement last, or will it evaporate soon after the initial contact is over? Is this improvement contingent upon the therapist's being present, like having another person nearby on a scary, stormy night, or is it based on something more lasting like a change in perspective, a new meaning that frames a problem or set of symptoms? The psychopharmacologist can do a great deal to soothe a harried individual by a thorough approach that does not jump to conclusions. He or she places the patient's history and current symptoms on a continuum with the normal and allows the patient, over time, to place them along that continuum and choose interventions. The psychopharmacologist is also guided by the dictum "first of all, do no harm" and must, with the patient, weigh the risks and benefits of any intervention versus no intervention at all. The following example illustrates some of the treatment options the psychopharmacologist needs to consider.

A lawyer comes for help. He feels he is getting depressed. He had a disagreement with his boss, a partner in the firm, who advised him to see a "shrink." The boss told him that he is losing credibility, that he is known for quick, scathing comments, and that others in the firm have all but written him off. The firm is downsizing; should he be looking for another job? The lawyer explains that for two months now his mood has been down, he hasn't been sleeping well, he has been overeating, has lost interest in sex and other pleasures of life, and feels overwhelmed by the simplest of problems. He has been thinking that life is not worth living, but has had no thoughts of suicide. In addition, he has two small children, and his wife has been diagnosed with a serious illness that might become debilitating over the next several years.

The lawyer has come to the psychopharmacologist by self-referral; he has read about antidepressants and is sure that he would like a SSRI, like Prozac. The psychopharmacologist recognizes that the patient meets the criteria for "major depression without psychotic features, single episode," but he also notices the lawyer's excellent ability to listen, to entertain another perspective, and to test it against his own. This process during the session itself marks a resilience, an ability to still swim freely in the sea of depression, that suggests the patient has the capacity to shift the mood state with the right shift in perspective. In addition, there are strong psychosocial stressors in the presentation: a critical boss, a wife's serious illness, trying to care for young children and still work full-time, and in the context of these, the lawyer's sudden belief that his colleagues see him negatively. The psychopharmacologist resonates with how much stress the patient is facing and observes his resilience in the face of that stress. This is both empathic and a simple reflection of the objective perspective of the psychopharmacologist. He notes that the lawyer's capacity to accept feedback is a significant strength and that given the corporate structure's flirtation with downsizing, it may be wise to "watch his back," to check out his status with others in the firm whom he can trust. The psychopharmacologist goes over the risks and benefits of the SSRI and writes an initial prescription, but he also mentions that psychotherapy sometimes helps when a person is depressed. The lawyer leaves the initial session more invigorated than when he entered the room.

Two weeks later the patient returns looking much better. His mood is upbeat and the tiredness gone; there is a background atmosphere of calm mixed with enthusiasm and hope. The psychopharmacologist is ready to sing once more the praises of Prozac. Yet the lawyer explains that he never took the drug. Instead, he decided to check with a few trusted colleagues in the firm, asking for feedback about his work with them. They remarked that he had aggravated them with his sharp, all-knowing attitude early on in his work at the firm, but he had developed a more open attitude over the last several years, earning their respect. His coming to them to ask was more typical of his changed attitude. It was his boss who was known for his scathing tongue, and rumors had it that significant conflict was emerging between the boss and the other partners. The younger lawyer's position in the firm was not in jeopardy. In fact, he enjoyed considerable support.

Over the next two months the lawyer returns for psychotherapy, which addresses the situation with his wife, the difficult decisions they face, the sharing of work in the home, and his hopes to follow a business interest which may give him greater independence several years down the road. His mood and sleep continue to improve.

The psychopharmacologist gave the patient the option of taking medication, which would have been completely consistent with the diagnosis, but he also intervened psychologically, giving support and noting with the patient the difficult circumstances that surrounded his shift in mood. The lawyer especially appreciated the suggestion to watch his back, and used that suggestion to actually seek feedback and obtain a more objective perspective on his situation in the firm. It is quite likely that if his boss's perspective had been corroborated, he would have returned more depressed, and the Prozac would have been needed. Yet his own resilience allowed him to make use of that support at work and the psychotherapy to cope with this particularly stressful moment in his life. In the initial session the psychopharmacologist noted the patient's strengths, his ability to shift out of the depressed perspective, and his lack of suicidal thinking. These all suggested that psychotherapy might help even without medication. Either option was reasonable. The patient was given the choice, and the psychopharmacologist used his relationship with the patient to "ride the bus" with the patient while the patient discovered the most appropriate treatment.

A second dilemma is common: if medication takes the edge off the patient's symptoms, will the patient have enough motivation to address a problematic social situation or psychological problem? An example is the middle-aged housewife who doubts herself and is under-appreciated by her teenage children and critical husband. We know that a SSRI will diminish her irritability and help with other symptoms of depression, but is her irritability also a signal that something is out of balance in her relationships? Is she giving too much of herself away, and if the SSRI works, will she simply continue to give herself away in a less irritated way? Initially, the psychopharmacologist does not yet know the patient well enough to sort this out in a tactful way. If the subject is broached without tact, the patient who is familiar with being deferential may simply take this as one more example of her failures and tie it to a self-negating perspective. The psychopharmacologist must either ride the bus for a while with the patient, build the relationship, and help psychotherapeutically when the time is right, or respectfully refer the patient to a trusted psychotherapist who recognizes the situation and will offer the needed support. With the latter approach, the psychopharmacologist might say, "There are two places where I can help. First, medication often restores energy and equilibrium when the body is tired like this. Second, people who give so much to others get tired out, and it is often helpful to have someone to talk with about your struggles to find something for yourself while still doing so much for others. This talking with another person sometimes works by itself or in conjunction with the medicine. Which approach sounds best to you?"

This problem of medication taking the edge off symptoms but leaving the patient with significant residual stresses also occurs with patients who have become psychotic or manic. We now have very effective antipsychotic and mood-stabilizing medications, and although they work to diminish the confusion and agitation of a psychotic or manic episode, the recovering patient is often left to struggle with an overwhelming loss of self-esteem and confidence in coping with the stresses of life. In addition, personal, familial, and work relationships have often been damaged during the psychotic or manic episode. The psychopharmacologist has a responsibility to recognize this situation and to refer the patient for individual and/or family therapy. This situation also requires tact, for the referral to another therapist is easily taken as one more rejection by a person whose self-esteem is extremely low. As much as psychopharmacologists may want to avoid getting too involved with these complex cases, these may actually be the ones in which it pays off for the psychopharmacologist to stay more closely involved. If done collaboratively with the patient, the work around the medication may allow for a slow, steady relationship to build, one that is the foundation for other areas of progress in the patient's life.

A third dilemma evolves from the split treatment model. If the psychopharmacologist develops an effective relationship at the right pace, the patient often feels comfortable talking with the psychopharmacologist, and the issues that require psychotherapy naturally find their way into the session. If the treatment is split, how does the psychopharmacologist get the issue into the psychotherapy? The most effective way is time-consuming, but in the long run, perhaps most efficient. The psychopharmacologist arranges a meeting with the patient and the therapist. This is conceived as a chance for "the team" to meet in order to share perspectives on the progress of treatment and to discuss any dilemmas that the patient, therapist, or psychopharmacologist is encountering. When undertaken with a clear sense of humility and mutual respect, this approach can be invigorating as each member of the team can use the others to hear a dilemma and offer suggestions. The value of a fresh perspective is often gained. An agreement with the patient that the psychopharmacologist will send progress notes to the psychotherapist, a conference telephone call with patient and therapist, or simply wondering with the patient how his therapist might approach this material will reduce the split and get the material for psychotherapy into the psychotherapy.

What if the patient recognizes that the psychopharmacologist might deal more effectively with the psychological issue? This situation may happen more frequently when the psychopharmacologist's therapy skill and experience are greater than the therapist's. The psychopharmacologist has a choice: call attention to this wish on the patient's part, with the attendant risk of shame for the patient at having brought something to the wrong door, or shame for the therapist if the matter is not handled tactfully. This should only be done, and done tactfully, if the psychopharmacologist believes that the therapist cannot really help the patient, and the treatment structure must change for the good of the patient. The uncertainties in psychological work are so great that it is somewhat rare for this first option to actually play out like this. The skilled psychopharmacologist must have a way to make use of the team and the sharing of perspectives to advance the treatment through these situations. This leads to the second choice, which is more common and preferred: to handle the matter without much fanfare, make some effort at addressing the material presented for psychotherapy, and then use one of the vehicles described above to get the material back into the psychotherapy. "Here's one take on [the matter just presented], but I'd be interested in [your therapist's perspective on this]; among the three of us we might come up with some interesting approaches." This attitude reinforces the importance of using multiple perspectives in approaching a problem and diminishes the personal authority of any one clinician that is an ever-present risk to the patient in psychological work. Unless the psychopharmacologist has the energy and capability to handle the whole treatment and is willing to fracture a working relationship with a colleague, it is usually more efficient and clinically accurate to follow the path outlined in the second choice.

A fourth dilemma deserves mention: how does the psychopharmacologist recognize when it is better to stop chasing his or her tail with polypharmacy and just to bear with the patient's suffering? Patients with severe recurrent major depression, bipolar disorders, posttraumatic stress disorders, and borderline personality disorders often present their therapist and/or psychopharmacologist with multiple sets of symptoms that are difficult to treat psychopharmacologically. When one symptom comes under control, another emerges. The stakes are high because the patient often feels that life isn't worth living, and indeed the risk of suicide is very real. If the psychopharmacologist forms an empathic relationship, she appreciates the patient's suffering and feels somewhat responsible for helping to alleviate it. It is not uncommon for these patients to present with combinations or alternating symptoms of depression, agitation, paranoia, panic, obsessive-compulsive disturbances, sleeplessness, and generalized anxiety. It is no wonder the psychopharmacologist often ends up prescribing a cocktail of medications: mood-stabilizers, novel antipsychotics, antidepressants, and benzodiazepines, not to mention more than one in some classes, and an augmenting agent such as methylphenidate or thyroid hormone. The treatment starts off innocently enough, with depression usually appearing as the main symptom, but mild improvement in some depressive symptoms is followed by the emergence of several others. The risk of suicide raises the stakes. In some patients the cocktail actually works, so there is hope that if one hits the right combination, life will be bearable enough for the patient that some areas of function will return. When the medication list reaches four or five, the psychopharmacologist often wishes that she had not been so hopeful at the start and had just stuck to a novel antipsychotic, explaining that some relief was possible, but not too much. Consultation is welcome in such situations. Because suicide looms as an ever-present risk, there is understandable caution about peeling back the lithium or the antidepressant. Electroconvulsive therapy is always an option, and for a brief period, will likely decrease the risk of suicide. It sometimes "clears the slate," making possible a fresh start to the medications, now informed by the complexity of the pre-ECT symptomatology.

It is our experience that split treatments make it more likely that these complex cases will receive polypharmacy. This may be good in some cases where the unusual cocktail seems to produce a reasonably positive result, but there is also a great deal of unpleasant trial and error, with significant side effects and expense. In these cases the psychopharmacologist must form an effective relationship with the therapist and the patient, and often with a patient's spouse or significant other as well. These relationships provide more information, some increase in security, and also a vehicle to wait out brief storms of anxiety or affect without jumping to a pharmacological solution. Experts in bipolar disorder recommend that a pharmacological intervention be evaluated for at least eight weeks or two cycles of the illness, and therefore a significant wait may be necessary to understand the effect of a pharmacological intervention.[4] A sound therapeutic relationship is necessary to weather such cycles without doing too many things at once. There will be less tail-chasing if these cases are identified early, and if the psychopharmacologist recognizes that a more significant investment of relationship will be needed to temper the expectation that a pharmacological solution will produce a completely satisfactory result.

Opportunities for Therapeutic Action

The role of the psychopharmacologist naturally creates an opportunity for several types of therapeutic action. First, the externalization of the problem and the focus on signs and symptoms that are not psychologically intrusive (such as sleep, appetite, and levels of energy) set the stage for developing a safe, non-intrusive relationship. Getting into matters that are too personally revealing before developing an adequate base of trust is discouraged by the very nature of the inquiry, so that patient and doctor follow the principle of respecting psychological privacy while trying to remedy a problem related to an imbalance of chemicals. The stage is also set for sound psychological work because an effective psychopharmacologist listens carefully to the information the patient brings about symptoms. He sets out possibilities for intervention, and then the patient chooses or modifies them. This interactive process is actually a template for a healthy psychotherapy relationship. After six or eight sessions spread out over the course of a year, the patient has formed an opinion about whether the doctor is trustworthy to handle more psychologically sensitive material. This is important for the patient's protection. It levels the playing field and gives the patient control over deeper self-revelation, thus offsetting the somewhat dangerous implication of some psychotherapy that it is healthy to immediately open one's heart to one's therapist. The patient will often say something like, "I know we've been working on finding the right combination of medications so I'm not so depressed, but I've been thinking about some stuff that happened when I went on a high school trip to Europe, and it's bothering me." At this point the patient has either done a brief psychotherapy with another therapist or has no therapist. The easiest way to handle the material is to open the field for a discussion, and this may lead to some deeper work regarding a traumatic experience or some other matter that warrants review, placing it in perspective from the safety of a good relationship. Chapter 7, "Working with the Borderline Patient," contains a vignette that illustrates the positive psychotherapeutic work which may occur once the psychopharmacologist has slowly established a dependable and non-intrusive relationship.

If the patient has no therapist at this point, she can be referred for therapy. If the prescriber is working in an HMO or community mental health center, it is important that his respect for the patient and his subtle knowledge of what might help therapeutically be passed on to the therapist directly or to the program director making the case assignment. Careful attention is required at this juncture, since what was unfolding naturally may be interrupted or dropped in the transition and assignment of the new therapist. This can set the treatment back, and it is also inefficient. A brief conversation among members of a working team can often keep the treatment moving smoothly, with little inconvenience to the patient.

If the patient has had a good experience with the therapist who did the HMO-sanctioned five to eight sessions a year ago when the depression set in, the psychopharmacologist may briefly survey the new material and suggest that the patient take it back to the therapist. This strategy will work if the patient has confidence in the therapist from a year ago and a positive feeling strong enough to warrant reconnecting. The psychopharmacologist gives a call to the therapist, preferably with the patient in the room, to let him or her know that the patient would like to come back to address a matter of importance. If the patient does not feel so positively about the original therapist, the strategy of referring the patient back for "psychotherapy" meets the HMO's operational plan to keep psychotherapy out of the hands of the person designated to supervise the medications, but it risks turning the patient away from the clinician with whom he has developed the steadier relationship. The patient then feels rejected and frustrated by the system. This is difficult for the patient and also less efficient. For the split model to work, the therapists must be very good at quickly forming effective, lasting relationships where the patient feels comfortable returning when needed.

Another opportunity for therapeutic action naturally moves toward work with the spouse or significant other. The patient will often say something like, "I know we've been working on helping my mood and my suicidal thoughts, and I know that if we hadn't added the lithium to the Wellbutrin I would have killed myself. It really helped. But I'm also thinking that if I can't get my husband to spend more time at home with me and with the kids, I will still feel depressed." At this point the patient is already getting much better and is able to articulate a level of concern with the quality of life she would like to lead. She likely has an individual therapist, and at this point the psychopharmacologist might wonder how she and the therapist are approaching this important realization. As a result of this discussion, the therapist and the patient may want the husband to come in for some sessions as a couple. The three of them can discuss whether there are enough marital concerns to introduce a third clinician. Sometimes it is possible for the individual therapist or the psychopharmacologist to do the couple's portion of the therapy.

Similar opportunities occur with families. This is especially true with the parents of an adolescent or young adult whose life trajectory has been significantly altered by a severe depression, manic episode, or psychosis. Parents and child are often relieved by a doctor who is willing to meet with them to field their questions and who can give them some sense of the prognosis. This is a matter to be handled with careful attention, however. How does one provide some sense of where the illness may head without going beyond one's very limited knowledge of what may happen for a particular individual? How does one respect knowing and not knowing? How does one convey hope while not minimizing the very real disorganization and suffering of the patient, and the fact that it may take a long time for the patient to begin to feel better? The psychopharmacologist also has a responsibility to make sure that the patient has an opportunity to have a relationship with a therapist who will be present during this period of recovery and new growth. Much good work remains to be done in exploring ways for the psychopharmacologist to handle the relationship with parents and children throughout all the stages of a difficult illness.

Finally, the recurrent nature of most anxiety, affective, and psychotic disorders means that the psychopharmacologist will often have the opportunity to provide intermittent treatment over many years. In a world with fewer extended families living in one geographic area and less likelihood that a person will remain with a given employer for any extended period of time, the possibility of a long-standing relationship with anyone is a potential treasure. The quality of that relationship can be a source of healing for the patient and a source of satisfaction for both the patient and the psychopharmacologist.

The Psychopharmacologist's Work with Other Treaters

Working with the Therapist

With the split between psychopharmacology and psychotherapy that is so common today, it is essential that the psychopharmacologist develop skills for working collaboratively with the psychotherapist. As noted earlier, there are many situations that evolve in the treatment of patients that require good communication between these two treaters. Perhaps the first hurdle is for the psychopharmacologist and the therapist to get past their natural competition to deliver the most effective treatment and, rather, to discover the value of their relationship as a source of added insight and emotional support to each other in the care of the patient. Once they begin thinking this way, they can relax, and creative possibilities unfold between them and among them and their patient. Communication, respect, support, and learning serve as the foundation of a relationship that enhances care and personal satisfaction. Simple measures such as a call from one to the other or a note to give information about a referral or a recent session are the starting points of the relationship. A useful rule of thumb is to let the other know when you've noticed something positive in the work he or she is doing with the patient. This begins to offset the self-doubt that often masquerades as quiet contempt or downright arrogance. The relationship is built by establishing a genuine basis for respect. Details of specific circumstances where interaction is common have been noted earlier.

Working with the Clinical Nurse Specialist

When functioning optimally, the RNCS-psychiatrist team brings the advantages of a two-person team to patient care. For example, with a highly suicidal patient with schizoaffective disorder, the patient may perceive one caregiver as more anxious and likely to hospitalize while the other is more tolerant of bearing significant anxiety. This split may be addressed in a joint session where the patient's own ambivalence about living or dying can be borne by all three parties. There may be more opportunity to understand the complexities of the patient's situation than one would have if working individually. There may also be some relief in sharing the immense burden that comes with treating a highly suicidal patient. The danger of the split can be addressed through the joint meeting. While the team must be consistent with respect to criteria for diagnosis and intervention with various types of medication, in clinical practice there are often several options that may bring about a good result, and having more than one perspective is often helpful. In addition, having two clinicians familiar with a patient's care allows greater continuity of coverage during each treater's vacations and illnesses and more opportunity for a timely appointment in urgent situations.

Some practical suggestions emerge from our early experience with this model. When we had the doctor see all patients first and then refer them to the RNCS, the doctor had a better handle on the case, but the RNCS felt she had to repeat the process of the initial evaluation. This could be annoying for the patient. There were also more patients to be seen than the doctors' schedules allowed, so if they all waited to see the doctor first, their care was unnecessarily delayed. On the other hand, if we had the RNCS see the patient first, there was a higher rate of no-shows for the follow-up visit with the doctor. This meant that the doctor was not really supervising the care. He or she had no direct experience of the patient and would have to rely on written reports without the clinical experience that makes them vivid. In addition, the medical staff of the acute (inpatient) services passed bylaws requiring physicians to do the initial evaluation and treatment plan for all patients seen by a physician's assistant or nurse practitioner. This seemed appropriate for the high-risk cases that present to the acute services, but the matter of which patients in an outpatient service need to be seen first by the psychiatrist was still to be resolved. From a practical point of view, and that of the physician, it is easier for the psychiatrist if she sees the patient first, so that she can establish a relationship, literally develop a first-hand view, and then be more available should the situation require it. It is also better from a risk-management point of view if anything untoward should unfold. The care is more likely to be perceived as thorough, and even if an adverse event occurs, there is the possibility of a good relationship with the patient if the supervising psychiatrist has actually met with the patient. A half-hour session within two weeks of the RNCS's initial evaluation is another way to get the psychiatrist involved in a real way early on in the treatment.

The fundamentals of a good relationship apply to the RNCS-psychiatrist dyad: trust, respect, and mutuality. Optimally, they share similar values such as the importance of establishing a good alliance with the patient, developing a thorough base of clinical information, and engaging the patient in the decision-making involving medication trials. These are three elements of sound clinical work as well as risk management, and knowing that one's colleague is attentive to these decreases the anxiety that stems from sharing responsibility for the care of a patient that one does not see regularly. Routine meetings for supervision and a shared interest in learning are key factors in ensuring that the relationship evolves and grows over time. It is also important to communicate to the patient the nature of the relationship between the RNCS and the supervising psychiatrist. A verbal explanation of the partnership working on the patient's behalf is often sufficient, although we have also found that a written document explaining the role of the RNCS adds to the patient's understanding and appreciation of having a treatment team.

Working with the Primary Care Doctor

As health care becomes more integrated over time and as the conceptualization of mental illness becomes better understood in terms of its physiological underpinnings, there is a growing awareness of the utility of having psychiatrists and primary care doctors communicating with each other. Third-party payers are aware of the fact that 27% of

patients in a primary care practice meet the criteria for a mental illness or substance abuse disorder.[5] A recent study has shown a reduction in medical expenditures when mental illness is identified in primary care settings and specialized mental health services are
delivered.[6] These sorts of observations have led many managed care
companies to use communication between primary care doctor and
mental health provider as a measure of the quality of care. In short, a
number of influences are converging to encourage communication between primary care doctors and psychiatrists. The primary care doctors seem to have two general tendencies, either wanting to refer the
patient for treatment by the psychiatrist or wanting to discuss the case
in more detail. More commonly, they wish to have an efficient, timely
consultation and effective treatment implemented by the psychiatrist.
Rapid, direct communication is essential. The rules of primary care
medicine prevail, whereby the doctor will allow interruptions in order
to have a brief telephone contact with another doctor. Let yourself be
interrupted, take the call, and keep it to two minutes or less. When
you call to speak with primary care doctors, let them know you will
need 30 seconds to two minutes to update them on the care of their
patient. They usually want to know your diagnosis and the recommended treatment. There is no need to divulge anything too personal,
just the basic outline. Primary care doctors are very appreciative of
concise information, such as medications and dosages, laboratory
data, and brief notes. The second, less frequent encounter involves
primary care doctors who would like to discuss a case in more depth
because of their interest in the complexity of a situation. Often they
have a very sound understanding of the biopsychosocial stresses on
the patient. Whatever the case, there is a growing opportunity for
psychiatrists to form brief, focused relationships with primary care
doctors around the care of their patients. Often this leads to increased
referrals, establishment of trust, and the seeking of help for themselves and/or family members. It may be the beginning of a destig-
matization of mental illness in the medical community.

The Pros and Cons of Split Treatments

"Split treatment" is a term used to describe treatments where the patient is seen by one clinician for psychopharmacology and by another
for psychotherapy. During the 1970s and 1980s when there were
fewer restrictions on delivering psychiatric care, psychiatrists themselves would sometimes "split" care, having one do the medication

part and another focus on the psychotherapy with a patient. The idea was to keep the boundaries clear between evaluation and management, the core of pharmacotherapy, and listening and interpreting, the core of psychotherapy. In other cases, a psychiatrist might have greater knowledge or talent for psychotherapy or for psychopharmacology. Despite these conceptually or practically driven splits, many psychiatrists did both psychotherapy and pharmacotherapy for the same patient. During the 1990s, the economic policies of the managed care industry made it less likely that a psychiatrist would do both psychotherapy and psychopharmacology for a given patient. Last year one of us met with an area clinical director (a social worker with a master's degree in business) for a large national HMO. He specifically said that he did not want psychiatrists doing psychotherapy with patients in his HMO. He wanted social workers, or occasionally clinical psychologists, doing the psychotherapy and wanted to limit the psychiatrists to evaluation and medication. He believed this was a more effective way to keep costs down. This concept has been popular in community mental health centers for many years. Recently, it has been challenged by one of the large national HMOs, which encourages keeping psychopharmacology and psychotherapy with a single individual. In a retrospective study, that HMO found it actually spent less money when it did not split the treatment.[7] We hope that this debate over the "value" of split treatments will undergo more systematic study.

If we were to articulate the pros and cons of the split model from a clinical and administrative perspective, without the value of the research that should inform our discussion, it would follow these lines. The split model allows for a more team-oriented approach. It provides the advantages of multiple perspectives and the opportunity for more support for the patient and for the treaters. It makes it less likely that a given individual will exert authoritarian control over a patient. It provides the opportunity for clinicians to see more patients and to gain something from that at the expense of greater depth of understanding of an individual. Both the therapist and the psychopharmacologist tend to spend fewer sessions individually with the patient than if the patient saw one person. Thus there is more opportunity for key information to be lost to the treatment unless the clinicians make a special effort to communicate. Split treatment may actually be more expensive, especially with the more difficult cases, since the lost information and the somewhat weaker relationships are more likely to require higher levels of care, such as hospitalization, to help the patient through especially difficult crises. There is less privacy with the split model. There is a greater chance that a psychiatrist will chase his or her tail with polypharmacy rather than wait out minor perturbations of affect or anxiety.

Relationship and the Future of Psychopharmacology

There are currently three generations of psychiatrists practicing. The majority of the oldest generation used medications sparingly, while psychotherapy was the mainstay of their treatment. The middle generation was taught by this older generation as well as by the minority who were psychopharmacologically inclined. During their tenure, advances in the field included neuroimaging, genetic research, and a host of new medications. These psychiatrists have had significant experience in practicing both psychotherapy and psychopharmacology. The newest generation of psychiatrists have had limited training and experience in psychotherapy and have been steered toward a practice of diagnostic evaluation and psychopharmacological treatment. At the same time, nurses with master's degrees in behavioral science have been granted the privilege to prescribe medication under the supervision of a psychiatrist, and clinical psychologists, though suffering some early setbacks, are mounting an all-out assault on the right to prescribe. This turmoil in the behavioral health field is taking place while primary care physicians with excellent medical but little or no psychiatric training prescribe the majority of anxiolytic and antidepressant medications. The outcome of these struggles is not clear.

It is an understatement to say that psychopharmacology has grown dramatically over the past twenty years. Many patients have lived better lives, and some have avoided an early death by suicide, as a result of its advent and wider availability. On the other hand, the widespread use of these new medications has not been entirely for the better. How many patients with bipolar illness have actually experienced a worsening of their affective states with a push toward rapid cycling through the indiscriminate use of antidepressants? There is some evidence to suggest that patients with obsessive-compulsive disorder or panic disorder will do better once they discontinue medication if they have had a cognitive-behavioral treatment. Will the use of medication without psychotherapy to fine-tune anxieties and irritability prevent some people from learning how to manage these by psychological means? These issues warrant our continued attention.

There are promising new developments that will soon directly influence clinical practice. Neuroimaging techniques such as positron emission tomography (PET), functional magnetic resonance imaging (fMRI), and single photon emission computed tomography (SPECT) provide opportunities to visualize cerebral metabolic activity and blood flow during periods of active symptoms and when symptom relief has occurred. As already shown in the studies of obsessive-compulsive disorder, these techniques allow us to assess the effects on the brain of new learning and medication. In addition, they can be used to study the effects on cerebral perfusion of normal emotions, such as a response to a sad thought. Cognitive testing can be performed on people with normal functioning and with specific illnesses such as schizophrenia to assess the effect of a specific illness on cognitive function during a test of concentration. Clear differences in brain activation have been demonstrated in the normal and schizophrenic patient. The effects of medication on cerebral perfusion can be studied in patients with a particular disorder. Preliminary studies hold promise for identifying which patients are more likely to respond to medication when they present clinically with depression. These tools may assist in determining who will respond best to medication and how long to treat them. In addition, the mapping of the human genome holds some promise that subtypes of depression may be identified. It may not be too far in the future when the patient who presents with depression will get a saliva swab for DNA much as one gets a throat culture for a sore throat. It may be possible for the psychopharmacologist to use this DNA profile to determine which medication is more likely to work for this particular subtype of depression. Greater specificity in our medication treatments is likely to occur through the use of these new tools.

As this specificity develops, there will be more pressure to achieve the prediction that the psychiatrist of the future will be a neuroscientist, a consultant to other treaters. The estimated need for these has been placed at 1 per 25,000 population. A neuroscientist who is not a psychiatrist loses the elements of *psyche* and *iatreia,* the Greek words for soul and healing. That would be a significant loss. With all this excitement about greater specificity of treatment, the question remains whether complex biopsychosocial problems really get that simple. For instance, new developments suggest that the hormone oxytocin functions like an antidepressant and is secreted in greater

quantities in socially connected mammals. Likewise, Substance P, a
pervasive central neurotransmitter, has been shown to have a prominent relationship to separation cries, depression, and its possible
treatment.[8] Are these biological clues that there is a biochemical healing value to a medical scientist having a relationship with his or her
patient, the "good chemistry" we mentioned in the Introduction? We
think so. Whether oxytocin or Substance P is the agent of this connection is not as important as the evidence that effective relationships
heal. We have tried to show the basics of how those relationships
work. As the psychopharmacologists of the future have more and
more refined tools at their disposal to target the mechanisms of illness, it is essential that they recognize the importance of what they
can do through their relationships with patients and the network of
people who treat them. Relationship itself may be one of the most potent pharmacological agents. The dialectic between science and relationship that psychopharmacology faces today is really a basic dilemma facing medicine itself over the next hundred years. Will
physicians through relationship continue to develop their capacity to
heal? Will those newly granted the right to prescribe do the same?

Notes

1. Stoll AL, Severus WE: Mood stabilizers: Shared mechanisms of action at
   postsynaptic signal-transduction and kindling processes. *Harvard Review
   of Psychiatry* 1996; 4:77–89. Stoll AL, Severus E, Freeman MP, et al.:
   Omega-3 fatty acids in bipolar disorder: A preliminary double-blind, pla-
   cebo-controlled trial. *Archives of General Psychiatry* 1999; 56:407–412.
2. White M: The process of questioning: A therapy of literary merit. *Dulwich Centre Newsletter* 1988; Winter.
3. Zwillich T: Anxiety builds over jump in liability for prescribing errors: In-
   surers pay more for prescribing error claims than for psychotherapy
   claims. *Clinical Psychiatry News* 1999; February, 27(2):1–5.
4. Potter WZ: Bipolar disorder: Specific treatments? Syllabus and Proceedings Summary, American Psychiatric Association Annual Meeting, May
   17–22, 1997, San Diego, California, p. 270.
5. Barrett JE, Barrett JA, Oxman TE, Gerber PD: The prevalence of psychiatric disorders in a primary care practice. *Arch. Gen. Psychiatry* 1988;
   45:1100–1106.
6. Pallak MS, Cummings NA, Dorken H, Henke CJ: Effects of mental health
   treatment on medical costs. *Mind/Body Medicine* 1995; 1(1):7–12.
7. Goldman W, McCulloch J, Cuffel B, et al.: Outpatient utilization patterns

of integrated and split psychotherapy and pharmacotherapy for depression. *Psychiatric Services* 1998; 49:477–482.

8. Kramer M, Cutler N, Feighner J, et al.: Distinct mechanism for antidepressant activity by blockade of central substance P receptors. *Science* 1998; 281(5383):1640–1645.

II How the Work Gets Done

Commentary to Part II

Leston Havens

Let us search these chapters for "pearls," for examples of unusual and generalizable ideas, what we need to keep at the back of our thinking for ready retrieval. The result will be less than the broadly systematic approach to the body that physicians pack into their minds in medical school, but perhaps more than many collect for psychotherapeutic work. We will also be looking for what *still needs to be done:* what problems defeat us, which situations are most troublesome to manage. For example, we may already sense the great difficulties that remain in evaluating an individual's health and strength.

Out of this survey comes a general point. There are many schools and opinions about psychotherapy, not so much because there is no one way to do the work but because the work itself requires contrasting attitudes and capacities. We need to be both accepting and skeptical, optimistic and realistic, detached but present, active and passive, intellectual as well as emotional, occupied with the past, the present, and the future. Red Auerbach, one of the greatest coaches, gave this recipe for managing a basketball team, "You have to know who to kick and who to kiss." A few of us can only kick, others only kiss; most are often uncertain which to do, or how much. We line up with our own teams on the basis of preferences (for kicking or kissing, thinking or feeling, exploring or training), or in an effort to offset, perhaps to balance, the preferences of others, or because of discovering new attitudes and ideas that need to be implemented. As a result there are many psychotherapies, which may, however, be more similar than different, like humans themselves and their bodies.

It is inevitable that therapists suffer such conflicts because everyone else experiences similar ones. Patients, too, need to be sometimes sociable and sometimes apart, eager but wary, idealistic and realistic, both hopeful and alert. Increasing evidence has shown that our brains are wired genetically as well as shaped by experience, so the individual human repertoire is limited, while life makes unexpected demands. No one "gets it right," no one's habitual repertoire works well in every situation, so we all have much to learn and change.

Awareness of the inevitable dilemmas permits making use of most of the competing psychotherapeutic schools. Gustafson has taught us that each of the schools emphasizes one side or the other of the principal dilemmas: societal demands or the needs of self, unconscious factors or existential humanness, the pull of disease patterns or of personality. And these same dilemmas are the source of patients' struggles, engagement with which represents a significant part of forming effective relationships.

Nowhere are the dilemmas more in evidence than around the issue of medicating. The deepest division within all our work is between those who look to brain and those who look to mind. In the preceding chapter, Sabo and Rand have set the pluralistic cast of the whole volume by balancing two conceptual frameworks in day-to-day decisions for specific cases and setting a relationship foundation under actions of whatever kind.

In the following chapter, Janna Smith plunges us into the problems of psychotherapy by describing patients and situations far from many people's life experiences. This is a fruitful place to begin because often the lack of such differences allows therapists to think they grasp more than they do. When the patient's experience is far from our own, we are immersed in "not knowing" and can learn how to work under those familiar conditions when we *think* we know.

But how do we gain openness to life events that may be what we fear most and have tried to escape? This is Smith's first challenge. It gets still more daunting as she stumbles upon the further horrors patients have kept from her. The most empathetic therapist cannot bear much of what is presented here; even trying to may burden the work intolerably. Then there is a place, she teaches us, for denial, humor, postponement until better circumstances or perhaps a still stronger relationship makes facing difficult things possible.

So we must be willing not to know and, on occasion, to not even want to know or assume, and certainly not to pry. And we must not hurry to interpret. What may look like paranoia, for example, may be an accurate reflection of life events, and the suspicion of paranoia only a reflection of our naiveté. We may also need to get accustomed to being ignored, to sessions missed and inquiries unanswered, without assuming these are signs of resistance. In fact, the patient's life circumstances can be overwhelming. And are we willing to *pursue* the patients when necessary, to go to them, into unfamiliar places? It may be amazing that they come at all, at great sacrifice, in terror.

Our own experience is that the largest difficulty is in tolerating helplessness. Particularly under difficult and dangerous circumstance, we press toward solutions, toward help we can provide, both to assist the patient and to master our own fear. Then treatment can dissolve into a quarrel because our anxious suggestions are ignored or rejected. We have not understood the situation, or that what we suggest may have long ago been tried and found wanting.

Janna Smith also challenges some condemnations of self-disclosure. She knows that many patients cannot be honest with us unless we are honest with them. Freud suggested that the unconscious operates on the "talon principle," an eye for an eye and a tooth for a tooth. Perhaps the same principle operates for self-revelation. Moreover, Smith illustrates how the therapist's honesty can reveal that patient and therapist have much more in common than either believed, so that what appeared to be unbridgeable differences are narrowed.

For these reasons, the situations Smith describes can be among the best ones in which therapists start their experience. Of course it is possible that in moving to more familiar settings therapists will believe they know more than they do, but it is likely that they will have mastered some of the unbearable, learned much about the real facts of life, and escaped at least a few of the traps that easy answers and ready interpretations offer.

With Scherling's study of violent men, we leap across a large psychological space, from the more usual concern for the victims of abuse to caring for the perpetrators. Perhaps such a leap is only possible within the structure of group work, so that in this chapter we have two contributions, the special demands of therapy with violent men and the remarkable ways in which the group facilitates that work.

Scherling begins with an important decision, to try to relax the almost reflexive decision to control men who are often out of control. This is an important modeling of what the men must come to do themselves—surrender control of others, which the power of violence has given them at the same time that it meant they could lose control of themselves.

We quickly see some of the striking advantages of the group structure. Authority and instruction are easily *distributed* away from the leader and among the group members themselves. "We" becomes the source of learning and guidance, not "him" or "it," with less danger of condescension and poorly informed advice. The ground is being leveled, with the result that there are more opportunities for sharing, increased openness, and comradeship, exchanges that quickly become part of the patients' own reflective process, and exchanges now of words and feelings, not harm and violence. Individual psychotherapy has been slow to learn these advantages of distributing authority in the relationship.

The possibilities of validation and support are also distributed, as well as the possibility of withdrawing support from those who are arrogant and denying. Group values are developed bit by bit, and then a sense of community itself. Just as psychotherapy is often the closest, frankest, and most supportive relationship that many people have ever experienced, group work often provides the first reliable community.

Psychotherapists are accustomed to people wondering out loud how therapists can tolerate the work. "How do you listen to that stuff all day long?" (Hence, the old joke: "Who listens?") Scherling's work, however, brings this problem to a new level. People wondered about his judgment in undertaking such a task. He is identified with these "bad" people and criticized afresh. Administrators worry about the furniture. Few worry about *his* strains. Meanwhile, he carries enough fears and uncertainties for ten therapists.

A final problem is that many perpetrators are themselves victims. How do we manage the delicate problem of abuse recollection in people who themselves are prone to violence? Here again the group can be invaluable, as other members may have been there before. There can be no more difficult balancing act in all our practice than exploring and acknowledging abuse while gaining control over the violence it has fostered.

The tension, and much of the excitement, of emergency work springs from the conflicting needs to form an immediate relationship with, usually, a stranger almost at the same time as decisions are made and actions taken on that stranger. The relationship is as important as the decisions, because without it there is little information or cooperation. Griswold writes, "Only authentic interventions will help." By authentic interventions he means those that carry the weight of the workers' understanding and concern, that seem to the patient, in some measure, *for him or her*. Griswold reassures us that we generally have more time than we think, but we seldom know or feel that. Happily, this is also group work. There is a group of workers available not only to the patient but, just as important, to the immediate therapist, too. Tension can be shared, help sought, and comradeship enjoyed.

There is growing awareness that emergency rooms are now at the center of both hospital and community life. With de-institutionalization and managed care, they function as outpatient clinics, sources of advice for therapists and psychopharmacologists, and the base of operation of many outreach teams. Inpatient units were once the heart of mental health care. This heart has moved to the new intersection point of hospital and community.

The chapter on psychoses is an extension of the earlier one on forming effective relationships. Here, however, many demands on therapists reach extraordinary intensity.

All therapists need to be able to give patients freedom. With people in psychotic states, fear and hatred toward authority may be so great that no communication is immediately possible. Many are so sensitive to others and so hidden themselves that anything like a spontaneous gesture is at best awkward and unreadable. How then is a relationship begun? The largest demand is on our capacity to be non-judgmental as well as receptive to the earliest feelings and movements of the other. Some workers seem to be born with these gifts. Most of us learn the hard way that we work in the dark. Discovering that we will bump up against sensitivities, we learn to move gently and be ready to apologize. Happily, the patients are often quick to appreciate good intentions whenever they exist and generous in forgiving blunders.

We must also be ready to recognize and interest ourselves in unconventional, sometimes very original points of view. The most general inhibition to doing so is the fear that we will encourage delusions. In my experience, the opposite result is far more common. Moreover, when unconventional viewpoints are encouraged and then further explained, we often discover their soundness. Thus open-mindedness to the unexpected joins "not knowing" and "not assuming" as critical attitudes for the work.

"Working with the Borderline Patient" may be the boldest of these chapters for entering and attempting to order the densest historical thickets in all psychotherapy. Sabo describes the principal recent workers and their methods, an attempt that is likely to earn him little but enmity. He addresses these classically most difficult patients, who are, like the grand hysterics that preceded them, the most attractive to theorists of every kind. And he sorts the theories out.

Sabo works from an advantageous position, being both a therapist and an administrator, moreover an administrator in a time when difficult patients cannot be locked safely away. He must find a way that works both for the individual patient and for the organizations endangered by the extraordinary financial demands such patients impose.

He begins in a place unusual for a literature preoccupied with pathology. He wants to find the patients' strengths, what they can do as well as what they can't. He recognizes their passion, their sense of justice, their frequent disdain for authority, including the authority of therapists. He does this to stabilize the clinical field as well as to render it more level. But many will resent this ceding of authority to the patient. We hope they will come to see the advantages.

He directs special attention to managing anger, perhaps the central problem such patients present. He describes different sources and types of anger, and the very different ways of handling them. He opens up the problem of fury, which has given the whole field one of its most famous names, the study of madness.

Then Sabo makes his boldest stroke: he insists that none of the various schools and approaches has a fully adequate answer. We require them all, and the ability to move among them in finding the particular answers that meet patients' needs. Ours is to be a pluralistic psychotherapy, holding the full riches of many strong lines of development.

Caren Plank presents what we believe is the central largely unaddressed problem in psychotherapy: How do we recognize and confirm *the person in the patient?* In contrast with general medicine, our work remains without routinely available tests of healthy functioning. The *host* of whatever disorders are found is poorly defined, elusive, often never mentioned. By "health" of course we mean capacities to work and love, or values that define who we are, or impressions of self-possession and reflectiveness. But the main study of medicine, quantifiable and precise physiological functions, has few equivalents on the psychological side.

Plank demonstrates a rare ability to sense and develop the person in the patient, under the most trying, soul-and-body-destroying circumstances. She notes that the first signs of life can be immediately repulsive—an odor, fears, self-protective withdrawal—so that one needs to move toward the patient even though one's first reaction is to flee. The reason we must be able to recognize, withstand, receive, and confirm the patient's intentions or signs of life, however off-putting, is that without such signs of life there is nothing to relate to.

How does one ensure the patient feels that something different from what has been experienced in the past can occur between herself or himself and others? Carol had been told she could hurt her child. She must often have wanted to. Can anyone support her better efforts, believe in her increasing mastery of them? Plank speaks for that better possibility, but most important, she conveys a quiet confidence which is a kind of miracle for its time and place. She meets the patient's quivering intentions with an intention of her own.

Through many of these chapters, we observe patients confronting dilemmas of human life. There is seldom an even balance to be found between conflicting wishes for society and solitude, giving to others and looking after oneself, following conventions and striking out on one's own. But what if the conflict is between loving a father and surviving his abuse, or between keeping silent about the abuse and testifying to it in a court of law? How does the mind contain the two sides of that dilemma? Plank saw Carol's ability to do just that as a remarkable demonstration of her strength. We believe its recognition operated as a stimulus to being believed in, an example of strength that would be difficult for anyone to surpass, and an enduring gift to the relationship.

Therapists, Plank suggests, need to acknowledge when they lack the resources to do what patients need, and yet not disappear psychologically or lose hope. This is more difficult than it may appear. The confession can be painful or not possible at all, and the silence may attenuate the relationship, blunting the patient's intentions and our own.

Development, Plank writes, "is inevitably a process which entails deep anxiety and profound hope." She is saying that anxiety can be healthy, even something to be celebrated, because of the great aspirations it signals. But observers may be unsettled by that anxiety, may try to take over the enterprise, direct or even discourage it, and squash the hope of independence. The reality of possible failure is not necessarily a morbid rumination. It can also be a sensible realization, an alerting to danger, and, if endured, one of the badges commemorating the difficulties of the fight. Thus old soldiers recount both their terrors and their triumphs.

Some will fault Plank for what may seem unprofessional places of meeting, self-disclosure, or sharing family life. And only a person with firm professional boundaries can practice in this way. But the fact is, there are cases that require it.

3 Psychotherapy with People Stressed by Poverty

Janna Malamud Smith

People who are poor are often badly served by psychotherapists and clinics. Since many mental health practitioners are from the middle class, and since American society is stratified, therapists who work in clinics that serve low-income citizens may have little personal knowledge of their clients' lives. This chapter looks at some of the dilemmas faced by people who are poor, and suggests ways of doing useful psychotherapy.

While the urban hospital where I work serves people who are poor for diverse reasons—those who lack money because they are psychotic, because they are physically ill, or immigrants, or students, or unemployed—I will focus primarily on the poor, alienated, and marginalized women I have known over the past fifteen years. Some are white, some Latino, and some African-American; most live in low-income housing; most have children. I will begin by describing the context of their lives, and then explore some psychological aspects of poverty. In the final section I will discuss treatment—including dilemmas for therapists and ways to adapt therapeutic technique.

The Setting

In 1978, as a graduate student in social work, I was placed in the psychiatry department of a hospital which had a satellite clinic in a housing project. I worked part-time in the clinic, and subsequently was employed by the hospital and worked in the clinic until 1992. I still meet with several patients who live in the projects, and the experiences I recount come from home visits, office sessions, and supervision.

The housing projects I worked in were mostly built after World War II to house young white soldiers returning from the war and hoping for a place to start a family. In the 1960s and 1970s they were integrated—somewhat to the dismay of the white working-class families, who responded by trying to move to the suburbs. Although these projects are small, well-managed, and more viable than most, by the late 1970s they had fallen into terrible disrepair. Several have since been rehabilitated, but they remain difficult places to live. Their residents often refer to them as ghettos. Families are largely single-parent and female-headed. Drugs and alcohol are abundant. Few people can find or manage regular work. People are trapped by many factors, one of which is the Kafkaesque nature of the welfare system. A small example: a poor family managed to send a child to college, where, in order to pay her tuition, she took a work-study job. Since she lived at home, her income was added to her family's total, and her family lost their food stamps—even though her income went to college expenses. When the family called the welfare office to object, a worker suggested that if the student became pregnant the food stamps would be restored. Unfortunately, attempts to reform the welfare system have tended to be equally ineffective.

Let me start with a story. In my mailbox at work is a message from Mary. Mary almost never calls. The message asks that I call her back at the "Night Owl," which is a bad bar—violent, down and out, druggie. But Mary—who stopped drinking ten years ago, and stopped taking drugs six or seven years later—still goes there to see friends and hang out. I feel frankly weird calling back a client at a bar, but I do. She answers the phone herself, her voice friendly and a little hesitant. "They're spraying my apartment [for cockroaches]. I had to get out." Mary has terrible asthma and bouts of agoraphobia. For the past dozen years I have been home visiting her. She pauses. She wants me to do something about our appointment, but I do not know what. I am hoping that she will say. For years she would never say, but lately she has been beginning to do so.

"I was wondering if you could come by and we could talk."

"In the bar?" I ask—my therapist's superego quaking off the Richter scale.

"No, in your car."

"How about if you walk over to the hospital to see me?"

It is an extremely cold, windy day in January; the bar is a mile away. I know she vomits if she gets on a bus, and feels lucky to have gotten out of her apartment at all. I suspect that she is wearing spike heels and an evening dress, because if she dresses up she has an easier time overcoming her agoraphobia and leaving her apartment. If she looks good, she feels less shame.

"You want me to walk over?" she asks.

"No, that's okay," I say. "I'll come." She is relieved.

"I'll be waiting outside."

We sit in the car. Mary talks about her neighbor who was recently evicted from the housing project for using cocaine. Her neighbor's kids have been taken by the Department of Social Service and are with the neighbor's sister. Mary doesn't think the sister is in much better shape than the mother. Mary is letting one of the kids stay at her house. We talk about how she deals with feeding everyone, and how she has run out of money. One of Mary's teenage daughters is up on charges for dealing cocaine. Since she was arrested, she has stopped dealing. We talk about whether she will get off. Mary is afraid that her daughter cannot take care of herself—has no idea how to survive. It is still a week until the next check day, so Mary is going to hit up some of the men she knows when they come into the bar after work. If she can collect thirty or forty dollars, she can make it through. After fifty minutes have passed, I tell her that our time is up. She tells me how relieved she feels to talk, and thanks me for coming. She goes across to the bar, and I drive home frankly hoping no colleague has seen me.[1]

Clearly, I am not describing your typical office visit. Rather, it reminds me of a poster I once saw of a frog whose legs became awkwardly tangled as he tried to inch along the bottom of a leaf without falling off. I'm the frog: the more alienated the person I am working with, the more I find myself bending in ways which—at the least—trouble my sense of form, and typically make me feel foolish. While most therapy with the poor women goes on in my office and uses conventional methods, the work pushes for accommodations. Psychotherapists are sensitive to the problems of patients (or therapists) who continually challenge the traditional prohibitions of psychotherapy (much is written about the importance of "maintaining boundaries"), but excessive caution may become a way of excluding patients who need flexibility. A useful way to think about flexibility is as a means of sparing a patient unbearable shame.

Contemporary Poverty

If we can justify grouping disparate human beings together as "poor people," it is because we find common elements of poverty manifest in their suffering. When people lack money in a culture where others have a lot of it, they face two overarching problems. The first, and more universal, is the dire nature of poverty: people without access to the resources that money provides live without adequate protection from dangers and traumas like hunger, homelessness, and violence. Their day-to-day survival is often an issue, and worry is never-ending. The second is that when poverty exists in a context of affluence, people tend to feel alienated, shamed, and angered by their marginalization. Attempting to survive in extreme circumstances, people without money make choices which are difficult for outsiders to comprehend and thus are subject to simplistic maligning—a process which increases alienation.

Some physical aspects of contemporary American poverty have improved during the twentieth century: more people get some medical care; almost no one out-and-out starves (though people are frequently hungry and eat malnourishing food); more people have some shelter and some clothing; a higher proportion of poor children live to adulthood. Still, much is unchanged, and situations are so difficult that people are repeatedly endangered. The easy availability of guns is an obvious problem.

Some of the ways in which poverty can force people to demean or endanger themselves have been consistent across time. For example, when leaving a city theater I saw young boys performing acrobatics on the street—doing flips and handstands on the hard asphalt with no mats to break their falls—hoping that theatergoers would throw coins. Seeing them reminded me of an account by an English contemporary of Charles Dickens who in the 1830s described small boys following after carriages on their thickly callused and filthy hands in the hopes of earning pennies. (A patient who read this paper pointed out that my analogy may be faulty since the boys I saw were performing a popular form of dancing—and thus were drawing satisfaction from demonstrating a skill.)

Many of the poor women I have known sell sex in order to get money for their families. When Victor Hugo wrote *Les Misérables* in the 1860s, he described similar scenes. The popular image in the media of prostitution is more likely to focus on flashy call girls, or teenage hookers, and less likely to include mothers trying to supplement their welfare checks.

A third continuity is hunger. Many families run out of food between welfare check days. I remember hearing of one desperate mother with seven children who chained and padlocked her refrigerator to ration the family's limited food. People who are not too ashamed make use of food pantries, taking home the day's leftovers from bakeries and restaurants. I remember a home visit I made where the only food in a woman's house was a pile of fancy but stale raspberry croissants.

The Psychological Impact of Poverty

Contemporary poverty may be even more psychologically harmful than poverty in the past, when there was less overall affluence, less advertising, and fewer commodities to consume. It is possible that under these conditions, poor people felt less intentionally excluded and deprived. The people whom I came to know while working in the clinic were aware that they were poor not because of an overall shortage of goods, but because of a lopsided and unfair distribution. They felt knowingly wronged. Like political refugees, they had to deal with the fact of having been rejected by their homeland.

Television—and the media generally—is a second forceful psychological pressure of contemporary poverty. All the families I knew in the housing projects owned several televisions. I have seen apartments without adequate beds that had a television in every room. It is a standard child's birthday present, and a popular resale item in the underground economy. Televisions stay on all the time—I think partly to manage fear and isolation—and the schedule of shows often organizes the day's activities. (If you wonder why a client is reluctant to come to an early afternoon appointment, check the soap opera listings.)

Obviously, televisions abound and stay on in plenty of middle-class or affluent homes as well, and most people have moments when they do not want to be interrupted—whether during "Masterpiece Theater" or "The Simpsons." Everyone who watches television is bombarded by the things that he or she doesn't have, and the fact that status, self-esteem, and overall worth are determined by their possession. So what is the difference? One difference is that middle-class people can afford a wider variety of activities and are thus less exclusively reliant on television as a window through which to see the larger world. A corollary is that the world portrayed in advertising is often one with which middle-class people have personal experience, so it is easier for them both to feel part of it, and conversely, to reality-test it and defend against it.

But more to the point, middle-class people watch an advertisement knowing that they can purchase what is advertised and thus reap the implicit status reward; they feel that the choice is theirs. For people without money and isolated in housing projects, television programs define much of their view of a world which excludes them. Furthermore, each advertisement serves as a reminder of the status they cannot have. I have seen more than one family use their last food money to purchase name-brand sneakers for a small child. The deprivation of food is less important than the deprivation for the child of living as a generic-housing-project baby. A gesture like this, which may seem foolish to an outsider, is an effort to rescue a child from the devalued status of not having. When her oldest daughter graduated from high school, Mary rented her a limousine for the prom even though it meant doing without necessities for weeks. She wanted her child to feel that she was as good as anyone else.

Another psychologically difficult dimension of contemporary poverty is the high degree of isolation—both social and physical. During the first six or eight years I worked in the projects, residents met with city representatives to beg that their address be changed from "Jefferson Park" to a neighborhood with streets like the rest of the city. (It was.) Women in one of the groups I ran spoke about having acquaintances drop them off blocks from home to hide where they lived.

Much of the isolation is economic. With little money, people can participate in few activities. Movies, museums, restaurants, harbor cruises, or trips to Disney World are only made possible by linking up with a working boyfriend, or buying a winning lottery ticket. But a deeper ramification is that what starts out as economic becomes social. A separate world is created which has its own ways. Consequently, many people feel inadequate or unwilling to participate in life outside the projects. A young woman whom I treated had been asked out by a man who was a little better off than she. The woman turned down the invitation because she was terrified that he would take her to a restaurant where she would have to order from a menu, and she did not know how.

When I first started working in the housing project, I had similar feelings. I developed culture shock because the world of the projects seemed so foreign. I felt tongue-tied sitting with people whose references I could not understand; it made me feel lonely and isolated, unsure how to behave. Once, when someone I home-visited insisted on preparing lunch for me, I felt half-paralyzed with discomfort. Not only was I violating the rules of psychotherapy (though not so much those of social work, which would honor such a gesture), but I did not know how to be her guest. Should I accept seconds? Should I help clear? Should I notice her child, awake and whimpering but unattended in a crib in the next room? Most of us must overcome a certain inhibition in order to leave our own worlds. The difficulty is heightened when one feels unwelcome and vulnerable to ridicule.

Another source of isolation resulting from poverty is more subtle. All of us extrapolate the larger world from our own experiences; they determine the generalizations we will make. I have often noted that my clients possess quite different—but perhaps equally unexamined—conclusions about the world from my own. For example, as the Iraq war began in 1991, my patient, Mary, prepared to be killed. She told me that she had no idea where Iraq was, nor how far airplanes could fly. But she knew that in her world—on the street—no one would challenge and provoke as Saddam Hussein had unless he was certain of winning. So she felt deeply worried. For my part, I believed the war was a mistake, and I participated in protests. Yet I felt quite sure I was going to live—protected by the defense system I disliked. We each felt a sense of isolation and alienation, but for very different reasons. Living with a greater sense of daily danger, Mary extrapolated more global danger.

An additional psychological pressure of contemporary poverty is that it necessitates endless involvement with bureaucracies—much of which feels devaluing. If you receive welfare, your eligibility is often reevaluated; you must visit an office and prove you still qualify. If you want WIC coupons—which help buy nutritious foods for pregnant women and young children—you need to go to another office, and to yet another to pick up food stamps. To gather enough food for the

Christmas holiday (when all cash goes to providing presents), I have seen women visit as many as eight or ten different programs and churches.

You are sent checks, Medicaid cards, and occasional vouchers. If your rent is subsidized, you are asked periodically to report your income, and if you live in a subsidized apartment, you will be inspected. If someone in your family is arrested for dealing drugs, you can be evicted and denied further access to public housing. The Department of Social Service is often involved in your life, monitoring the way you raise your children. You have to buy "durable goods" on time, paying large amounts of interest. For my clients, that often meant buying from RENT A CENTER where they would end up paying over $1500 for a $700 washer/dryer set, but with a year or more to pay. Saving is not only impossible, but impractical: if surveillance of your bank account reveals more than a minimal balance, you lose your benefits. Whatever the pros and cons of specific measures, they shame people psychologically by forcing them to endure demeaning encounters, often with suspicious or rude people. Clients feel exposed, not trusted—not fully adult. They become guarded. Over time, this erodes self-esteem and increases a weary helplessness. When Mary was a child, instead of food stamps, government workers distributed surplus food such as cheese, flour, and butter. When Mary's mother sent her to stand in line for the food, she felt utterly ashamed. Another patient who qualified for food stamps chose to not eat four or five days a month rather than use them, because he felt too ashamed handing them to the cashier at the food store.

Adaptation and Defenses

How do these women experience their lives? Poverty is traumatizing; inevitably it exposes people to more violence, more violation, more illness, more hunger, more loss, more hopelessness and helplessness. There is little choice. Women struggle constantly with the question of how responsible they are for their circumstances. Privately, many take an inordinate share of the blame, feeling that their own badness must make them deserve their fate. They feel enormous shame about what their lives have come to and enormous guilt not being able to provide more for themselves and their loved ones.

The severity of poor people's circumstances makes life a tightrope without a safety net. There is little margin for error. Spend twenty dollars the wrong way, and everyone is hungry. Such environmental severity, and the mutual blaming and criticism it generates, gets simplified and internalized as a disapproving other. People who live in dire circumstances often castigate themselves harshly and unfairly when they fall short of impossible goals. American platitudes about individual responsibility are punitively internalized. Women believe what they have too often been told: that their circumstances are their own fault. Ironically, in some ways, this preserves a kind of hope. People vacillate between an exhausted lassitude and short, frantic, self-defeating efforts to function at an impossible level. It is common for more affluent people to have many of the same feelings of responsibility when trouble comes into their lives, but having more money helps hold trouble at bay, and helps offer mitigating choices when it appears. Furthermore, more affluent people are less likely to receive messages from all around them which reinforce self-imposed blame.

People's bad feelings about themselves have to be managed somehow. Whereas more affluent Americans frequently project feelings they disown onto poor people, immigrants, and people of different races, the women in the housing project used to project a lot of negative feelings onto their neighbors. A psychiatrist who started the clinic I worked in once explained how he had secured members for a group. At first he simply invited people to come and talk about their lives, but no one came. So he posted signs that said: "Are your neighbors' children out of control? Are other people's dogs making the place dirty and unsafe? Are you being kept awake by other people's boyfriends screaming?" By externalizing the problems, he found women willing to attend the group. Already devalued, the women had viewed the label of psychological problems as an additional burden, an unacceptable price for membership.

Externalization offers a kind of ironic justice, since one awful part of being poor in America is that the society relates to you almost exclusively through projective identification. Those of us who are more affluent often unconsciously project upon the poor the feelings that cause us shame. We do not want to know the reality of people's lives, but prefer to maintain a titillating (and punitive) fantasy of the poor as licentious, weak people. Such a fantasy spares us guilt and political responsibility. It is a truism worth repeating that in housing projects and poor communities, Americans publicly notice all the drug use, family violence, inadequate parenting, crime, and antisocial behavior that we tend to overlook in the rest of the culture.

I was startled when I first realized that poor people knew this, and felt burdened by it. For instance, I witnessed women embracing the projection counterphobically in an effort to master it. The second meeting of a mothers' group I was running began with half the members showing up late and several not coming. I had inherited the group—of middle-aged white women—from a much-beloved community worker who had left to go back to school. No one was happy to have me as the replacement. So when I asked if anyone knew where Linda—a missing member—was, everyone chimed in, "Oh yes, she went to the hospital to visit her boyfriend. He got shot during a 'B & E' [breaking and entering]." The statement of how difficult it felt to come to the group with a new leader was framed as a challenge in the vernacular: "Do you have any idea how tough and bad we are?" Feeling probably more vulnerable and abandoned than anything else, the women first let me know that they were able to handle a world where boyfriends were robbers who got shot. Could I handle their challenge?

Toughness is certainly one effort at adaptation. Poor women feel the need to be tough because the society asks them to withstand so much. In addition, to be known as tough is extremely helpful in the community because it keeps other people from preying on you—stealing from you, bothering your kids. Furthermore, pummeling and being pummeled offers a temporary release from the unbearable tensions of everyday life. Mary and I had many conversations about our different views of violence. My concept of safety—a space safe from violence, where feelings are permitted to make their way into words—for a long time epitomized for her my utter ignorance about her world. Suggesting that she curtail her fighting was like touting unilateral disarmament—something only plausible if you are not the foot soldier on the front line.

Eventually, Mary would tell me about someone she was going to get, and I'd remind her that I wouldn't make home visits to prisons no matter how much the bitch (or bastard) deserved what was coming— a remark which usually made her grin and offer a grudging, "I'm hip." Our success was that she became much better able to choose her fights, to reserve her fists for occasions where someone was being unfairly attacked and there was no other route to justice. What she got back for her increased restraint was status; she became something of a stateswoman in her neighborhood, someone who negotiated disputes and possessed authority. She liked the role.

Behavior that outsiders might deem antisocial is another adaptation. For example, disposable diapers are among the most valuable items for women with young children. They are expensive and cannot be bought with food stamps. Most women have a hard time affording them. If they are lucky, their boyfriend—or a friend's boyfriend—will bring some by. Otherwise, women sometimes trade sex for money to buy them—or to buy other unaffordable items: kid's bicycles, CD players, and so forth. In fact, one ironic angle on the drug trade is that addicted women sometimes trade sex for drugs instead of less transient commodities.

People describe stealing, label changing, hoisting goods, buying stolen goods, and so on. They also con bureaucracies. For instance, many women have trouble paying their phone bills and keeping their phones on. Yet phones are particularly important because mobility is so limited. My patient Mary's solution for a year was to claim to the phone company that her baby used a "breathing machine." The baby did have bad asthma, but Mary knew that the phone company would maintain her phone only if the child used a machine. I heard about several women who bought household items on payment plans, and then intentionally broke them before they had finished paying. Knowing that they had been forced to pay twice the common amount for the item, they felt they were owed a new replacement. To manage such maneuvers, people often play dumb, a consistent adaptation of oppressed people throughout history, but one which fuels self-doubt and invites demeaning projections from outsiders.

An overlooked motive of behavior deemed antisocial is people's wish to give instead of take, their wish to care for those they love. When one of Mary's teenage daughters made money dealing drugs, she immediately bought a fancy Christmas tree and presents for her little brother. Mary stole bandages from the hospital for her downstairs neighbor, who had an open sore on her leg. (The neighbor was diabetic, but she worked in a doughnut shop and continually ate doughnuts. She felt too ashamed to face the doctor.)

Poor people often describe feeling both terrible and justified in breaking rules and laws. They feel entitled to do so because the world treats them badly, but they also feel guilty, and frightened that they might get caught. They often feel deeply ashamed. Even though writers like Helen Block Lewis, Helen Lynd, Heinz Kohut, and others have made us aware that shame is ubiquitous in human society, for the women I knew in the projects, it was the unspeakable plague. Not only did they feel shamed by their poverty, but they felt ashamed because the poverty continually forced them to compromise themselves. If a drunk man offers you $30 for sex, your answer will depend on whether or not you have food in the cupboard. If you don't report the income from your part-time job, you end up always worried that someone will report you.

Generosity and sharing are also responses to the harshness of this life. If it is your check day and not your friend's, you will lend her money, and she will pay you back when you run out. If you have two diapers and your neighbor needs one, you will give it to her. Other mothers will take your kids for weeks at a time if you have trouble. If you are out of food, someone will try to feed you. Do you need to dress up? Someone will lend you a blouse. Do you need a place to sleep? Take the couch and put your kids with my kids in one bed. But the sharing also means that people who have almost nothing are always being asked to part with it. A woman who gets a few extra dollars is immediately hit up by kin and friends, who, if she spends the money on herself instead of them, may be quick to criticize her.

In my experience, middle-class and affluent people are much less generous, and more careful about what they offer. Several people I spoke with who grew up in housing projects and moved into the middle class missed the sharing. Why is it so different? A historical study of witchcraft may offer insight. In his book, *Witchcraft in Tudor and Stuart England*,[2] the historian Alan MacFarland argues that the witch hysteria included this pattern: A poor woman would go to a more affluent family in a community and ask for help—food, clothing, firewood. The family would turn her down. Soon they would accuse her of being a witch. One explanation of this behavior was that the community's economic frame was changing. Rather than seeing extra goods as allowing them to care for others, people were beginning to stockpile to accrue entrepreneurial capital. This may be an incomplete explanation of the witch trials, but it illustrates an ironic shift that I've witnessed during treatments: as people move beyond basic survival, they often stop sharing so much.

A woman who grew up in the housing projects and then trained as a therapist described missing the sense of immediacy and excitement of her original home. Since, aside from drug busts, there is little police presence in poor communities, many disputes are handled privately. This woman recalled the excitement and sense of justice she had felt as a child when a friend's father fired his gun at an obnoxious and noisy ice cream truck driver—who had refused to move from beneath the window—and managed to scare him away. My colleague found her middle-class life more comfortable, predictable, and safe, but also more distant and reserved.

Treatment

The ideal cure for the effects of poverty is money, social justice, and a social order which minimizes the distances between classes, and which brings the greatest possible number of people into the middle class. Since such change is not imminent, groups or milieu programs are probably the preferred methods of helping poorer patients, since groups can work well to fight devaluation and oppression. Unfortunately, joining a group takes enormous up-front trust. Most of the women I have known would not attend a group without first making a strong individual relationship. Most available programs—whether to detoxify people from drugs and alcohol, treat trauma, or treat families—require people to risk putting faith in an alien and frightening system.

Beginning a Relationship

When clients arrive for treatment—possibly because the Department of Social Service has said it is the only way to keep their children, or the court has sent them as part of probation, or a nurse practitioner has recommended they get help—it is hard to overstate the degree of distance usually experienced by both therapist and patient. The issue can be one of race or culture, but often it is primarily social class since the majority of psychotherapists with advanced degrees come from middle-class families.

The therapist's position, modest but worthwhile to the therapist, is likely to be viewed very skeptically. People rightly assume you are not street-smart and wonder what helpful knowledge you could possess. At the same time, they know you have the power to harm them. If they let you know how crazy they feel, you can lock them up. If you find out how they parent, you can remove their children. If you learn about their boyfriend who sometimes helps out, you can get their benefits pulled. Because therapists working in public institutions must also fill out disability forms, sign welfare forms, and report child abuse, the issues of trust are enormous, and sometimes only partially resolved after years of treatment. For instance, a patient who spoke readily about her incest history waited six years to discuss her family members' involvement with drugs.

If treatment is going to have a chance, you must be willing to force the form of psychotherapy to accommodate the people—even as you are trying to help people learn to accommodate the form. Oftentimes, when women come to therapy they are in crisis. Sometimes they will tell you more than they meant to, feel terribly ashamed by what they have revealed, and disappear. Other times they will present themselves in a way they think the therapist will approve—as one-time sinners who have forsaken their evil ways. People tend to think of a therapist as a combination school principal, minister, salvation army worker, extraterrestrial being, and dupe. Often they miss their second, third, or fourth appointment. Therapists complain about—and feel their self-esteem challenged by—the constant skipped sessions. Preoccupied with schedules, therapists fail to comprehend the enormous obstacles a client must overcome to appear at all. How will she get to the office? Who will take the baby? How will she explain where she is going? How will she pay back the favor if someone drives her? Why should she expect that the therapist will do anything but demean and criticize her? And what possible reason does she have to predict that a relationship with a psychotherapist will be anything other than unpleasant, judgmental, and shaming?

For a therapist who undertakes this kind of work, there are endless tests. Some are similar to those of other treatments. Some are different overall or in degree. It seems to me that people test a lot to see what kind of psychic stamina you possess. Will you pursue them? In Margaret Wise Brown's children's book, *The Runaway Bunny,* a baby bunny transforms himself into many shapes to hide from and test his mother. She pursues him. When he transforms into a sailboat, she becomes the wind; when he is a flower, she becomes a gardener; and so on. The book has become a classic because it captures the importance for a child of having caregivers who can psychologically pursue him. Many people in depleted environments have been deprived of the opportunity of such pursuit, the sense that they matter enough to have someone come after them. Too overwhelmed and burdened to respond even when very young children need them, poor women may insist that the child come to them—and feel angry when the child cannot always manage it. Therapists repeat the problem unless they temper their notions of what constitutes motivation. I feel puzzled when professionals too readily question a client's motivation.

Rather than explore resistance too much, it works better to genuinely marvel with people how they manage to make it at all.

The Therapist's Position

Your clients view you as "other." You might not be street-smart, but they imagine you have everything but trouble in your life. They may have fabulously distorted notions of your wealth, or, conversely, they may assume that if you work with them it is only because you cannot manage anything better. Each situation is different, but often it helps the relationship if you answer questions forthrightly. People need (and deserve) to know what planet you come from. Do you have children? Do you live with someone? Where do you go when you take a vacation? Will you send a postcard? Or as someone asked a therapist I supervised, "Why do you have welfare hair?" meaning, why don't you dye the gray out of your hair since you can afford to do so?

Sometimes you need to minimize differences, but usually it is more useful to acknowledge them. If you behave disingenuously, people know. I remember a therapist working in another poor community who made a point of driving a battered car and wearing old clothes, as if that would undo the real distance; it failed. Acknowledging the differences makes common ground possible. One woman I see who is often a little psychotic as well as poor has frequent conversations with me about the differences between being affluent and poor, and white and black. She loves clothes, and sometimes the obvious ease with which I purchase a new pair of shoes feels unbearable to her, and uncomfortable to me. Sometimes she is furious and envious, other times admiring. Sometimes, her anger and envy cause her to withdraw. Other times, she brings the subject up as a way of disguising her other reasons for withdrawing and isolating herself from the relationship.

Sometimes you search hard for shared experience. The same patient called one night thinking she had to go to the hospital. She was terrified of the hospital, but maybe she needed it. She was too anxious. Her boyfriend was out drinking and hadn't come home. She couldn't do her housework. I asked what she couldn't do. She said she couldn't do her laundry because she had recently put too much bleach in a load by accident and ruined a pretty shirt.

"Is that what worries you most?" I ask.

"Yes."

"You know," I say, "I don't use bleach but sometimes I send pens through the laundry."

"Pens?" she asks. "You do?"

"Yeah, and do you know what happens when I do that?"

"Ink everywhere?" she asks—her voice becoming mildly hopeful.

"Everywhere," I agree. "The whole load gone."

She roars with laughter, then says, "You don't know any better than to do that?"

"I guess not."

"Thank you for talking to me, I don't need the hospital. I'll do my housework."

This example illustrates two other approaches I find critical to doing therapy. The first is humor. People whose lives are overburdened are inclined—if the therapist asks them to experience more of their pain than they can bear—to make the therapist the projected bearer of their pain and grief. If the therapist cannot stay out of that role, a patient will flee, hoping to leave the bad feelings behind in the consulting room. The danger of humor, however, is that it sometimes hurts feelings, and if you are inattentive or neglect to apologize, the hurt will go underground and fester.

The second approach is to use stories. You tell them, listen to them, and analyze them in displacement. People often feel better able to let you know their unconscious process through a vivid story. And it often feels more bearable if you respond by speaking to the story rather than too directly interpreting it.

While I tend to favor humor and storytelling with all patients, I emphasize it as particularly useful with people who have so much pain in their lives. Furthermore, traditional kinds of interpretations are more fraught in these psychotherapies than in ones with more affluent, educated patients, who may be more aware of what they have signed up for when they pursue therapy. Interpretations that are not respectful make people feel exposed and ashamed, not understood. But the power of an interpretation to harm rather than help is increased by the social disparity between therapist and patient, and by the degree of shame most patients feel.

Difficulties for the Therapist

One reason therapists are reluctant to accommodate treatment to fit the needs of the poor is that the work is very difficult, and when clients drop out it can be a relief. If they stay, the therapist must witness an unremitting world, and experience her own pain and guilt. When people have so little and are suffering so much, it is hard not to feel both horrified and guilty. Unrecognized, such feelings distort the therapist's judgment, or tempt her to become complicitous with pathology, to make excuses for behavior that needs to be challenged, and unwittingly to increase hopelessness. Conversely, to avoid the discomfort, therapists often ask too much of clients and drive them away.

It is harder still to witness people being harmed, and to bear one's own helplessness. Years ago, I treated an adolescent girl from a very troubled family. Her mother's boyfriend had drowned, but that was the least of it. One time when she couldn't get to the clinic I made a home visit and watched her baby-sit her two-year-old half-brother. She was by turns kind and quite sadistic—taunting and thwarting the child. She dangled a cookie in front of him when he was hungry, pulling it away as he reached for it. Laughing hard, she maneuvered so that he lost his balance, tripped, and hurt himself. When the child could bear no more and dissolved into tears, she comforted him by filling his bottle with orange soda. Glancing into the refrigerator, I saw only large bottles of soda.

My patient thought she was doing a good job. This was life as she knew it. Since she dismissed the questions I raised, I was unsure what else to say. Several hours later, home and eating dinner with my husband, I started weeping unexpectedly, overwhelmed by painful feelings from the home visit. I wanted the toddler to be shielded from her sadism. I wanted the refrigerator to have nutritious food. I wanted the girl to share or accept my views of behavior and relationships. I wanted to be shielded myself.

Another difficulty for therapists unfamiliar with the terrain of a patient's life is distinguishing intrapsychic issues from contextual ones. Because the patient's world seems foreign, the therapist is deprived of the guideposts which she takes for granted in other treatments: the subliminal familiarity of the patient's life. If a patient talks about the difficulty of writing a paper for a course, anxiety about buying a house, concerns about career or children, the person's experience may be vastly different from the therapist's, but the landmarks are recognizable. Working with people who as a group seem very different from oneself, the therapist loses the landmarks, and consequently must spend time orienting herself.

I have found it particularly perplexing to sort out when a situation in which a patient finds herself is really dominated by circumstances, and when it is not. Did a woman fail to come to an appointment because she lacked bus fare, or is that her way of saying that you said something during the preceding session that she perceived as critical? Or maybe her boyfriend was high so she didn't trust him alone with her children. Or maybe she was simply scared of something she was feeling. The circumstances of people's lives impinge so much that it is a constant challenge to insist on space for the intrapsychic, to honor people's experience while still offering an alternative perspective. While one must do this with all clients, the possibility of behaving insensitively is greater here and, conversely, more inhibiting.

Listening to all the semi-legal or illegal things people are doing can be unsettling. It is difficult to decide how and when to comment. People's behavior sometimes makes you angry, sometimes envious, sometimes incredulous. I've had the same feelings working with wealthier people when they describe ways they are cheating, but because I perceive them as having more options, I find it easier to explore the behavior earlier in the treatment.

All therapies are a process of building a shared language, but it is harder when the experiential distance between people is greater. The women I worked with often did not have a lot of words to describe intrapsychic experience, and their language tended to be part of a different frame. For example, a patient told me that she was just "lazy." What is lazy? A piece of a moral construction which from my perspective seemed vestigial and punitive. A second example is a mother who said of a traumatized child, "Her only problem is that she doesn't show me or anyone else respect." Or what did Mary think when I first suggested that it would probably make her feel safer if she could stop getting into fist fights? Throughout her life, the only safety she knew was provided by her fists. Theoretically, all such ideas are ripe for exploration, but in fact, people often quickly clam up, feeling stupid or defensive if you ask them much about what they mean. Questions can feel like authoritarian challenges designed to humiliate.

Some people feel at home with language, but often words seem cheap, or important feelings are inaccessible to language, and are enacted rather than recounted. A patient who had held me at arm's length arrived unannounced in my clinic office one evening as I was getting ready to leave. Her glasses were broken, her face swollen, and her little boy was panic-stricken. A drunk boyfriend had just beaten her up. When we had spoken about her troubles, it wasn't meaningful to her. She had to show me *in vivo*. Words would not convey her experience adequately.

In all psychotherapies I am interested in what patients choose not to tell. Middle-class patients generally feel increasingly open as the treatment proceeds. This is relatively true with poorer patients, too. Yet, no matter how well and how long I have known the women in the projects, they continue to shield parts of their lives. Sometimes, a crisis will cause them to tell me something they have hidden. Sometimes I will just stumble on it. For a while, Mary was buying stolen jewelry—something I found out during a home visit when a boy appeared at the door to sell her gold chains. (I remember feeling oddly proud when she reassured him that "it was cool"—they could do business with me there—yet simultaneously slightly compromised, envious of the ridiculously low price she was paying, and worried that the gold had been stolen from people I knew.) Similarly, during the couple of years when Mary used cocaine, she steadfastly denied to me that she was taking the drug. She knew I might alert people who would take her children, and only told when she felt ready to stop and wanted my support.

All patients have a tough time telling you things they think you will disapprove of or take action on. They also are often reluctant to say things they fear will hurt your feelings. Even with encouragement, most of my poorer patients felt frightened to criticize me directly, or to initiate criticism. To signal me about my empathic failings, they skipped sessions or clammed up; sometimes they could acknowledge my many mistakes when I brought them up. But sometimes I did not think to ask. The disparity of social power is so great that I am not sure it can ever be completely overcome. I can imagine what ambivalent and difficult feelings I would have about someone who offered me support, invited me to confide, yet who I knew could take my children away from me, or jeopardize my income.

Goals of Treatment

The goals of treatment depend on the clients' wishes, the problems they bring, and the length of time you have to work. Often, as I came to know people, I found that they felt depressed, traumatized, ashamed, angry, and desperate. At the beginning of treatment it is good if the therapist can avoid behaving like a cop—or avoid a patient's inclination to perceive you that way. That means dodging projections, surviving loyalty tests, and not trying to address too much at once. The goal is to establish enough trust so that the patient feels safe to continue coming. You try to offer people an explanation of their circumstances which places less blame on them than they do, but which gradually names actions that are self-destructive. You help them experiment with small steps of taking control over massively out-of-control lives. You speak frankly if you think you know why something is going awry. Usually you must help a person give up an addiction. In many states, the law requires you to report instances of child abuse or neglect. If you must file a report, explain clearly to the client what you are doing and why—before you do it.

If the patient decides that therapy is useful, and if there is a way to fund it, long-term work is often beneficial. At first, the therapist is likely to encounter many crises. Gradually, if the patient feels a little more in control of her life, therapy can focus on some of the intrapsychic problems—the trauma, the abuse, the numerous losses, the enormous shame. Another problem, stemming directly from the massive deprivation, is what Ivan Boszormenyi-Nagy calls "destructive entitlement"—the feeling of being owed a debt which you feel entitled to extract from inappropriate parts of the environment. For instance, because a woman's mother neglected her, she may be asking her five-year-old to make lunch for the younger children. It is worth exploring the pros and cons of such an arrangement. It may be necessary, and it is not always pathological; but it might be. Is the mother thanking and admiring the child, or merely assuming that the child's service is her due? Does the child more often feel competent and proud, or resentful and overburdened? Do both the mother and the child realize that the child is assisting rather than serving or replacing her mother?

If therapy succeeds, you will often see patients increase their ability to make stable relationships—I'm not sure why. Maybe the comfort of talking and getting predictable support eases other exchanges, maybe it is because substance abuse and acting out diminish, maybe it is because people recognize something positive they want from a relationship, or feel a little more hopeful. Whatever the reasons, with more stability the patients' finances tend to improve a little. Eventually, you try to help clients feel less alienated, and help them connect or reconnect with social institutions: to work if they can; to attend support groups like Alcoholics Anonymous; to attend church; to pursue a high school equivalency degree; to join a tenants' organization, or whatever their own interests and needs warrant.

Coda

My patient, Mary, grew up in adverse circumstances. Her mother dealt heroin, and, when the police came, she sometimes hid the drugs on the children. They moved frequently and suddenly. Mary never lived with her father—in fact, she met him only once, in a chance encounter on the subway. Her one ally, a grandmother, committed suicide when she was nine. Her brother started setting fires, and burned down their home three or four times. There was a stepfather Mary liked who seemed to stabilize things a little. But one day her mother came home and announced that she had just married another man. The stepfather left. The new husband turned out to be an alcoholic boxer who beat his wife. Mary moved out when she was about sixteen, worked in a bar, and lived with different men.

She was homeless when I met her in 1979. She owned nothing. She was subject to terrible drinking binges, where she would consume hundreds of drinks, get into bar brawls, and take drugs. Her two children had been taken away. She had no interest in therapy, but she wanted her children back. I immediately liked her willingness to fight the system, her warmth, and her wry humor.

Fifteen years later, one of her children, who graduated from high school, has an apartment and a baby of her own. Two other children continue to live with Mary—one attending college, the other in grade school. Mary has been sober for over a decade. She has completely given up heroin, cocaine, and hallucinogens. It has been several years since she last laid a fist to anyone, and she prefers not to fight. She lives in an apartment that she has furnished fully: it has beds, a sofa, chairs, a washer and dryer, televisions, pictures on the walls, photographs of children, lamps, a coffee table. Thanks to a colleague who voluntarily taught her for many years, she has mostly learned to read. She participates in a women's group, pays most of her bills, and some nights cooks for her family.

There are problems. The oldest child has had two psychiatric hospitalizations, and has a dissociative disorder—probably because her early childhood was so traumatic. Though only in her twenties, she is unable to hold a job, receives disability, and is struggling as a new mother. At one point rumors surfaced—never substantiated—that the second child was molesting younger children. Mary still has times when it is difficult for her to leave her apartment. She still prefers to stay up during the night and sleep during the day. She still dissociates ("loses days") after stressful events. She still has bouts of depression. Her physical health is bad, and it is unlikely that she will ever be able to work. But she is alive, a fact which continues to amaze us both.

Notes

1. I originally published this part of Mary's story in the "A Week in the Life" column in *The Family Therapy Networker,* July/August 1992, pp. 69–71.
2. A. MacFarland. *Witchcraft in Tudor and Stuart England.* New York: Harper & Row, 1970.

4 Group Psychotherapy with Violent Men

Donald Scherling

At times people have asked me why I would want to work with violent and abusive men. "They should be locked up and never let out again." "How can anyone beat a child or his partner or spouse?" People have strong reactions to violence. I have had similar reactions to interpersonal violence and have worked hard to avoid conflict and violence in my life. Generally I've found it easier to identify and empathize with victims than with perpetrators of abuse and violence. Before I started my group for violent men, many of my clients were from the other side of violence and abuse: adult victims (mostly women) or families with adolescents and children who had been or were currently involved in relationships marked by physical violence, psychological maltreatment, and sexual abuse.

Having seen the devastation in the lives of victims of violence, I have struggled to make sense of my own considerable disgust and anger directed at both real and imagined abusers. At times I have had to work hard to restrain my own polarized position and my frequent fantasies of revenge and rescue. I have struggled to understand and accept the complex issues of loyalty and commitment that my clients often felt toward their abusive family members. Like others, I was sometimes quick to criticize victims who chose or felt compelled to remain in dangerous relationships despite considerable outside pressure or support to leave (from extended family members, police, social service agencies, and therapists).

This mixture of feelings, combined with my interest in family therapy and treatment that addresses whole systems (including both victims and perpetrators in the context in which they live), drew me to work directly with men who have used violence in their relationships. I have also been interested in research confirmed by my clinical experience which indicates that a majority of perpetrators of violence were themselves victims of violence and abuse. In approaching this work I hoped to find a way to be balanced and respectful in my attempts to intervene in the total drama of violence in families.

Since I had done a lot of group work involving addictions and believed in the strength of group treatment, I expressed an interest in starting an outpatient men's group when I began my doctoral internship. A number of clinicians encouraged me, confirming the community's lack of treatment resources for men, especially those who had been hospitalized for safety in the wake of troubled, conflicted intimate relationships. A special need existed for men who had threatened or been violent toward themselves or their family members, but were not involved in the criminal justice system, where they could be mandated to a batterer's treatment program.

After reading as much material as I could find about treatment with traditional-role-oriented men, violence and battering relationships, the men's mythopoetic movement, and clinical treatment of anger and explosive problems, I began the group. In an attempt to contain my own anxiety, I initially made the mistake of trying to exercise tight controls in the group, by structuring both the content and process rigidly. After a series of power struggles and marginal compliance, I was able to relax my attempts at social control and to encourage the members of the group to exercise their responsibility to work together to develop group rules and culture. This approach was more effective and provided more opportunities for them to practice and be caught in the act of assertive, direct communication. Gradually my anxiety has become more manageable, but the work remains delicate and challenging.

This chapter will focus on some of my experiences working with violent men in group psychotherapy in an outpatient mental health clinic. It will not be a comprehensive or state-of-the-art review of treatment for batterers, nor will it necessarily address methods of treatment in specific settings (prison, jail, court-mandated batterer's program, victim shelter). Rather, I will discuss my experiences and reflections in the hope that a more general audience will be stimulated to extend and apply these ideas in their own thinking and clinical work in a variety of settings. Since the most commonly encountered violence occurs in families, homes, and intimate relationships, this "domestic violence" will be the focus of the chapter. While protecting the identity of the men involved, case vignettes will be used both to illustrate my clinical approach and to provide a background for the discussion.

Why Are Men Violent?

Although each person is unique in both temperament and experience, work with violent men quickly yields common themes that may explain why they continue to use violence in their relationships, despite laws and public opinion that condemn it. A minority of violent men are coldly calculating and planful, using violence and oppression in a predatory way (plotting and stalking, threatening and intimidating others), but the majority become violent in the context of passionate emotions. When anxious, threatened, angry, or afraid, they often erupt into violence in an unpremeditated, impulsive, and explosive way.

Violence and its consequences are marked by paradoxes in both the intrapersonal and interpersonal worlds. While violent men often describe their violence as an experience in which they lose control, they may also come to see a violent outburst as a coping strategy that helps them to regain control. By discharging or diffusing the intense, overwhelming emotions of anger, shame, and fear, violence serves as a psychological and physiological release that aids them to restabilize their sense of self. It also "works effectively" in relationships by exerting power and control that forces others into compliance with their wishes, at least in the short term. Violence creates a power imbalance in relationships, by forcing either distance or intimacy, thus unilaterally controlling the outcome of any interaction. This is so reinforcing that violent men become dependent on violence as a coping and control strategy, thereby ceasing to learn other more equitable, assertive, and adaptive options for regulating emotions and resolving conflicts.

These two interwoven strategies (coping with intense emotion and relationship control) are the motivators of continued violence for most of the men that I have seen. As with substance abuse, however, what works as a short-term solution is destructive in the long run. When a man gets violent he tends to hurt himself, destroy his things, and drive away friends, effectively isolating himself from his most important connections. Violence erodes the basic building blocks of healthy relationships: trust, equality, and communication. Although the violent man may eventually realize that his victims remain in the relationship out of fear and compliance, fearing abandonment, he knows no other option than to progressively tighten his control by escalating his threats and violent behavior. This can both sadden him and fuel his rage at the fear of losing them. Feeling desperate, he might rationalize the violence to himself and to his victims as necessary to maintain the relationship. Although usually denied, his shame and fear of abandonment may lead him to believe that his victims are to blame for actually provoking him to "necessary" violence. Eventually, the emotional and physical violence may result in a series of incarcerations: complete loss of freedom and the destruction of all that he hoped to possess.

Although he would not discuss it openly, Joe, age 42, had a very difficult childhood, filled with occasional violence and emotional isolation. His parents were killed in an auto accident when he was seven. He was adopted by an aunt and uncle who were hard-working, hard-drinking alcoholics on a rented dairy farm. Lacking parenting or communication skills, his aunt and uncle ignored his school failure and self-imposed isolation. He was completely unsocialized and had no friends until he began drinking alcohol as a teenager. The alcohol worked like magic; now he could relate to people without the terror he'd always felt. For 15 years Joe bummed around the country in a drunken, substance-induced haze. Finally one treatment worked. After a successful halfway house stay, he has maintained abstinence from drugs and alcohol for 18 years. Yet he continues to struggle with chronic depression and anxiety. Other than his 20-year relationship with a woman who also struggles with depression and debilitating arthritis, Joe remains very isolated.

Joe joined the men's group to work on social skills. He continues to struggle with his great fear of relationships and uses verbal attacks and threats of violence to distance himself from others. When someone identifies with him or compliments him, or when he feels some affinity to another person, he is filled with anxiety and then rage. In an attempt to manage this rage, he attacks them with a verbal barrage of insults and threats. If the other person backs down he is able to calm himself, but if they defend themselves or counter, Joe quickly escalates, makes numerous threats, and then leaves the group, slamming furniture and doors. He may then go home and trash his apartment in an attempt to lessen his anxiety and rage, but this is not always effective.

If Joe continues to feel threatened and enraged, he sends further insults and threats through the mail. Although he knows that this is illegal and often creates more problems for him, he maintains that this behavior is necessary. He states that threatening others discharges his anxiety and rage and holds him together. Since he pictures the other person becoming distressed by his nasty, threatening notes, he feels he has transferred the negative emotion. Ironically, Joe has even employed this method to distance himself from me, other mental health professionals, and other helpers, when he feels known (and threatened) or when they have been engaging or helpful.

The Context of Violence in Society and Culture

Violence is supported and encouraged by many traditional male norms in the culture and is present in virtually every ethnic group in this country. While paying lip service to nonviolence in public forums, many men continue to hold violence as a male "right" to enforce their will in their homes and relationships. Violence is widespread, condoned, and even glorified in the entertainment media and held up as a necessity by many people. It is prevalent in both overt and subtle ways, embedded in language, culture, and institutions.

In some families, angry outbursts may be the only way to get attention, solve problems, or demand respect, and anger/rage may become the only emotion that is allowed to emerge, especially for males. In these families all feelings may eventually be disallowed and lost to awareness, except for anger. All negative emotional sensation may eventually be identified as anger, and violence may become reinforced and justified as the way to deal with it. It becomes the automatic behavior in any uncomfortable situation.

When a boy learns that violence works (to get his way), and when he has been shown over and over that violence is the first choice in any kind of relationship or conflict resolution, he doesn't stop when he grows up and leaves his original family. He takes that view of the world into the school, the workplace, the street, into his politics, and most especially, into his intimate relationships. Gradually people who exercise more healthy assertive behaviors avoid the chronic violence of these men, who are then left surrounded by compliant victims or by other equally or more violent people who overtly or covertly encourage and support their violent behavior.

Although he may attempt to take a different course, a man may become trapped in a family pattern where violence has become the only means to command respect. Moreover, violent contacts or being punished may have been the one sure way while growing up to get attention from emotionally distant or absent fathers. A number of the men in the group have described situations in which their fathers were continuously absent or focused on other things. They learned at a young age that if they could act up sufficiently to overwhelm their mother, their father would be called in to punish or control them, often with physical violence. This contact was seen by some as preferable to no contact at all, although in the long run it made real connection and intimacy impossible for everyone in the family. It also left them bitter and full of rage.

> Chris, age 35, described a history of continuous family violence when he was growing up, the oldest of five children. His father would disappear on alcoholic binges for days at a time, only to show up unexpectedly and dramatically in the middle of the night. Chris witnessed his mother being battered and was frequently challenged by his father to go out and "kick some butt." "Anger was the only emotion that was shown or allowed for the boys and men in my family." Chris's brothers and sister took up the family banner in their early teens, gaining reputations as the toughest and meanest people around.
>
> Despite Chris's attempts to escape his family's reputation, he described many times when people came to him looking for a fight because of this reputation. He would feel desperately trapped because of his father and younger brothers taunting and encouraging him to defend his own and the family's honor; what he really wanted to do was run away. In fact, he described staying away from home as much as possible during his teens, trying to avoid identification with and reenactment of his family's reputation. However, when he was really stressed at the end of his marriage and one other relationship, he found himself threatening violence in order to hold onto the relationship, almost by reflex.

Group Therapy: The Core of Treatment

As is often the case with marginally motivated or treatment-mandated populations, I have found that group treatment is vital to the delicate task of building and maintaining a therapeutic relationship with historically violent clients. While I frequently do individual and family therapy in parallel to the group, the group format is the major ingredient of effective treatment. Although mandated batterer's treatment programs usually prescribe a specific, structured content, time limit, and set of behavioral tasks, this group is an open-ended, ongoing group without a predetermined formal focus, structure, or time limit. It is not promoted exclusively for the treatment of violence, nor is it designed to provide contracted, mandated treatment for batterers. Several of the men in the group have previously completed mandated batterer's treatment and have described the flexible design of this group as helpful, enabling them to feel more self-motivated and less defiant.

The open-ended group format has enabled senior members of the group to do much of the orientation and confrontation of newer members, during the time when the latter are less stable and denying responsibility for their behavior and its consequences. The group also helps to decrease and diffuse anger at the perceived injustices of the law, forced treatment or recent arrests, and gender biases in the courts. A brief review of individual stories, during orientation of new members, allows for identification, emotional attachment, and trust. This also creates an opportunity for more senior members to both model and begin to confront the new members on their attitudes and behaviors. It also challenges all group members to face the dilemmas of life and examine more closely what they can't change: the past, the reactions and behaviors of others, and what they can change: their own attitudes and behaviors.

Group Utilization of Legal Involvement

A number of the men in the group are on probation, or are otherwise involved in the legal or criminal justice system (restraining or protection orders). This necessitates regular discussion of their legal mandates in the group and frequent reporting to probation and other agencies. Making these reports a part of the group agenda provides an opportunity for the men to regularly examine their progress in treatment. I have often engaged the entire group in formulating a progress report or letter that a group member needs for court or probation. This allows the men to hear direct feedback about both positive changes and areas of concern from other members of the group. Further, it teaches them to be more assertive and direct in asking for help in making changes and in reflecting on and communicating their assessment of themselves.

Feedback from peers also serves to moderate and balance those who are either completely self-condemning and self-depreciating (seeing only their difficulties), or those who arrogantly report only success and deny all of their problems. Sometimes the group members become so engaged in this process that they accompany each other to court to offer support. Sharing this experience strengthens their trust and often serves to moderate their sense of shame and isolation. This also allows them to return to the group with a more balanced and richer description of the experience based on their multiple perspectives.

This reflexive process has increased the bonds of connection and moderated the sense of isolation and victimization that many of these men feel. I believe it also tempers their tendency to deny or justify both past and current violence, thereby preventing rationalization of additional violence. In addition, the men now regularly solicit feedback from others as they wrestle with self-defeating thoughts, actions, and major decisions.

The Group as a Container to Manage Emotions

Group support is also vital in providing a container for managing strong emotions, which may initially present as anger and resistance. Once the men begin to trust that they are not unique, their sense of demoralization, shame, and guilt begins to emerge. This identification with others' vulnerability also encourages them to own their fear and anxiety about abandonment and loss of relationships. Working with these emotions which have been disguised behind the initial presentation of anger, rage, and violent threats is critical to establishing and maintaining a relationship with violent men.

> George, a 37-year-old man whose ex-wife had remarried several years ago, was persistently depressed and enraged that he was restricted from seeing his children. His past threats of assault and thoughts of homicide had resulted in a series of restraining orders and his being cut off from all contact with his children (two girls, ages 7 and 9, and two boys, ages 10 and 12).
>
> On the basis of past reports from his oldest son, he believed that his children were being neglected and at times physically abused by both his ex-wife and her current husband, who reportedly were chronic alcohol-

ics. Since his wife's family had a lot of money, they could afford legal representation, while George was destitute and lived and worked at the YMCA. He entered the group having been repeatedly hospitalized for suicide attempts and frequent threats to harm his ex-wife. He was particularly angry that the hospital staff had felt it their duty to warn his ex-wife of his threats, and he had recently been served with another restraining order, which prohibited all contact with his children as well.

Although George was not trusting enough of helpers to connect with me, he was able to connect with other group members who shared similar emotional and legal struggles. He was able to make a weekly commitment of safety and to consistently attend the group, thus allowing further trust to develop. By sharing the story of his childhood of traumatic abuse and contrasting this with the special relationship he had with his children, George became more responsive to the group's encouragement to let go of his attempts to control by threatening violence. Slowly he began to focus on himself in the present in the hope of being stable enough to have a relationship with his children later on, when they were old enough to exercise their own choices.

Learning Alternative Behaviors

I have found many opportunities in the group to expose clients to the style of control and manipulation that they may be using in all their relationships. Catching them in the act of making a threat or escalating toward violence during a disagreement with another group member provides powerful learning. When a man experiences the emotional rush of energy and becomes aware of how quickly he resorts to threats and posturing in the group itself, he cannot as easily deny his need for help. When group members can observe first-hand their own physical and emotional sensations in the face of another's escalating rage, and then participate in a firm and supportive de-escalation and processing of the experience, they can begin to generalize these in-group experiences and implement their new skills in other areas of their lives.

Frequently someone will share examples of how he applied his learning in situations of conflict with family members or others during the week. This may prompt others to reflect on their own successes and diminish the tendency to focus solely on frustrations about situations beyond their control. The group also provides a place to practice tolerance, assertiveness, and communication skills. All of the members benefit by bearing witness when an enraged member can successfully take a time-out, return to the group, and then assertively discuss and negotiate a resolution to his conflict. Such an emotionally charged encounter enhances both confidence and skills as members prove to themselves that they can manage intense feelings and communicate their concerns without threatening anyone. The group is also a forum where assertive communication can be practiced as both sender and receiver. The effectiveness of direct, specific requests and feedback can be contrasted with the ineffectiveness of global demands or aggressive threatening communication on both sender and receiver. In this way communication skills are connected to real experience and forged in a positive learning context.

Cognitive, Behavioral, and Psychoeducational Components

Although the group is not structured exclusively for the treatment of batterers, proven components from model batterer's programs are often used, applying both the structure and content in the group. Psychoeducational presentations are combined with discussions, worksheets, and practicing. Units on emotional awareness, labeling, tolerance, and regulation; assertive communication; conflict resolution; anger management; gender roles; relaxation and meditation; and writing (journals, letters, and diaries) as both a coping and communication tool have been used regularly. Resistance to these subjects is lessened because the members' current struggles inform the choice of the structured presentation or group exercise. For example, if one of the men presents an experience of an argument that escalated into threats or violence, his experience would be used to analyze and teach. This personalized application loosens rigid thinking and encourages the men to more openness about the entire drama of violence as it moves from triggers, through escalation, to the violence, to the aftermath of shame, rationalization, and remorse. Alternative options can then be reviewed and tested to determine where earlier intervention can diffuse the escalation before the man erupts into violence.

Some subjects are so universally useful that they are periodically reviewed, applied, and practiced in the group. These include the Duluth Model–Domestic Abuse Intervention Project's Power and Control Wheel and the Equality Wheel; anger management techniques; breathing and relaxation exercises; assertive communication worksheets and practice in group; logging, analyzing, and practicing alternatives to each man's unique triggers (both intrapersonal and interpersonal) and his process of escalation to rage; time-out and development of written rules for fighting fairly; writing letters and journals to reflect and communicate without threats or control. Members are also encouraged to share resources that they have discovered or invented to aid in their recovery. A number have shared self-statements that they use to soothe and ground themselves when they are triggered into an escalation of anger, thus preventing the rage and the usual violence that accompanies it.

Several self-help books have been tested by the men and are now regularly recommended to newer members of the group: McKay, Rogers, and McKay (1989), *When Anger Hurts;* Potter-Efron (1994), *Angry All the Time,* and Paymar (1993), *Violent No More.* Suggested exercises from these books are sometimes completed and shared in the group. This enhances understanding and deepens identification and bonding within the group, because it creates a common vocabulary and elicits more sharing of parallel experiences of coping and communicating.

Avoiding Power Struggles in the Group

When used effectively, the group format itself is useful in preventing power struggles. When six to ten people are present and given responsibility for the group, conflict can be diffused more easily than when a breakdown occurs in individual therapy. Furthermore, senior members of the group are able to both model resolution of conflicts and contain the emotional outbursts of newer members. When a man is able to experience and resolve a conflict without losing control, it provides a rich learning experience for the entire group.

A positive approach that focuses on progress and successes is also helpful in avoiding or moderating the frequent power struggles that occur in relationship with violent men. By contrast, I have found that men bound to traditional male gender roles will turn off or become defensive when approached with criticism. While not ignoring or dismissing the problems and dilemmas that have brought them to treatment, we instead highlight and build on successes by catching clients in the act of some positive behavior and affirming it. When someone communicates assertively and directly, avoids a potential conflict by letting go or giving in, or takes a time-out from an escalating argument to collect his thoughts and then returns to the discussion, this experience is validated and reviewed in depth.

Descriptions of outside events as well as interactions that occur in the group are grist for the mill. Feedback is given in very specific and concrete terms, and is always connected to the goals and experiences that have been shared in the group. This quickly becomes a group pattern and is often initiated by the group members themselves as they begin to develop a more balanced, hopeful perspective and sense of self. I have found that group members are more likely to give honest and difficult criticism to another man if they can first identify and discuss his positive changes and progress.

I have found the following question helpful in moving men toward greater accountability and less defensiveness: How do people react to you when you talk/act this way? This question can be used in any context and for any observable behavior. It is useful in preventing power struggles over issues of social and behavioral control because it encourages a man to reflect on his behavior and its consequences in a nonjudgmental way. It also lowers his defenses and encourages him to request reflections and feedback from others on the impact of his behavior in the present context. Here-and-now feedback also provides for more powerful learning, which can then be generalized to similar situations outside the group.

Substance Abuse and Violence

Research shows a consistently high correlation between substance abuse and violence both in families and in other contexts. A large percentage of the men that I have worked with in this project are either actively abusing substances or are in recovery from addictive use. Having been an addictions counselor for a number of years and knowing the value of abstinence as a foundation of change, I find myself frequently caught in a major dilemma with men who are violent in the context of substance abuse. Of necessity, both batterers' programs and addiction treatment programs exercise rather rigid abstinence requirements in order to remain in treatment. However, working with these men, even those who are undergoing court-mandated treatment, is very problematic if one is excessively rigid from the outset. Although they may initially respond to external pressure, they frequently drop out or bounce around between different helpers, never really engaging in treatment of their own volition. As a result, neither the violence nor the substance abuse is addressed. In addition, issues of rejection and loss of control felt by men in these treatment settings seem to exacerbate their sense of alienation and perception of the self as inadequate. If one can avoid power struggles, a more workable treatment alliance can be established.

While clearly and directly addressing abstinence from substances as the foundation and goal of reclaiming control of one's life, I have found a flexible approach to be more workable, particularly while engaging the men in the initial phase of treatment. Once they are attached and committed to the group, the peer relationships in the group encourage an examination of their own substance abuse and confront them with a powerful group expectation of abstinence. This flexible approach causes more anxiety and worry for me as a therapist, however, because I cannot as easily soothe myself with rigid rules and controls and must also tolerate a more unstable and unpredictable group. Some of the men miss groups frequently because they cannot time their abstinence periods with the meeting days, and they forget or ignore the group schedule in pursuit of numbing themselves with substance abuse.

Despite these problems, a mixture of men who are abstinent from drugs and alcohol and active in 12-Step programs (in recovery) and others who continue to use or abuse substances has proved helpful to the men in both of these subgroups. Those in recovery can validate their progress by describing how abstinence from drugs and involvement with the self-help groups (Alcoholics Anonymous/Narcotics Anonymous) have helped them to deal with their emotions more effectively and decrease their use of violence in relationships. Those who are still using (drugs or alcohol) can begin to see the association between their substance abuse and their violence abuse as they hear and relate to the stories of those in recovery. In addition, 12-Step program principles like powerlessness, loss of control, and letting go are useful in discussions of both violence and substance abuse.

Discussions of the dilemmas and paradoxes in relationships also prove valuable in providing more options for all the men. They are often surprised to discover that power, control, and force are ultimately destructive to relationships, while vulnerability, honesty, and powerlessness often result in better and deeper relational connection. Some may be challenged to apply 12-Step recovery principles in relationships; often they are amazed at the results. One man whose wife is actively abusing drugs and alcohol has made impressive use of the addiction model with his own violent behavior. He calls his violent behavior his drug and points out how it offers a quick fix, a brief high followed by even more pain and problems. He borrows the frequently quoted metaphor of Dr. Jekyll and Mr. Hyde (his terms: Mr. Mean and Mr. Nice) to illustrate the polarities in his behavior and often portrays his struggle to avoid using violence as parallel to an addict attempting to avoid drug use.

Those still using substances are frequently invited to 12-Step meetings, where they hear people honestly sharing their shameful experiences and taking responsibility for change. This helps them to begin to feel hopeful about themselves and their future. While the ideal of abstinence should always be held up, negotiating more realistic, less ambitious goals implicitly teaches flexibility and compromise and provides opportunities for incremental change and more consistent success. The men also learn to assess and accept their limitations and begin to develop the skills to establish a balance between realistic goals and their own ability to meet the challenges of change. This can prevent the demoralization and shame that frequently occur when they make grandiose promises of change before they possess the motivation or resources for success, thereby setting up repeated failures. Some of the men may need addiction treatment, but if this is forced before a relationship is established, the violence may never be addressed, even though the addiction is treated successfully. Consider the following case.

Brian, a 32-year-old man, sits in my office with his leg bouncing rapidly, an angry scowl on his face. Two weeks earlier he had been released from the county jail after serving a nine-month sentence for resisting arrest and assaulting two police officers. After jail he spent several weeks in a short-term inpatient psychiatric hospital unit with acute anxiety. After a few exchanges, he notes that he is here only to fulfill the mandate of his parole and to continue to obtain his medication. Brian continued to struggle with frequent relapses and binge drinking and began to jeopardize his job because of tardiness and absences.

Relying on his mandate to treatment, I was able to gradually build a relationship with Brian by ignoring his provocative comments and verbal challenges, highlighting instead his brief periods of abstinence and success at holding onto his job. In both group and individual sessions, I refused to join him in his own condemnation of himself because of his problematic behaviors. Instead I pointed out his successes: abstaining from alcohol for several weeks at a time and his parallel progress in avoiding fights and violent encounters with old rivals on the streets. If no present successes were available, I remained interested in his past success and asked questions about his special talent as an award-winning auto body artist.

I also gained Brian's trust because I responded quickly and actively to his crises when he ran out of medication and had withdrawal problems and when he was fired from his job, as a result of being hospitalized. He was also intrigued that I encouraged him to talk openly about his dilemmas in relationships, a topic he had considered taboo in the light of his legal problems with restraining orders and parole. By offering options, while consistently encouraging addiction treatment, I was able to avoid the kinds of power struggles and impasses that marked his chronic history of intermittent treatment and relapses. Eventually he accepted my recommendation of longer-term addiction treatment, since he had sufficiently tested our relationship.

Over the next six months Brian taught me a lot about humility and flexibility as he continued in individual therapy, while living and receiving treatment in an addiction treatment program and halfway house. During this time he advocated a split in treatment focus in which he worked on his addiction in the other program and focused on his relationship issues, sexual concerns, and violence issues in his therapy with me.

Despite my challenges to this split, he insisted on it. Therefore his halfway house counselors focused almost exclusively on his recovery program and day-to-day management of emotions and relationships in the halfway house. Psychotherapy simultaneously provided a safe haven to contain and sort out his other, more historical issues without the numbing effect of alcohol (unresolved relationships with several women, whose indecisiveness agitated and enraged him; issues of sexuality which resulted from early and chronic physical and sexual abuse as well as emotional neglect by his adoptive mother, who suicided when he was 10, and a girlfriend who suicided the night he ended his relationship with her when he was 24).

Brian recently shared his feeling that his tough, angry, threatening exterior protects him so that no one messes with him. When I challenged that by saying that women often mess with him, he was able to acknowledge that they can see through the exterior, and that I am the only man he knows who has been able to see through it. I was encouraged by this disclosure and his capacity to tolerate this degree of intimacy.

Counselor/Therapist Fear and Anxiety

At first I struggled with issues of my own safety and feared that I was at risk in working with this population. I was the only therapist in a room with six to eight very large and muscular men who have all used violence to resolve relationship impasses. At times they get into arguments and escalate into physical posturing and verbal threats with lightning speed. Rules and guidelines about the group are useless when several men are escalating rapidly. One has to intervene firmly and quickly, utilizing the group strength to diffuse these situations.

In addition to fear for my physical safety, my fear was also related to professional scrutiny and embarrassment about the work. Some professional colleagues questioned why I would ever want to work with such despicable characters. Once the work was under way, I frequently worried about failure and feared at times for my professional future. "Did you hear how Scherling lost control of his group the other night?" was a quote I often rehearsed in my head. A cartoon provided an excellent illustration of my fear. It pictured an empty room with holes in the walls and broken and upset furniture scattered about; the announcement on the board read "Today's group is about Managing Anger."

It is sometimes difficult to be identified as a local expert on violence. Prejudices frequently emerge in both overt and more subtle ways, and I become associated with these prejudices. A number of times during a case conference or a staff meeting, when violence is an issue, jokes are directed at me: "Oh, this is one of Don's guys." When a loud noise is overheard, or shouting comes down the hall, people look at me and point, suggesting that I go take care of the situation. A colleague holds up a newspaper headline about a spouse abuse story, and I overhear several others talking about how it must be one of my men. If something gets broken in the office, one of my violence-group clients is often accused either directly or indirectly. When word filtered back to the senior clinician of a new unit where the group was meeting that one of the men had become threatening and "thrown his chair," I was called into the office and asked for some guarantee that nothing would get broken. If any more incidents came up, I would have to meet somewhere else. Meanwhile, no one asked about my feelings or safety. I have become acutely aware of the shame and blame that my clients feel from others, which in their case often tends to spawn more anger, resentment, and rationalization to use violence to deny or avoid this emotional pain.

It is the third meeting of the newly formed men's group, initiated to assist men in their transition from the inpatient psychiatric treatment. The men in the group eye one another nervously, as it has just been noted that all of them except for myself are currently under restraining orders from spouses or agencies.

Sam, a muscular, tanned 35-year-old man, begins to shout about his anger at the helping systems for keeping him alive and begins to share anecdotes about his reckless driving and excessive drinking, stating a hope that he can provoke someone into killing him. He shares morbid details of an intentional accident on his motorcycle in which he tried to die, and is now left with memory loss, trouble in walking, and seizures. I notice his arm muscles bulging as he tries to break the arm off his chair, and tears well up in his eyes. I attempt to calm him and diffuse his escalation, when he explodes suddenly, blaming me for making him cry in the group. He jumps up and hurls his chair against the wall, drops his pants to show the grotesque scars from his accident, swears wildly and walks out, slamming the door, stating, "You assholes don't need to worry about me, you'll never see me again."

This incident was so frightening that it left me shaken, and other group members became quite agitated. In the light of Sam's volatile history, I didn't know if he would use this as another excuse to suicide. It was difficult to prioritize the things that needed to be done: the need of the other group members to process their reactions, my need to deal with my own fright, and the importance of attempting a follow-up with Sam. After the group calmed down some, I left them to process the situation on their own, so that I could alert the crisis team and Sam's mother that he had left agitated and might be at risk. After completing the group, I was able to debrief the experience with colleagues on the inpatient unit.

> Mike, a 35-year-old man living in a halfway house, complains that his medication is not sufficient to help him sleep. He describes becoming more and more impatient with other residents and their "petty bullshit complaining." "If something doesn't change or I don't get out of there, I might lose it and really hurt someone." His history contains many incidents of his "really hurting" other men. He has often picked fights or taunted and provoked others into fights to release his anger. He complains that the halfway house staff gets into power struggles with him and "they won't win." The group works hard to keep Mike engaged and talking in the hope that his anger will decrease. The following week he reports that he had used suggestions and commitments to the group to keep himself out of fights.

Since the group meets in the evening, it is usually the last clinical session of my day. On the way home from work I frequently find myself asking difficult questions. Should I have confronted a particular man more to test his dangerousness? Should I have gone easier with him and not challenged his thinking so directly? Will he be safe tonight . . . should I have tried to force him into involuntary treatment in the locked unit? If I force him into treatment, will he get the message that I don't consider him capable of dealing with his emotions and containing his behavior? Should I call his probation officer, the crisis team, the psychiatrist who prescribes his medication? Will his wife be safe, or should I warn her and call the police? Will I see him again so that I can intervene, or will he be too angry to return? Will he be jailed again this week? Will he tell the police that I did the wrong thing, or didn't help him in the right way so he got violent? Will I be the target of a revenge attack, because I am blamed for the loss of a relationship? Is my family safe? Is my professional career safe?

Contextual Supports for the Therapist

I believe this kind of work is best done in an agency that can provide relatively easy access to emergency and crisis services. It has been helpful to develop a rapport with the emergency room staff, the inpatient psychiatric unit staff, other key clinicians, and the police. I have found it crucial to obtain regular supervision and to discuss my fears and concerns openly. As noted earlier, at times I have needed to consult with a peer immediately following a group, so it is essential to have other clinicians available for consultation following every group. Interaction with professional colleagues at training workshops is another valuable resource both to validate the challenge of this work and to provide fresh ideas that counteract burnout and hopelessness.

Safety: Assessing Dangerousness

In addition to my fears about my own personal and professional safety, I have struggled to assess and design interventions dealing with my clients' dangerousness. Since these men have historically used violence both to manage intense emotional experience and to regulate and control distance in relationships, their level of safety or dangerousness in a specific situation is difficult to assess. Studies of battered women show that women are at greatest risk of battering and homicide when they are in the process of leaving a relationship. I have found that the risk of suicide is also much higher for historically violent men when an important relationship is threatened or ending. Since men tend to use more lethal means of harming themselves, assessments of safety are crucial. Four of the men in the group have attempted suicide when their intimate relationships were ending and their efforts to control or hold on to their partner or children ceased to work. All four nearly died in intensive care from severe drug overdoses; two continue to have heart rhythm problems as a result of their attempts.

Again, the group itself is a valuable resource in assessing risk and providing a safety net to those who become distressed and dangerous to both themselves and others. I have regularly engaged the group members in discussions of risk and safety and enlisted their involvement in setting up crisis intervention plans and no-harm contracts as a part of the group process. To date, they have accepted this challenge and provided excellent support, encouragement, and even firm coercion when needed. When a man at risk has contracted for safety with the entire group, his commitment to keep his word seems to be strengthened. The multiple perspectives and collective wisdom of the group also enhance both the assessment and the safety planning in crisis situations. Several of the men credit the other men in the group for saving their lives, since they became aware of the risk and intervened immediately by calling for emergency assistance in hospitalizing them.

These experiences have built strong bonds, decreased the level of shame, and encouraged an appropriate sense of pride in group membership. I believe that these bonds have also served as a safety net in preventing further violence and have helped to lower the risk of additional suicide attempts. Since the men at risk were able to return to the group to discuss their experiences, they have learned additional accountability and have taken pride in their commitments to one another. As a result, they are increasingly bold in challenging and confronting one another and offering their opinion about the level of danger they see in situations. The senior members are also proactive in proposing contingency plans and safety contracts when they notice a member slipping and have assisted in hospitalizing group members at risk. This sense of shared responsibility for safety and change has also helped me to maintain a more balanced perspective of my own limitations in the group.

> Greg, a 28-year-old man who is separated from his wife and daughters, ages five and two, enters the group room to announce that he has developed a plan to kill his wife's new boyfriend. He has had a long history of alcohol and drug abuse and an even longer history (back to his early teens) of incarcerations for fights and other violent assaults. He has been hospitalized three times in the last year with suicidal thoughts. He is currently on probation for two violations of a restraining order which restricts him from entering his wife's home. He is bruised and has stitches on his face and hands from jumping head-first out of a second

floor window of his wife's house when the police were in the living room waiting to arrest him.

After an hour of intense negotiation and considerable caring confrontation by the group, Greg agrees to give up his new shotgun to his father and to allow my contact with his father to verify this. I have agreed not to call the police or his wife if he does this immediately after the group and verifies everyone's safety within the next hour. It was a long hour.

Group Leader: Active Interpersonal Style

In order to engage and maintain relationships with these men, I have had to become more proactive and assertive in my clinical approach. If a man does not show up for the group, I usually pursue him with a call during the next week to find out what happened and to invite him to the next group. I have found it useful to ask new members to commit to a trial of three to four group sessions before they make a decision to continue. This allows them to feel more in control and less coerced and gives the group a chance to engage and include them. At times I have encouraged contacts between members of the group between sessions to aid their networking and relating. This has caused some problems when some of them have had conflicts or disagreements outside of the group and then refused to be in the group together. However, these problems have also provided many opportunities for them to process and learn about other options for negotiating and dealing with conflicts.

Use of Humor

Careful use of humor has also proved to be an enjoyable and powerful tool in diffusing tension in the group. Rather than asking intrusive, directive questions in the face of some difficult crisis, humorous statements allow the men to discuss very serious concerns in a more direct and open manner. The humor must not be hostile, humiliating, or invalidating, but should allow the men to laugh at their own and others' life dilemmas.

> Jack, a 43-year-old man who suffered from chronic depression, talked about his persisting suicidal thoughts. He went on to share an elaborate fantasy in which he would sail his 25-foot sailboat on a solo voyage. While not actively plotting his own death, he would hope to be caught in a storm or run down by a ship or involved in some other event in

which he would die at sea. He had thought a lot about this and had built this fantasy up into a relatively concrete plan. He told about it with a sense of glee and laughter, despite his obvious severe depression.

Several of the other men in the group were bewildered and threatened by his flippant lightheartedness in discussing his own suicidal thoughts. In the spirit of joining his tone and perspective, I commented that his story was very helpful as well as entertaining, because it gave us direction in helping him. I went on to suggest that if we heard him talk about or saw that he was working on his sailboat, we would be alerted to intervene. If we noticed that he was provisioning or preparing for launch, we would know that it was time to lock him up. Jack laughed in appreciation of the humor and the respectful empathy for his struggle.

For several weeks Jack continued to mention how much he appreciated this sensitive and empathic comment, because it encouraged him to laugh in the midst of his emotional pain. Despite Jack's expressed appreciation, another man in the group was scandalized by my "joking" about such a serious subject. He became agitated and exploded in a dramatic, harsh, and angry rebuke of me. This took me by surprise, and I became angry and defensive myself. However, I recovered and was able to hold and validate the perspectives of both men. The group members were able to see for themselves how I struggled and then engaged my own strong emotions in a firm and assertive way. We took this opportunity to discuss the seriousness of suicide as well as my clinical judgment and intervention. This open discussion allowed others to comment on their own surprise and fear in the experience. They were also able to experience the power of flexibility and diversity, and to see that different people required different approaches. We often use humor in the group in more mundane circumstances as well, especially when offering feedback or to temper someone's self-pity.

Victim Stories: The Core of Therapeutic Alliance

Although studies vary, research shows that a high percentage of men who become violent in their adult lives either witnessed or were victims of violence and abuse in childhood. I have found that one of the most important aspects of building and maintaining a relationship with these men is being with them and encouraging the telling of their own stories of victimization. This is one of the most difficult parts of the work, for it requires that one hold a balance between support and accountability, between a man's own history as a victim of violence or sexual abuse and firm boundaries of accountability for his behavior as a perpetrator of violence.

Work with these men has required that I adopt a both/and approach and live with the paradox, always struggling to maintain a balance in the tension of dynamically engaging both aspects of interpersonal violation. If one ignores their own stories of victimization, they will be unlikely to engage in therapy beyond the most superficial compliance. The telling of these stories provides many opportunities for me to show respect and care for the men as people who have been violated themselves. Building an empathic relationship around their victimization increases trust and makes them more willing to engage in responsible discussions about their own use of violence. Motivation for change and recovery has been initiated, owned, and strengthened for some of the men by telling the stories of their own victimization. This storytelling has increased their ability to empathize with the victim experience and has loosened their usually rigid self-righteous rationalization about their own violence.

> Fred's father, a Korean War veteran and career military man, was killed en route to his second tour of duty in Vietnam when Fred was 9 years old. Fred was devastated, but was reprimanded and punished in his attempts to grieve his loss because it was upsetting to his mother, who subsequently had a series of "nervous breakdowns," psychiatric hospitalizations, and suicide attempts (in two of them she held her children hostage for more than 12 hours while holding a gun to her own head, refusing help and forbidding them to call for assistance). In addition, his mother remarried a very large, angry, alcoholic man who routinely beat and tortured Fred on a daily basis (the torture included being locked in a dark shed for several days at a time without food or toilet facilities).
>
> When he was about 14, Fred escaped from home at times only to fall prey to a "kind, understanding" neighbor who sexually molested him and swore him to secrecy under the threat of telling his stepfather. Fred himself began to fight and abuse alcohol and drugs by age 17 and continued until age 39. Although not physically violent with his wife, he was verbally abusive and continuously absent on alcoholic binges and extramarital affairs. Since then he has sobered up, but he now struggles with an impending divorce, which devastates him primarily because of the separation from his own four children, with whom he is quite close. He never abused or even touched his children in anger. His guilt and shame are now directed at himself, and he struggles with chronic thoughts of suicide.

My experience with other survivors of trauma has proved helpful, because sometimes an individual may need to be cautioned and assisted in pacing his revelations to avoid retraumatization or shaming. When men are being screened and oriented to the group, this storytelling process is mentioned as a voluntary option that many of the men choose to engage, if their participation continues beyond a few sessions. The men are reminded frequently that sharing of childhood and other traumas is completely optional. When one of them does request this process, he is offered one or more individual sessions to test his feelings in the process of the sharing, since the telling often triggers additional, unexpected memories. Some of the men have taken advantage of this individual telling as a preparation and screening process before exposing such sensitive material in the group. This has allowed them more choice in editing aspects of their story to protect the confidentiality of family members and to prepare themselves emotionally.

Whether it is planned or spontaneous, when a man begins to talk about his own victimization, I have found it helpful to interrupt him and initiate a direct reminder about his control of both the content and the pace with which he shares his stories. Group process and guidelines are discussed concretely and explicitly, with a number of cautions and options offered. It is critical that no one be pressured into premature revelations that may trigger guilt, shame, or rage. As previously noted, if they begin to feel shame, these men may react with dramatic violence and blame the therapist for humiliating them.

At the same time, some need encouragement to share more details since they have rarely felt it safe to discuss their own vulnerability and pain at all, especially not with other men. The group format helps immensely here as more senior members of the group are able to actively support the telling, without pushing or intruding. Since the senior members have usually shared stories of their victimization in some detail and with some frequency, they are able to provide the newer member with acceptance and support, often by again discussing their identification with the experience of victimization and providing brief examples of their own experience. Following a story that has been emotionally intense, each person should be checked to make sure that he is grounded and oriented in the present. It is important to monitor the group members carefully to guard against anyone becoming stimulated into aggression or violence as their memories get stirred up.

Occasionally one of the men requires additional reassurance or individual time with the therapist to regain perspective, following the group. This was true of Paul, described below, who used individual time to make powerful comparisons between his own and his father's violence. This allowed him to mine rich meaning from his own multiple perspectives as both victim and violent abuser. Having worked these issues through in a more private setting, Paul became willing to report his reflections and learning in the following group session, thereby extending his own and others' healing.

Paul was the oldest of eight children, so he often received the brunt of his father's almost daily outbursts of violence and verbal abuse. The only thing he reports being proud of in his childhood was his role as the family "lightning rod," deflecting his father's wrath onto himself, thereby protecting his mother and siblings. Paul's victimization extended beyond the family. Once when he was nine he was humiliated by being hit and spanked in front of his class. This experience was so shaming that it reversed his previous view of school as a haven from the chaos of home.

With no place of safety or reason in his life, Paul began to view the whole world as hostile. Since he was systematically humiliated and beaten, even when he carefully followed his father's numerous rules, he lost hope and the spirit to try. Knowing no other strategy, he escalated his misbehavior and gained satisfaction from his reputation as a trouble-maker and fighter. He approached every relationship and interaction as a contest of wills and control.

Paul enlisted in the army but was discharged early, being labeled incorrigible because of his binge drinking and violence. After discharge from the army, he went on a four-year binge with alcohol and drugs and was arrested and incarcerated intermittently for violence. Paul never connected his own patterns with those of his father until his wife filed for a protective order and divorced him, after an incident in which he threatened her with a machete.

Paul's separation from his wife and young son triggered even more rage and escalated his substance abuse. He reports being obsessed with revenge and homicidal thoughts. Seeing no other solution to his emotional pain, he developed a number of elaborate plans to murder his ex-wife and then kill himself. Only when Paul was jailed for barroom violence did he begin to develop the insight that he was repeating the pattern that his father had used in his childhood. He became involved in religion and studied the Bible for four years, which helped him to grow more reflective and moderated his quick temper and impulsive reactions.

More recently, in danger of losing yet another job for verbal abuse and threats toward his boss, Paul began treatment. He credits the individual and group sessions with helping him to understand and redirect his violent urges into more adaptive assertive communication. "I now understand where the rage comes from, so I can hold myself together until I calm down enough to go back and talk about it." He has even begun to visit his father again, trying to let go of the past in order to "get some of his technical knowledge of mechanics, without all the bullshit that he dishes out emotionally." These visits have increased Paul's empathy for others' perspectives, even in the midst of a confrontation. He has recently described a heated argument with his wife in which he was able to interrupt his urge to threaten and was able to fight fairly to the point of resolution.

While I have found it central to the therapeutic connection that the men share their own histories of victimization, a note of caution is also warranted. Stories of abuse can be very distracting and can cause the therapist or group members to lose focus or excuse current behaviors as an inevitable outcome of earlier victimization. Like the spouse or partner, one can get so invested in caring for the remorseful, needy little boy that the violent, abusive adult is tolerated or ignored. The most difficult men to treat are those who routinely use their own victimization as a rationalization for their violence. The group is often helpful in moderating this rationalization by consistently challenging each person to accountability in the present.

These discussions are tense emotional experiences for the group members and make for powerful bonding. Group members should be cautioned that this kind of bonding, while generally a healing experience, can be frightening to some. It has been important to remind the men that they have a choice in how close they allow others to be, and they are encouraged to verbally request some distance rather than to bail out by acting up. The group has picked up on my initiation of a decompression ritual, so that they will check in and lighten the emotional tone of the group with humor or more mundane material before ending a group session in which someone has discussed some details of his victimization.

Dealing with Sexual Intimacy

An area of relationship that is even more hidden and sensitive than the violence for these men is their sexual intimacy. Since coercion has often been used in their sexual relationships as well, the men may have a special need to deny this. In addition, sexual intimacy is often a part of the cycle of violence, when in the aftermath of a violent episode the man seeks forgiveness and reconnection, as described by

Walker (1984). It is during this phase of the relationship cycle that the man comes closest to experiencing his own dependency, which is usually vehemently denied. Awareness of this vulnerability and dependency prompts the men to avoid exploring any aspect of their sexuality. In addition, many have been emotionally, if not physically, separated from their partners and have not been sexually intimate for some time. This often weighs heavily on their fragile sense of self as men, making their fear, shame, and rage overwhelming.

To avoid triggering their shame or pressing them to share, at regular intervals I introduce a psychoeducational segment on sexual intimacy. Depending on the issues being raised in the group, I focus the presentation to discuss their concerns. These might include dilemmas of both the men and their partners in the cycle of violence, overwhelming feelings, and the heightened importance that sexual activity carries for their sense of themselves as men. I also discuss other issues and provide additional depth in areas that I know are current concerns for them: (a) impotence; (b) date rape and coercion in sexual relationships; (c) safe sex; (d) sexually transmitted diseases, especially HIV and hepatitis; (e) side effects of medication, especially impotence; (f) irrational fears of their partner's infidelity; (g) guilt over the effect of their own infidelity on themselves and their relationship; (h) concern about managing the safety and sexual activity of their teenage children, who want no part of their coercive control. I have found it helpful to review these topics and provide information in a generic fashion, cautiously keeping my comments general enough that no one feels singled out. This neutral, matter-of-fact approach has reassured them about the commonness of their problems and has sparked some men into a deeper exploration and questioning of their own identity. Some have sought more information, support, and referrals for issues that they had avoided in the past. Often the group is motivated to respond with surprising candor about these issues. It is important to check in with them as a group and to provide individual time following the group for those needing to process strong feelings provoked by these subjects.

Summary and Conclusion

The group has been functioning for close to four years. While referrals have numbered about 75, only about 40 of these men have attended even one group, about 20 have attended more than three sessions, and about 10 have been involved for six to twelve months. I note these figures to illustrate the frustration and challenge of working with this group of mostly involuntary clients. Though the work is difficult, patience and persistence pay great dividends as one is given the opportunity to integrate wisdom on both personal and professional levels. This wisdom does not come quickly or easily, but is provided by respectfully observing and participating in the multidimensional healing that sometimes occurs for these men and their families.

I have come to see that there are many perspectives to each person's life story. It is important to note that everyone is to some measure a victim and deserves the love, caring, nurture, and respect that allows him to gain the insight to see who is responsible for the pain and hurt that he has experienced in his life. However, all are more than victims, for each is also responsible not to abuse and victimize others. It is rewarding to watch the men develop a sense of themselves as capable, accountable people who have exchanged their desperate use of violence for an ability to nurture, support, and love others.

My work with violent men remains difficult and challenging. At times it is so frightening that I carry more anxiety than I like to hold. However, the continuous reminder of my own vulnerability and lack of control has been humbling in a positive way. I believe that this humility has enhanced my respect for the right and responsibility of all my clients to determine their own timing and values in guiding the work of their recovery. It has made my work with both victims and abusers a more mutually creative, cooperative process in which I try to work as hard, but not harder than, my clients. I often remind them that I serve as a consultant to them. I can share my knowledge and experience, which is constantly updated by both clients and colleagues. They have the choice to use or reject these resources. I strive to remember that a client's change and success are not things that I can ensure or control in any of my clinical work. While I would prefer to live in denial of this humbling realization, I find that work with this group of clients demands honesty and integrity at the highest level.

References

Campbell, J. C. (Ed.). 1995. *Assessing dangerousness: Violence by sexual offenders, batterers, and child abusers.* Thousand Oaks, Calif.: Sage Publications.

Dutton, D. G. 1998. *The abusive personality.* New York: The Guilford Press.

Dutton, D. G., with Golant, S. K. 1995. *The batterer: A psychological profile.* New York: Basic Books.

Edleson, J. L., and Tolman, R. M. 1992. *Intervention for men who batter.* Thousand Oaks, Calif.: Sage Publications.

Farrell, W. 1993. *The myth of male power.* New York: Simon and Schuster.

Gelles, R. J., and Cornell C. P. 1990. *Intimate violence in families,* 2nd ed. Newbury Park, Calif.: Sage Publications.

Gilligan, J. 1996. *Violence.* New York: G. P. Putnam's Sons.

Goldner, V., Penn, P., Sheinberg, M., and Walker, G. 1990. Love and violence: Gender paradoxes in volatile attachments. *Family Process, 29,* 4, 343–364.

Harway, M., and Hansen, M. (1994). *Spouse abuse: Assessing and treating battered women, batterers, and their children.* Sarasota, Fla.: Professional Resource Press.

Herman, J. L. 1992. *Trauma and recovery.* New York: Basic Books.

Hunter, M. 1990. *Abused boys: The neglected victims of sexual abuse.* Lexington, Mass.: D. C. Heath (Lexington Books).

Koss, M. P., Goodman, L. A., Browne A., Fitzgerald, L. F., Puryear Keita, G., and Felipe Russo, N. 1994. *No safe haven: Male violence against women at home, at work, and in the community.* Washington, D.C.: American Psychological Association.

McKay, M., Rogers, P., and McKay, J. 1989. *When anger hurts.* New York: MJF Books.

Meloy, J. R. 1992. *Violent attachments.* Northvale, N.J.: Jason Aronson.

Miller, D. 1990. The trauma of interpersonal violence. *Smith College Studies in Social Work, 61,* 1, 5–26.

Paymar, M. 1993. *Violent no more: Helping men end domestic abuse.* Alameda, Calif.: Hunter House.

Pence, E., and Paymar, M. 1993. *Education groups for men who batter: The Duluth model.* New York: Springer.

Potter-Efron, R. 1994. *Angry all the time: An emergency guide to anger control.* New York: MJF Books.

Potter-Efron, R., and Potter-Efron, P. 1995. *Letting go of anger.* Oakland, Calif.: New Harbinger Publications.

Prochaska, J. O., Norcross, J. C., and DiClemente, C. C. 1994. *Changing for good.* New York: Avon Books.

Rooney, R. H. 1992. *Strategies for work with involuntary clients.* New York: Columbia University Press.

Tavris, C. 1982. *Anger: The misunderstood emotion.* New York: Simon and Schuster.

Walker, L. E. 1984. *The battered woman syndrome.* New York: Springer.

5 Psychotherapy in Emergency Situations

Todd Griswold

Emergency situations, so full of intensity and danger, challenge clinicians to overcome their own fear and connect with frightened patients. The stakes are high: there may be very immediate risks of suicide, violence, irreparable damage, or departure from much-needed treatment. While psychiatric emergencies often call for treatments such as medication or hospitalization, most interventions are in fact verbal. Effective psychotherapy in an emergency means connecting with someone in severe distress, and using that connection to help manage the issues of fear and control which are so prominent in a crisis. An alliance which is built on understanding and caring will help provide hope and minimize the immediate danger.

Emergencies arise in ongoing outpatient treatment, during inpatient treatment, and outside of treatment settings. While the ideas in this chapter are broadly applicable to emergencies in a variety of settings, some specific attention will be paid to clinical encounters in an emergency room or psychiatric emergency service (PES), since these sites have become increasingly important in effective crisis management.

Characteristics of Emergency Situations and Their Implications for Psychotherapeutic Approach

Emergencies are as variable as the people involved in them, but they share certain features which have a direct bearing on psychotherapeutic approach. Fear and issues of control can dominate the clinical encounter. Other intense feelings or states, such as despair, shame, or dependency, may require special care. Exigencies such as time constraints and the involvement of third parties must also be effectively managed.

Fear

Emergencies involve potential danger, usually both real and imagined, and danger is frightening. Fear exerts powerful effects on patients *and* clinicians in emergencies, and it is probably the most crucial issue in crisis psychotherapy. Patients often fear they are losing their mind, or that they will lose control and hurt themselves or someone else. They may fear that the clinician will overpower them, sadistically mistreat them, or incarcerate them. Clinicians, on the other hand, often fear being physically attacked by a patient (this, in fact, is regularly the salient experience of most trainees when first venturing into an acute psychiatric treatment setting). However, verbal attack and devaluation can be nearly as fearsome as physical assault. Clinicians may also fear bad clinical outcomes, and the ensuing guilt and regret, shame, or legal proceedings. Finally, clinicians may fear their own emotional reactions to an intense crisis, or may simply fear that they will be unable to effectively manage an emergency.

Since patients often fear the clinician, one must try to make oneself less fearsome. An unassuming, low-key bearing is a good way to start. Avoiding prolonged direct eye contact, permitting plenty of personal space, and arranging seats so as not to block egress are useful practical measures. Care should be taken to avoid comments which might be misinterpreted as suggesting a hidden agenda. Reassurance can help relieve fear, too, but it is not effective without first establishing a bit of connection or trust. When patients fear they may lose control, fall apart, or overwhelm the clinician, the approach should emphasize quiet confidence and authority, and faith that the situation will improve.

When a clinician is extremely anxious about being hurt by patients, or about patients hurting themselves, then his own overriding worries prevent him from understanding the patient's experience. Patients perceive this anxiety, and they become more distressed. Often the anxious clinician will distance himself from the patient, and then will be unable to use empathic support to help stabilize someone in distress. He may even avoid as much as possible talking with the patient.

Under these circumstances, the clinician feels pressed to do something before considering all aspects of the situation. The evaluation will be cursory, the alliance will be nonexistent, and efforts will be directed toward shuttling the patient away as soon as possible, either by abrupt discharge or by transfer to another clinical site. These premature decisions may lead to commitment and restraint being used unnecessarily.

> At 12:00 midnight, the police were called by the manager of a local coffeehouse after Mr. M. refused to pay for his meal. His somewhat disheveled appearance and his bizarre comments led police to bring him to the hospital, where he was immediately triaged to the psychiatric emergency service. The clinicians in the PES ascertained from prior records that during his last admission he had punched one staff person and thrown hot coffee at another. When the psychiatry resident spoke with him briefly, the patient was somewhat irritable and clearly delusional, but his behavior was in good control. Nonetheless, the history and the patient's irritability frightened the PES clinicians. The psychiatry resident quickly decided that the patient should be medicated and hospitalized. No effort was made to speak with him about having been seized by the police or about his distress. When the resident suddenly walked into the room carrying medication, the patient became agitated and knocked the medication out of his hands. Mr. M. was then placed in restraints and hospitalized involuntarily. Soon after being hospitalized, it was clear that the patient was in much better clinical condition than when he had been assaultive during the previous admission. He was discharged after a couple of days, but he remained extremely angry about his treatment in the PES. He told people he would never seek help from the PES, no matter how desperate he felt.

This outcome might well have been avoided had the resident and nurses been less fearful. Then someone might have made the effort to try to connect with the patient, do a careful assessment, and come up with a plan that would have helped the patient.

Issues of Control and Voluntariness

Because fear is so prominent in crisis situations, issues of control and voluntariness often become central. The patient and the clinician both may wonder whether everyone will be able to control themselves enough so that nothing terrible happens. Must the clinician step in and assume control, which might involve involuntary treatments? Perhaps the treatment is already involuntary from the outset. Some patients are brought to a psychiatric emergency service against their wishes. They are not seeking psychiatric help but instead find themselves facing a clinician who is urging them to talk.

The possibility that a clinician can immediately restrain, medicate, or commit a patient has immense implications for psychotherapy in the emergency setting. It can make alliance impossible, or conversely can permit an alliance which otherwise would be destroyed by fear. Many patients, especially those who are paranoid or who have been traumatized by others, profoundly mistrust clinicians' intentions, especially in a crisis. On the other hand, those who are terrified that they might lose control of their behavior and act on powerful impulses may feel much less fearful when they know that someone will step in and keep the situation safe if necessary. Similarly, clinicians who would feel too frightened of a patient in other settings can sometimes connect with a patient if they meet in a psychiatric emergency service.

Effective crisis psychotherapy requires the clinician to be comfortable and therapeutic with his power to impose involuntary measures, and to maintain the perspective to use these measures only when appropriate and necessary. The clinician should strive to permit patients control and autonomy in all circumstances except those severe enough to require coercive action. One should not let one's power distance oneself from the patient. At the extreme, one must not see the patient as an adversary.

Because some emergency interventions are coercive or involuntarily applied, clinicians must be vigilantly aware of their own aggressive impulses. When a clinician is so uncomfortable with power or force that he cannot effectively restrain or commit a patient, harm can result from inaction. On the other hand, when a clinician enjoys overpowering patients, he may act cruelly in using unnecessary force.

What about a situation where a clinician decides he must try to keep a patient in the emergency room (or in his office) despite the patient's expressed wish to leave? How does a clinician talk empathically with a patient about involuntary treatments, such as the plan to commit him, or to administer involuntary medication, or to restrain him for safety? These are challenging situations which call for the utmost respect, understanding, and clarity. As mentioned previously, patients often feel misunderstood, overpowered, or mistreated. The clinician should acknowledge the patient's distress, explicitly explain the therapeutic intent of the involuntary measure, and offer hope.

For example, when involuntarily hospitalizing a depressed suicidal patient, one might acknowledge the patient's pain and suffering (as well as his wish not to be hospitalized), emphasize that hospitalization is necessary to maintain safety, and explain that treatment can help. The patient may not understand, or may disagree, and in these circumstances it may be helpful to acknowledge the disagreement: "I know you may not see things the same way, but I think you're in a very dangerous situation and I know that hospitalization can help keep you safe until you feel a little better." It is also helpful to be respectful of the patient's stated reasons for opposing hospitalization; family, work, and financial obligations are all very real constraints which should be acknowledged, but which must yield to safety concerns in a crisis. Patients often have unstated fears or fantasies about hospitalization, which can contribute to a powerful sense of stigma, so a matter-of-fact description of treatment on a locked inpatient unit will help provide a clearer picture of what is ahead. Finally, the clinician should explain the legal process for review of the commitment to minimize the patient's fears of being locked away forever.

Restraining a patient, like commitment, is an involuntary treatment full of potential for fear and symbolism. The same principles of acknowledging the crisis, explaining the therapeutic purpose, and defusing the fearful fantasies apply. If a clinician has decided that a patient may become assaultive and must be restrained, one might say, "I can see you're upset and you're frightening me. We're going to put you in restraints so that no one gets hurt. We are not going to hurt you. We just need to make sure everyone stays safe." By acknowledging that a patient is scaring you, a clinician can reduce his own fearsomeness to the patient, which may decrease the patient's fear and thereby decrease the impulse to strike out. (Acknowledging being frightened is only useful, however, if adequate force is available to restrain and contain the patient's aggression.) Again, it is important to be respectful and clear about the therapeutic purpose.

Talking effectively with someone in restraints requires close attention to the feelings and fears commonly experienced by the patient. He may fear attack or sadistic mistreatment. He may be panicked by confinement. Quite often, he will feel deeply humiliated by his recent behavior or by having been subjected to such a crude means of control. He may be enraged at being overpowered. Sometimes, he may feel relieved that someone has taken control, or he may feel safe to "lose control" and may scream or thrash. While it is important to assess an individual's reaction and tailor one's approach accordingly, some generalities apply. Once again, a clear and respectful and helping attitude will help prevent further distress in the patient. For example, thank the patient for cooperating with restraints if he was cooperative. Ask if the restraints are causing any pain. Offer a pillow and a blanket, and always make sure that clothing or bedding adequately covers a patient who is wearing a dress or skirt or who has little clothing on. If you leave the room, explain why you are leaving and when someone will return.

> A teenage girl was brought to the hospital in restraints after she had told staff at a residential school that she felt suicidal and then fled from the school. She was furious, hurling profanities and thrashing. She was also sweating profusely and appeared to have slightly dilated pupils. While it was important to assess her for possible intoxication or withdrawal, it would have been impossible to take vital signs or perform a physical exam without agitating her further. Enough history was available to know that she was furious after seeing her boyfriend with another girl that day, and that she had never been diagnosed with a major mental illness. Rather than using a chemical restraint, one of the female staff spoke to her in a quiet, understanding way about her boyfriend, and she quickly felt much calmer. It was then possible to complete the medical evaluation and take off the restraints.

When someone is very agitated in restraints, try to sort out why, and therefore how best to talk with the patient. However, there are some limited situations in which trying to engage the patient in conversation will worsen the situation, regardless of skill and sensitivity. If the patient is intoxicated or acutely manic and irritable, talking may be of little help and the best approach is simply to be firm and clear, to decrease stimulation, and to use medication when necessary.

> When the clinician addressed a manic woman in restraints as Ms. P., she immediately yelled back, "That's *Ms.!* Not *Miss!*" and she proceeded to accuse him of sexist disrespect. His efforts to clarify only aggravated her further. Her esteem had probably already suffered such injury that she was bound to hear disrespect in any approach, and to return it in force.

> A manic man who was known to frequently use drugs was brought to the emergency room in restraints. He was hostile and agitated, and the clinician felt the most important matter was to sort out if he was acutely intoxicated or withdrawing. The clinician entered the room and said, "Hello, Mr. Jones." The patient instantly retorted, "Say Nation! Say

Nation! My name is Robert Nation!" The clinician bluntly asked him if he had used any drugs or alcohol that day, and he promptly spat at the clinician. Mr. Jones likely felt insulted already by being brought into the hospital in restraints, and the impersonal questioning about his misbehaviors was clearly not well-received. However, given the acute mania, it is unlikely that a more cleverly worded approach would have calmed him. In both these cases, verbal interventions were of limited usefulness.

Time Constraints

By their very nature, emergencies generally mean that time is limited: decisions must be made and action must be taken. Some situations do indeed require a swift response, but in most circumstances there is less immediate urgency than it may seem at first. Managing one's own anxiety about time, while not taking unwise risks, is crucial. Samuel Shem describes this concisely in his classic novel about medical internship, *The House of God,* when he explains that the first step for an intern during a cardiac arrest is to take his own pulse.

When does a psychiatric emergency require immediate action? First, something clearly must be done very quickly if the patient is on the verge of hurting himself or someone else. Second, an emergency exists when a serious medical condition manifests as, or accompanies, an apparent psychiatric emergency: for example, an acute alcohol withdrawal delirium or an overdose. These are true emergencies. Almost every other clinical situation, no matter how confusing or worrisome, merits taking time to talk with the patient, to think with him about his situation, without making a premature decision regarding involuntary treatments or discharge.

Sometimes we can know when a patient is on the verge of hurting himself or someone else, but often we are not sure. The clinician should start by directly asking patients if they are having urges to hurt themselves or anyone else right at this moment. In general, if the danger of violence toward others is imminent, then the patient is often quite agitated and distraught. Physical agitation is probably the best clue to potential imminent violence (more so than diagnosis, or the presence or absence of psychosis); a history of violence is another important risk factor. It is harder to anticipate imminent self-harm. If a patient acknowledges impulses to hurt himself, then the patient and his belongings should be searched, and he should be under fairly constant observation. Sometimes, however, patients will not be forthcoming, and overdoses and self-cutting can occur right in the emergency service and take clinicians by surprise. Probably the best way to reduce this risk, short of thoroughly searching all patients who enter an emergency room, is to minimize long waits and other impersonal frustrations, and to be vigilant when delivering disappointing news.

Medical emergencies presenting as psychiatric and behavioral disturbances require rapid recognition. If abnormal vital signs, shifting level of consciousness, or obvious neurological impairment are present, further medical evaluation is urgent. The interview should reflect serious concern for the patient's well-being as a basis for connection and should focus on gathering information about medical problems, medications, possible overdose, drug and alcohol use, head injury, and so forth. Concealed overdose is an especially vexing problem. When overdose is suspected but denied, the clinician must decide whether further efforts at gathering history will be fruitless, and if so to proceed with medical monitoring and toxicologic screening. The rationale for taking these steps should be explained clearly.

Time constraints other than urgency have significant implications for crisis psychotherapy. In an emergency room, the contact with a patient is generally short-term. Usually the patient and clinician will be meeting for the first time, and they may never meet again, or may plan to meet for a limited number of follow-up sessions. (A long-term relationship can develop, however, between a clinician and a frequent user of a psychiatric emergency service, and sometimes the PES is the best site for long-term treatment of the most difficult patients.) Because of the time constraints, it is important to establish an alliance as quickly as possible because stressful interventions might be required soon. Often the focus of the interview is to identify problems and recognize real external stresses, and then to look for practical and immediate steps which might alleviate the situation. While a psychodynamic formulation can be indispensable in planning an intervention, the interview itself has a here-and-now focus with less attention given to exploring feelings about the past.

Intensity

In addition to fear, psychiatric emergencies often involve other intense, even overwhelming, states such as hopelessness and despair, shame, rage, regressed dependency, or paranoia. The emotional intensity of the crisis challenges the clinician's ability to connect, or even to simply communicate, with a distressed patient. Here, the approaches are often similar to psychotherapy in other settings.

Hopelessness is common in psychiatric emergencies, especially those involving demoralization and suicidality. Despair may be acute and overtly painful, or it may be quiet and empty, almost invisible. Unfortunately, hopelessness and despair are not always easy to recognize, nor are they easy to relieve in an emergency situation. Finding the person inside the despair and really wanting to help are the best first steps. Only authentic interventions will help. The clinician can communicate his sincere belief that treatment will help, and this may provide important hope. Involving family and friends may sustain someone who has quietly withdrawn from social supports. Much of the section on "The Suicidal Patient" later in this chapter is generally relevant to approaching despair and hopelessness.

Shame can be extreme and calls for exquisite attention to treating patients with dignity and respect. It may help to genuinely admire the patient's strengths. "Counterdependent" patients have to overcome tremendous resistance to asking for help, and the difficulty of seeking help should be acknowledged. Sometimes one can lessen the acuity of a patient's shame by engaging him in the important process of making sure that a medical problem is not causing his condition. Certain explanatory models of psychiatric difficulties, particularly trauma and medical models, may lessen shame acutely and help build an alliance or initiate treatment.

The patient who is rageful should be recognized as likely having good reason, and this should be stated explicitly. As in other settings, enduring the angry verbal attacks of an enraged patient without retaliating or fleeing can help establish an alliance which permits other sorts of interaction later. Of course, careful attention must be paid to issues of dangerousness, and when the anger is intense enough to frighten the clinician, he or she must make a decision whether restraint is required for safety.

The patient who is regressed and desperately dependent may benefit from support and understanding communicated in a simple but not overly emotional way. The clinician should focus on practical matters, such as what the patient can do today to soften the crisis. One may have to be quite frank and disappointing about one's inability to provide an instant cure, or even to help at all.

Severe psychotic symptoms can make it challenging to connect with a patient. Disorganized thought, distracting hallucinations, or extreme withdrawal make it hard to establish an alliance, or even to communicate. Yet the clinician should persevere in a simple and clear conversational approach even if the patient is not answering any questions.

> A young woman with schizophrenia had been growing gradually more withdrawn and quiet over a period of months. She was brought to the emergency service when a home visit found her to be sitting motionless in a nearly empty room. She was very thin, pale, and mute. She had not left her apartment for days, and the refrigerator was empty. In the emergency room, she sat motionless and mute for 10 minutes as the resident attempted to elicit any response. Finally, he decided that he needed to perform blood tests to assess her medical condition. Still, he took the time to carefully explain what he was going to do and why, and she proceeded to quietly lift her arm and place it on the table for the blood test. The resident had thought she was unreachable and had not registered a word he said, but she was listening closely. He was able to build on this initial contact and went on to treat her for three more years, during which time she became less constricted in her life and began a part-time job.

Third Parties

Emergencies regularly involve other people besides the traditional doctor-patient dyad, and therefore assessment and treatment frequently involve contact with a number of different people. Many patients will be referred to an emergency room by someone else who has recognized danger and defined the situation as an emergency. For example, patients may be accompanied by treating clinicians, friends, family members, neighbors, employers, teachers or school officials, medical doctors or nurses, clergy, attorneys, local politicians, and of course police and ambulance workers. These third parties may be an enormous help or a major hindrance to the patient and the clinician. On the positive side, they can provide important historical information, offer immediate support in the crisis, and assist in establishing an alliance toward treatment. Conversely, they may distort history, fuel the crisis, and undermine treatment. With so many interested parties, the clinician can easily feel pulled to one or another version of the "truth," since people in these situations have different perspectives and may even make efforts to discredit one another or to split allegiances. Clinicians must always remember that they are treating the patient first, but must also remain open to, and respectful of, the concerns of others who are closely involved.

Psychotherapy during the crisis frequently involves meeting with the patient and others together. If one plans to meet with the different parties separately, it is generally advisable to meet with the patient first. Doing so allows the clinician to hear the patient's perspective first and will help communicate that the patient's well-being is his first priority. More details regarding working with third parties will be reviewed in the sections on "Working with Families" and "Working with Third Parties."

Techniques of Psychotherapy in Common Emergency Situations

Four important principles derive from the characteristics of psychiatric emergencies just described. These principles will help make psychotherapy as effective as possible in a crisis situation. First, recognizing and managing one's own feelings, especially fear, is crucial. Second, involuntary interventions, used only as a last resort, can be made from an empathic position and need not destroy an alliance. Third, there are actually few *immediate* emergencies in psychiatry, so time can usually be taken to listen, to try to understand, and to think clearly and carefully. Fourth, one must maintain one's allegiance to the patient when working with third parties. These principles together are directed toward establishing and maintaining a connection with the patient despite the turbulent forces inherent in the crisis.

Since emergency situations involve fear and danger, time constraints, intense feelings and states, and urgency to act quickly and decisively, a clinician's own feelings may influence the clinical action more than the patient's needs. Powerful affect in a patient readily elicits strong feelings in the clinician. Thus clinicians regularly find themselves having to effectively manage their own intense affect when facing an emergency situation. Although this is true to some extent in all treatment settings, the risk is especially high in crisis situations.

Perhaps the most common error in an emergency is that the clinician's own fear and anxiety lead him to abandon (or never even entertain) an attitude of respect, thoughtfulness, and support toward the patient. Instead, the clinician becomes authoritarian, controlling, impersonal, even adversarial. This approach usually intensifies the patient's sense of crisis and danger, and thereby creates an unfortunate cycle which can easily culminate in restraint, commitment, or the patient fleeing.

Certain situations commonly arise in psychiatric emergencies: suicidality and self-injurious behavior, potential violence, working with third parties such as families, and collaborating with other treaters. Particular techniques of psychotherapy can be used in each of these situations to establish an alliance and help stabilize the crisis.

The Suicidal Patient

Suicidality is in some ways the most difficult yet the most routine condition in psychiatric emergencies. Assessing and reducing suicidal risk is a challenge, and is subject to any number of confusing distortions and misunderstandings. How can a clinician use psychotherapy to reduce the risk of suicide in an emergency? The goals are to understand and accept the patient's pain and to provide hope, while recognizing that one's own feelings may pose obstacles.

Eliciting the presence of suicidal thoughts and impulses is the first step. One can't be helpful with a patient's suicidality if one doesn't know it is there. Patients may not be entirely forthcoming about their suicidal thoughts. They may be frightened, ashamed, quietly enraged, or hopeless. So the process of learning about a patient's suicidality requires building an alliance.

Helping suicidal patients express the intensity of their pain may be easier if the issue is approached gently. Sometimes language should initially be more general and then progress smoothly into the more charged material: for example, "I know you've been under a tremendous amount of pressure. Have you ever felt like giving up? Do you feel like life just isn't worth living anymore? Have you had any thoughts of hurting yourself? Have you thought about ending your life?" and so on.

Try to understand what the patient's deep feelings are. Buie and Maltsberger have written that the most pressing impulses fueling suicide may be "murderous hate, and an urgent need to escape pain and find peace," while desperate feelings of aloneness and worthlessness may make patients particularly vulnerable to suicidal crises.[1] Psychic torment may involve intense feelings of shame, guilt, self-loathing, rage at others, and despair. Psychotic patients may feel compelled to end their life to escape persecution, or for more cryptic reasons.

Acceptance of the patient in his or her acute pain is crucial. Criticism and irritation, which come so easily to overworked crisis clinicians, will destroy any possibility for an alliance.[2] Since the patient may feel alone and worthless, full of unacceptable impulses, then uncritical acceptance by the clinician can provide relief and the hope of further connection. Do not try to talk patients out of their suicidality by remarking on their strengths or how much they have to live for. This will be heard as definite evidence that the clinician does not understand how terrible they feel.

When patients feel accepted, they are more open to consider that a clinician might really want to work with them. An emergency clinician can act as an accepting, non-critical, problem-solving ally in helping patients resolve their suicidal ambivalence.[3] When a desperate patient has found someone who understands and wants to help, he or she may begin to feel some hope in the face of despair. The clinician also provides hope when he conveys the knowledge that treatment helps and that the patient truly can feel better.

Suicidal ambivalence need not be an obstacle to understanding. Ambivalence is almost universal among suicidal patients seen in emergency settings, so it should be expected and understood. Evidence of ambivalence in word or in action does not mean that the patient is not at risk, however. It means that an important part of the person wants to live, and this can be the basis of establishing a connection.

Clinicians must be aware of their own feelings, which can interfere with establishing an alliance. These are notoriously problematic when a patient's anger seems to be fueling his suicidality. The clinician must recognize anger when it is playing an important role, but should not personalize it as a reproach. Becoming angry at apparent reproachfulness will distance the clinician from the predicament and pain of the patient. Responses of punitiveness and moralism arise naturally but are obviously not helpful. On the other hand, a different sort of problem arises when the clinician overidentifies with the patient. Overidentification usually leads the clinician to underestimate the risk of suicide. The patient will feel misunderstood, and tragic consequences may result.

The Aggressive or Violent Patient

Psychotherapy with potentially violent patients can quickly tax a clinician's energy and patience. Potentially violent patients are often afraid, and they instill fear in clinicians. The earlier remarks on fear and control apply here. There are additional techniques, however, which may be useful in reducing the risk of violence by establishing and maintaining an alliance.

Reminding oneself that the patient is suffering and needs help to contain overwhelming feelings can help provide focus and establish a connection. The intense feelings underlying violence can be conceptualized as arising from either rageful anger or fearful panic, "usually prompted by an actual or threatened injury or loss, which may be real or imagined."[4] Verbal and other measures can often decrease the tension that precedes violence. These approaches have been reviewed elsewhere.[5] A non-threatening physical approach is crucial. Offering food or water may clarify the clinician's role as helper. A straightforward professional bearing is useful. Attention to the patient's self-esteem, autonomy, and legitimacy of grievance must be clear. One should never attempt to deceive, negotiate, or promise something that can't be delivered. One must be clear about limits and behavioral expectations without being challenging or condescending. Finally, when a clinician is significantly frightened of a patient, a working alliance cannot be established, and steps must be taken to ensure safety so that clinical work can continue.

Working with Families

Since many crises directly involve family members of patients, it is important to work with the family in a way which best helps the patient. Many different family forces may intensify during a crisis, and the clinician's approach should vary with the situation. Family members may identify the crisis and bring a reluctant patient in; they may fuel the crisis and designate the patient as the sick one; they may oppose treatment sought by the patient; or they may offer a patient crucial support. In any of these situations, the challenge is to ally primarily with the patient while viewing the crisis within the family context.

A general principle in working with families is that, just like the patient, the family members are often overwhelmed with intense feelings during a crisis. They may be very frightened, or may feel a great deal of shame, or may be extremely frustrated and enraged. They usually understand that a clinician's attention will initially be directed toward the patient, but they may be quite anxious for reassurance. When gathering history from the family, a professional, attentive, and non-blaming approach will offer support to the family system and thereby generally help the patient.

The threat of violence or suicide (or actual violence or self-harm) in a family creates the greatest challenge in working with patients and their family members. Gathering history in these situations is subject to more than the usual limitations. Fear and shame may lead to coercion, concealment, and other distortions. When family members recognize danger but the patient does not want treatment, they find themselves in a dilemma in terms of seeking help. They can continue to try to manage the situation without help and thereby risk danger, or they can contact the police or the psychiatric emergency service and face charges of betrayal.

> Mr. T., a 45-year-old man with schizophrenia, had lived with his parents all his life. He had not been able to manage well in the world, and his parents had cared for him at home. His parents eventually became more elderly and frail, and during a recent deterioration he began to intimidate them and deprive them of food and water. After several weeks, he struck his father in the face. His mother, obviously terrified, called the psychiatric emergency service and described what had happened. She asked that he be hospitalized immediately. When an ambulance and police arrived to transport the patient to the hospital, his mother screamed at the police and ambulance workers to leave the house: "Don't you dare hurt my son! He didn't do anything wrong!" She later explained that she had indeed been frightened of her son and wanted help, but she also feared he would be hurt by the police or doctors. She felt guilty that she had reported him to the "authorities," and also feared her son's reaction if he knew she had called the police.

A different problem arises when the patient describes family problems but the family members will not come in to speak with clinicians. This can lead to an impasse in treatment.

> Ms. M., a 45-year-old married mother of two grown children, frequently came to the psychiatric emergency service reporting suicidal thoughts and requesting hospitalization. She had a long history of chronic depression with psychotic features, and she was never able to identify any precipitants to these episodes. Multiple hospital admissions involving various medication trials and individual therapy had not improved her condition. Her family regularly refused involvement in her treatment. Only after much time was she able to recognize and explain that she sought hospitalization when her husband was angry at her. Indeed, she felt responsible for exasperating her family and wanted to be in the hospital to offer them respite from her burdensome presence (and perhaps to provoke some sense of guilt in them as well). A decision was made to contact the family every time the patient came to the psychiatric emergency service.

Through steady, gentle, and non-blaming outreach, the family gradually got to know the PES staff and began to meet with them. Although subsequent treatment with the family was not easy, it was at least clear that involving the family was crucial to stabilizing any of the patient's suicidal crises.

Working with Third Parties: Confidentiality and Tarasoff Duties

The involvement of "third parties" during a psychiatric emergency often raises questions about confidentiality. Some general principles apply; Beck has reviewed these issues thoroughly.[6] Maintaining confidentiality is central to psychotherapeutic work, and confidentiality is also the rule in emergency work. However, there are more exceptions to the rule in an emergency situation than in an ongoing outpatient psychotherapy. A true emergency, in and of itself, constitutes an exception to the presumption of confidentiality. When danger may be imminent, and when communicating with someone against the patient's wishes could reduce the risk of harm or substantially influence emergency treatment, then the clinician should certainly proceed.

> Ms. B., a college student facing final exams, came to the medical emergency room after taking approximately 15 aspirin tablets when distraught over the exams. She was evaluated medically and determined to be medically stable. When she initially arrived in the emergency room, she was sobbing and frantic, but she became serious and reticent by the time she was being evaluated psychiatrically. She denied that she had been trying to end her life, and she generally minimized the whole incident as "just flipping out." However, she refused to give the clinician permission to call her roommate or family. The clinician decided that the potential danger warranted calling her roommate against her wishes. The roommate recounted an alarming week in which the patient had become increasingly tearful, had been giving away her belongings, and had spoken of suicide as the best way out of her difficulties. Once the patient learned what the roommate had said to the clinician, she again became tearful and was able to talk about how desperate she felt. She agreed to hospitalization.

Although the overdose was not particularly dangerous, the clinician rightly suspected that the patient was quite suicidal, but had "sealed over" after some time in the hospital. The decision to call the roommate was a difficult clinical judgment call, as these decisions always are. In this case, speaking with the roommate provided the most important information needed to help the patient.

When working with third parties, one must distinguish between gathering history and disclosing confidential information. Information provided by third parties is generally quite helpful in a crisis, and gathering history does not violate confidentiality. An emergency clinician can, and should, listen freely to any information provided by family, police, therapists, and so on. For example, when a patient does not give permission to talk with family, but family members already know the patient is being evaluated, then a phone call to gather information in no way violates confidentiality if one does not disclose details about the patient. On the other hand, if the family does *not* know the patient is being evaluated, then a phone call will disclose that the patient is being seen psychiatrically. The clinician must make the judgment whether the degree of danger presented by the crisis warrants this disclosure. If the clinician does decide to speak with the family, he can keep the disclosure of details to a minimum. In the absence of an emergency, however, the clinician generally should not disclose any information about the patient without the patient's consent.

An important exception to maintaining confidentiality is the so-called "Tarasoff duty." This duty has been established and expanded in a series of legal decisions. The original Tarasoff decision stated that psychotherapists have a "duty to warn" specified potential victims if their patient poses a risk of harm to those victims. After the original decision, the Tarasoff duty was expanded to become a "duty to protect." Beck states that courts have generally found a "duty to protect" if two of the following are present: (1) a history of violence; (2) a motive; (3) a specified threat and victim. Depending on the situation, the duty to protect can be discharged in a variety of ways, such as hospitalizing the patient, warning the potential victim, or notifying the police of the danger.

Reporting situations of potential abuse or neglect to state social service agencies also frequently involves disclosing information against a patient's wishes. State law requires clinicians to report, so there is a statutory obligation which mandates this disclosure as a legally protected exception to confidentiality.

These entirely appropriate contacts with third parties against a patient's wishes do present major breaches, not of law but of the traditional framework of psychotherapy. These breaches may be experienced by the patient as violations and breaches of trust. In crisis psychotherapy, the clinician must try to convey that any communications with others are made in the interest of helping the patient and understanding the emergency. Generally patients can understand a clinician's decision to call someone to gather information. They are less likely to understand and approve of Tarasoff warnings and reports to social service agencies. These disclosures cause great anxiety for patient and clinician alike, in part because of their uncertain and potentially serious consequences. Clinicians are understandably uncomfortable when they feel that the law requires them to put a third party's interest above that of their patient, and in so doing, to possibly destroy the therapeutic alliance. There are no foolproof ways to protect an alliance in the midst of these grim dilemmas, but certain approaches can help. If a Tarasoff warning or report to a social service agency is made, the patient should be informed and should be told that the law requires the clinician to act. If the clinician feels torn, he can describe his dilemma to the patient. The clinician should say explicitly that the disclosure is not intended to harm the patient. In fact, the report is intended to help prevent the patient from harming someone, and preventing harm is clearly in the patient's interest. If the patient is particularly paranoid, the clinician may decide to make the phone call with the patient present, so the patient knows just what has been said. Sometimes patients will be able to see the potential benefit of the disclosure.

Crises in Treatment: The Emergency Clinician as Consultant to Ongoing Psychotherapy

Clinicians working in psychiatric emergency services are increasingly providing a central part of the comprehensive treatment that a patient might receive in a "system" of care. Emergency service clinicians often perform the initial assessment and formulate the treatment plan when a patient first seeks treatment. And even if the patient is already receiving outpatient treatment, in a crisis it is often the emergency clinician (rather than the outpatient clinician) who assesses the patient and formulates the treatment plan. Both de-institutionalization and managed care have contributed to this expanded role. This means that now more than ever, emergency room clinicians are uniquely situated to offer consultation to outpatient therapists.

Frequently, a psychiatric emergency arises primarily from a crisis in an ongoing psychotherapy. These situations have been described from the emergency clinician's perspective in the literature.[7] The patient comes to the emergency service in acute distress, and little information may be present initially to indicate a difficulty in the outpatient treatment. The causes of such crises are many, and may be simple or complex. For example, therapists' vacations can trigger painful feelings of abandonment, anger, and despair. Sometimes the therapy may be overwhelming the patient, for example by moving too quickly into intense material or by not offering enough support and structure for a disorganized patient. Patients may stop taking medication when angry at their psychiatrists, and then become acutely symptomatic. Patients may be dissatisfied with their current treaters and may be looking for a second opinion to address unanswered questions, or to provide reassurance that their therapy is not going awry. They may be looking, perhaps unconsciously, for a new therapist. Sometimes a patient's crisis communicates anger at the therapist by declaring the therapy a failure and thus discrediting the therapist before his or her colleagues. Finally, a therapist's incompetence or exploitation of a patient may precipitate a crisis.

These situations present challenges and opportunities. The biggest challenge is recognizing that the primary problem lies in the outpatient treatment, and then developing an understanding which is reasonably close to the complicated reality. It is important to ask patients what they feel about their therapy, and to contact outpatient therapists when developing a formulation. The perspectives of the patient, the outpatient therapist, and the emergency room clinician may diverge quite a bit. This may signal a problem in the therapy, so one should try to make sense of the discrepancies.

An opportunity for learning and change exists if an understanding can be reached. The emergency clinician can sometimes use a fresh perspective and clinical distance to help sort out an impasse in which both the therapist and patient are deeply embroiled. For example, a more dispassionate clinician, less distracted by strong feelings, may be able to see the situation more clearly. Similarly, a patient and therapist may both reveal thoughts and feelings to the emergency clinician that they have difficulty addressing directly with each other. On the other hand, patients and therapists may conceal from others something in the therapy that troubles or embarrasses them. Nonetheless, there may still be clues which can assist in formulating the problem.

Mr. K., a middle-aged man with paranoid schizophrenia, had been out of treatment for several years until recently starting psychotherapy with a psychiatrist in private practice. He came to the emergency service with acute paranoid fears that his psychiatrist had implanted a transmitter in his ear and was broadcasting messages to him. Mr. K. described meeting with his psychiatrist six days a week, and recounted that the psychiatrist would transcribe the contents of the sessions carefully. As he was feeling more distressed, he asked his psychiatrist for medication, and he reported that the psychiatrist told him he was too sick to be taking medication. The patient told the emergency room clinician that he wondered if the psychiatrist had problems similar to his own. He was clearly frightened and distressed by this situation. Phone calls to the psychiatrist were not returned, and Mr. K. was relieved to come to the emergency service for follow-up appointments and for antipsychotic medication.

In this case the potentially awkward step of consulting with the outpatient psychiatrist was not possible since he did not return calls, but usually communication with an outpatient therapist is possible. When providing consultation to outpatient therapists, emergency clinicians should present their opinions clearly yet diplomatically. Thoughtful insights presented respectfully may benefit the treatment substantially, whereas insensitive consultation is unlikely to help either the therapist or the patient.

Ms. V., a woman with borderline dynamics and a long history of treatment, came to the emergency service on a daily basis for a week, describing suicidal preoccupation and frustration that her medications weren't working and were causing a variety of side effects. All questions about precipitants to the crisis were fruitless. A thorough review of her medication was undertaken, but her responses to questions were vague and she seemed to show little interest in examining her medication regimen. The emergency room clinicians who saw her were frustrated with her, though they offered regular appointments if she wanted them for support. When asked about her psychotherapy, she revealed that she had begun therapy with a new therapist two months previously. The therapist was called, and she was very concerned about the worsening crisis her patient was experiencing. She had been receiving increasingly frequent urgent phone calls from the patient, and therefore had set up several extra appointments that week. The therapist explained that she was leaving for vacation the following day, but she wanted to leave her vacation number with the patient so she could call if she needed extra support. The emergency service clinician was able to commend the therapist's good intentions but to wonder with her if Ms. V.'s crisis might reflect anger about her therapist's upcoming vacation, and the patient's increasing fears that her dependency needs would overwhelm the new therapist. He described how exasperating the patient could be, and wondered if the therapist might be feeling guilty about going away, and was perhaps trying to make up for it by trying to be available when on vacation. The therapist insisted that she loved working with the patient, but was open to considering various treatment plans. In collaboration, the therapist and the emergency room clinician decided that the emergency service would follow Ms. V. during the vacation, and that when they resumed therapy they would meet weekly, with the emergency service available for additional support at other times. Ms. V. became substantially less distressed after this plan was developed, and her suicidal preoccupation resolved.

Facilitating Transition to Other Treaters

Patients often begin treatment with an emergency clinician and then need to continue treatment with a different outpatient therapist. Facilitating this transition is extremely important because patients frequently don't pursue referrals from emergency services. When referring a patient to outpatient treatment after a single emergency interview, setting up a specific outpatient appointment is preferable to just providing a name or number. It is even better if the patient can speak briefly by phone with the outpatient clinician or service.

In the public sector, outpatient waiting lists can be as long as weeks or months, so immediate referral is not possible. At Cambridge Hospital, the PES routinely provides ongoing short-term crisis follow-up for patients until they can begin regular outpatient treatment. The transition to outpatient treatment after one or two months of follow-ups in the PES can be particularly difficult. Often patients establish a strong connection to the emergency clinician whom they first met at the height of the crisis. If this same clinician has provided the follow-ups, then a substantial alliance has been built over several meetings. Why would a patient want to change treaters just as things have stabilized a little? Patients are at risk of dropping out of treatment when they are referred under these circumstances.

There are steps, however, that can be taken to help patients with this difficult transition. Successful transition to outpatient treatment must be one of the treatment goals during short-term crisis stabilization. The crisis clinician must take care not to foster too idealizing or intense a connection. With patients prone to dependent attachment, focusing on pragmatic here-and-now issues and tempering the intensity of empathic, supportive comments will help. Regular reminders of the need for referral to other treaters should be given. Sometimes scheduling one of the PES follow-up appointments with a different clinician can decrease the intensity of the focused attachment. Often it is helpful to schedule a final PES follow-up appointment after the initiation of outpatient treatment. This provides an opportunity to confirm that the outpatient appointment has been kept, to offer further encouragement to stay in treatment, and to say goodbye.

Common Dilemmas in Psychiatric Emergencies

Certain dilemmas which arise frequently during emergencies call for particular psychotherapeutic approaches.

Assessing and Engaging the Paranoid Patient

Paranoid patients who are not in treatment may walk into an emergency service, or may be brought in by a community member or agency. Engaging the paranoid patient challenges even the most capable of clinicians. Respect, attention to personal space, minimizing intrusiveness, maximizing autonomy, and counter-projective techniques can all be useful. Generally it is best to be clear and matter-of-fact with a paranoid patient, especially regarding such delicate issues as communication with others, confidentiality, security guards, medication, restraints, or commitment.

A particularly sensitive predicament arises when, in conversation with a paranoid patient who came in voluntarily, the clinician comes to suspect that substantial danger might be present just as the patient wants to leave. For example, the patient may make allusions to exacting terrible revenge on someone. As the conversation turns toward more affect-laden material, the patient may become more uncomfortable and the clinician more anxious, with the result that the patient may decide to leave abruptly. The clinician must attempt to prevent the patient from leaving, and may have to make the difficult decision whether or not to hold the patient against his will. Suddenly the clinician is no longer a supportive listener, an ally, but instead becomes someone who wants to deprive the patient of his liberty. This shift in the relationship often angers and outrages the patient. It may culminate in the necessity to restrain the patient. But it does not necessarily completely destroy any alliance. The clinician must explain that the situation sounds quite serious, that his job is to assess the situation and make sure things are safe, and that he wants to help prevent a situation which would get the patient in trouble or which the patient would regret. Patients can sometimes ally (at least partially) with an approach such as the following: "It sounds like you're so angry you could do something you might really regret. If you hurt someone, you'd be in a lot of trouble, and the last thing you need is more trouble in your life."

Sometimes the patient is not in the emergency service but instead is creating some friction in the community. A community agency, family member, or neighbor may contact the psychiatric emergency service asking for help, which may be a veiled request to lock the person up. Frequently such a person is not in treatment, is quite paranoid, and is surrounded by an enormous amount of upset. The task is to assess the patient, with more or less urgency based on what is known about the situation. Yet often the patient will not want any contact. Indeed, almost any contact will be perceived as an intrusion, a violation, or further persecution. How can one introduce oneself gracefully into such a situation? It is helpful, insofar as it is possible, for the clinician to locate the source of persecution outside himself. For example, if a home visit or phone call to the patient is planned, the clinician should be specific about the reason for the call, which is usually some complaint or concern from someone else. What the clinician must communicate is that he is not an agent of whoever made the complaint, but he is just doing his job in evaluating a concerning situation. Also, since some people likely *are* harassing the paranoid patient by this time, the clinician can often ally with him by acknowledging how terrible it is that people are giving him such a hard time. As always, the sentiment must be sincere or it may be seen as a ruse and will heighten paranoia.

Provocative Self-Destructiveness

Many patients in crisis hurt themselves. Probably the most common examples are cutting or small overdoses. The intent and degree of actual harm vary tremendously. While some patients are attempting to commit suicide, for most it is not so clear. These patients can cause intense frustration and anger in clinicians. The term "provocative" emphasizes two points: that such self-harm can sometimes be understood as an effort to affect others, and that such behavior regularly provokes anger in clinicians. It is important to remember that the intent of the patient in hurting him- or herself is not usually to irritate the emergency service clinician, although the clinician may react as if it were.

Crisis psychotherapy of patients who have just hurt themselves must focus first on trying to understand what led up to the act. What were the patient's feelings and thoughts? What did he want to do? What did he hope would happen? It is crucial to distinguish suicidality—thoughts of wanting to die—from other states. An attitude of curious exploration and implicit recognition of distress is most helpful. For many patients, cutting or other self-harm serves to discharge or relieve painful affects, and can be viewed as a coping mechanism. In these cases it is important that the clinician not present himself as one who will punish the patient for misbehavior, or who will try to take away the coping mechanism without offering anything in its place.

When a patient repeatedly acts self-destructively, one must formulate why. One possibility is that the self-harm does express a message to treaters. Is the patient desperate and out of control, and saying that he or she needs further "containment" to prevent suicide? If so, hospitalization and other supportive interventions should be considered. Or is the self-harm primarily a rageful reproach directed toward disappointing treaters? In this case, one should address the disappointment in such a way as to not promote further regression, while neutralizing the fantasy that one might be the patient's special savior. For example, one might offer the following observation: "People have really disappointed you. No one has been able to help you as much as you feel you need. I bet I'll disappoint you too. But one thing is clear: I can't keep you from cutting yourself. Together we can try to figure out other ways to manage your pain, but I can't prevent you from hurting yourself." Even when patients leave angrily, feeling that the clinician is useless too, they have a more realistic sense of the roles that they and their treaters play.

Conditional Suicidality: "Admit Me or Else!"

A 25-year-old man arrived in the emergency room in great distress, requesting a detox admission. He had a five-year history of heavy drinking, but had been sober for a nine-month period after a detox two years ago. Over the last several weeks, his drinking had increased after he was fired for absenteeism. On the day he came in, his girlfriend with whom he lived told him he couldn't stay with her any longer. He had no psychiatric history and had never felt suicidal. The clinician recognized he was in a crisis and that the best treatment was detox. However, not a single detox bed was available. When told the dismal news, the patient promptly said he felt suicidal, and said he would kill himself unless he were admitted *somewhere*. However, he assured the clinician that if he were admitted, he would not hurt himself.

This situation can be described as conditional suicidality: the patient says he will become dangerously suicidal unless something specific can be provided (often detox or hospitalization), in which case he is certain he will be safe. These situations exasperate and enrage clinicians, often leaving them feeling manipulated, exploited, or even overpowered. Needless to say, such feelings can easily interfere with treatment. A certain perspective can help. First, it is possible that the patient is describing his situation accurately; not uncommonly, people who are homeless and addicted are indeed overwhelmed and suicidally desperate, yet the support of detox or hospitalization will offer hope and relief. Should we be incredulous that support and treatment can stabilize the crisis and reduce the danger? Second, one must realize that even if the presentation is in fact a gambit to achieve hospitalization, then the patient's situation must be fairly grim and desperate if a psychiatric unit is the place he would like to be. Sometimes a clinician's sincere understanding will permit the patient to recognize and acknowledge that he will not in fact hurt himself, but instead was terrified that no one would help. Offering temporizing alternatives, such as a shelter for the night with a follow-up appointment the following morning, is a practical approach which demonstrates the clinician's concern and willingness to continue working with the patient.

Denial of Illness

Patients with limited insight into their illness often stop taking medication and drop out of treatment. While some degree of impairment in insight may reflect neuropsychological deficits, often patients are unable to accept the reality of their illness because of fear, stigma, and overwhelming losses. Emergencies often arise when patients have dropped out of treatment, and each new crisis presents an opportunity to try to engage the patient again.

When stigma is a major obstacle, sometimes patients can connect with treatment that is framed within a biological, psychoeducational model of learning how to manage a brain disease. This explicit discussion of illness, however, can frighten many patients. Often a more subtle, indirect approach is most useful. Patients who deny they are ill when asked explicitly often have some level of awareness that they might benefit from psychiatric treatment. Such patients will sometimes engage in crisis stabilization which is focused on acknowledging and relieving "stress" or "problems." Delicately worded phrases may permit a gentle discussion of illness. For example, psychotic patients who deny symptoms can sometimes acknowledge "difficulty concentrating" and "distracting thoughts." While somewhat indirect, this approach does not deceive the patient or collude with denial, but instead spares the patient the intolerable pain of being asked to baldly acknowledge that he is crazy. If asked directly about diagnosis or medication, however, the clinician must be factual and clear.

Regressed Dependency

Many patients who are treated in a psychiatric emergency service openly express their intense dependency. They are suffering profound distress and want relief. They feel entirely unable to survive without tremendous support. More specifically, they may come in and insist that they are utterly unable to manage any longer outside of the hospital. One's approach to these clinical situations depends in part on how one views the risks of iatrogenic harm in further hospitalization. Patients will rarely understand the statement that hospitalization may be detrimental, but in some cases patients have begun to notice this themselves and may not be confused or frustrated by a direct remark to this effect. More generally, one must strive to understand the acuity of the patient's distress and to communicate that understanding. If the emergency service is one which undertakes follow-up readily, then it is helpful to make the PES limitlessly available to the patient as the best treatment in this situation, while declining hospitalization as something that most likely wouldn't help. Patients will be angry, which is fine, as long as the clinician continues to stress his interest in working together with the patient to try to manage the crisis. Daily follow-up appointments should be arranged, and therapy should increasingly focus on finding practical ways to cope with the stresses at hand, such as scheduling some satisfying activity, taking walks, listening to music, and so on.

Relentless requests from patients, day in and day out, for hospitalization and detox and medication begin to tire out emergency service staff. Overworked clinicians may unconsciously envy these patients who seem to relinquish the burdensome responsibilities of life at the first obstacle, and simply enter the hospital to have their every need met. Clinicians have some typical responses to this situation: with-holding and sadism. Given the increasing difficulty of accessing inpatient treatment, staff in psychiatric emergency services can come to see themselves as the guardians of a precious resource, withholding the delicious reward of hospital admission from all those they deem unworthy. Sadism can be explicit in any number of ways, such as making patients wait to be seen, or bludgeoning them with indirect allusions about their being ineffectual. Once again, the emergency clinician must be vigilant regarding countertransference feelings which will disrupt an alliance and interfere with therapy. Humor shared with colleagues can be a healthy outlet for discharging some of these strong feelings.

Conclusion

When an emergency is the precipitant for someone seeking treatment, it may be the patient's first contact with psychiatric treatment. The clinician should keep in mind that the management of this initial encounter can greatly influence the patient's attitude toward treatment and help-seeking. An early positive alliance can draw someone into treatment, just as an unpleasant experience can keep someone away from much-needed psychiatric services for years.

Emergencies are taxing, but they can indeed be opportunities for substantial change and growth. Psychotherapy in emergency situations is never boring. In the midst of an extreme crisis, psychotherapy can truly make a difference in patients' lives when clinicians connect with patients, treat them respectfully, stay aware of problematic countertransference, and stick with them in their fear and pain.

Notes

1. Buie, D. H., and Maltsberger, J. T., *The Practical Formulation of Suicide Risk* (Cambridge, Mass.: Firefly Press, 1983).
2. Hillard, J. R., "Suicide," in Hillard, J. R. (Ed.), *Manual of Clinical Emergency Psychiatry* (Washington, D.C.: American Psychiatric Press, 1990).
3. Meyerson, A., Glick, R. A., and Kiev, A., "Suicide," in Glick, R., Meyerson, A., Robbins, E., and Talbott, J. (Eds.), *Psychiatric Emergencies* (New York: Grune and Stratton, 1976).

4. Menninger, W. W., "Management of the Aggressive and Dangerous Patient," *Bull. Menninger Clinic,* 57:2, Spring 1993.
5. Menninger, W. W., "Management of the Aggressive and Dangerous Patient," *Bull. Menninger Clinic,* 57:2, Spring 1993; Rice, M. M., and Moore, G. P., "Management of the Violent Patient," *Emerg. Med. Clin. North Am.,* 9:1, February 1991; Hughes, D. H., "Assessment of the Potential for Violence," *Psychiatric Annals,* 24:11, November 1994.
6. Beck, J. C., "Current Status of the Duty to Protect," in Beck, J. C. (Ed.), *Confidentiality versus the Duty to Protect: Foreseeable Harm in the Practice of Psychiatry* (Washington, D.C.: American Psychiatric Press, 1990).
7. Skodol, A. E., et al., "Crisis in Psychotherapy: Principles of Emergency Consultation and Intervention," *Am. J. Orthopsychiat.,* 49:4, October 1979; Kass, F., et al., "Emergency Room Patients in Concurrent Therapy: A Neglected Clinical Phenomenon," *Am. J. Psychiatry,* 136:1, January 1979.

6 Treating Psychoses

Leston Havens

This chapter focuses on painful and demoralizing experiences that people with psychotic symptoms have, experiences that can be relieved or even removed by psychological means. I will also discuss psychological problems arising in the course of medication use, notably non-compliance, and means by which they can be overcome.

The term "psychosis" has a broad application. It originally meant condition of the psyche as opposed to condition of the nerves, or neurosis, an etiology reversed at present. It referred to incomprehensible mental and behavioral events, also called "bizarre." Today such events are partly understood, so the term refers to extreme emotional states, for example seemingly inappropriate emotional states, great excitement, flatness or lack of emotion, and sometimes extremes of terror or despair; also marked deviations of thinking, especially in paranoid or megalomaniac directions, as well as scattering of thoughts; also persistent perceptual anomalies, illusions and hallucinations in particular; and finally behavioral disturbances, sudden violence, extreme withdrawal or rigidity, and various bizarre mannerisms that were once termed "catatonic." Many times what impresses observers most is a loss of centeredness that may be seen as a loss of will or coherent selfhood. Psychosis then returns to its first meaning, condition of the psyche, or, in the popular phrase, "losing one's mind." An important partial exception is extreme states of oppositional or paranoid self-will that are also termed "psychotic."

One of the most painful experiences many patients have is being thought or called psychotic. This often early experience may be a self-judgment and can result in rapid demoralization. At other times the judgment is pronounced in family, work, or social circumstances. Perhaps most demoralizing are professional judgments to this effect, made without attention to their psychological impact; such pronouncements often destroy budding relationships between patients and helpers. It is important to note that "psychotic" or a related term like "schizophrenic" is the supreme negative judgment available in many societies, carrying an even larger weight of opprobrium than "criminal," "perverted," or "retarded," and sometimes a greater sense of doom than being diagnosed with cancer.

What may either accompany the judgment of psychosis or stand alone is the psychotic person's experience of *contempt*. Commonly it has three features, each of which deepens the resulting demoralization. First, the experience of being held in contempt may seem very general, after which can follow the charge of being paranoid. It is seldom easy to decide how delusory the patients' convictions actually are. My own observation of people prone to psychosis is that they often are held and know they are held in general contempt, so that the further charge of being without insight is also unsound. Second, the psychotic person often feels contempt or hatred back toward those who are seemingly contemptuous. This may be a distasteful feeling in that many psychotic persons, having long experienced the pains of contempt, dislike extending it to others. The ensuing further contempt for themselves is added to the judgment of society, comprising the third feature, self-loathing. It is valuable to emphasize that self-loathing may not be expressed directly, indeed may be covered by attitudes of superiority or again contempt toward others. The self-loathing person predictably works to distance himself from himself, being convinced that any close observation of himself will confirm his bankruptcy. What I am asserting is that the social experience of being psychotic adds immeasurably to the handicaps imposed by whatever disabilities underlie it.

Countering the patient's expectation of contempt is therefore a first principle of forming effective relationships. It requires an acute sense of how the patients feel about themselves and a strong urge that they not feel that way. As I will emphasize repeatedly, a lively sensitivity to the positive aspects of the patient and a willingness to acknowledge them should come first and should occupy the earliest and extended part of any intervention. This is often best done by finding a common interest between therapist and patient, such as sports, music, or the movies, during the discussion of which each can enjoy the other's opinions, share pleasure, and move the emphasis of the relationship away from the pathological and contemptible. Some observers find it hard to note what is admirable about many psychotic people. These observers are often far from believing that the most apparently pathological among us still have much more in common with the "normal" than they have features that are different. Such observers may also be slow to note the determination, idealism, and often, generosity of spirit that have survived or even grown in the patients through years of pain and turmoil.

I emphasize again, as I did in Chapter 1, that a thorough training in the pathologies of human nature often crowds out attention to what is vital and healthy in others. This has a particularly noxious and destructive effect on work with the sickest patients.

It is a surprising and unwelcome conclusion from prolonged observation of human interactions that some of the most lovable features of our species have sad results. Sullivan was fond of saying that schizophrenic patients tend to be drawn from the ranks of the "non-suave," that is, the socially awkward, relatively direct, and openly idealistic. These are people who "wear their hearts on their sleeves" and hence are vulnerable to criticism or manipulation. Therapists like Sullivan, sympathetic to such qualities, readily ally with psychotic people, and are then well-positioned to share the abuse they receive and able to undertake the long-term task of rendering the patients less vulnerable. I will suggest some means for achieving the latter when I discuss long-term goals later in this chapter.

Generally less lovable is the rigidity of ideals so common among psychosis-prone patients. Ethical judgments tend to be black or white, so that while the patients' idealism seems noble, its application is adversarial and often unsuccessful. An alliance can be built around the idealism, which is quickly shattered by the impracticality. This problem may be overcome if therapists are willing to share some of the patients' fury at social injustice and their naive impatience for good people to understand what the patients value. In this way an opportunity is provided to begin to deal with patients' rage. It is no accident that a synonym for psychosis is "madness." Indeed the patients are often furious, a fact easily forgotten when, between outbreaks, they return to the passivity, even tenderness, that is a longer-term state. Plainly the maintenance of a practical, steady aggressiveness is a central failing for many psychotic people. In other words, their anger needs to be mobilized and put to sensible use when they are passive, and shared, that is, divided or apportioned between patient and therapist, when they are furious, so that they do not self-destruct. A second and very difficult long-term goal is this lessening of the polar extremes of passivity and fury toward a workable midpoint.

The naive openness of many of these patients also calls for early attention. This may not be immediately apparent if the patient is overtly paranoid, scattered, or removed. It has been repeatedly observed that many paranoid psychotics have been earlier in their lives *not paranoid enough,* that is, they have trusted blindly and been deceived; this was often a repeated occurrence. Perhaps as a result, many have become chronically paranoid. A particularly striking example is the occasional patient who has learned that he or she cannot enter a relationship without "getting lost" in it; "boundariless" is the expression used today. A close understanding of this tendency is helpful. Difficulty in maintaining self-possession during a warm romantic relationship is not restricted to psychotic people. In fact, "falling in love" has often been compared to a psychosis in its merging with the beloved, losing oneself in adoration of the other, plus intense jealousy and suspiciousness even among the normal. Memory of such experiences should help therapists understand the boundariless plight of the patients. What may need to be added in the understanding of psychotic patients is the experience of trying to survive intense love in the absence of resources of supportive others who are able to right the resulting imbalance.

Some psychotic people resolve never to expose themselves to the same terrors again, limiting their relationships to impersonal objects or animals. This results in the well-known "schizoid" adjustment that may seem very odd to others. Still more striking are the usually affectless, heavily mannered individuals who are victims of lifelong autistic states, that is, states of marked emotional withdrawal. Some have the resource of special talents that permit commerce with professional worlds. All of the adult autistic persons I have known report storms of intense affect that, because of their fear of others, they are unable to calm by the usual methods of human closeness and holding. An occasional patient devises methods of mechanical holding that provide comfort. No task is more formidable or at present predictably lifelong than luring such patients back to the human world.

To the experiences of being called psychotic, treated with contempt, lacking suaveness, and acting from a rigid idealism and naive openness must be added a group of experiences that can be described as loss of control and/or meaning. By loss of control I mean the very common (and perhaps definitive) experiences of, for example, having thoughts snatched away, being commanded by voices or illusions, and automatic obedience, a reflex-like following of others' commands. By loss of meaning I refer to a timeless, futureless state in which the idea of effective action is at most an occasional, fleeting thought. Both losses offer fearful glimpses into the possibilities of psychological life and chances for interventions against them.

Experiences of loss of control have often been thought to be definitive of schizophrenic psychoses, as in the "Schneiderian symptoms." There is little doubt that they constitute, from the patient's perspective, some of the most alarming and debilitating features of psychosis. To be ordered and insulted by insistent voices throughout one's time awake (not generally in sleep) is a suffering that transcends all but the most hellish interpersonal experiences, as when the orders and insults occur in everyday life. "Thought-capture" refers to a disruption in thinking marked by an almost palpable sense of one's thoughts being pulled out of the mind. More difficult to describe is a general sense of having all of one's movements and thoughts controlled. On several occasions I discovered that this, which had been the patients' long-term experience, was only noted after the patients had gained a degree of independence that could then be contrasted with their previous state. God is often named as the moving and controlling party, affecting the smallest details of daily existence. In this there are similarities to Julian Jaynes's account of the human world before the emergence of consciousness and independent selfhood.[1]

The existence of automatic obedience, a feature of catatonic psychoses, makes these extreme losses of control unmistakable. Today automatic obedience (or command automatism) is tested by placing a limb in a certain position and observing that the patient does not move the limb again until commanded. Early in the twentieth century the testing was done by means of a pin shoved through a throat stick. The patient was ordered to put out his or her tongue, and the tongue was then struck with the pin; a quantitative measure of obedience could be established by counting how many times the procedure was repeatable. In training I heard it said that the testing sometimes had to be stopped because the tongue was a bloody pulp. Automatic obedience may be followed or preceded by automatic disobedience (negativism). In either case, the patient can be said to lack an independent center of volition, only acting for or against the observer.

It is as if everything comes into the patient: there is no protection from the world; the condition of boundarilessness extends to every aspect of life. Some patients report that reading poetry is the aspect of accepted life closest to this experience. Poetry breaks down conventional barriers to the communication of feeling states by imbuing natural objects and events with power. Not infrequently patients report being stopped and held by powers felt in nature, as manifestations of godliness do to many more. Cassirer argued that the word "god" was in fact the first expression in all languages, brought to speech by just such experiences.[2] Jaynes has speculated that these experiences reflect a particular stage of brain development before the breakdown of the "bicameral brain."

I will describe four interventions, helpful by the measure of patients' reporting increased control as well as feeling understood and allied with: sympathizing with the terror and awesomeness of the experiences, validating their similarity to a poet-like sensitivity, helping establish some distance from the god-like powers, and asserting patients' rights as individuals against the powers. Medications are particularly helpful in reducing the strength and intrusiveness of voices as well as the patients' sensitivity to experience. But just this sensitivity may be what some patients value most about themselves (or are commanded not to interfere with), so that an adequate trial of medication must often wait until the patients are helped to gain a fresh perspective.

Sympathetic concern for experiences that have generally resulted in the patients being called psychotic (if not also forcibly hospitalized and medicated) requires that one not add to the intrusiveness. (Of course this waiting may be impossible under emergency conditions.) Because standard medical practice is a kind of enforced close contact, many of these patients have avoided professional assistance for years. Finding helpers who are knowledgeable about the patients' plight and not themselves terrorized by it can be a significant relief. If added to this is a confidence that the situation is neither hopeless nor to be blamed on the patient, a useful relationship can begin.

Second, renaming phenomena called bizarre or psychotic has a strong remoralizing power. For example, referring to the patients' experience as evidence of sensitivity, even a potentially creative sensitivity, not only naturalizes the trait but points to its usefulness. The commonest objection to this arises from the fear that patients will not see themselves as sick, will refuse medication, and will fail to follow doctors' orders. The opposite has been my experience: compliance with medication increases, and therapeutic suggestions are taken more seriously. Moreover, the sullen compliance (if in fact there is real compliance) and demoralized attitudes so common among obedient psychotic patients can sometimes be replaced by even joy in life. It is not known how much the so-called "negative symptoms" of schizophrenia, for example apathy, are functions of being named schizophrenic, with all its implications of a negative future and having no place in society.

Third, establishing distance from the powers, that is, gaining autonomy, depends first upon an emerging self-consciousness. I believe that many of these patients have been unaware of their subservience, like fish unaware of the water they swim in. It is as if their consciousness and self-awareness were largely in the hands of the voices, displaced outside themselves and not their own. A few patients, in my experience, do protest against the intrusions, sometimes silencing them for a while, but this is exceptional.

Helping psychotic people gain self-consciousness is, once again, a function of respect. This should not be surprising if it is understood that by acknowledging and regarding others, we routinely help them come into their "own." One patient I knew had swum in the water of her obedience as long as she could remember and, having come to a realization of this when it was partly over, fell into despair and experienced "nothingness," now being without the meanings her previous orders had given to every last detail. (I will take up this loss of meaning shortly.) Consciousness of herself was a consciousness of "emptiness." On the other hand, I felt her, both her sensitivity and the lostness, together with a presence that she could experience only through its impact on me. She said others were laughing at her or turned away. I wanted her to hear and hopefully feel the different response that I experienced toward her. At first she could hardly hear my words; I seemed far away; she would stop, puzzled; I had not seemed real. Gradually she felt my presence, but she herself felt empty. Then she felt real with me. I wondered if she was learning a new language characterizing her self.

This patient's emergence was still more evident in the changing account she gave of her relationships with those around her. As long as I had known her, she radiated a quiet power to influence people when the cause she espoused was not in her own interest but that of someone else. She did not seem aware of this power; perhaps it was in the service of the orders. What changed was her capacity to act not only for others but in protection of herself. For example, she set limits on the demands of a fellow-worker and arranged that a roommate leave when she took advantage of her. Later I will discuss the terrible problems many patients have in not being exclusively the servants of others—automatic obedience in the social and work spheres. This patient surprised me by the rapid growth of her self-protection.

But the meaninglessness, the futurelessness of her life persisted. Sometimes she yearned for the old god-filled days. This is a commonplace in the account of modernity—this despair and yearning at the "death of god"—but her despair was so outspoken, her sense of nothingness and emptiness so direct and complete as to make me wonder if Nietzsche and Heidegger had experienced what she had. I recalled Heidegger's lament for the modern age: too late for god, too soon for being. Here was a predicament that she and I could share with each other. Sometimes, she said, it seemed enough just to get through the day. Perhaps she will go back, perhaps to a god less severe in commands. Once she told me she envied me my work: to be helpful and, at the same time, to enjoy myself. I wished that for her too.

The problem of meaninglessness and lack of future is an appropriate point to discuss the most difficult part of the work, the long-term part. Symptoms may pass, especially with effective medications, but the patients may be left *in an unproductive relation with life*. They can survive outside hospitals, live in group homes or halfway houses, even work long and hard, but without the vitality and purpose that luckier people have. We know the prognosis of psychotic states, followed over long periods, is extremely varied, and we lack firm predictors of different outcomes, so that working and hoping for the best outcome is not quixotic. Further, the tragic plight of people lost to either servile compliance or bootless freedom should be motive enough.

The first long-term goal I mentioned was overcoming naiveté, helping the patients gain a little suaveness or the "false self" that Winnicott suggested was necessary for the protection of "true self" (the former not to be confused with "false personality" or character armor).[3] Gathering awareness of this problem confronts the patients' frequent hatred of suave people, from whom they may have had only contempt. Many patients have told me that they would rather die than be like that. This is a problem for much therapeutic change, some women hating to become overbearing like men they have known, the aggressive fearing to be "passive wimps," and so forth.

The fact is, few changes that we achieve will be very great, so I tell the patients: don't worry, you'll always be an honest soul, just add 1 percent of cunning, or else the suave *will* kill you!

These patients do not easily find a place between openheartedness and isolation. Beginning a relationship slowly, observing behavior coolly, allowing a sense of the other to develop—all of these are impeded by floods of sensations that obscure, for example, the gut verdict needed. Again, a central focus of attention and action seems slow to form. Therapists can be helpful by sorting the materials presented and transmitting their own sense of the other in any relationship. A main principle of therapeutic action is exercised here: on the one hand, accepting the patient's difficulty, understanding where it comes from, not being critical; on the other hand, having confidence that progress will be made. A great peril for the therapist is being patronizing, that is, talking from a position of superiority. Being older than most of my patients, I can recall many similar mistakes of my own and how slowly I learned, if I did at all. Throughout one wants to *illustrate* the very relationship being recommended, a relationship marked by equality, respect, sincerity, and listening to each other. The medium of exchange must carry the message: how therapist and patient get to know and perhaps come to trust each other is the very process needed in everyday life. A great obstacle to such results is therapists expecting to be trusted and thereby encouraging the very naiveté at issue. We have to earn patients' trust, even warn them against trusting us.

A structure of therapeutic action now is evident: deciding what needs to be done (in this instance, learning some suaveness); understanding and appreciating the patients' difficulty in doing so; therapists filling in for the patients (thereby modeling what is needed), but doing so while confessing and recapitulating therapists' own, often far from successful learning experiences, throughout guarding the desired interaction from behavior subverting the very capacities needed (for example, by encouraging trust). Much of therapy is practice like musical practice: going over and over the same material to get it right, growing to feel one's strength, the task becoming second nature, all for the more important performances of life.

We need to appreciate a feature of repeated practice and successful performance, which is that the actual performance is by no means given in the practice. What my patient in fact did, to remove the roommate and guard herself, required creative steps nowhere learned or implied in the course of our interactions. These had to be improvised. One result was that *the performance was her own.* Note what this does to her experience of all the failures, arduous practice, and persistent despair that preceded: these become a measure of her victory and of the change in her self-esteem, a large change for those who previously owned at most defeat. Old soldiers carry their wounds as proudly as they do their medals because one is the measure of the other.

Confidence cannot be given; it can only be earned. Granted that therapists' confidence in patients (when sincerely given) sets the stage for practice since the confidence *is already a success* for the patients in the interaction. But this must be lacking in the performance when the audience may look on stony-faced until they have been won over. At the start, performers have only their learned skill and memories of past success to support them. Of course the familiar demons of failure and despair will appear. Helen Hayes is reported to have vomited before performances even late in her long theatrical career. One learns to expect the demons, even to welcome them as signs that there is much at stake. I have seen some very defeated people reach that point. There is an incomparable sweetness in the result.

Therapists can savor such results as long as they remember how little they have contributed to them. This is not to say that they do nothing. What they add may be small but, like vitamins, essential: an observation or two (this person is naive); a sympathetic body nearby now and then directing attention (to help focus); and the willingness to persist in leaning against, for example, overtrusting, and toward the goal of a viable relationship. It is also sobering for therapists to note that these interactions are not experiments, in the sense of exact repetitions, but part of an ongoing historical process which means that what the patient did might have happened anyway, with nothing from us at all. There is no way to know in the individual case.

The same structure of therapeutic action is useful in leaning against either passivity or fury and toward a practical aggressiveness. Again, one directs attention, in this second long-term objective, to what is being neglected during the passivity and then noticed too late in the fury. The patients usually have excellent reasons for the neglect, perhaps having long protested in vain or worse, and found that protesting only deepened their humiliation. One therefore begins, not with urging protest, but with a steady sharing of whatever aggravations will eventually lead to fury. Curiously, I have found that such a sharing prevents the fury, although no actual headway has been made against the aggravations. A full acknowledgment plus the presence of an ally seems enough to do at least a temporary job. Gaining a practical aggressiveness capable of correcting aggravations is much more difficult and should not be approached without a timetable measured in years. The central principles are parts, now greatly extended, of the structure of therapeutic action described: modeling what needs to be done; describing one's own failures (for the patients must fail many times in such efforts); and, above all, not repeating the patient's experience of being humiliated, this time by the therapist, when the patient is either unable to act or unsuccessful. Few tasks are more formidable or less likely of complete success than taking command of one's life, so that even a small measure of gain is worth the long haul.

This does not require intensive therapy in the sense of regular, frequent contacts, but instead occasional, sometimes brief visits with someone seen as an ally. Frequent visits may be contraindicated because great personal closeness is not well tolerated and because too much is being promised and spent when the task is a slow, long one.

The third long-term goal is the most daunting of all in those chronic autistic states where patients have withdrawn from every human contact. While the therapeutic principle is simple, its implementation is complex, requiring extraordinary creativity and patience. One needs to make human contact appealing in the face of its flat rejection and without recourse to reason, because the patients generally have better reasons for withdrawal than any we can bring against them. Here may be the most salient instance in all psychotherapy of explanations and interpretations destroying the work. Explanations are a form of instruction; for these patients, personal instructions are a form of domination and intrusion. Every explanation is at least partly an argument; an argument to these patients is the very definition of intrusion. Therapeutic charm, so widely depended upon, is equally destructive. It is a lure and a tease for those many patients who have gone that way tragically before. This leaves respect, but respect at a level of delicacy and tact seldom attained. Years ago I began to observe an occasional individual going through training programs who could sit with autistic patients in such a way as to leave them unperturbed; he or she had a rare sensitivity to others' sore points, so that the patients felt at once attended to and protected. Patients who had spoken to no one for long periods spoke to these young people; and others who had left every previous encounter distraught and angry looked forward to their visits. Here was the start of a reconciliation with human life. Therapists, as I wrote in Chapter 1, need to provide analgesics for psychological pain, one of which must be their own presence. The test is, can therapists make the patients feel better?

Much else will be needed over any long haul, but respect remains the center. It can also become the center of the patient as well, moved from the experience of the relationship to a changed experience of the person's own self. This new *self*-respect serves as a counterweight to the supremely tactless and intrusive disrespect of hallucinatory commands. I have even noted instances in which a therapist's supportive voice replaced the old condemnatory voices. In one case the patient reported meeting life difficulties in a new spirit; where once any impasse or setback was accompanied by volleys of hallucinatory abuse, now she felt a calming presence and sometimes a word or two of encouragement that she associated with the old therapist.

The final long-term task is less formidable. Many psychotic patients retain human contact, but of a particular kind. Their relationships mirror the obedience dramatically represented by command automatisms. In work situations they spend long, often unpaid hours, may never go on vacations, undertake the most difficult assignments without protest, and are both highly valued and exploited by employers naturally eager to see the patients' relapses as signs of illness rather than the exploitation. It is astonishing how much of some organizations' work gets done by one or two of these obedient people. Therapists would be wise, however, not to attempt rapid programs of economic liberation. The patients are characteristically glad of the work opportunities and are identified with their employers. That these work attitudes are part of the psychotic process is suggested by the same attitudes being held toward the inner authorities, that is, identification with the commands and denial of any right to indignation or protest. The same attitudes are generally also held toward parents. This gives therapists little room to move: they cannot be fully sympathetic with the rage, and if they ally with the authorities, they increase the enslavement.

The patients are ashamed of any rage they feel ("I have no right to be angry"), and both fearful and in awe of the authorities. In the days when psychological processes were considered part of the study of schizophrenia, this so-called rage-need conflict was one candidate for causing the massive breaking and scattering of mental function that occurs in schizophrenia. I am using the conflict here to structure one set of long-term approaches to these patients. I have already discussed the problem of finding a middle course between blind rage and passive resignation, by gently noting aggravations in the latter state and sharing some of the fury in the former. These actions also bear on overcoming enslavement. What I suggest now recapitulates this structure of therapeutic action with a new emphasis: one needs to call attention, very quietly at first, to the question "what's for me?" (as opposed, for example, to the lack of suaveness). No response other than bewilderment is to be expected for a considerable period until there emerges some *personal interest*. I do not mean personal entitlement, which takes still longer, entailing a direct confrontation with previously all-powerful authorities. The claim of a personal interest is less bold and seems to many self-evident; an occasional patient will express surprise at not having considered it before. Once again the medium must not contradict the message; therapists are not to press their own interests, for it is the patients' interests that must be kept at center stage. In fact, one hopes to be contradicted and argued with— strong signs of these personal interests.

The emergence of personal interests and, later, entitlements provokes a resurgence of voices in some patients, and in all the fear that they will be hated and condemned. That is, having personal interests does not mean the structure of authority is gone. What has gone is the monopoly of authority. The patients have entered, however gingerly, the normal human state of conflict between one's own authority and that of others. As a result, therapists can then share their own experiences with this dilemma, their own failures and successes, so that the patients can take, through the resulting companionship, one more step into the human world.

A note on mania: while I have seen favorable results of psychological action on almost every type and phase of psychosis, I have not seen this in regard to full-blown mania; nor have I seen it described by others. This is not true with lesser degrees of mania, perhaps because they may be indistinguishable from excitement. In regard to the latter, I have observed a number of allegedly manic people who have been able to turn their "excitement" into productive behavior, with relative calm, when their projects were understood and supported, as I illustrated in Chapter 1. This is an example of a widespread problem, arising from the ease of confusing pathological states with normal anxiety, sadness, or excitement.

Today we face a happier but different problem of "awakenings" from psychotic states treated by new, more effective medications. Some of these awakening patients find themselves faced by a world from which their lack of confidence, inexperience, and often self-loathing make them shrink. They may even stop their medications, occasionally reporting that they prefer the old delusions; suicides have also occurred. I suggest providing an ally and companion to these patients to help confront the seemingly new and bewildering world. Here again, therapists need to acknowledge the patients' fears while standing for the possibility of a better future. As always, great patience is needed together with recognition of a problem seldom met with elsewhere so clearly. The recovering patients may feel that they have no future because they have no lively dreams, nothing that points to a viable future. Such a vision of the future may never have been fostered in their pasts; they may think the time for it is gone; it may even be unimaginable. And if it does appear, it may seem to therapists grandiose, perhaps a return of the psychosis. Let therapists recall that the dreams of the young often seem extravagant or arrogant ("I want to be President"), and that these awakened persons may be psychologically very young indeed. I like to talk of my own early dreams—how I cherished them, and how I had to learn to keep them alive while enduring the time, effort, and disappointment needed to bring them to fruition. Nothing can repay our efforts more solidly than taking such patients into the new possibilities that they, perhaps beyond all others, deserve after years of bearing with and surviving their torments. Then our work can be a successful union of pharmacology and psychotherapy, so like the best results of, for example, orthopedic surgery combined with the slow and sensitive physiotherapeutic mastering of muscles and movements long neglected.

Notes

1. Jaynes, J. *The Origin of Consciousness in the Breakdown of the Bicameral Mind.* Boston: Houghton Mifflin, 1976.
2. Cassirer, E. *Language and Myth.* New York: Dover, 1946.
3. Winnicott, D. *The Maturational Processes and the Facilitating Environment.* New York: International Universities Press, 1965.

Additional Reading

Garfield, D. A. S. *Unbearable Affect: A Guide to the Psychotherapy of Psychosis.* New York: John Wiley and Sons, 1995.

7 Working with the Borderline Patient

Alex N. Sabo

> No great progress in this field of study can be made until it is
> realized that the field of observation is what people do with each
> other, what they can communicate to each other about what they
> do with each other. When that is done, no such thing as the
> durable, unique, individual personality is ever clearly justified. For
> all I know every human being has as many personalities as he has
> interpersonal relations.
>
> Harry Stack Sullivan, "The Illusion of Personal Individuality"

Several years ago I accepted a clinical/administrative position which
required that I facilitate the development of an integrated mental
health and substance abuse delivery system for a catchment area of
roughly 140,000 people. I began by convening regular meetings of
leaders of the various clinical programs for the purpose of discussing
difficult cases. I had hoped to gain some measure of the perspectives
they brought to bear on their work, and from this to help them col-
laborate toward the purpose at hand. After several meetings it became clear that the bitterest rancor was evoked by cases involving patients who formerly would have been described as borderline, but
who now had modern therapists fully versed in multiple personality
disorder. Some insisted that the most helpful approach involved recognizing the borderline dynamics and holding the therapists and patients "accountable" for their behavior. Others stressed that if a more
tolerant attitude were adopted the patients would become more ma-
ture, would ultimately integrate their "alters," and peace would be
restored.

I had heard such discussions before at elite institutions which consider themselves expert at these treatments. Lines are drawn and battles fought. But this work is more complex than these formulas allow.
What amused me in the current situation was that our leadership
group named itself the "Integrated Treatment Team." As Huck Finn
might have said, "That was a stretcher." Each program had a leader

who believed he was right, and each would intervene with the patient according to his version of the truth. The result was that our integrated team functioned more like a multiple personality disorder, with one side contradicting the other, programs not communicating with each other and acting as if the others did not exist. Anger was expressed at the "borderline/multiple personality disorder" patients—they held a mirror to our team, which did not like its reflection. These patients teach us about ourselves: that we have deep needs to feel connected to others, that we become afraid when alone, that under enough stress we think in black-and-white terms, that we each want our own way most of the time, and that we behave differently with different people. Sullivan considered these principles so basic that he placed them at the heart of psychiatric work.

Psychotherapy with borderline patients is difficult, the outcome uncertain, and the stress great. Talented and knowledgeable therapists have watched with dismay as their best efforts yielded nothing more than stagnation, more often great turmoil and pain, and sometimes utter disaster. Each decade heralds at least one enlightened new approach which, more often than not, finds itself in disrepute or, at best, more soberly regarded by its successor. Some have labored solo; others have developed distinguished doubles teams; while another recruits an entire army. Consider Knight, Kernberg, Gunderson, Breuer and Freud, Buie and Adler, van der Kolk and Herman, Linehan, to name a few who have thrown their hat into the ring. Writer, beware! Love and Hate, Good and Evil, Politics and Science, Trauma and Vulnerability, Victim and Perpetrator, the Bounded and the Unbounded create tensions that may undo those who amble in this minefield. Yet the difficulties exist, the patients come for help, and hope springs eternal. With this caveat, I will provide a sampling of key contributions to relationship-based work with borderline patients, outline an approach to the psychotherapy, and make practical suggestions.

Overview of Key Contributions

For nearly two decades, many looked to the work of Otto Kernberg for guidance. Kernberg focused on the borderline patient's reliance on "primitive" defenses such as splitting and projective identification to ward off severe anxiety related to anger and separations. While most of us use these defenses sometimes, especially under great stress, the borderline patient is likely to use them regularly and with less frequent recourse to more adaptive defenses. Kernberg taught that splitting was related to the borderline patient's inability to tolerate the anxiety associated with bringing together positive and negative representations of self and object. He considered a constitutionally based intense anger to be a fundamental problem for borderline patients. In a field where the patient regularly discovers what he or she is feeling by eliciting strong, similar emotions in the therapist (projective identification), where rapid shifts of idealizing and devaluing others occur regularly, and where intense anger is the most common currency, the therapist will need strong principles to anchor the treatment. Kernberg urged therapists to adhere faithfully to the three tools of psychoanalytic treatment: interpretation, technical neutrality, and transference analysis.[1] He hoped that these tools would accomplish the important task of allowing the therapist to keep his or her feet, to preserve a place to think, in the midst of a stormy emotional sea. They sometimes did.

While balance was sometimes possible, the constant bringing of therapy material into the interpersonal context (transference analysis) and the imbalance in the power relationship of the therapy implied by interpretation actually amplified the unmanageable interpersonal field they were meant to manage. One recalls Sullivan: "For all I know every human being has as many personalities as he has interpersonal relations." When one emphasizes these three tools in the work with borderline patients, one accentuates the distancing, the imbalance of power, and the frustrating nature of psychoanalytic therapy in a way that is likely to intensify the anger the patient feels. The anger may in part be "constitutional," but it is also field-dependent. The therapist unwittingly hardens or accentuates some of what is called "personality." Partly to offset these problems, two subschools of psychodynamic therapists emerged and emphasized different dimensions of a complex problem and different approaches from Kernberg's. These subschools are embodied in the work of Buie and Adler[2] and Judith Herman.[3]

Buie and Adler argued that borderline patients lacked a "soothing introject": they suffered from a deficit in the capacity to self-soothe under the stress of separations. Emanating from this fundamental problem, three broad psychological developments would unfold in their treatments. First, as the patient grappled with the problem of aloneness and separations, the patient and therapist would be exposed to intense rage and anger. The patient would communicate these experiences to the therapist using the defense of projective identification, eliciting the feelings in the therapist that the patient himself or herself was experiencing but was unable to feel and articulate. The therapist has the opportunity to work creatively with this highly energized emotional material to better understand the immediate feelings of the patient and the historical circumstances under which they were shaped. The task of this phase of the therapy is to survive the rage of the patient without retaliating. This phase may require months to years of work, and, if successful, results in the patient's internalizing a soothing introject available during times of stress. A successful outcome of this phase allows the patient the capacity to tolerate being alone. The patient can now call up images of a person who represents a benign helping presence. This is not so different from the soothing introjects depicted in recent popular myths. Consider E.T. just before leaving earth, pointing his finger at Eliot's forehead and stating, "I'll be right here," or Ben Kenobi appearing in a vision to Luke Skywalker during times of stress in the *Star Wars* adventures. The presence of a guardian angel or the promise of a rainbow after a storm represent similar soothing introjects taught regularly in non-psychoanalytic contexts to large numbers of people.

If successfully traversed, the first phase of treatment gradually gave way to a second phase which addressed the "narcissistic" aspects of personality development. Issues of worthlessness and incompleteness are worked through using Kohut's model. The therapist allows herself to serve as an idealized figure to accept the projections of the emerging self of the patient. The therapist serves as a mirror to the patient, reflecting back a sensitive awareness of the patient's feelings and experience. Empathic understanding is central. Inevitably, the therapist makes mistakes in understanding, and the patient becomes frustrated. Kohut considered these moments essential to the treatment and to the development of new psychic structure and called them *optimal disillusionments*. Disillusionment is essential to psychological growth, as in the poems of William Blake where a person matures by moving from songs of innocence through songs of experience, but the disillusionment should be manageable in the context of a caring relationship and not shattering. The patient comes to realize that nothing dire results from these failures by the idealized figure, and that he can probably solve the problem at hand better if he did not rely so much on the idealized figure. Kohut called these realizations the *transmuting internalizations* that lead to a stronger sense of self.[4] If this phase of treatment goes well, the patient emerges with a solid sense of self-worth and completeness. The third phase of treatment involves efforts to consolidate a sense of love for the self that will allow the patient to function and enjoy work, play, and relationships. Much of the work here focuses on the stuff of everyday life. The therapist validates the patient's achievements in the real world. Success in this phase allows the patient to leave treatment with a stable set of values and ideals. At the core of Buie and Adler's approach is the assumption that the therapist and patient form an effective relationship that carries them through these difficult stages of development.

Herman's work represents another effort to reconceptualize the core difficulties of borderline patients and to devise more helpful approaches to their psychotherapy. Herman draws on Erikson's stages of psychosocial development and emphasizes the importance of basic trust being established with the first caregiver. She draws on the many retrospective studies between 1985 and 1995 which associate high levels of early physical and sexual abuse and caregiver neglect with the development of Borderline Personality Disorder. Basic trust is shattered by severe trauma: "When trust is lost, traumatized people feel they belong more to the dead than to the living."[5] This feeling is common for borderline patients during the most demoralized phases of their lives. Herman places the condition of the borderline patient in the context of those subjected to severe trauma by human hands for long periods of time, calling the condition a Complex Posttraumatic Stress Disorder. She states that prolonged exposure to totalitarian control leads to alterations in (1) affect regulation, (2) consciousness, (3) self-perception, (4) perception of perpetrator, (5) relations with others, and (6) systems of meaning. In this context, disempowerment and disconnection are central events leading to a disturbed sense of self.

Herman's treatment emphasizes the quality of the relationship and attention to three phases of recovery: establishment of safety, remembrance and mourning, and reconnection to ordinary life. For her, the quality of the therapeutic relationship is the key to recovery, and she articulates a set of values that inform the relationship: persuasion over coercion, ideas over force, and mutuality over authoritarian control. This conceptual framework is very powerful for establishing alliance and externalizing blame, so that safety within the relationship can emerge. Many patients value the support and respect implied in this model. (See Chapter 11 by Newman for a more thorough exploration of work with severely traumatized persons.) In practice, some therapists using this model avoid the constructive place of anger within the dyad of the therapy, and to this I'll return in a moment. One can easily see similarities in Buie and Adler's and Herman's models of recovery for borderline/complex posttraumatic stress disorder patients. The first and third stages are almost identical. It may be that, for the patients in whom trauma was a greater factor, remembrance and mourning are more essential, whereas for patients in whom the developmental problem was more in the range of lack of affective attunement, the narcissistic issues require greater attention. In many therapies, attention to both will be necessary in the middle phases of the work. Marsha Linehan's practical suggestion that therapists routinely prioritize the content of each therapy session by addressing life-threatening issues first, therapy-threatening issues second, and quality-of-life issues third may actually build into each session a preview of where the therapy is headed. (See Chapter 10 by Robins and Koons for a more thorough explanation of Linehan's approach.)

The Value of a Normative Context

As a college undergraduate, I developed my first real interest in psychology through intensive reading of Freud and Jung. I admired Freud for his clarity of thinking and the lucid style of his writing. Yet, when I analyzed my dreams and thought of my life from his perspective, I couldn't help construing myself and my family as full of pathology. It was a dark world that I grew up in and continued to live in through my unconscious life. I felt pulled down partly by real experience but partly by Freud's framework. Jung, on the other hand, juxtaposed thoughts and images like a poet gone mad; his writing was a sea of chaos. Yet his references to myth, religion, and the archetypes had an uplifting quality. The dark, frightening nature of my dreams took on a new light. I could be Odysseus traveling to the underworld to learn, through struggles with mother and father, the secret that would allow my survival on the island of the sun. There was something healing about confronting one's shadow as a normal process of human conflict and development. This confrontation has been celebrated in different cultures and places throughout the ages. I was not alone.

In much the same way that patients with psychoses develop a deep sense of self-loathing (see Chapter 6 by Havens), patients with borderline disorders frequently loathe themselves, especially by thinking of their desire for others as poisonous or dangerous. Work with borderline patients is often stormy, frightening, and difficult. Therapists need a way to conceptualize their work which allows them to endure the difficult phases. Yet even more than the therapists, the patients need a respectful context within which to understand their situation. Kernberg provided a model which sometimes allowed the therapist to keep his or her bearings, but which very few patients find appealing. Buie and Adler's conceptualization is kinder to the patient, but is still very therapist-centered in its language. Herman's formulation integrates psychodynamic concepts with an awareness of the effects of political repression on human development and revisions from the women's movement. Patients find her language much less blaming of them and acceptable as a way of understanding painful and confusing experience. Shay has also done this through his work with Vietnam veterans and has argued that an individual's personality changes when those in authority betray what is right. The parallel he draws between the traumatized veterans and the tragedy of Achilles achieves the uplifting effect that is at the core of Jung's work.[6] Herman's and Shay's efforts go a long way toward offsetting the stultifying effects of shame. Yet, lest we wrap our patients too tightly in a victim role, I suggest we take the movement toward a normative context one step further.

From a scientific and evolutionary perspective, the problem of the borderline patient brings us to the work of Paul MacLean and John Bowlby, who provide us with a normative context which dignifies the "borderline" struggle. MacLean used comparative neuroanatomy and studies of reptilian and mammalian behavioral routines to arrive at several conclusions. First, there are only three behaviors which distinguish mammals from reptiles: nursing in conjunction with maternal care, audio-vocal communication for maintaining maternal-offspring contact—the separation call—and play. These three behaviors evolved with the appearance of early mammals 180,000,000 years ago and are associated with changes in central nervous system structure and physiology that committed mammals to a family-like social structure. All mammals have a characteristic separation call with a characteristic frequency and duration. The purpose of the call is to keep young offspring in contact with their mothers, since prolonged separation is likely to result in death. In squirrel monkeys, small amounts of morphine, which do not otherwise affect the level of arousal or other behavior of the young monkeys, will extinguish the call and naloxone will reinstate it. Opiate receptors abound in the cingulate cortex of rhesus monkeys, and lesions to the cingulate cortex will eliminate parental behavior and play in various mammalian species. Hamster pups raised by parents with cingulate lesions have only a 12% survival rate.[7] Oxytocin is another natural hormone associated with bonding and a sense of well-being. It has been shown in animal models to function like an antidepressant, and it is capable of turning off the stress response by shutting down adrenocorticotrophic hormone (ACTH). Thus, the adaptive survival value of a family-like social structure for mammals (extended parental care for the young, separation calls, and play) has committed us to a physiology based on oxytocin-related and opiate-mediated attachments to each other.[8]

I mentioned earlier that borderline patients often loathe themselves, feeling that their strong urges to be with others and the desperate calls in the night to engage support are symptoms of their dangerous and poisonous nature. In the framework of MacLean, they might represent the debt of mammalian biology to an evolutionary survival strategy. Mammals gained hegemony over reptiles because of this social strategy. Carl Sagan used to joke that our egg for breakfast was a daily celebration of this mammalian victory. But it comes at a cost. All mammals can be terribly stressed by separations from their attachment figures and soothed by reconnections with them. Some speak of borderline patients as having pathological love addictions. Perhaps they represent the dramatic tip of our iceberg, yet take the rap for the rest of us. I am reminded of how difficult it is for our "integrated treatment team" to look in the mirror. When I consider the borderline patient's frantic efforts to avoid aloneness, I am reminded of MacLean's work. It calms me, removes me a bit from the immediate tumult, and I think in a more clear-headed way. I often tell some version of these stories to my borderline patients as illustrations of our mammalian physiology. I find this helps in three ways: some are interested, others are amused, while our own areas of conflict are dwarfed by the great battles between mammals and reptiles. Humorous and not-so-humorous illustrations of snake, rat, and good mother abound in the world around us. Finding ways to "cool" the transference, while forming a useful relationship, is a key aspect of work with borderline patients. They can sometimes see their own situation with dignity or a little humor rather than as a shameful shortcoming. The anger de-escalates. This approach also gives us a non-pejorative framework in which to open a discussion about separation calls and who substitutes might be—friends, family, crisis teams—elements of what Newman describes as self-care. Effective relationships with borderline patients are formed when one discovers a normative context that makes sense to both the therapist and the patient and when one can talk simply and directly about the repetitions that make the relationship unbearable for either party.

What MacLean elucidated at the neuroscientific level, John Bowlby clarified at the psychosocial. Bowlby considered a safe home base the fundamental condition for normal attachment and human development.[9] He defined attachment figures as those who seemed stronger or wiser and to whom one turned when sick, injured, or afraid. Attachments span the lifetime. One doesn't grow free of them; they are a natural lifelong process. Bowlby eschewed the term "regression" because he thought it was normal for people to seek the comfort of the home base when in trouble.[10] Life itself is a dance of regulating distance from one's attachment figures. When secure, one makes forays out into the world, exploring, discovering, and shaping new possibilities. When wounded, sick, or afraid, one returns to the home base for nurturance and recovery. With borderline patients, one should respect the normal process of attachment and the need to regulate distance. The task for the therapist is to avoid too ambitious a role. Attachment is necessary for psychological development, but the therapist need not be the only attachment figure.

Approach to the Psychotherapy

Psychotherapy with borderline patients is likely to take a long time. Whatever the physiological components of the disorder may be, much of the work is developmental and occurs in the context of relationships and learning. Major questions for the therapist are how intense a level of work he can tolerate and what level of intensity is useful. These therapies are difficult to manage in any case, but for the most part the more often one meets in a short period of time, the more heated the interpersonal field becomes. Ambitious therapies have involved as many as four sessions per week for five to ten years, while more modest treatments have consisted of one session per week for a number of years. In the era of managed care, many treatments are limited to no more than 26 sessions per year. With the exception of Linehan's data,[11] there is little controlled research concerning the superiority of one form of treatment over another. The therapies are notorious for falling apart. In a study we conducted at McLean Hospital, borderline patients had averaged 32 months of prior therapy with a number of therapists before entering the study through a hospitalization.[12] Some were considerably better five years after that; some were not. I have personally conducted psychotherapies of both the ambitious and the modest sort and have mixed results. I currently prefer the more modest interventions, but I am not sure whether this is because I have lost the energy to do the ambitious treatments or because the more modest treatments are more efficient. I have had patients who did very well in the five- to ten-year intensive mode, with three or four sessions per week for several years followed by gradually tapering sessions over the years. I have also had patients who did not do well with this mode or who dropped out of treatment. I have had equally mixed results with the more modest treatments. One of the decisive factors appears to be the quality of the therapeutic relationship. Did the relationship allow the patient to experience enough anger to be constructive and grow? Or was the anger too much for the relationship, dispersed through either persistent paranoia or unuseful blaming of others, or turned on each other so that neither the therapist nor the patient could stand the other? Too stable a relationship is not helpful either. I have seen patients who form a stable relationship with a therapist for ten to twenty years, but the nature of their complaints changes little. They never get better.

This brings me to an important point. With some borderline patients, it is easy to form an initial alliance. Some of these patients quickly arouse a supportive and empathic response from the therapist. Winnicott described such cases. He felt that it was quite possible to form a supportive relationship, but that nothing would change unless a characteristic development occurred one to two years into the treatment. He described it as an attack upon the therapy. This might occur as a suicidal crisis or as a paranoid transformation of the patient's experience of the therapist. Winnicott saw this as a useful development which, if handled well, would lead to essential psychological development for the patient. He asked the therapist not to retaliate in such cases, but to act like a heavy rock which the sea crashes against, but which does not move. He believed that the patient was actually using this experience to differentiate her internal world from the external world. The attack upon the therapy or the therapist was the process by which the patient began to realize: "I am not you, but I am glad you are out there." If the patient never had this experience, she would forever retain an essentially psychotic inner core. She would go on insisting that whatever she thinks is the reality of others. She could read another's mind; she always knew the other's motives. The outer appearance of being stuck in this trap would be a supportive therapy that lasted many years, but where no essential change took place.[13]

Through consulting on many cases that have gone well and on many that have gone poorly, I am convinced that there is merit to Winnicott's idea. I think of it as a way that a primitive, intense experience of anger must be felt and used constructively for the purpose of psychological development. This development requires a sound relationship and a skillful therapist. It may be easier to achieve through a group structure (consider Newman's and Scherling's chapters for ideas in this regard). I would add that the therapist can be a rock without retaliating by saying, "Ouch, what you're doing hurts!" rather than enduring so much storm that he chooses to flee the work. The trick is to tolerate enough storm to understand the patient and to permit the developmental process, but not to endure so much that the therapeutic relationship gets irreparably damaged. The therapist (or conceptual framework) who flees this anger, or who consistently turns it into projections against others, prevents the patient from finding a way to make this developmental leap. The therapy is friendly and goes on forever, but nothing ever changes. The "ouch" lets the patient know she has her own mind, as does the therapist. The relationship endures, and the patient is ready to move on to the next phases of her development. I think of the type of anger expressed by the patient and the reciprocal experience of anger of the therapist in this situation as normal accompaniments of the first phases of treatment described earlier in the models of Buie and Adler and of Herman.

Another way to conceptualize this anger emerges from the work of Lacan[14] and Bion.[15] In this framework, one can imagine people existing in three realms: first, the fused state, represented by the number one, where the mind and affects between two people are one. Next is the dyadic state, represented by the number two or the concept of mother, where there are nurturance and empathy, the feeling is warm, and communication is often clear through gesture rather than words. Finally there is the triadic state, represented by the number three or the concept of father. This is the place of language, law, and the social order. It is a cooler place. (See Chapter 9, where Gustafson refers to these three realms as the three fields of observation.) Successful work with borderline patients involves balancing the time spent in the dyadic and triadic spaces. Anger is an orientation tool toward this balance. If too much time is spent in the warmth of the dyadic state, anger is a possible ticket out from the danger of fusion and psychosis. Movement from the dyadic toward the triadic, such as ending a session on time so that the next patient's session is not late, often arouses anger as the patient in session experiences a desire to stay in the dyadic warmth. One can run a check on the therapy by asking how much time is spent in each state. Most borderline patients need a balance of the dyadic nurturance, and the cooling stability of language, law, and social order. This framework is useful for evaluating day-to-day flows of affect and putting their meaning in some perspective—a compass of sorts.

Anger has other constructive functions in the therapeutic relationship with borderline patients. I mentioned earlier Kohut's concepts of optimal disillusionment and transmuting internalizations. These moments are usually signaled by the patient feeling frustrated or angry with the therapist. If the relationship is sound, one need not do too much with the anger which naturally accompanies these moments. The task is to be present and to listen respectfully to what the patient learns through them. This type of anger, which is usually milder and less scary, accompanies developments in the second phase of Buie and Adler's model. A third type of anger is in reaction to social injustice. For example, cultural suppression of anger in women contributes to their negative self-image and perhaps their greater vulnerability to depression.[16] While acknowledging this will help the relationship throughout all phases of the work, it is a type of anger that should not be confused with the desperate need for an object that Winnicott identified so aptly. When a therapist confuses these two types of anger, the therapy can become interminably stuck or can be destroyed when the anger of phase one erupts with too much fury.

A fourth type of anger involves patients who have experienced severe abuse at the hands of another who was meant to care for them. It is especially important to handle this type of anger skillfully and tactfully through the therapeutic relationship. Some of it is rightfully assigned to the perpetrator of the abuse, but that perpetrator is often an ambivalently held object, so that the patient has mixed loving feelings as well. The therapist respects the patient's psychological predicament and allows a safe place for both sets of feelings to be expressed, held, and explored. The patient's freedom is maintained, and her ingenuity for solving this predicament is a surprise for the therapist to discover. The therapist approaches each patient on an individual basis rather than prescribing a moral formula. If the abuse occurred early in life, these patients usually need, as Winnicott described, to go through an experience of anger related to differentiating the internal world from the external world. If this need is present, the therapist must not shy away from that anger or mistake it for the natural anger of a victim against the perpetrator of humiliation or violence. The therapist allows this anger to be experienced and metabolized through the dyad of the patient-therapist relationship, where it belongs. If it is projected outside the relationship, the patient may never make the needed psychological development.

A fifth type of anger permeates the work with borderline patients: the anger that is integral to valuing relationships. As Bowlby points out, a mother who gets angry at a child running into the street does so because she values the relationship and wants to protect the child from danger. The spouse who becomes angry in the context of a partner straying does so in the context of wanting to preserve the relationship. It is useful to remember this natural function of anger to protect relationships as one attempts to understand the constructive place of anger in valued relationships.

I mention the constructive place of anger in the therapeutic relationship because most conceptual models of borderline personality disorder place excessive anger or inability to manage anger at its core. Consider Kernberg, Linehan, the serotonin hypothesis,[17] or DSM-IV. As in bipolar disorder, we treat the severe swings of mood, but we must also leave a place for the normal experiences of anger, sadness, despair, and elation that accompany all of us through life. With borderline patients we may find useful help in treating unmanageable anger through serotonin reuptake inhibitors or dialectical behavior therapy, but we must also respect the natural place of anger in the development of a healthy and strong person. This brings us to the question posed by Havens to modern psychiatry: What are the tests of normality that allow us to know what is pathological? How does the interpersonal field we create with a patient contribute to what we call borderline? I am convinced that one can sometimes identify through a history and interview patients who are likely to develop a full-blown borderline presentation if certain types of stressors or interpersonal situations develop. How one engages in the relationship can have a profound effect on "how badly borderline" the patient ultimately appears. The therapist is never quite sure how much he or she contributed to the "personality disorder" in a case that goes badly. It is natural to take some solace when one observes the same mess occurring with someone else, but this avoids the question of whether some other approach might have prevented the disastrous development altogether. In some cases where I greatly feared a long, nearly impossible mess, the patient ended up doing well, with only the minor ups and downs of everyday life. How could that happen?

Havens has described the invasive nature of some people, and how interpersonal language is the tool for finding the right working distance in these situations.[18] When borderline patients look back, they often describe their mothers as not being present enough, and then being present too much ("low maternal care and high over-protection" on the Parental Bonding Instrument).[19] This may be a persistent perception of how we all feel when overtired, hungry, or frustrated by something we can't get quite right. Perhaps this is the normal variant of the low serotonin state—irritable, whining, lashing out against an image of mom as bad guy—that is played out innocently enough even in situations where the best parenting is available for a child. How does a mother find balance in these situations? Winnicott described the task of a child learning to be alone with his mother. The mother balances the child's immaturity and dependence, and she is present without making demands. She lets the child be. Perhaps when the potentially borderline patient can find a relationship balanced in this way, he does not appear so borderline. How do we get there?

Havens has described empathic language as "credulity operationalized," where the goal is to be taken in. The potentially borderline patient has powerful, emotionally invasive capabilities, and the therapist requires skills of another sort: interpersonal language, "skepticism operationalized," where the goal is not to be taken in, not to allow the patient to settle assumptions or projections upon the therapist. If one can parry these, it may be possible to "clear the field" so that something fresh can happen. Havens gives a primer on the types of projective and counterassumptive statements that allow a therapist to prevent projections and assumptions from landing too squarely and derailing the treatment before anything useful can happen. For example, for a patient wary of doctors, he suggests starting with the old German proverb, "A young doctor means a new grave-yard," or the milder version attributed to Ben Franklin, "God heals, and the doctor takes the fee."[20] When one sees the anger and the attack coming, such proverbs can be quite useful to utter. They contain a kernel (sometimes more) of truth, which both the patient and the therapist know, but they are also funny, acknowledging and discharging the anger and the fear about to be placed on the therapist. Such statements can work very well in early sessions to help set the tone of a balanced relationship. A counterassumptive gesture by the therapist such as fumbling about, being unable to find a pen, or forgetting to tie one's shoe might help to offset the assumption that the therapist should be all-powerful or all-knowing. These approaches often work to offset invasive assumptions or projections. Havens is trying to achieve a balance of power in the relationship: "Patient and therapist need to be defended against one another . . . neither . . . should overwhelm the other."

When this balance is struck, the field is clear for the therapist and patient to engage in the push-ups or jogging of therapy, the give-and-take that builds the self. Havens calls this "random speech," a tool for letting the patient take or leave what the therapist has to say. "It occurred to me . . ." is a typical statement. The therapist offers thoughts, nothing too grand or grave, simply an easy flow of ideas, "possibilities [that] can be mentioned, considered, and dismissed with the same freedom in which they were conceived." In cases where the potentially borderline patient never became borderline, I was able (or stumbled) to offset projections and assumptions so that we moved regularly into the world of random speech. The therapy then took on a tone of two passengers riding the bus together and commenting on what we noticed as we rode along. Such relationships were often low-key ones, continuing over many years, but with sessions held less frequently—biweekly, monthly, or less often. The patient came to value the relationship, as evidenced by maintaining it for many years and, if need be, traveling long distances to have a session, but the heated interpersonal drama (transference/countertransference) had a milder, less frightening, less life-or-death quality. Were these patients simply at the healthier end of the narcissistic-borderline continuum that Adler described? I am not sure, but I sometimes think some might have gone the other way had I behaved differently. While I offer this possibility, I also think that other patients may just need to draw that bead on their therapist, the situation that Winnicott described in his

"Use of an Object" paper. In some cases, no matter how I labored to keep the transference cool, it heated up and moved through the perilous attack on the therapy that must be survived. The therapist may hold a trail-map, but the patient has his or her own destination. The fellow travelers will influence the quality of their journey.

The following vignette illustrates some of the issues I have been discussing.

A middle-aged woman arrives at the mental health clinic asking for medication to help with sleep and anxiety. She has been away from the clinic for several years, but has a 15-year history with the clinic which includes several aborted psychotherapies, five hospitalizations for suicidal behavior including three attempts (two life-threatening), and several years of self-inflicted small wounds. Her diagnoses have ranged from paranoid schizophrenia to adjustment disorder, with PTSD, borderline personality disorder, and bipolar disorder sprinkled in between. She is a plain, somewhat worn-out looking woman who is pleasant enough and reasonable in her requests to the psychiatrist who is assigned to her care. She wants to keep it simple: no talk therapy, just some medication for sleep and a persistent, nagging sense of anxiety. While the psychiatrist knows that it is not usually so simple, he goes along with the request, and the two agree to tackle the "chemical imbalance" behind such troubles. He lays out symptom profiles based on her current and past history and discusses what might work, what might be problematic. They begin the task like team members attempting to solve the riddle of the chemical imbalance. The work goes on quietly for a year, 30 minutes together once a month, with modest gains. One day the woman walks in, stating: "I really have to talk with you about something. My mom really pisses me off."

She asks if she can come in more frequently to talk; the medicine only does so much good. The psychiatrist has limited availability of time, but they agree to 30 minutes once a week. She comes punctually each week, looks forward to the sessions, and speaks in an enthusiastic and urgent way. It's as if she has been waiting a long time to sort things out. At first the talk is of a critical mother who will not let her raise her daughter freely. The story shifts to childhood, the mother's depression, and years spent in foster care. At this point the woman begins to recall traumatic events, with unsettling anxiety, deterioration of sleep, and some confusion as to what is real and what is not. The psychiatrist acknowledges that past trauma can often create the types of symptoms she is now experiencing. He also reminds her that he has only 30 minutes per week, that she has been holding herself together rather admirably, and that the work they do will be more useful to her if she can maintain her current capacity to take care of herself and her daughter. He mentions that she may want to remember at her own pace and in her own way those experiences from the past that are necessary to her health in the present and future. Nothing more, nothing less. This framework is at once reassuring and containing for the woman. She starts with anger at her mother for falling into a deep depression, and then moves toward anger at her father for giving her and her sister to foster parents. She brings in vivid material of physical abuse by the foster parents, including a memory of being half-buried in a dark cellar, the fear and helplessness of being trapped there. The woman does not return to therapy for two weeks after vividly recounting this event. When she does, she is angry at the psychiatrist. She accuses him of making her recall things that she does not want to recall, stirring this up. He simply repeats the prior invocation to recall at her own pace and in her own way as much as is necessary to her health in the present and the future. The signs of helpful remembering will be her ability to keep functioning and leading her life herself. She is angry with him for several months, but continues to come and to sort out past and present.

The anger subsides. She moves forward urgently, coming punctually, having put much thought into what she says and conveying that she wants desperately to tell her story: the marriage to a paranoid man who physically abused her, his dangerous attachment, her escape, the fear, her sweet daughter, now ten, her current partner, an alcoholic who is kind when sober but vicious when drunk. What can she do to find a free, safe place? Life is hard, but she has some hope. She misses several sessions, then comes in one day with slightly pressured speech. She asks that the psychiatrist write a letter to a judge absolving her of responsibility for shoplifting because she is mentally ill. She states she has never stolen before, but it was Christmas, and she had no money. She needed presents for her daughter. At the drugstore, she tried to steal a stuffed animal and a radio to give her daughter, but she was inept. She was arrested. During those two weeks when she was absent from therapy, she described higher energy, racing thoughts, and poorer sleep. It sounded like hypomania, and the psychiatrist told her that lithium might help. She agreed. With regard to the letter, he was stern with her, saying that he did not expect that she would use her illness to do illegal things, that though she loved her daughter, this was a dangerous path. The psychiatrist said that this one time, he would write the letter stating he knew of no previous lawless behavior, and that what appeared to be hypomania was now properly medicated. She glared at him and took the note.

The therapy moved forward over the next two years. The woman was always punctual; sometimes she had much to say, other times she was reflective about feelings and perceptions she had held during the week, and was eager to bring these to the session to share. The therapy was not much work for the psychiatrist. He came to admire the woman's strength and resilience. He enjoyed being with her, listening to the fresh experience of her thoughts and feelings, and how she put them in perspective. They had started so modestly, talking of chemical imbalances and subtle adjustments of this and that, and now such a poignant story had unfolded, as if she had been waiting so long, and carefully watching for the moment when she could tell what she needed to tell. She studied over a period of many months and achieved her high school graduate equivalency degree. She got a job. She put down her foot with the alcoholic partner: he could not live with her and her daughter if he was drinking. She offered him help through the clinic, but he refused. He was convicted of his third driving under the influence charge, and just before he was to serve a year in jail, he hanged himself. This shook the woman terribly, because she had loved him. She felt sadness, fear, and guilt. She used the therapy with the same intensity, bringing strong feelings to the sessions, and talking over what it meant. She came to some peace about this tragedy, and she put this event into perspective with the other tragedies of her life. She arrived at a balance in both her perception of and relationship with her mother, and found a way to raise her daughter in her own loving way. When the therapy was ending, she remarked one day that the key moment for her had been the day when the psychiatrist had been so stern about the letter to the judge. She had been angry at him, but she felt that the clarity about his holding her accountable was crucial to her understanding the limits of what he would do for her.

If I were to describe metaphorically what took place in this therapy, I would do it simply. The psychiatrist and the woman took a cab ride together. For the first phase of therapy (the pharmacotherapy), the passenger (the woman) discussed with the cabbie (the psychiatrist) possible routes to her destination. Then she signaled that there was a longer trip, more to discuss. In the second phase (the psychotherapy), the two were fellow passengers on a bus trip cross-country. They shared what they saw along the way, and each offered the other a supportive ear, endured the crankiness of prolonged travel, developed the respect and friendship of fellow travelers. At the end of the trip, they wished each other well. For both it had been a memorable passage.

Practical Suggestions

I draw upon the concepts discussed in this chapter to make some practical suggestions for therapists working with borderline patients.

1. Develop a perspective that works for you and the patient. The therapist must believe in it; it must resonate with what is real for the patient; and yet it must be broad enough for the individual experience. As much as the therapist feels anchored by the perspective, it must be altered by what is unique for the individual patient and offer opportunities for freedom and surprise.
2. Build a treatment frame that is realistic. An effective therapist must anticipate and know something about the answers to the following questions: How much time and over what duration is the therapist really willing to work with the patient? What resources are available to pay for the treatment? What does the therapist really know about what intensity or length of treatment is valuable? How do the therapist and patient acknowledge and respect others whom they may need to help bring about a successful outcome?
3. Understand and balance the amount of time you work in twos and threes, the dyadic and the triadic or social modes. Regular consultation with a sensible colleague is a useful practice (an example of engaging the triadic mode).
4. Some anger and hate must be contained within the therapy in order for the patient to grow. Understand it and use it. The three-stage model may help orient you.
5. Use counterassumptive speech or gestures to offset the projections of therapists as omniscient, all good, or too much of a good friend. Spend much time in random speech mode: "What if . . .? How about . . .?" This is the aerobic exercise and body-building mode of psychotherapy.
6. Discuss and/or teach skills early on, if needed, for coping with anger or dissociation.
7. Practice patience.
8. Maintain steadiness.
9. Learn something new from each person.
10. Do not expect too much too soon.

Notes

1. Kernberg O. 1984. *Severe Personality Disorders: Psychotherapeutic Strategies*. New Haven: Yale University Press, p. 101.

2. Buie DH and Adler G. 1982. "The Definitive Treatment of the Borderline Personality." *International Journal of Psychoanalytic Psychotherapy,* 9: 51–87.
3. Herman JL. 1992. *Trauma and Recovery.* New York: Basic Books.
4. Kohut H. 1971. *The Analysis of the Self.* New York: International Universities Press.
5. Herman, *Trauma and Recovery,* p. 52.
6. Shay J. 1994. *Achilles in Vietnam: Combat Trauma and the Undoing of Character.* New York: Atheneum.
7. MacLean PD. 1985. "Brain Evolution Relating to Family, Play, and the Separation Call." *Archives of General Psychiatry,* 42: 405–417.
8. Sabo AN. 1996. "The Stress Response and the Separation Cry in Medical and Psychiatric Illness." *Berkshire Medical Journal,* 4(4): 5–10.
9. Bowlby J. 1988. "Developmental Psychiatry Comes of Age." *American Journal of Psychiatry,* 145: 1–10.
10. Bowlby J. 1984. "Violence in the Family as a Disruption of the Attachment and Caregiving Systems." *American Journal of Psychoanalysis,* 44: 9–27.
11. Linehan MM, Armstrong HE, Suarez A, et al. 1991. "Cognitive-Behavioral Treatment of Chronically Parasuicidal Borderline Patients." *Archives of General Psychiatry,* 48: 1060–1064.
12. Sabo AN, Gunderson JG, Najavits LM, et al. 1995. "Changes in Self-Destructiveness of Borderline Patients in Psychotherapy: A Prospective Follow-Up." *Journal of Nervous and Mental Disease,* 183: 370–376.
13. Winnicott DW. 1971. "The Use of an Object and Relating Through Identifications," in *Playing and Reality.* New York and London: Basic Books, pp. 86–95.
14. Miller JA (Ed.). 1988. *The Seminar of Jacques Lacan.* New York and London: W. W. Norton.
15. Bion WR. 1984. *Second Thoughts: Selected Papers on Psychoanalysis.* New York: Jason Aronson, pp. 146–148.
16. Miller JB. 1991. "The Construction of Anger in Women and Men." In Jordan JV, Kaplan G, Miller JB, Stiver IP, and Surrey JL, *Women's Growth in Connection.* New York: Guilford, pp. 181–219.
17. Coccaro EF. 1989. "Central Serotonin and Impulsive Aggression." *British Journal of Psychiatry,* 155 (suppl. 8): 52–63.
18. Havens L. 1986. *Making Contact: Uses of Language in Psychotherapy.* Cambridge, Mass.: Harvard University Press.
19. Maughan B and Rutter M. 1997. "Retrospective Reporting of Childhood Adversity: Issues in Assessing Long-Term Recall." *Journal of Personality Disorders,* 11(1): 19–33.
20. Havens, *Making Contact,* pp. 88–116.

8   The Psychotherapy of a Desperate Situation

Caren Plank

I recently came upon this bit of conversation from Robert Coles's biography of Anna Freud. Coles asked Freud how she might approach working with poverty-stricken American families, particularly young women with children experiencing many social and psychological problems. She replied: "There is no point trying to talk about their pathology. The longer we do that, the more hopeless the whole situation will seem to be . . . I don't know what I'd do. I'd want to turn around and leave, I'm sure. But I doubt I could do so. I think I'd try to get away from the feeling of helplessness and immobility by looking around, and then getting up and trying to do something. Do the floors need a sweeping? Is there some cooking to do? . . . I'd try to show that I have an interest in the people, and am ready to work."[1] As the director of an inner-city Early Intervention program for high-risk families with young children, in which case management, advocacy, and home visiting are mandated aspects of the primary therapist's responsibilities, I am often asked how clinicians manage to create a space for psychotherapeutic work in the face of overwhelming needs for assistance. The red thread connecting the multiple levels of the work with such families, I would suggest, is an inner orientation (initially almost entirely on the part of the therapist, but later more nearly shared) away from inevitability and certain knowledge, most particularly the knowledge that the future will be just like the past.

At the most critically needed time, the therapist envisions about the other precisely what the other cannot envision for herself: who this person might become. This requires both a staying put by the therapist and an essential mobility. By staying put I mean an ongoing commitment to engagement in a developmental process. By essential mobility I mean the competence on the part of the therapist to work in the subjunctive, where what might be is not so much determined, as discovered.

The belief in a future (as other than the past and present), which may at first be introduced as an imaginative element in the therapist's mind, enables the therapist to sustain, without being so overwhelmed, his presence in the real. I do not believe that empathy or the taking on of the other's perspective, even if it could be done, will necessarily lead to structural change. Rather, the leverage of the therapist lies in his relative freedom to think somewhat better of the patient than the patient has been able to muster on his own and to face down all the circumstances in which such a fuller self-knowledge is still impossible to feel. The quiet introduction of difference, in the form of hope, may be the key factor in initiating change.

I mention this particularly because some practitioners and theoreticians, concerned over possible enmeshment and boundary questions in such work, miss aspects of what is fundamentally a process of individuation and therefore boundary-establishing for such patients. It may well be that the most difficult efforts of the therapist will be directed toward the recognition of the patient as "someone more than he is at present." The superego, as "the imagined inner future of the ego," says the notable psychoanalyst Hans Loewald, establishes the character of futurity.[2] I agree with Christopher Bollas that there are many patients who, by dint of severe traumatic past experience, have repressed not only the past, but the future.[3]

In such situations, the graver danger is not "boundary violations," but failure of the therapist to help her patient establish the idea of a future, because the many places where the present is still not sufficiently different from the past make any notion of futurity intolerable. In the absence of a viewpoint of potential growth, the present does become painfully, even disastrously, unbounded. Without the superego, we might say, there is no work. Without the future, the present is unlivable.

How does psychotherapy contain, mitigate, and transform the patient's anxiety, helplessness, and dread that things may not get better?

The therapeutic relationship itself, with the developmental possibilities it affords, is obviously one such container. But for the container to hold, the context in which such work is authorized becomes tremendously important. There is great debate in the therapeutic community and in the public mind over the efficaciousness of current models of care. I believe that programs of early intervention, such as the one in which I worked therapeutically, afford us an opportunity to examine the way in which decisions about caregiving and risk-taking can be made in these difficult times.

I first met Carol and her 8-month-old daughter, Jeanie, when the family was referred by the family doctor to the early intervention program located in an inner-city neighborhood in which they lived. The Massachusetts Early Intervention (EI) system, privately vendored across the state by programs certified and funded by the Department of Public Health, is a comprehensive, community-based approach to the care and treatment of families with children under the age of three years who are at high risk for adverse developmental and psychological outcomes. Mandated by State Law M.G.L. 111G in 1982, the DPH Operational Standards for EI represents the consensus the Commonwealth reached over what negative events or contingencies families should or should not be able to protect themselves against on their own. The "things which can happen" needed to be serious enough in terms of actual or potential outcomes, as measured by normed instruments and sound judgment by certified EI clinicians, to warrant intervention. The implicit assumption was that if such things happened, families deserved whatever protections the system of EI could afford. Within this framework of eligibility, it was at least potentially possible to shape adequate responses to a broad range of environmental and biological risks. More severe contingencies could be responded to with a more comprehensive array of integrated services, which might include infant-parent psychotherapy, individual and group therapy, discrete (for example, speech and physical) therapies for the child, advocacy, case management, and non-didactic developmental guidance. This flexibility in provision afforded the system a high degree of responsiveness to differing needs and changing life circumstances. Moreover, therapeutic services were to be provided in the natural environments in which the family lived their daily lives, mediated through an interpersonal context of care and attachment. In early intervention, with its central focus on the emergence of self, relationships become the means through which new developmental possibilities are explored and realized. Do you think I can take this step? Can I take it with you here today?

The sharing of risks and responsibilities over potentially negative outcomes is both necessary and terrifying. Public policy is formed within this context of paradox: neither connection nor disconnection appears to be a permanent or adequate response to the problem of exposure. Even when institutional practices have authorized involvement, there is a tendency to minimize need because of our uncertainty over how much we can, wish to, or should provide. I make the assumption that failure of recognition is re-traumatizing to the patient. It is all too easy to "confirm the patient's terrifying fear that they need too much and have to be disciplined. One of the reasons therapy takes so long is that it is hard for the therapist, let alone the patient, to arrive at the place where they both understand, by feeling it, that the need for what is happening is legitimate, appropriate, necessary, and that it is enraging that it has not been seen until now."[4] The time, the effort, the cost, and the fear associated with recognizing how much care is needed touches our disinclination to realize how much has been, and may yet be, lost. The family is obviously the first, most encompassing, generative, and conflict-ridden context for the sharing of loss. Therapies are somewhere down the road, but, if they are good enough, they always almost capture the complexity and richness and terrors of undertaking a new beginning. Every pair, be they parent and child or therapist and patient, depends on the collective understanding of what is at stake in the process of growth.

These situations demand that the therapist muster hope and courage to counterbalance the pressure of despair and fear. When the therapist brings such a strong commitment, there is always danger that he will become lost in the pair (the dyad of the therapy) or will put forward his own projections of fear, helplessness, or possibility onto the patient and the clinical situation. If not recognized and addressed, the patient may never individuate. Or the situation may deteriorate because the therapist becomes exhausted and resentful. It helps enormously for the therapist to also work in a context larger than the dyad. The EI program provides such a context, one that has authorized involvement after public conversation and debate over contingencies and has built in the supports of supervision, consultation, field training, and team process to affirm the primacy of a therapeutic relationship in the service of growth that might not otherwise occur. The dyad of intense therapy is subject to the third perspective of these other supports. This third perspective offers balance and lessens the possibility that the therapy will have an adverse outcome.

Our current health care environment is dominated by concerns about cost, and we have moved dramatically toward "translating moral questions of responsibility into instrumental questions of cost."[5] Perhaps "instrumental questions" have become the most affordable language in which to frame the vulnerabilities of the human condition: scarcity, risk, need, and limitation. But it is because of our concerns, not simply our costs, that we risk connection. In the intermingling and transfer of these vulnerabilities, we make ourselves susceptible to losses that are not, properly speaking, only our own. Yet it is also connection which makes losses more supportable than they might have been otherwise. If the communal is established through the sharing of loss, we are protected, to the extent that we can be, by the risks we take in finding each other.

Case Study

You will probably never be able to eat off the floor in Carol's house. A sticky tapestry of dust, crumbs, and fallen debris runs waywardly throughout her apartment. I follow one trail into Sam's room, where Carol shyly unwraps the Ninja Turtles curtains and bedcovers she has purchased in anticipation of her son's return. But the room looks dismal, much as another did that afternoon years back, when she asked, half-heartedly, if we might paint it blue. I can still remember how much I wanted to leave: the grime, the crumbling plaster, the aura of futility making me next to useless. Only an illusionist could have convinced herself she was making much progress. Somehow we went on anyway.

"Yes, yes," I manage to say, "Sammy will like them," picturing, from a fold of memory, the large speckled turtles that Carol's husband Gene, when alive, had brought home from his trips fishing on the local pond. Carol would lie in bed, sleepless in the summer nights, she said, the muffled sounds of arguments and occasional gunshot penetrating the closed window glass as she waited. But in the morning a fresh netting of life filled the tanks. On my visits I would gravitate toward their swimming bodies, intending, perhaps, to catch and align myself with the suggestion of movement. Every so often one or another would rise to the surface and break through one medium into another. Was Carol now doing so too?

For a long time she did not. In those first years, even the receptionist spoke to her in the whispers reserved for the gravely ill. Once, coming to work, I had picked up a small bird lying on the cement outside my office, its bones so fine as to be almost an abstraction in my hand. Yet the body felt heavy, as if a tiny lead plumb were pulling it down and down. I remember moving my hand up and around trying to find the source and center of weight in so porous a frame. It took time to fathom. Lifeless, without the ability to hold itself up, the bird was merely a register for the force of gravity. I think Carol somehow felt like this to me when I first met her.

Perhaps for such reasons, I welcomed her odor. For a brief while, I even thought of the smell as peculiarly her own, a way to signal, when she could not otherwise, that she was there. I knew she was generous; she might be offering me a tool of navigation. Without this help, I could well have missed the deep vein of conviction that permeated her life. True, the conviction seemed one of fear. But with so much else about her stifled, here was an atmosphere we could work together if not quite with, at least in.

Like any air, it took some getting used to, some time to adjust to conditions. I did not want to ignore whatever intention she might have had to keep her distance; certainly the potential was there for repulsion and a lonely safety. But there was also something distinctive and tangible to share. Her baby daughter and the clothes on their bodies were stagnant and soiled. After our meetings, so was I. In her apartment I could see there was often no hot water or way to wash. Dishes piled up in the sink and clothes on the floor. Even in the cold of the refrigerator, it seemed, food went bad. I could, I suppose, have persisted in perceiving these conditions as emanating solely from her. But the compelling nature of olfactory transmission and transferential process quickly obliged me to acknowledge them as ours as well—the way, for now, we could stay connected in a place or to a context once gone rotten.

I already knew the nineteen-year-old girl before me was anything but rotten. But surrounded by malignancy, the camouflage of odor may well have kept this truth hidden. I had the strong suspicion that this was a matter of survival; that she could not dare to convey herself otherwise. But living required that she might have to try. It helped considerably that even when her personality and desires were apparently most suppressed, she still could not keep from me completely either her kindness or her acuity. Gradually, we worked our way into the crawl space such intelligence allowed.

I couldn't force much. You don't want too much pushing and shoving in so confined a space. It was enough that week after week she would come, usually with the baby in her arms, and settle onto the carpet. Only very rarely would she look at me. Occasionally, she would speak, but more often not. Sometimes, it was an effort just to leave her alone. I thought of how the mothers of sleeping infants sometimes wake them to make sure they are breathing. Was I feeling like this? If so, perhaps the emergence of tender concern was reassurance enough that we were viable.[6]

Carol was not so sure. One thing she did want to know right away was whether it was destined that she would hurt her child the way she had herself been hurt. She had been told she would. "No," I said, "often something very different occurs under such circumstances." I doubted that she believed me. The little girl was profoundly deaf secondary to a viral infection transmitted from mother to child during the pregnancy. The left side of the girl's body had also been affected, resulting in a mild hemi-paresis. I wanted the confidence to grow in Carol that what might pass between us could be decidedly less lethal. I was almost wrong.

There was no mistaking the appropriateness of Carol and her daughter for joint psychotherapy. Not only did the child have significant biological problems, for which the mother felt deeply responsible, but the family was living in extremely impoverished conditions, lacking the rudiments of adequate shelter, economic resources, and viable family and social supports. There were indications of drug use and violence in the home by the child's father, and an immobilizing depression in Carol. Isolated by the overwhelming realities of her day-to-day existence and a history of pervasive abuse, she could barely tolerate being in the presence of another person. But dissociated from many aspects of her interior and external environment, she had little way of feeling what it was she might need or want. This psychological state, as much as anything happening to her, created a particularly high-risk situation for herself and her daughter.

Together with referral for pharmacological assessment, there were many ancillary therapeutic and support services which the program could and did offer. But how was she going to discover that she might wish for something different? For Carol, to whom the world looked unrelievedly dangerous, who had to survive on her own in the most terrifying of circumstances, there was missing that experiential base of trust in what Winnicott calls "use" of the other for growth. But with such a desiccated internal working model of relatedness, how was she going to engage in a therapeutic relationship and, of immediate concern, how was she going to mother her child?

And here we find an instance of just how our patients so often give us revealing clues as to how to proceed. Here certainly was a mother filled with the dread of contamination from parent to child and without a sense of a realizable future for herself. But she did, if only barely, have hopes for her daughter. In fact, the very state of foreboding contained, in nearly undiscernible form, whatever hopefulness she could afford. The work began in this place where she had the most at stake in staying alive.

When I could let it, the contours of destruction did take shape for me. A father who had briefly held her began to beat her. He hit her with a stick between the knees and the ankles for nameless infractions. (Later, I learned of a male child born after Carol who died unexpectedly at a very young age.) At six she was raped by the father's brother and again at nine. The second period of assault lasted a year. The uncle would follow Carol into her bedroom. Apparently, much of the time the mother was at home, but profoundly absent. When Carol found the words to tell her mother what was happening, the mother protested. Why had she not been told earlier? Remarkably, Carol did not quite lose her mind then. But in school she was so stunted and silent that teachers put her in a class for the mentally retarded. Opening her mouth, she told me, made her sick.

At home she kept vigilant watch over her seven younger siblings. She called them children and was certain they needed her protection. She had been right. A month after Carol moved out at age seventeen, a sister was brutally raped by the father. Then the girl tried to take her life. In court, the mother spoke up for the father. Carol provided the only testimony there was against him, the sister being far too frightened and incapacitated for speech. When the judge committed the father to a hospital for the criminally insane, Carol felt the act as her own.

"As soon as he comes out," she would say repeatedly, "he's going to come after me." I was ready to believe this. The family was one of the most threatening I had encountered in over twenty years of experience. For several weeks, the mother and a brother-in-law had been calling to warn me off. I'd better watch it, the brother-in-law said. One night, when I left work, someone might just come after me. Who was I, anyway, to help Carol and her children? Therapists had no place in their lives. They were the only ones who could tell her how to raise her kids. If she couldn't get it right, the family would take them. They would see to it that I could lose my job or worse if I spoke with her again. I took the threats seriously. The feelings they engendered were tremendously informative and suggestive, particularly of what Carol may have had to give up as a child to survive in her family. The transference of the likelihood of harm onto what she and her child might expect seemed highly possible. I thought that here might be a place to take a stand against these expectancies. With due consideration, I decided to stay put.[7]

Issues of safety and betrayal are likely to feel urgent. Inner-city programs for high-risk families deal with these problems often enough to have established protocols of signing out and calling in, beepers, cell phones, special codes to obtain help in an emergency. Relationships with community police, street workers, emergency response teams, and other experts on defusing potentially violent situations can provide support, on the spot, if needed. Criteria and procedures for when to call for help, including from one's immediate supervisor, are all most useful when they are settled in advance. All of that helps the worker attend to the work at hand.

For therapists who are working under the auspices of an agency, as I was at the time of this encounter, support is provided both by the availability of ongoing clinical supervision and consultation and by the presentation of case material for review and discussion by peers to help sort out these dilemmas. At Boston Children's Hospital, where I later developed and directed a new EI program, situations in which the worker might be in some physical danger are brought to the attention of the General Counsel for thorough discussion and review. Complex treatment decisions involving child safety are also brought before several Child Protection teams.

Throughout this work, I also sought clinical supervision from highly experienced psychotherapists in the greater therapeutic community, especially those who seemed to have a talent for not being overwhelmed by particularly difficult conditions. I found their support heartening. Establishing a network of such connections would obviously be extremely helpful to the sole practitioner. At the Boston Institute for Psychotherapy where I have taught, practicing therapists can participate in clinical fellowship programs specifically directed toward providing community-based therapeutic services for families. University and institute training programs in parent-child psychotherapy, early intervention, and infant mental health are now flourishing as even experienced clinicians seek guidance on how to expand their practice.

However conscientiously the work proceeds, the therapist's involvement does not preclude absence. During one particular August I was away. Carol and Gene's families were spending a few weeks at a local bungalow colony. The prior August had seen trouble enough: heavy drinking, belligerence, and casual sex building to near combustion in the heat and close quarters. Before I left this year, Carol told me she did not want to go back. We talked about alternatives, but I imagine none of them felt very real to her. When the time came, she went along. Not surprisingly, one night turned particularly wild. In the morning, a woman staying in the camp accused Gene of sexually abusing her young son. A commotion spread across the colony; people took sides. Carol did not know exactly what she believed, but she could not quite keep herself from knowing what she feared. She turned to Gene's mother, who somehow had not heard, and told her of the accusation. In disgust, the mother walked away. Carol's responsibility, she admonished, was to stand by her husband. "I really tried," Carol would tell me months later, still not certain she had tried hard enough.

The first call when I came home was from Gene. Carol, he said, was acting very strangely. A day or two before she might have taken some pills. "Bring her in immediately," I said. By the time I saw her, she was almost frozen. Could this be self-preservation in extremis? At the hospital she robotically went through the physical exam, the questions, the room assignment. She did, however, make one concise statement: Her family wanted her dead. Who could survive what was true in this and remain sane? I imagined she had to be psychotic to absolutely loathe herself. She was in mortal danger. But would each horror, the psychotic and the real, hold the other in check?

At such times, the requirements for the protection of the self become more complex. Staying alive might depend both on the structure afforded by hospitalization and on the continuity of a facilitating relationship in which Carol "could go on being." If trauma consists of the absence or interruption of a facilitating containing relationship, was there any way, under the circumstances, in which a non-intrusive developmental process might be kept alive? I thought it made sense to try. On the wall of her ward, a sign read: "Needs will be met on the half hour and the hour." What would it mean if we were a little off?

In those first disoriented, frightening days after being admitted, she would run urgently toward me whenever I stepped onto the floor. As she flew down the corridor, my first thought was of an infant needing to nurse. However psychotic, she remained connected. However archaic, her need for sustenance revealed a competence.[8] She wanted to live.

It is my belief that despite her apparently inchoate, archaic, and fragmented state of mind and communication, Carol was striving for an "integrative experience." We should be as prepared to read ambiguous, archaic, and potentially disturbing signs for the sometimes deeply buried competent hopes, wishes, and needs they might contain as we are prepared to see evidence of disorder and disintegration. Such disintegration is often a defensive holding action until the person can bear the pain of knowing that someone important to their protection and development had neglected or misread whatever clues to their striving after recognition, health, and self-knowledge they were capable of making at the time.[9]

Carol did not make such strivings easy to detect. I don't imagine anyone would have been heartened by routine measures of mental status. She was considered dangerous to herself and unresponsive to staff. But one evening I brought her young daughter with me on my early evening visit. In Jeanie's right hand was a tea set to play with, and on her left foot a shoe with an untied shoelace. I left the shoelace as it was. I cannot say precisely from what distance Carol noticed the untied lace. But in a movement graced by memory and intention, she bent and tied and double-knotted the lace. I am, her eyes suddenly clear and focused announced when they sought mine, still her mother. So you are, I nodded, less afraid than I had been for weeks.

Such moments of familiar recognition were brief. Keeping this in mind undoubtedly helped me through the weeks to come. I did trust what I knew from them. But what else, outside the sphere of our mutual understanding, was Carol experiencing? Was there a way to create a still, quiet, safe space in which she might find out? I thought it important to manage the trust for this as well. I took to moving my chair over near hers and settling in, as Carol sat in what, from a more distant perspective, could be taken as mute isolation. I wasn't so sure. A certain calm, one with which I felt reasonably comfortable, enveloped these hours. I didn't ask her questions or push myself to speak. I noticed that her breathing, which often was rushed and labored when I arrived, would slow and become more regular. Perhaps mine did so too. For an hour or so in the late afternoon, we would sit like this in each other's company. As much as possible, given the circumstances and the surroundings, I hoped both of us might become relatively free from the coercive elements of therapeutic investigation. What would be there if she wanted to give an accounting to no one but herself?[10]

I mentioned earlier that staying alive for Carol depended both on the structure afforded by hospitalization and on the continuity of a facilitating relationship in which Carol "could go on being." In my efforts to help Carol in the hospital, I tried to work enough with the staff to let them into my relationship with Carol. If I were successful in this regard, perhaps her net of support would be strengthened. If I failed, I would risk revealing too much of her to others, who did not have the time, or for some, the commitment to share in her developmental crisis.

There was little disagreement that Carol was suffering from major depression with psychotic features and that she was at high risk for suicide. Reaching her, I suggested, would involve appreciating that she was struggling with a lifetime of abuse and horror, fearing that she would never be free of the past, and trying to find some desperate way to make passage to a life where she could be herself and yet be free of that past. The crisis of loyalty with her family, combined with my absence, had left her with only her mind, the psychosis, as the place to stay alive. Any way you looked at the situation, this was a life-and-death matter for Carol.

In these situations, it is worth a try for the therapist to explain his perspective to someone on the unit, be it a committed nurse or the attending psychiatrist. One identifies a staff member who is receptive to such a view, and asks their observations, validates them, and shares an intuition of one's own. One works with that key staff member to build an alliance to the therapy that goes beyond the time when the therapist is present at the hospital. At best, this deepens the staff's understanding of the patient, conveys a bit of hope, and allows the hospital, not just the therapy relationship, to become a place where the patient can "go on being," if only for a few days or weeks. At worst, the staff rejects the therapist's hypothesis, and the therapist experiences, for a moment, the isolation or shame that our patients often feel.

By a slight lingering emphasis in her description of their encounters, Carol herself suggested to me the staff person on the unit whom she had begun to trust and with whom I also found it helpful to confer. His ease and naturalness with Carol appeared to decrease her anxiety, promoted a sense of normalcy, and, I believe, contributed to her growing readiness to explain the meaning of her psychosis to me. Her fondness for him perhaps even made accessible certain old, but rediscoverable, affects. For the first time she spoke of love for a father. Burying this need for love and attachment had paralyzed her spirit and sequestered her desire. Her father's long-term commitment to a state hospital signaled the removal of her right to hope, or so it seemed. Now it appeared she came to find him; possibly from guilt, but much more profoundly to recollect her capacity for love. The reconnection to her father was necessary to life, but, given his destructiveness, simultaneously life-threatening. She might choose to stay just where he was.

This was a hard time for everyone. On the ward, conferences were held and plans made. One recommendation was to move Carol to another, more distant extended care hospital; another recommended ECT. There was a very real danger that she could be lost. Still, Carol found it impossible to give the doctors the reassurances they sought. I thought she might be sorting out her father's destiny from her own, deciding whether she was entitled to exist. Why speak before knowing it was for herself she was speaking? Having a pretty fair sense of the devastation wreaked on her sense of agency, I wondered if there was a way to wait her out. But you don't get a lot of time on an inpatient psychiatric unit these days to do the slow work of self-definition, even if, as here, definition was a matter of survival. Could she be given the consideration to feel it as a birth?

Probably not. Because of the most commonplace of contemporary problems, insurance coverage, the distant hospital turned her down. ECT was ordered. In a panic, Carol refused. A guardian ad litem was hurriedly called in. But this was someone she would need to talk with if she wanted to have a say in what would happen next.

I thought she might. She was often courageous. There was her recent acknowledgment of tender feelings for me. She hadn't realized, she said, in some amazement when she did. What did I feel about this, she wanted to know. I suggested she had reclaimed some of her right to care, and that was a very good thing. Still, there were reasons to worry. Carol would also need to show recognizable signs of life to someone with authority for discharge. Our times together became increasingly difficult. She pleaded with me to get her out of the hospital. I could do this easily, she insisted. I thought she had learned this strat-

egy of staying alive by surrendering agency a long time ago. But playing dead in a hospital is a dangerous business; it can be taken for real.
You can, with the best of intentions, be overrun.

Finally, an appointment between Carol and the guardian ad litem
was arranged. Even now, years later, I remember going home that afternoon not knowing whether she would be able to feel what she had
to do. "Why do I have to speak to him? You can get me out of here if
you want to," she repeated one last time. I already knew this was not
true. The discovery that one's therapist is not omnipotent is often a
defining moment. What would the discovery mean for her? With
mounting concern, I felt that something critical for her future and our
relationship was at stake. Our conversation turned sober. "I've done
what I think I can, for now," I said quietly. This had been a genuine
and not altogether easy discovery for me, as well. Probably, it has to
be that way to be felt as real. Affective competence is something you
can go a long way to support, but ultimately cannot live for someone
else.[11] But timing and specificity matter tremendously. Just try handing over too much responsibility for a life to someone who hasn't had
the chance to dream and taste of what that life could be, and they will
sensibly hand it right back to you. It's a way of saying, wait; I still
need you to hope and invest in a future I cannot quite see and feel as
real for myself yet. I thought this could well be the case with Carol. I
also knew she would not be given the time she needed for belief to in-
cubate. If she was coming out, she was coming out prematurely. We
would have to deal with those consequences later. As it happened, I
never learned all the specifics of the conversation Carol held with the
guardian ad litem. But late that evening he called with the gist. The
hospital was ordered to move toward discharge. In five days we
would greet the rush of life.

Part 2

The transition toward health would, in fact, take considerably more
time. Two years after Carol's discharge from the hospital, I sit in my
office waiting for Carol to park her car as anyone might park their
car. I can't help myself. I am delighted. Would I like to see it? she
calls breezily, from the hallway. I grab my jacket and run outside. I
wouldn't miss this ordinary moment for the world.

There it is. The car is red as a ripe tomato. "I couldn't find one pur-
ple," she laughs. It is an old joke, this business of bright and strong
color, but something else too. A blossom heaved up from a harsh soil.

I run my hand along the hood and take a closer look at Carol. I have not seen her for all of August. Her black hair is growing out and is almost shining; she is slimmer. From her eyes, I catch a light. She has known some joy, I think in amazement, then slow myself down. The hard-won therapeutic gains of the last two years pass through my mind like an old and heavy freight train. I let the train of thoughts carry me back to the day Carol left the hospital.

At the nurse's station, there are heartfelt good-byes, wishes for recovery, and some concern as to whether Carol will be back. Who could not have doubts? If anything, she looks a little worse than when she first arrived four months before. I quickly pack her puffy frame, her few belongings, into an elevator. Will someone stop us? Should they? Carol is silent as a mouse, and I am worrying, worrying again, will she be safe? There is nothing triumphant about this exit, only a strained relief that she has escaped some danger, perhaps for another. Where is Gene, I think in frustration, as we walk into an empty house. He did not come to the hospital to pick her up as promised, nor did her mother. By late in the afternoon, the hospital administrator calls me to ask if I might pick her up. "We simply can't keep her another day," he reports, succinctly. I think briefly of the careful discharge planning meeting, everyone on their good behavior, the too easy smiles. As if none of this has anything to do with her, Carol falls asleep almost immediately on the couch.

Trying to settle myself, I think of the day my mother and I practically carried my father home after his quadruple bypass surgery. Almost everything that could have gone wrong during those weeks in the hospital did so. I had been afraid he would die while still on the respirator; his neck was so swollen you could not see where it ended and his head began. Then came the arrhythmias, nausea and bleeding, another surgery. He looked so ill so much of the time that I found it hard to picture him ever well again. That had not exactly been a triumphant exit either; we were all much too weary for celebration. But within a few months, he was back walking through the hemlock forest.

Given everything, Carol would take a little longer. But it helped to know just how terrible illness can look and recovery still be possible. Could I see any signs of health? I thought I might. At the day treatment center, Carol showed a new capacity for assertiveness. She came late, made her own schedule, turned down activities. She told me she did not fit in. In one sense, I had to hope she was right. Almost all the other patients had spent long years in the mental health system and lived, when they were not in the hospital, in staffed residences. "I have a home of my own and two children to get on buses," she told them, when suspension was mentioned. My own sense was that something terribly important and original might be going on. Could she be attempting the gestures of liberation from authority (particularly the authority of naming and defining) in what could be, if treated as a transitional moment and not a threat, a relatively safe way? This is the kind of thing you have to do with teenagers. If you become too threatened by their emerging powers, you either force them underground or to outrageous acts. Still, I did not want her to have to leave: there was very little new that could be found at home, alone.

Could she be left to discover what she needed to find and then move on? The staff of the day treatment center and I consulted over whether there was a way they might keep her on. Luckily, the young and committed staff became interested in this young woman who seemed to have a plan for treatment they did not have to write. The rules would be relaxed and she could have a chance. And quite naturally, something did happen. She made a friend.

There never had been friends. Carol had gone her whole life without going out to the movies or into the city shopping. She had never been to a party or spent the long night in close camaraderie. Her house had always been too dangerous to invite anyone in. She was missing the critical experience of friendship the way the body lacks a crucial nutriment. Now she found it. There were daily confidences and weekend sleep-overs. One magnificent endless night, Carol and her friend Laura stopped at every ice cream parlor they passed for blocks. I could see them: trying out chocolate and strawberry and pistachio, rainbow-colored sprinkles, hot fudge and butterscotch sauce, hour after hour. "I've never done anything like this," Carol whispered to me conspiratorially in the morning when she called. This will change her, I mused, pleased, if a bit belatedly. For the person I thought I had once known was already slipping from sight and now reappearing, less and less as someone she had been before and more as someone she could become.

Perhaps this is an overstatement. Hope certainly plays a part in the "something more" that therapists, like parents, envision for their children. But gradually the provision and assimilation of new conditions and experience can make for a fresh impression, much in the way that you see, without realizing exactly when, green overtake brown in a spring garden. Psychologists enjoy being accurate about this process of just-noticeable differences.[12] But it may be that one genuine marker of change is the way it throws you, at least temporarily, off balance. In psychotherapy, the parlaying of time and effort into repetitious enactment kicks up the unexpected. What appears to be only apparent motion becomes real, and someone, hopefully the patient, gets a real leg up.

Fortunately, Carol and I fell out of step in just this way. For the first time in our long association Carol missed her appointments. When she did come, she was often late and a little impatient, as if I had already missed her point. But, occasionally at night, my phone would ring and without any preliminaries of "hello" or "this is Carol" or "is this a good time for you?" she would launch into a detailed recital of her day, those small matters of apparently slight significance to which, in ordinary life, one listens patiently only because they happen to someone for whom we care. I thought she might be saying, "I have you," in a way which finally could feel more durably ordinary, than extraordinary. In Carol's circumstances, the ordinary was a monumental achievement. Even more important, I thought the non-compliance over appointments and the calls might be evidence of her evolving self-worth, evidence that she was willing to both risk and share. If the calls were clues to her hopes for a less stultifying and false compliance, I thought it important to ask myself if we were at one of those nodal points in the work, those moments when the therapeutic relationship might achieve enough leverage to become the means through which a new developmental possibility could be tried and realized. Can I take this step? Can I take it with you today?

This isn't always the case. There are other situations in which I have used planned phone calls as a transitional holding action, a temporary means to provide a reliable experience of safety at a particularly difficult time. But in this instance, planned calls would have taken away from Carol the opportunity to risk asking for something she had never been able to ask for before. Hadn't I learned to trust her intuitive capacity to lead us into just the work that needed to be done? I knew, given the circumstances, that a case could be made for her resistance, entitlement, or unacknowledged hostility. You hate to miss these things. But I also knew a case could be made for my own. After all, it's a lot more convenient for the therapist to entertain spontaneous gestures at ten in the morning than ten at night. It is my experience that once a person experiences the capacity for generative expression as truly her own, she will not need to continue to inform someone else about it around the clock. The first flush of excitement, however, we might do well to share.

For the child to feel what the parent cannot is a tremendous risk. Affective originality, especially from a child, can be terrifying. Such movements are often put down, their potential for discovery stalled.[13] But for the child to feel this clearly, as loss, may be a developmental achievement that neither the relationship nor the child can afford. What may be sensed is that a great deal about oneself is at stake, repeatedly. Probably, there is no way to avoid this entirely. Development is inevitably a process which entails deep anxiety and profound hope. For a more or less protracted period, parents contain these creative and destructive possibilities with and for their children and themselves. Like their children, most parents cannot avoid the anxiety and hope that the "something more" that they, as parents offer and the child largely grows in identification with, can itself undergo transformation. In this sense, the negotiations between parent and child must be real and flexible enough to admit of a new agent as well as a familiar one.

This isn't easy. Parents cannot help expressing through the "idiom of caretaking,"[14] as Christopher Bollas calls it, their own particular rules for being and relating. Every child receives the particular idiom of caring, the "rules" for being and relating, as simply the way things felt and were. To imagine otherwise entails loss, a loss of the relationship insofar as the relationship depended on the inevitability of life being felt the way it was. Repetition undoubtedly obscures the pain of knowing that what seemed inevitable was simply one's history. It may be next to impossible to give up completely the lifelong wait for the parent who could recognize the deeply real person one didn't, but might yet, become. It is gut-wrenching for the patient to leave the parent behind, while making the passage to a richer life.

Part 3

The self is changed through a meeting with another. For the traumatized person, it is difficult to trust that the interaction with the other will bode well. Trauma inflects perception in such a way as to coerce the impression that you know, before you know, what is going to happen next. The result is sameness, or what amounts to it psychologically: the loss of agency and desire. It had taken years for Carol to emerge from the paralysis of certain knowledge to chance the uncertain discovery of what life and relationships could offer. Therapy can extend, but cannot "fix," these offers. On Carol's way to inhabiting a self she was beginning to recognize as her own, Gene died, catapulting her back to a place uncannily familiar, fated and perverse.

Even the death was not quite unexpected. There had been an earlier heart attack, the result of cocaine use. Afterwards, there was a steady gain in weight, continued drug use, an increasingly ominous silence alternating with desperate violent outbursts and attempts to control. There had always been battering, a continuous barrage of orders and prohibitions prescribing what could be thought and said. Now the sound of Gene's voice kept everyone on edge. Sam, at age two, would cover his ears as soon as his father walked into the house. Jeanie, the vibrations apparently penetrating the shield of even profound deafness, would run to her mother. For years Gene refused all offers of help. Even so, I thought of the turtles swimming in the tank. When had he turned away?

There was a flurry of activity, of promises, right before his death. He broke down and sobbed. If Carol would give him another chance, he would stop his drug use, he would change. But somewhere in the middle of the night, he must have lost hope. In a few hours, he was dead from a massive coronary, from another overdose of cocaine, from what may have been an inescapably lonely premonition of failure.

Carol fell dormant. Within days, she moved back into her mother's house. Then, in less than three months, that arrangement fell apart. Carol moved out, only to find an apartment in the mother's town. I thought she might well not be ready to come back to what we had been doing together. For several months, I traveled across the city to meet her. One day she announced she was returning to the neighborhood where I had my office. I was relieved and wary. Both of us knew there was going to be more between us. What were we in for?

Within a few weeks, the new apartment deteriorated. Mornings, Carol could not rise to put the children on the bus for school. (Many months later, she confirmed my sense that keeping them home was a way of making sure they were all alive and still together.) Often she missed our appointments, and frequently did not make the move to let me know in advance. These absences had little of the happy rebellion of earlier times. When I would finally call her at noon or later, there were only the half-muffled sounds of a mind asleep, trying to remain so. I had to be worried. Connection, the activity of life, was now a disturbance. But I also reminded myself of how living things, during the cold of deep winter, stay alive by conserving energy. They do not grow, but they are not dead. You can get this wrong. More than once, until I learned otherwise, I've pulled up some apparently dead stem only to discover, underground, a viable knot of roots and bulb. Is there, as a novelist I admire suggested, some unexpected "aeration down below" which we can't see, but which keeps life going?[15] "Start with the idea that things want to grow, that they have to be actively dissuaded from growing."[16] No one I had ever met had been as pervasively dissuaded as Carol. The real astonishment was that she was alive at all.

There was a bare, stripped-down quality to what she could manage. Maybe she could breathe only for herself? The children were placed, first with strangers, then with relatives. Both carried threats of terrifying disconnection and loss. But her capacity to stay with her children emotionally did not collapse. When almost everything else fell by the wayside, they still could be who they were with her. Away from them, however, and their need of her, she sleepwalked through the days. I knew she was trying to decide, again, whether she had the right to go on. Finally, there was no way to avoid knowing that if she chose to live, it was what she intended for herself. For years, she had vigilantly, shamefully hidden her aliveness by shunning the most common markers of viability. She had used appearances (I'm tempted to say "brilliantly" if it were not at such cost) to distract others from and preserve her life. This gave her a margin of room in which to exist. Now there were ways in which her life was potentially more her own, freer, with Gene gone. She could decide to turn down what this offered.

She did, almost. For a frightening period I could feel (whether from her or from me at this point really didn't matter) a powerful, dangerous appeal to turn away and an equally powerful appeal to take over. I tried to do neither, but to feel each as a version of what had already happened and might now, between us, happen again. Here we were, in what could become some common final pathway of loss of striving. Except that she wanted, if only just, for me to share in what this would do to her (and to me). It was this shared potential for feeling something together that previously had been hers alone (and perhaps mine alone) that seemed most real and important to stay with. You cannot "know" this. You will not be "told." Nonetheless, the imaginative allowance that conceives therapist-patient enactment as a living form of telling, as symbolic action and not mere action, is at the heart of the therapeutic alliance.[17] If the therapist cannot feel and trust in the potential "something else" of re-presentation, it is unlikely that the therapeutic process can convincingly unfold. The therapist is simply too lost and scared to join in the action. He will or should be scared anyway. It is not as if the symbolic were the opposite of the real. Symbolic action draws upon and brings into connection more and more of what experience feels like, not less. Ernst Cassirer, in *An Essay on Man,* tells us that "man cannot escape from his own achievement. He cannot but adopt the conditions of his own life . . . He cannot live his life without expressing his life."[18] The expression can, in fact, go badly. It is from within these real conditions of risk that any extra piece of mental freedom is won.

However they say so, what therapist and patient stake is their hope. This is a fine and tangled weave. Could Carol hear the heartening echo of her own hope amplified in me? Could she trust that my intimation that she had already decided to live came from her? What did it mean for me that so much of what seemed valuable between us was precisely because it entailed trust rather than certainty? I had a dim intuition of what the philosopher Martha Nussbaum calls the "fragility of goodness." "Human excellence," she says, is "a growing thing in the world that could not be made invulnerable and keep its own peculiar fineness."[19] Therapeutic gain awaits such general discoveries.

We began to make them. We each held on. And doing so became its own signal, a gesture of will we could reciprocate. This led to a subtle, but significant change. Now our agreements, including the agreement to continue, became more transparently marked by choice. Something of the moody, amorphous quality of our being together disappeared. Carol herself seemed to acquire solidity and shape. Over the years, I had gotten used to not particularly looking for her in her body. But now Carol walked in with enough lilt in her steps for me to look at where she, in fact, was. I thought this meant she might have plans worth carrying out.

The children came home that year a few days before Christmas. There was a loving, tumultuous rendering of this in my office some weeks later. But it was a little hard to keep clear. Mixed in was a conversation about taking a trip in a car the following summer. "A car!" I exclaimed in surprise, searching out Carol's eyes for confirmation above the tangle of arms and words. "Oh yes," she replied, with all the aplomb of a seasoned traveler. "Didn't I tell you? I'm studying for the road test."

Postscript (Two Years Later)

"Don't drop it now," I hear myself saying. But really, at this point, neither of us needs the reminder. Together we ease the desk out from under our fingertips onto the landing just outside Carol's apartment. Sam swings the door wide open, and with one last heft we are inside. I can feel Carol's gaze following mine around the room as I stand frozen, blocked and dazed by an apparently impenetrable disarray. "You'll never be able to eat off the floor," she graciously mumbles. I smile and tuck the remark away for when I can think more about our profound and distant synchrony. But the comrades-in-arms feeling is back. Then slowly, in what I've come to think of as a process akin to dark adaptation, I begin to see again. There in one corner of the crammed living room is an open space. It is a small space: rectangular and perfectly sized for the narrow wooden desk that Carol so carefully measured a few weeks back at my old office. Ever since Carol received the letter from The College offering admission, we have been propelled by the momentum of wishes near to coming true. The atmosphere is heady and hints at expanse. But the herald of intention may come in the making of a one-of-a-kind gesture. This is rarely a grand affair, although in Carol's case, it was against great odds. As I muse, I notice that Carol has maneuvered herself over by the far corner beside the window and is excitedly waiting for me to find a way through. I want to give myself another moment to silently fathom the logistics of belief, the precise calibrations of trying, and how a clearing in the mind has, just for now, assumed the size of a desk. But I need to answer the remains of a question. "It's going to fit, isn't it?" "It is, it is."

Not too many months ago, Carol walked into my office with the following dilemma. She didn't know, she said, whether to write about Sophocles' Antigone or Ibsen's Dora for her English class assignment. She made a case for each and then appeared to lean toward writing about Dora, feeling apparently that Dora's experience in some manner of speaking both connected with her own and simultaneously offered a vantage point from which to see herself and her situation from another perspective. She might, she then added, try to write about Antigone as well, but later, after she had a chance to reread the play. She then allowed that something in this experience gave her joy and that she felt freer than ever before.

I would suggest that she attained, if only fleetingly, that state of reflective memory wherein we encounter ourselves in our diverse dimensions. Gone, for the moment, was that all-consuming vigilance, that conservatizing, immobilizing concern for safety, which had usurped all her energies and held most of her spontaneous gestures in check. In this new encounter, we were joined, not by ghosts, but by our companions through time, whose struggles for freedom and value, at once universal and particular, illuminate our own.

Loewald, in his paper "Perspectives on Memory," says the following: "Becoming an idea means that the unconscious structure loses its unitary, instinctual, 'single-minded' character and becomes reinserted into a context of meaning, i.e. into a context of mutually reflecting and related mental elements. The linking is no longer one of merely reproductive action; it is one of representational connection . . . We are led back to the intricate relations between memory and mourning. In some sense, the sadness and grief of mourning perhaps also concerns that loss, that giving up of the unitary single-mindedness of the instinctual life that tends to preserve in some way the primary narcissistic oneness from which we have to take leave in the development of conscious life and secondary process mentation. That development involves being split from the embeddedness in an embracing totality, as well as that internal split in which we come to reflect and confront ourselves. By virtue of the secondary process, the ego exercises its functions, including that function by which the individual becomes an object of contemplation and care and love to itself and can encounter others as objects in the same spirit."[20]

To know ourselves as historical beings, to make both a past and a future, will take as long as the patient (or any of us) needs to stop refusing ourselves the knowledge of reality we already possess. If the knowing of what is real cannot occur in childhood, the later work of recognition will take great effort and courage. For a long time, it probably will not be able to be done alone. The loss of what might have been is simply too painful. When I am asked if the care and time that went into the work with Carol is justified or if the connection between us has made it hard to part, I answer that the developmental process through which the self becomes real to itself is the process of individuation and emancipation. "The therapy that works best is the therapy that becomes seamlessly interwoven with the patient's own development, that is the patient's own development."[21] As the self and others come into mind, leave-taking becomes, more genuinely and simply, the course of life.

Notes

1. Robert Coles, *Anna Freud* (Reading, Mass.: Addison-Wesley, 1992), p. 91.
2. Hans Loewald, "Internalization, Separation, Mourning and the Super-ego" (1959), in *Papers on Psychoanalysis* (New Haven: Yale University Press, 1980), p. 275.
3. Christopher Bollas, *Forces of Destiny: Psychoanalysis and Human Idiom* (London: Free Association Press, 1989), p. 43.
4. Paul Russell, unpublished paper, presented to The Consortium for Psychotherapy, 1995, p. 7.
5. Theodore Lowi, "Risks and Rights in the History of the American Government," *Daedalus* (1990), 119: 31.
6. Clinical treatment in early intervention often draws upon models of infant-parent psychotherapy in which "therapists treat mother and child together using a flexible, psychodynamically oriented treatment approach that can include home visiting, advocacy, and non-didactic developmental guidance . . . The meanings that the child holds for the mother and the interactions between them offer a window onto the mother's internal world. In using this joint psychotherapy with high-risk mothers and young children, the therapist gains the opportunity to attend with immediacy and specificity to the ways the child is at risk and simultaneously to address the mother's history and psychological experience." See Robin Silverman and Alicia Lieberman, "Negative Maternal Attributions, Projective Identification, and the Intergenerational Transmission of Violent Relational Patterns" (1999), *Psychoanalytic Dialogues* 9(2): 164.
7. Psychotherapy can profoundly realign existing family and social structures. "Psychotherapy of any depth or intensity will reach a point where it challenges the structure of existing attachments, existing attitudes, mind sets, shared beliefs, structures of feeling, networks of relationships. For it not to do so will inevitably leave the individual unchanged." (Paul Russell, unpublished manuscript, "What Is Radical about Psychotherapy?", 1995, p. 1.) The stress of these changes can challenge the therapeutic relationship as well. "Therapies in which the therapist betrays the patient cannot be that rare. I suspect it is only a matter of degree. The work requires personal courage on the part of both patient and therapist. It is best to know this. The therapist who does not is liable to betray his patient." (Russell, 1995, p. 2.)
8. For two related texts on levels of mentation and the integrative activity of understanding, see Jonathan Lear, *Love and Its Place in Nature* (New York: Farrar, Straus and Giroux, 1990) and Hans Loewald, *Sublimation* (New Haven: Yale University Press, 1988).
9. Insofar as the therapist is attuned to what is in need of organization, even the transference of infantile "instinctual" wishes can become an integrative experience. I agree with Loewald that the greater organization (of

mind) of the therapist (by virtue of his own past experience of being understood before fully knowing for himself what it was he was communicating) allows the therapist to appreciate the strivings of the patient, however apparently inarticulate, as meaningful. "The patient, being recognized as something more than he is at present, can attempt to reach this something more by his communications to the analyst, which may establish a new identity with reality." (Loewald, "On the Therapeutic Action of Psychoanalysis" [1956], *Papers on Psychoanalysis,* 1980, p. 243.)

10. We can get so caught up in the bold schemas of treatment plans, goals and objectives, that we forget it is very much the almost imperceptible moment-to-moment adjustments and attunements of attention and affect through which the experience of being in a relationship is built up and internalized. Attention to these microprocesses of relationship building were particularly important with Carol, for whom safety and protection from impingement were always in the foreground. During this period, when many of her fears about being violated and held against her will were revived (not an uncommon experience for hospitalized patients with her history of sexual and physical abuse), I found myself hoping we might achieve that delicate equilibrium in which presence is not experienced as intrusion and absence is not felt as loss, something close to Winnicott's key concept of the capacity to be alone, that is to say, oneself, in the presence of another.

11. For a fuller explication of the concept of affective competence see Paul Russell, "Process with Involvement: The Interpretation of Affect," in Lawrence Lifson, ed., *Understanding Therapeutic Action* (Hillside, N.J.: The Analytic Press, 1996), pp. 201–216.

12. See the proceedings of the Developmental Process and the Enigma of Change Conference, Boston, March 7, 1997, for a review of contemporary, nonlinear, systems models of change, particularly the paper by Daniel Stern, "Developmental Process and the Reordering of the Intersubjective Environment in Treatment."

13. It may be that however unmistakably every child is someone new, for the parents she is also felt as someone known. Not every developmental possibility or childhood initiative survives such presumption. In some families, it's almost as if the parents are too convinced of what they know. The representation of the child, organized through the logic of the parent's caretaking, cannot allow for some crucial aspect of the child's generative acts of self-regulation or affective expression. In such circumstances, the child too may foreclose or sequester possibilities that cannot be recognized and guided within the context of the relationship.

14. Christopher Bollas, *Forces of Destiny: Psychoanalysis and Human Idiom* (London: Free Association Books, 1989), p. 15.

15. James Hamilton-Patterson, *Griefwork* (New York: Farrar, Straus and Giroux, 1995), p. 37.

16. Ibid., p. 59.
17. "A symbolic relationship . . . impresses us as one in which we have a hand." Loewald, *Sublimation,* p. 45.
18. Ernst Cassirer, *An Essay on Man* (New Haven: Yale University Press, 1944), p. 224.
19. Martha Nussbaum, *The Fragility of Goodness: Luck and Ethics in Greek Tragedy and Philosophy* (Cambridge: Cambridge University Press, 1986), p. 2.
20. Loewald, "Perspectives on Memory" (1972), in *Papers on Psychoanalysis,* 1980, pp. 170–171.
21. Paul Russell, unpublished manuscript, "Why We Must Continue to Do What We Do," 1994, p. 8.

III Rethinking Psychotherapy

II Rethinking Psychopathology

Commentary to Part III

Leston Havens

Now we move from real-life situations to ways in which the work can be more generally understood: Gustafson's dilemma theory, Robins and Koons's description of dialectics, Newman's approaching trauma as a central therapeutic problem, and Margulies' account of a psychoanalysis that takes in so much of what has been learned. In the first chapter of this section, Gustafson introduces a broad, powerful design. He sees the central problem of psychological life as that of balancing the demands for conformity and individuality. There can be no restricting our therapeutic concerns to intrapsychic life, the interpersonal, or the dominant pressures of the day. The *dilemmas* of everyday life touch the whole span. He wants to liberate individuality while not letting that liberation be destructive of the individuals who must live in the real world. To that end, he rides with his patients the deep currents carrying them toward this goal or that. The currents must be both confirmed and withstood, accepted and balanced, and the patient's life constructed from among them. This practical-minded man also seeks the counsel of *dreams,* but dreams understood from all the principal points of view: as disguised wish-fulfillment (Freud), as compensations for the limits of waking thoughts (Jung), and as accurate perceptions of the real conditions of the patients' lives (existential). In addition, he proposes a structure for psychotherapy which is not bound exclusively to short-term or long-term work, but which matches the needs of patient and situation. It is a great liberation.

Not only does this structure include the contributions of the principal schools, but it provides a powerful method of forming effective relationships. Because every patient struggles with these dilemmas and delivers them into the clinical encounter, Gustafson's tactic of engaging the patient in the struggles engages them where they centrally are.

Robins and Koons represent pluralism of a different kind. The word here is *dialectic,* to describe this very self-aware effort to include both acceptance and change, validation and confrontation, behavioral analysis and being genuinely open, operant conditioning and Zen. The great strength of this approach seems to us the realization that no one type of relationship meets the various and changing needs of the particular patients addressed, nor are therapists always able to engage their patients in the variety of ways they require. Here we meet the clearest contemporary statement that too much is often asked of individual therapists. So this is a group effort in both senses in which we have used the term: groups of patients and groups of workers. Note the relevance of such variety to the patients particularly addressed: they tend to *polarize* relationships, with therapists, for example, being quickly switched from loved to hated. The treatment is concomitantly *de*polarizing. Every idea is used to invite consideration of its opposite, one worker balanced by another.

The overall goal is to create a *learning* environment. This requires managing the patients' experience, through different types of influence and in moment-to-moment control of the relationship. Such is the basic orientation, rather than, for example, interpretation or the opening up of the relationship to many possibilities, as in some interpersonal work. The approach is also distinct in giving less attention to historical and unconscious discoveries than some schools do. Robins and Koons know, in advance, much of what they want to accomplish. Even such an apparently divergent framework as that of Zen Buddhism is brought in for *specific* purposes, notably to teach tolerance of painful realities. (Much of the Buddhist approach is termed "existential" elsewhere in these chapters.)

Hence, one importance of the emphasis given in this chapter to validating patients. This helps balance the emphasis on learning, which necessarily implies that the patients have much to learn or have not learned. Similarly, the goal of this work, to construct a life worth living, depends upon the patients' accepting that they have not already done so—something that may not be accepted even when the life in question is an apparent shambles. But this goal, a viable existence, helps validate what patients *can* become, and each step toward that goal provides evidence of their success.

We have placed Newman's discussion of treating the chronically traumatized in this theoretical section because it demonstrates how many methods and conceptions are necessary to treat a relatively specific, common problem. Newman's is a broad, systematic attack using individual and group contacts, steady and intermittent meetings, analytic and cognitive concepts, and a subtle, persuasive sense of the work's dangers, with suggestions for offsetting them.

The professions and the population at large are still struggling to come to terms with physical abuse, especially intra-family abuse, and we are only beginning to engage with the problems of psychological abuse. Many roles exist for therapists: acknowledging and empathizing, interpreting, guiding, coaching, and reconstructing the patient's aspirations and ideals. Newman points to another role that is sometimes overlooked, the therapist as *witness*. There is a natural tendency to deny what humans can do to one another. Family members may too often have looked away from what another family member has been doing. There may have been no real witnesses ready to "go on the stand." One casualty of a situation like this is the patient's sense of reality. Few can see the world for what it is when important matters are consistently denied. Therapists as witnesses therefore help restore the patient's capacity to hold on to reality as well as to make it less easy for the rest of us to turn away.

Margulies makes an eloquent plea that psychotherapists not turn away from psychoanalysis. He means to deliver its whole and evolving tradition, which in his telling encompasses both interpersonal and existential ideas, for the foundation of psychotherapeutic work in general. This seems to us a unique and invaluable approach. Implicit in it is a plea to psychoanalysis itself: Do not huddle in little enclaves of self or ego psychologists, interpersonalists, or Kleinians. Recognize that these differences make up a broad, many-faceted effort, no part of which can stand for the whole. Of course analysts disagree, Margulies states, but there's much more on which they agree. Just as patients must recognize their warring elements and reach a self-possession that acknowledges conflict while refusing to let it destroy the individual, so psychotherapy and analysis must keep in touch with *their* warring elements and not let disagreements undermine the work as a whole.

9   The Field of Brief Psychotherapy

James P. Gustafson

In the hundred years since the publication of the first book of brief psychotherapy by Breuer and Freud (*Studies on Hysteria,* 1895), the field of brief psychotherapy has gradually shifted from a psychotherapy of the subject in psychodynamic theory, to a field between subjects in interpersonal theory, to a field of objects in cognitive-behavioral theory. Nevertheless, there remain a great many practitioners of the inner world, as of the interpersonal world, as well as of the dominant outer world of our times (Havens, 1973).

Each of these worlds has its own virtues and therapeutic advantages, which I propose to show. Centered in its own perspective, each also has gaps, which I will also discuss here. When I was writing this essay, I was involved in conducting a week-long workshop on "Advanced Training in Brief Psychotherapy" for the Door County 1997 Summer Institute in Egg Harbor, Wisconsin. I spent the first three days presenting the three worlds of inner, interpersonal, and outer, their key authors, and the key concepts to my audience of experienced practitioners. I also showed each day several videotapes of my own cases by which they might judge what the perspective of the day could illuminate and what it missed in the actual interviews. This essay could be considered the joint work of our discussions.

The ultimate outcome of the pull for objective psychotherapy in our times is what is called single-session psychotherapy—the very ideal of the health maintenance organization arranging for the minimum of expenditure. A group single-session psychotherapy would be even more ideal from an economic standpoint, if an entire auditorium of mistaken patients could be converted from their mistaken ways to well-being. Thus, I felt obliged to consider this venture in my fourth day of the Door County Institute. While there are instances of such conversions, from error to rectitude, aplenty, I find it much more down to earth to propose a single session that can be repeated on demand in the way shown by Winnicott (1991). The patient remains in a dilemma, even if he has a better way through it after a first session (Gustafson, 1995a, 1995b). He is apt to slip back, and thus the need for a follow-up session on demand.

The attentive reader must be wondering by now why the field should be split between these perspectives. Why should there be separate schools or subsocieties (Bergson, 1900) of the inner, the outer, and the interpersonal? My reply leads into the very center of difficulty in Western culture itself, in which the subject and object have been so difficult to reconcile. In America, we have had a series of cultures in the last three hundred years that reflect this difficulty in a succession of ideologies: first the Puritan, then the American Enlightenment, then Transcendental Romanticism, and finally the American Pragmatism in which we now dwell (Mumford, 1926; Mosier, 1952).

These religions or philosophies or myths have oscillated between the excesses of the subject and those of the object. Now that we are in the American pragmatism of the "cash value" of objective practices, as William James put it (Mumford, 1926), we are in the greatest danger of losing the subject, or the inner world. However, those in touch with their own subjective worlds are in great danger of foolish romanticism. In other words, there is no way around the necessity of getting back and forth between the subjective and objective worlds. All our patients, and we ourselves, must negotiate this, or we become one-sided and grotesque (Anderson, 1919).

For this passage, I believe that dreams are indispensable, when they are balanced by an adequate account of the structures of the objective world. Thus I will conclude this essay, as I concluded my five-day workshop, with some remarks on the use of dreams in brief psychotherapy as maps of the entire daily passage between the inner and outer worlds. We must do this adequately, or we are going to be in serious trouble.

Brief Psychotherapy within the Inner World of the Subject

The field of brief psychotherapy commences in 1895 with the publication of *Studies on Hysteria,* with the first two, of Anna O. and Frau Emmy, illustrating the kind of hysteria, or somatoform disorder, that proliferates when given a theater, and the next three, of Lucy, Katherina, and Elizabeth von R., illustrating the kind of hysteria that can pull itself beautifully together in one, seven, or a half-year of sessions. Whenever I ask audiences of experienced therapists if they have read this book, only a handful of people reply that they have studied it. Every day I spend on our consultation services in the hospital, I rely chiefly on this map.

The subsequent elaboration of the psychodynamic point of view of the inner world can, I think, be adequately summarized through a reading of Freud (1909), Reich (1933), Melanie Klein (1959), and the existentialist Binswanger (1963). The modern versions are more or less rediscoveries of the same ideas in the 1960s and 1970s in the work of Mann (1973), Malan (1976), Sifneos (1979), and Davanloo (1980). Lesser known are Semrad (1966) and Margulies (1989), who take up where Binswanger left off in the existentialist tradition.

The key ideas in this perspective turn around the concept of an elevated ideal which takes a fall into actual failure. Anxiety is the signal of the danger of the fall that is at hand, and depression, grief, pain, tears, and rage are the signals that it has already taken place. Conflict is the gap between the ideal and the actual; resistance is the sign of defenses to run away from it; and transference is the very conflict projected between the patient and doctor, usually with the doctor as the ideal, and the patient as the faulty subject. For example, the hysterical line of defense so amply illustrated in *Studies on Hysteria* moves the patient from raw anxiety into a kind of distraction based on attending to the physical symptoms that arise in bodily anxiety, such as tightness in the chest, lightheadedness, and so forth.

Now it may be possible to conduct successful brief psychotherapy by strict use of *interpretation* within this classical set of concepts. Mann, Malan, and Sifneos have argued exactly this, with follow-up studies to prove it. What they cannot exclude, however, is what else the therapist may have been doing *besides* interpreting the core concepts. I am inclined to believe that arousing the patient's subjective world works best by means involving more than interpretation. Semrad was my first teacher of brief psychotherapy, and he demonstrated the power of the presence of the doctor in every hour I watched him consult to our patients. Freud (1913) himself said that you could not relieve a conflict if you could not mobilize it and get near it.

In other words, I think the classical psychodynamic concepts are important for understanding how the patient falls from his or her own grace of the ideal, but additional means are necessary to get near the patient in his or her distress.

The Case of Basilar Artery Migraine

I have written about this case before, and provided a two-year follow-up (Gustafson, 1995b). The reader may want to refer to this text for more background, because here I am going to confine myself to the technical problem of access to the patient's inner conflict.

The patient was referred to me by the neurologist of our University Health Service, who was concerned because this young woman was getting prednisone injections for a rare form of migraine from her neurologist in New York City. Our neurologist could find nothing in his examination and doubted the diagnosis and the radical treatment, and wanted a second opinion from me.

When I met this 19-year-old woman in her first year at the university, she said that she had come for this second opinion. She only wished that her parents were there, because they could give me all the details. I said that I wished they were too, but since they were not, perhaps she and I might simply take the history. That was fine with her, and we began with the first episode, which occurred around Christmas time in her junior year of high school.

All she seemed to know was that one day she became "spacy, light-headed, paranoid, you name it." I startled her by replying that that was always a distraction. She had been upset about something, and was attending to the physical sensations that came with it. What could she have been upset about? "School," she answered just like that, and we began descending into her predicament.

It was this. Her sister was so good at school, and she wasn't, and yet her parents told her it was crazy to be upset about this. I responded that, perhaps, she wanted to beat her sister. "Oh, yes," she answered, showing her beautiful teeth. "And once she did get a C!" she fairly shouted back at me. I responded that I was glad for that, and she gave me a huge smile, again showing those fierce teeth. But soon she was pointing two fingers of accusation at her head (Gustafson's sign, 1986;

see also Gustafson, 1992, 1995a, 1995b), and, curiously, putting one of the fingers in her mouth as if to suck on it as well.

The patient was showing how much she accused herself for her rage at her sister, and how much she wanted comfort, while I am simply responding to her graphic expressiveness and bringing out what her body is trying to say. Freud and Breuer (1895) used to say that the feeling was "strangulated," and the job was to take the patient's hands off her own neck. Reich (1933), Sharpe (1951), and Semrad (1966) all follow in this line, technically, of addressing the expression of the pent-up body. While Freud changed from being very responsive to being like a blank screen, many of us have continued what he began. Certainly, this approach risks misleading suggestions to an already highly suggestive patient. Yet it also gains the beauty of being in tune with what a desperate young woman is trying to let out. As Winnicott (1971) would say, in such cases, it is a matter of responding to what the patient herself has been looking for: "If it (the special occasion) is wasted the child's belief in being understood is shattered. If on the other hand it is used, then the child's belief in being helped is strengthened" (p. 5).

Brief Psychotherapy within the Interpersonal World

Jung (1916) provides the first interpersonal theory, and he is followed by the developments of Alexander and French (1946), Sullivan (1956), Balint (1968), Winnicott (1971), and Kohut (1971), in the psychoanalytic school which becomes ever more interpersonal in its perspective (Gustafson, 1986). From Sullivan's line comes all of the development of the family therapists, like Haley (1966) and Selvini-Palazzoli (1989), and all of the solution-focused therapists, including Milton Erickson (1980), Watzlawick et al. (1974), de Shazer (1985), O'Hanlon and Weiner-Davis (1989), and Hoyt (1996).

Jung introduces the idea of a persona or social mask, and the idea of a shadow self which carries the seeds of invigoration and the risks of psychic inflation. Alexander and French (1946) call this return to vigor a corrective emotional experience. Sullivan's (1956) contribution centers on the phenomenon of selective inattention to the means by which the persona is deflated, and the shadow is inflated. Usually the patient and the doctor fail to attend to these two vital matters.

Balint (1968), Winnicott (1911), and Kohut (1971) all address the need for a holding environment within which the return or regression to the early vitality can be backed. The family therapists pose the chief mechanism of the deflation, which is the perverse triangle in which any third thing of benefit to others is hard on the patient and depletes him (Haley, 1966). In its most malignant form, it is the imbroglio described by Selvini-Palazzoli et al. (1989), in which a child is drawn into being an ally of a parent in a war with his or her spouse, and then betrayed. The solution-focused therapists become skillful at finding the overlooked capacities in the patient hidden by selective attention to all the pathology.

The Case of Flashbacks

Winnicott (1971) always emphasized that you ought not to reach to the distress of a child if there is no holding environment to take good enough care of her afterwards. I think this applies equally to adults. Interestingly, this opens up a large set of possibilities for brief psychotherapy when there is a professional holding environment that includes the pharmacological psychiatrist, the psychologist therapist, the inpatient service, the emergency room call system, and so forth. Increasingly, I find that our residents and our staff are bringing cases for consultation to my Brief Psychotherapy Clinic that are very disturbed and carry classical pathological diagnoses like bipolar affective disorder, borderline personality disorder, and so forth. If these patients have a benign response to understanding (Balint, 1968; Gustafson, 1995a, 1995b), I can give a single session, and even repeat it on demand, as Winnicott used to do with children and with some adults (Gustafson, 1986).

A 30-year-old patient with the diagnosis of post-traumatic stress disorder, secondary to childhood incest, was brought to me by one of our senior residents from our inpatient service. He had been following her in the outpatient department for about a year, and was very concerned that she was in continual danger of suicide for the last several months for no apparent reason. As an attending psychiatrist in our outpatient clinic, I had met this patient several times.

Her outpatient therapist also came to the consultation, and wanted to know what to do about going into all the flashback material that had been overwhelming in these last several months during which she had been so suicidal. Should they be going into it, or leave it alone?

As Sullivan (1956) used to say, my job was very simple, in that I needed to take a history of her stability, which had suddenly become a history of instability. Yet no one seemed to have an idea of the dynamics that had altered the history so dramatically. This was clouded in the fog of selective inattention, which almost always occurs when there is a great deal of anxiety.

The story turned out to be very simple, as it almost always turns out. The patient had started a new relationship about nine months ago, and had felt a great comfort in this close connection. It all began to get anxious when they moved in together, because she was depending on the person a great deal more. It got dramatically worse when they had their first fight, over the partner being somewhat neglectful of the cleaning chores. Now the memories of incest began to break in at night in the form of nightmares. Although she got comfort from her partner at first, the more she told her, the more anxious she became that her partner could not endure the burden. The private holding environment was coming apart, and the basic fault was yawning open once again.

Now the disturbance fell upon the professional holding environment, and the same thing happened there. The patient began to dread that her psychologist was getting worn out as well. It was all of one piece.

As we came nearer to the end of the hour of consultation, I still needed to reply to the question of what to do with the flashbacks. I asked the patient if she would be willing to tell me something about them. We went into several of them, with my sense that we might well need to have her go back to the hospital after the session (she had planned on discharge that day). The flashbacks were simply unbearable, about being a sexual object for her father, culminating in his death by a heart attack soon after having had sex with her.

She did need to go back in the hospital after the session, but she had gotten some relief on two vital matters. One is that she began to understand how she had had such a stable period, and how the fear of burdening her partner had then become overwhelming. The second is that she began to understand how the same thing had happened with her psychologist, and how her dread of alienating the psychologist had been exaggerated. The holding environment was now in better shape. Also, I could recommend simply to attend to her fears about being a burden in the present (interpersonally) and to leave be the overwhelming material from the past (psychodynamically). If the first were attended to, there would be a lot less of the second.

Brief Psychotherapy within the Objective or Outer World

Behaviorism has a long history going back to the nineteenth century. Its strictly objective point of view was that of nineteenth-century psychiatry, as in Kraepelin's distinction between dementia praecox and manic-depressive psychosis. It was greatly reinforced by the behavioral studies of animals, such as those of Pavlov, who started this line of objective science. It was augmented, in its transfer to America, by a line of psychologists starting with Watson, who argued that it was the only legitimate scientific psychology of the human being.

Classical behaviorism is built upon the idea of conditioning to rewards and punishments. It is ideally suited to experiments, by specifying the schedule of conditioning and measuring the results. There is no need for a subject, only an object responding to a schedule. The subject becomes a ghost in the machine, who is no longer of relevance to science.

Contemporary behaviorism reintroduces the subject to some extent, insofar as some aspect of the subject can be handled objectively. Thus Marks (1987) is a classical behaviorist, who deconditions anxiety by exposure. Yet he allows that a quarter of the subjects refuse to engage in the experiment. The subjects can be recalcitrant.

Aaron Beck (J. S. Beck, 1995) goes farther, by handling the beliefs or assumptions of the subject as generative of depression. The subjects externalize their negative ideas about where their lives are going, which allows the clinician to operate upon these *externalized ideas* to change them into more hopeful perspectives. This is the beginning of so-called cognitive behaviorism.

Social behaviorism in White (with Epston, 1990) and Linehan (1993) *externalizes the career* of the subject as an objective and deteriorating pathway. Thus, White addresses schizophrenia not as schizophrenia but as the "in the corner lifestyle" (White, 1989). The patient is invited to telescope time, to see where his career in the corner is going to take him. This often arouses rebellion against the career, which is motivation to take a path more desirable to the subject. White finds "unique outcomes" to show the subject that he is already living out of the corner, occasionally, and challenges him to consider when he can have more of them. Linehan's work with borderline patients is similar, and very common in groups. It relies on specifying the behaviors which continue the borderline career, versus those which lead out of the career.

It is no accident that sophisticated behaviorism has taken over as the brief therapy par excellence of the major disorders of psychiatry, including schizophrenia, borderline personality, alcoholism and drug abuse, obsessive-compulsive disorder, depression, panic disorder, and so forth. By and large, it is the second line of treatment, the first line of treatment being psychopharmacology. The latter is even briefer, in terms of time spent by the doctor, and could also be considered a kind of brief psychotherapy.

I would like to explain why I think psychopharmacology and behavioral therapy are so well suited to the major disorders of psychiatry. The reasons are structural, and the argument oddly is made by Freud, Jung, Winnicott, and others in the psychodynamic tradition, as well as by William James, Sullivan, Bateson, and others in the interpersonal tradition.

To put it very simply, all of the major disorders of psychiatry—indeed, all of DSM-IV—is constructed on a very simple logic (Gustafson, 1999). Namely, the patient is depleted or worn down by his role in the social world, and this drives a desperate attempt to seek restitution (Freud's word) or compensation (Jung's word) for his suffering. Thus, megalomania is restitution for being a nobody (Freud, 1911), mania for depression (Jacobson, 1953), antisocial forcing for being taken (Winnicott, 1971), hysterical sickness for being neglected (Freud and Breuer, 1895), borderline entitlement for having no rights at all (Main, 1957), alcoholism for relief from unbearable tension (Bateson, 1971), obsessions about cleanliness for those who feel dirtied (Freud, 1909), and so on.

I asked my colleagues in the Door County Institute to name a psychiatric disorder that did not have this structure, but they and I could think of none. Notice that this entire set of disorders can be taken objectively, without any reference to the subject or to the interpersonal world. The object can be observed to wear down. The object can be observed to fire up.

Now, this allows the brief therapy of psychopharmacology a tremendous simplicity. In general, it revives worn-down objects, by charging them up with antidepressants. In general, it tones down fired-up objects, by cooling them down with antipsychotic, antimanic, or antianxiety medications. More often than not, the patients utilize antidepressants to get going in the morning, and antianxiety agents to go to sleep. They are both depleted and fired up.

The behavioral brief therapies do the same thing using behavioral schedules instead of drug schedules. The worn-out patients need release from their hopeless assumptions, and the over-demanding patients need to learn to check themselves. To some extent, psychopharmacological or behavioral training accomplishes these objectives, as measured by extensive studies, with statistical verification.

This is not to say that the objective perspective is altogether sufficient for the major psychiatric disorders. I see hundreds of patients a month with our residents in the outpatient clinic, and fewer when I cover the inpatient service, who are handled in this thoroughly objective way. Some get better, some do not, while most wax and wane. Often, I am able to reach out of this objective field to the interpersonal and subjective fields, to find what is holding up the case. This is a kind of brief therapy, in the sense of a single session to locate the relevant forces.

The Objective Case of "Problem Saturation"

As Michael White put it (1989), these patients are almost always "problem-saturated," like solutions saturated with solute. Add one more thing, and you precipitate a huge reaction. Our clinic is full of these patients, and they are all more or less the same case, with minor variations. They are taken advantage of by everybody. The world is endlessly perverse, at work and at home, giving others what is good for them, which is bad for the patient. Others rule them, and they are silent (Freire, 1970). I have called it "the exploding doormat problem" (Gustafson, 1995a), but Robert Louis Stevenson preceded me in this by more than a hundred years in his case of *The Strange History of Dr. Jekyll and Mr. Hyde* (1886), which was proposed by its author as the general condition of Western man (see Gustafson, 1995a, chap. 11). In brief, the protagonist is depleted as Dr. Jekyll, giving everybody else what they need, and he explodes out his back gate in the dark of night as Mr. Hyde, stopping for no one.

Piaget (1968, pp. 64–70) argued that all adolescents are megalomaniacs in their egocentrism about getting the world to be reformed to fit their grand idea. Rightly, he says that putting these reform ideas to work, "undertaken in concrete and well-defined situations, cure[s] all dreams" (p. 69). But it is odd of him to say that "professional work definitely restores equilibrium" (p. 69). Yes, it decenters the subject into being a correct object in the in-group of the professional world, like Dr. Jekyll, but it only invites a compensatory rage worthy of Mr. Hyde.

So many patients founder in this chasm between an egocentric world of the subject, and a decentered world of the object. The latter gets you in and dispirited. The former gets you as out as an outlaw. In other words, Dr. Jekyll by day, and Mr. Hyde by night. Many cannot do any better than this, and the television reflection of the average viewer conveys exactly this two-dimensional situation. He is pathetic in the sitcom, and violent in the murder mystery, and this is the endless cycle of his life. I consult to this situation all day long in our clinic. The best I can do, briefly, is to acknowledge the grief of being badly used, and to witness the humor of getting one's own back. Certain comic expressions of revenge bring these patients alive for a few generative seconds, such as the patient who laughed at the resident's idea of asserting herself to her tyrant husband. I responded, "Yes, God will not abide that for long," and she laughed again, and then disappeared into her culture of silence (see Freire, 1970).

It is not a good idea to overcome the selective inattention of these patients to the cycle they live in, for it makes them desperate. They get flooded with anxiety, or despair. A little window into a little feeling is all that they can bear. This is why they bear with the objective doctors, who do not look too closely, who always have other ideas for improving things, who bear therefore and to some extent with them. Better to keep things in an objective blur, when the interpersonal and subjective fields are altogether disturbing if visited for more than a few minutes, or, in some cases, seconds.

Single-Session Psychotherapy, or Single Sessions Repeated on Demand

Single-session psychotherapy (SST) has become extremely popular in these days of economical medical care. It is not difficult to ridicule, and this ridicule is often deserved. Yet I think there is some value in it (see Hoyt, 1996). It is worth examining what it can do, and what it cannot. It turns out that there is much to be gained from considering brief psychotherapy as a single session, repeated, as Winnicott (1971) used to say, on demand.

The simplest way to make the argument for single-session psychotherapy is to notice that it has been observed since time immemorial. The Old and New Testaments are full of examples, and William James (1902) documented hundreds of cases, and explicated their mechanism, as the dynamics of conversion.

The situation is very simple. The subject is lost, and sinking, into despair. In other words, he is convinced that the direction he is going in is only going to get worse and worse. It could be called sin, it could be called alcoholism, and so forth. This makes him ready to be saved, especially insofar as he has a vision or a profound experience of being accepted. This draws him into a new community, with a new practice, and a new confidence.

Alexander and French (1946) discuss this very dynamic in the case of Jean Valjean from Victor Hugo. He is a brutal thief, who is shocked by the kindness of a bishop. He is then cruel to a little boy, but can no longer stand to be wicked. His entire career is disrupted by clemency.

The very argument for conversion in a single session exposes its own weakness. For there are many thieves who are not moved by clemency, unlike this one Jean Valjean who was. The same is true of alcoholics, who can convert suddenly, but more often have not hit bottom. Conversion depends upon very specific conditions—of despair with the descending path, and of hope with the ascending community (James, 1902). It is a social event, with highly specific social conditions. It involves group psychology, of being lost from the group and found by the group. Its power is attested by the huge growth of fundamentalism in this country in the last several decades.

I would rather not practice on a daily basis, with very difficult cases, hoping for this remarkable breakthrough. The rule is that they go around the same circles as they did before, and I would not like to depend on the unusual exception. Rather, I would like to take the single session as a complete whole, which can then be repeated on demand (Winnicott, 1971). This has the advantage of reaching into similar powerful forces, while being ready for return to the status quo. It awaits developments between sessions.

The technique is not mine, and it is available to anyone who can ride the emotional currents, which are very powerful. I will try to make it as explicit as possible, but the reader may want to refer to Winnicott's (1971) text for further examples. Most often, the patient is being handled objectively by others, when I see him in consultation. He is run down by the world, and he is demanding in his turn.

In general, the patients and their doctors do not understand the dynamics of the situation. As Sullivan (1956) would say, they have selective inattention for the mechanism of their depletion, and they have selective inattention for the mechanism of their excitement. My job is to see the obvious, by going over how they are being worn down. Almost always, this will come into focus on the interpersonal field, in which the needs of others are coming ahead of the needs of the patient, and are thus highly perverse for his well-being. But I have had to reach beyond the objective field, to this interpersonal field. That is why I see something that the patient and doctor have missed. They were looking externally, objectively, behaviorally, and could only see the depleted outcome.

Once I bring this plight into focus, the patient will almost always become very upset, cry, and often get angry. Now, we are within the subjective field, where the patient is falling terribly short of his own ideal. Often, he will accuse himself with Gustafson's sign (1986, 1992, 1995a, 1995b), of one, two, or three fingers pointed at his own head. If I cannot notice this bodily sign of self-accusation, he will stay stuck in his own court of self-blame. If I do notice it, the defense almost always rises to defend the patient.

Now, this simplest of techniques is sometimes not enough, as I will illustrate in the following two cases. In both, the technique described shook up the patient, to prepare what followed. However, I also needed a dream in the first case, to *reach*, as Winnicott would say, to what was so dissociated because it was so painful. I needed a shared sense of beauty in the second case, also to make what was so dissociated and so painful something which was bearable.

The Case of the Missing Lion, and the Case of the Witness

"The Case of the Missing Lion" is quoted verbatim as a single session of consultation in one of my recent books (Gustafson, 1995a, chap. 8). Here I will only take it in passing, as an illustration of the structure of the single hour. The single hour is a matter of entering a field with the patient (and doctor, when it is a consultation) because of their distress for which they want help. Access, or entry, is granted only because of this hope to be helped. In this case, it was a matter of the patient pulling out her eyelashes. This had been helped some by the cognitive-behavioral treatment, but it threatened to come back as the therapist ended the treatment relationship. I got a little way with the patient, by taking the trichotillomania as a common way to relieve tension. Yet she remained very guarded.

The middle part of the interview acknowledges her need for perfect control, and then asks why she needs it so much, and thus reaches, in Winnicott's phrase, to her vulnerability as an awkward child. Once we are there in this distress, I can take the dream dive, and find the missing lion of her own outrage.

In the middle of this distressing confession about being an awkward child, I ask her for a dream. At first, she insists she has none. Appealing to her stubbornness, I say I bet she has never had a single image in her whole life from the dream world. She relents, and says she has had just one dream. She dreamt there was a murderer in the family, and it made no sense.

If it made no sense for *her* family, what family did have a murderer? I was looking for the context from which the image was drawn, along the lines that Jung used to go. That question woke her up, for it fit the family of her fiancé, in which the father was being cruel. Now we had reached the missing lion of her rage, for she was full of anger at her father-in-law and his injustice. Now she recalled that she had dreamt this after talking with her mother-in-law on the telephone. The dream had been a search for her delayed reaction, delayed by her controlling character.

Now it is time to come up, and close the field to something small that she can bear. She has been "riled and rattled" by her coming marriage into a family rife with injustice. I compare her situation to that of the nesting herring gulls, who pull up grass when enraged with their neighbors. She can do that with her eyebrows. If she would rather not, then she can either keep her distance or she can object. I leave her with her dilemma.

Thus, the single hour is an opening, a reach, and a closing. Often, it opens with an objective and even medical complaint, and the reach is to the interpersonal perversity (as here) of the family, and to the subjective experience (as here) of the dream. But overcoming selective inattention to how the cycle works is daunting, and is often only undergone because of the company of the doctor. When the doctor leaves, he had better close to something manageable.

"The Case of the Witness" is extremely moving to me, because it is the plight of a remarkably articulate 92-year-old woman in a partial care facility. We can all identify with her fate, which could be ours in a matter of time. She is very alert, and very troubled by what she sees in her peers at the home. She suffers from intractable nausea and intractable sleeplessness.

She has been taken care of by one of my most able students, who hears her out and tries valiantly to find remedies for her nausea and insomnia. Little works, and so I am asked to consult. It turns out that the nausea has not been so bad lately, but the sleeplessness is still very bad, and so I begin with her by my interest in what she thinks about all night. Her husband has died some years ago, her children are dispersed, and so it is not out of tune when I add that I certainly don't know "because I've never spent a night with you." In print, that sounds rather bald, but it seems to go across quite naturally, as if another groom is actually wanted.

I qualify this by noting further that the night mind is like a crow, and can fly anywhere. She knows, and takes me along, to all her regret about the past and her terror of the future. We reach as far as the worst thing, her fear that her children, now in their seventies, might die before her.

As Winnicott would say, something was now due from me, and I said I had just been reading *The Witness of Poetry* (1983) by Milosz, her countryman. He wrote that the nightmare of history is only bearable to him because he can be the little boy again, looking backwards, as he rides along in the hay wagon, at the beautiful oaks. She gave a little cry, and exclaimed that she knew exactly what he meant. She wanted to tell me a beautiful story, from the same period of her early life. A little girl from her circle of little girls bringing back the milk in milk cans had spilled hers in tripping over a rut. They all poured a little of their own into hers, and she went home with a nearly full can like all the rest. That was the beautiful kindness. That was what made life bearable.

We went on from there, but that was what secured the reach into the night of past and future. She could go back to the beautiful, and thus have a dream screen on which to dwell.

Dreams as Maps in Brief Psychotherapy

Certainly, it is uncommon to hear of dreams being reported in brief psychotherapy. Objectively, they would be irrelevant. Interpersonally, they would be out of focus. Even subjectively, they would not be the chief interest of the psychodynamic doctors, who interest themselves in feelings. You will hardly find a dream in the books of Mann, Malan, Sifneos, and Davanloo.

Yet, I will assert that I find dreams the most powerful vehicle that I have for mapping the dilemma of the patient. The healthier the patient, the more I rely on them. I have many cases of this kind, that I see once or twice a month, which simply are a series of dreams, analyzed.

The convention in psychotherapy is that dreams are for long-term or analytic psychotherapy. I have no objection to this convention, but I find it too limiting. Now, there are sound reasons for why dreams have been so confined. One is that the theories of dream interpretation require such an elaborate treatment of the dream that only long-term and frequent psychotherapies give enough time for the work-ups of the dream material.

I am not going to recapitulate the entire text of my book (Gustafson, 1997), but I will outline a few key ideas which give access to dream material in brief contexts. In general, there are three traditions of dream interpretation which depend upon the context of long-term psychotherapy: the psychoanalytic ideas of Freud, those of Jung, and those of the existentialists. I will outline these ideas briefly before proceeding to my own.

Freud's (1900) idea was that dreams were elaborate disguises of wish-fulfillments. His technique was free-association to each of the elements of the dream text. Generally, this took a great deal of time.

Jung's (1933) view was that dreams were compensations of the unconscious for a distorted conscious idea. This is why dreams were so often absurd, in making a *reductio ad absurdum* out of the patient's conscious point of view. Thus, if the patient were confident in an unreliable way, he would have a dream of an extreme disaster. Jung's method of working up the dream is more economical than free association, for he draws the patient back to the text, to complete it. His question for each element is not "What comes to mind?" which leads everywhere, but "How do you know about this ——, and when did you first learn of it?" This establishes a kind of autobiography in relation to the text.

The existential ideas, best exemplified by Binswanger (1963), simply take the dream as metaphor, with particular attention given to the space and to the time of the dream. This gives the patient a picture of his own world, relatively undisguised, if metaphorical.

More recently, the ideas on dreams of Freud, Jung, and Binswanger have been most highly developed in Erikson (1954), Hillman (1979), and Margulies (1989). Erikson develops the manifest or sensory dimensionality of the dream, Hillman the dream as a necessary destruction of dead notions, and Margulies its inscape peculiar to the individual dreamer.

My unifying idea is that all of these methods are *searches* of the unconscious, with varying intents and varying circumstances. The key is to locate what the patient is searching *from,* and *for.* Where is he lost, objectively, interpersonally, subjectively? As one of my colleagues in the Door County Institute put it, a dream is an answer for which there is yet no question. Therefore, the key to the riddle is to find that question. Remarkably, the material falls into place, very rapidly.

In general, I find Jung's work-up to be the best way to start. For each element of the text, I ask how the patient has come to know about such a thing. If I do not have a great deal of time, such as only a quarter of an hour, a few such elements worked-up will often suffice to converge the argument of the dream, *if* the departure point or the question of the search is established.

The Case of a Remarkable Birth

A young woman in her late twenties in graduate school had suffered a great deal of intrusion from her Italian parents, in the kind of game described by Selvini-Palazzoli et al. (1989) as an imbroglio. By this, Selvini-Palazzoli meant that the weaker parent, often the father in Italy, draws in the daughter as his true partner, only to drop her suddenly when the mother calls his bluff. Often, this precipitates a great deal of disturbance in the daughters, but our patient was made of sturdy material and was mostly outraged, and amazed.

She had a number of sessions with one of our residents, who asked for my consultation because the patient continued to be outraged and amazed by the antics of her parents. Whereas before her mother had feigned a heart attack to draw her home to Italy to get her away from the boyfriend, now they had shifted tactics and insisted that she marry him! Evidently, they now seemed to have him in their pocket, and she was to get in there with him, to be secure for life.

I listened to her usual amazement in our hour. For example, they had come for New Year's and condoned her fiancé's drinking their home wine, while she was not allowed more than one glass! And so forth and so on. Now her question to me was, what ought she to do? Should she accept the marriage? Or risk going her own way? Already, she had put it off by a ruse, but she would be pressed soon for her reply.

If she was consciously amazed, her unconscious was not, and her dream was perfectly clear. She dreamt that her mother is pregnant, and she rushes to the labor room with her father. She looks down from the top of a staircase at the door of the labor room, and out comes her fiancé. Her mother has given birth to her fiancé. In other words, it was all her parents' conception!

What a remarkably helpful dream this was. It was at once a wish-fulfillment of Freud, a compensation of Jung, and a metaphor of Binswanger. In Freud's search for a wish-fulfillment, the dream states that her mother ought to have the fiancé herself if she wanted him so much. In Jung's search for a compensation, it states that there is nothing amazing about her parents at all, except for arranging their own offspring. In Binswanger's search for a metaphor, it is she up high looking down the stairs into the hell of what was being cooked up for her.

I saw her about a year later, and she had refused the marriage proposal. Now she had a boyfriend who pleased her very much, but she was concerned about his correct parents. Her dilemma was now whether her boyfriend could sustain his rebellion with his passionate Italian lover, or whether he would recant to suit his parents when it was time to get married. Nice problem.

Conclusion

It is time to close, and I only want to say one thing more about this remarkable field of brief psychotherapy. I can accept that it will continue to be divided between its objective schools, its interpersonal schools, and its subjective schools. After all, this is the very condition of our Western culture, in which specialties each have their own markets. There is no higher court than the market, which counts the winners by the numbers of their sales.

Of course, it is not all a horizontal world in which everything is leveled to its "cash value" in this American Pragmatism which seems to be world-conquering. Objectivity is not everything. But the appeal is only to the individual patients, and to the individual psychotherapists, who know what depth is, and what height is, and yet how to survive, getting between the vertical of the gods and the leveling of man.

In the end, the technical problem of the three subsocieties of brief psychotherapy is resolvable in a relatively simple way for those who have an interest in seeing in all three ways. The problem is well known in ecology (Allen and Starr, 1982), where it is widely recognized that the lens of the observer determines the grain and extent of

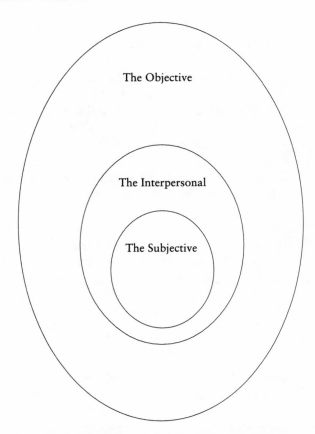

The embeddedness of the three fields of observation

the field that he can bring into focus (Allen et al., 1984). Thus, a wide-angle lens sees a wide field and groups of organisms, an ordinary lens the individual organism, and a telephoto lens into particular gestures of an individual. Similarly, the objective lens in psychiatry sees the cycle of the human group between depletion and restitution, the interpersonal lens the perversity of particular organisms for others, and the subjective lens into the conflict of the individual being. In other words, the objective field has *embedded* within it the smaller and finer-grained fields of the interpersonal and the subjective (Allen and Starr, 1982).

Make these three lenses and their relevant fields of observation your own, or not. You will get rewarded enough by the subsocieties

(Bergson, 1900) that serve each of them, if you stick to just one of them. You will be a great deal more helpful to your individual patients if you can use all three.

References

Alexander, F., and French, T. M. (1946). *Psychoanalytic therapy, principles and applications.* New York: Ronald Press.

Allen, T. F. H., O'Neill, R. V., and Hoekstra, T. W. (1984). Interlevel relations in ecological research and management: Some working principles from hierarchy theory. *USDA Forest Service General Technical Report* RM-110, July 1984.

Allen, T. F. H., and Starr, T. B. (1982). *Hierarchy, perspectives for ecological complexity.* Chicago: University of Chicago Press.

Anderson, S. (1919). *Winesburg, Ohio.* New York: Viking Press, 1960.

Balint, M. (1968). *The basic fault, therapeutic aspects of regression.* London: Tavistock.

Bateson, G. (1971). The cybernetics of self: A theory of alcoholism. *Psychiatry,* 34: 1–17.

Beck, J. S. (1995). *Cognitive therapy. Basics and beyond.* New York: Guilford.

Bergson, H. (1900). *Laughter.* In W. Sypher (Ed.), *Comedy.* Baltimore: Johns Hopkins University Press, 1980.

Binswanger, L. (1963). *Being-in-the-world: Selected papers of Ludwig Binswanger,* J. Needleman (Ed.). New York: Harper and Row, 1967.

Breuer, J., and Freud, S. (1895). *Studies on hysteria.* New York: Avon Press, 1966. Also *Standard edition 2.*

Davanloo, H. (1980). *Short-term dynamic psychotherapy.* Northvale, N.J.: Jason Aronson.

De Shazer, S. (1985). *Keys to solution in brief therapy.* New York: W. W. Norton.

Erickson, M. H. (1980). *The collected papers of Milton H. Erickson,* E. L. Rossi (Ed.). New York: Irvington.

Erikson, E. H. (1954). The dream specimen of psychoanalysis. *Journal of the American Psychoanalytical Association,* 2: 5–56.

Freire, P. (1970). *Pedagogy of the oppressed.* New York: Herder and Herder.

Freud, S. (1900). *The interpretation of dreams.* New York: Avon Press, 1965. Also *Standard edition.*

Freud, S. (1909). Notes upon a case of obsessional neurosis. *Standard edition, 10,* 153–318.

Freud, S. (1911). Psychoanalytic notes upon an autobiographical account of a case of paranoia (dementia paranoides). *Standard edition, 12,* 3–84.

Freud, S. (1913). Further recommendations to physicians on the psychoanalytic method of treatment. On beginning the treatment. The question of the first communications. The dynamics of the cure. *Standard edition,* Volume 12.

Gustafson, J. P. (1986). *The complex secret of brief psychotherapy.* New York: W. W. Norton. Reprinted in paperback, Northvale, N.J.: Jason Aronson, 1997.

Gustafson, J. P. (1992). *Self-delight in a harsh world.* New York: W. W. Norton.

Gustafson, J. P. (1995a). *Brief versus long psychotherapy.* Northvale, N.J.: Jason Aronson.

Gustafson, J. P. (1995b). *The dilemmas of brief psychotherapy.* New York: Plenum.

Gustafson, J. P. (1997). *The new interpretation of dreams.* Madison, Wisconsin: James P. Gustafson.

Gustafson, J. P. (1999). *The most common dynamics of psychiatry.* Madison, Wisconsin; James P. Gustafson.

Haley, J. (1966). Toward a theory of pathological systems. In G. N. Zuk and I. Boszormenyi-Nagy (Eds.), *Family therapy and disturbed families.* Palo Alto: Science and Behavior Books.

Havens, L. L. (1973). *Approaches to the mind.* Boston: Little, Brown.

Hillman, J. (1979). *The dream and the underworld.* New York: Harper and Row.

Hoyt, M. F. (1996). *Constructive therapies,* Volume 2. New York: Guilford.

Jacobson, E. (1953). Contribution to the metapsychology of cyclothymic depression. In P. Greenacre (Ed.), *Affective disorders: Psychoanalytic contributions to their study.* New York: International Universities Press.

James, W. (1902). *The varieties of religious experience.* New York: Mentor, 1958.

Jung, C. G. (1916). The relations between the ego and the unconscious. In J. Campbell (Ed.), *The portable Jung.* New York: Penguin, 1972.

Jung, C. G. (1933). Dream-analysis in its practical application. In C. G. Jung (Ed.), *Dreams.* Princeton: Princeton University Press, 1974.

Klein, M. (1959). Our adult world and its roots in infancy. In M. Klein (Ed.), *Envy and gratitude and other works,* 1946–1963. New York: Dell, 1975.

Kohut, H. (1971). *The analysis of the self.* New York: International Universities Press.

Linehan, M. M. (1993). *Cognitive-behavioral treatment of borderline personality disorder.* New York: Guilford Press.

Main, T. (1957). The ailment. *British Journal of Medical Psychology,* 30: 129–145.

Malan, D. (1976). *The frontier of brief psychotherapy.* New York: Plenum.

Mann, J. (1973). *Time-limited psychotherapy.* Cambridge, Mass.: Harvard University Press.

Margulies, A. (1989). *The empathic imagination.* New York: W. W. Norton.

Marks, I. (1987). *Fears, phobias, and rituals, the nature of anxiety and panic disorders.* New York: Oxford University Press.

Milosz, C. (1983). *The witness of poetry.* Cambridge, Mass.: Harvard University Press.

Mosier, R. (1952). *The American temper.* Berkeley: University of California Press.

Mumford, L. (1926). *The golden day.* New York: Horace Liveright.

O'Hanlon, W. H., and Weiner-Davis, M. (1990). *In search of solutions: A new direction in psychotherapy.* New York: W. W. Norton.

Piaget, J. (1968). *Six psychological studies.* New York: Vintage.

Reich, W. (1933). *Character-analysis.* New York: Farrar, Straus and Giroux, 1949.

Selvini-Palazzoli, M., Cirillo, S., Selvini, M., and Sorrentino, A. M. (1989). *Family games, general models of psychotic process in the family.* New York: W. W. Norton.

Semrad, E., Binstock, W. A., and White, B. (1966). Brief psychotherapy. *American Journal of Psychotherapy,* 20: 576–579.

Sharpe, E. F. (1951). *Dream analysis.* London: Hogarth.

Sifneos, P. (1972). *Short-term psychotherapy and emotional crisis.* Cambridge, Mass.: Harvard University Press.

Stevenson, R. L. (1886). *The strange case of Dr. Jekyll and Mr. Hyde.* New York: Puffin Books, 1985.

Sullivan, H. S. (1956). *Clinical studies in psychiatry.* New York: W. W. Norton.

Watzlawick, P., Weakland, J., and Fisch, R. (1974). *Change: Principles of problem formation and problem resolution.* New York: W. W. Norton.

White, M. (1989). *Selected papers.* Adelaide, South Australia: Dulwich Centre Publications.

White, M., and Epston, D. (1990). *Narrative means to therapeutic ends.* New York: W. W. Norton.

Winnicott, D. W. (1971). *Therapeutic consultations in child psychiatry.* New York: Basic Books.

Acknowledgments

I am indebted to the fifty-five colleagues of the Door County Summer Institute of 1997 for their remarkable help with this material, and to Dr. Carl Chan of the Department of Psychiatry, Medical College of Wisconsin, Milwaukee, Wisconsin, who organized the Institute and brought us all together. Their names are: Kay Adams; Richard Adelman; Mary Androff; William Arnold; Lisa Becker; Kenneth Berg; Michael E. Berger; Eric (Carl) Bergh; Stephen C. Billingham; Marcia

Bradley; Sandra Braine; Jerry Burand; Carrie Danhieux; Nina Dexter; Trudy Doppmann; David S. Dowell; Kathleen M. Ertz; Zvi Frankfurt; Geraldine Frossman; Bradley C. Garson; Terri Geraghty; Michael E. Griffith; C. J. Gunnell; Mark R. Hansen; Thomas Harbaugh; Zoe Hazenson; William Hilgendorf; Murvil R. Hurd; Barbara L. Jensen; Randolph P. Johnston; Veronica Jordan; Margaret B. Kellog; Danielle Kizaire; Roy Kletti; Gregory N. Lewis; Phil Lomas; Michael Mandli; Chuck Milliken; Michael L. Minkin; Karen Nelson; Richard C. Ney; Alexander E. Obolsky; Steve O'Neill; Robert Piper; Therese Ransel; Marilyn Reinhardt; Teresa B. Rosales; David J. Schibline; Barbara J. Schramm; Richard Schramm; Emmanuel M. Tendero; Tony Waisbrot; Randy Wallace; Steven G. Warner; and Joseph B. Webb. I am also indebted to Dee Jones for her skillful help in preparing the manuscript.

10 The Therapeutic Relationship in Dialectical Behavior Therapy

Clive J. Robins and Cedar R. Koons

Introduction

The degree of focus on, and treatment of, the therapeutic relationship is one of the more important ways in which dialectical behavior therapy (DBT) differs from behavior therapy in general. This is due largely to the nature of the population for whom the treatment was designed, chronically suicidal and self-injurious women, most of whom met criteria for borderline personality disorder (BPD). In the first section of this chapter, we discuss how features of patients diagnosed with BPD influence treatment in general and the therapeutic relationship in particular, and summarize evidence that DBT may be an effective treatment for these patients. Subsequent sections describe the theoretical foundation, structure, stages and goals, and strategies of DBT, with an emphasis on how they both influence, and are influenced by, the therapeutic relationship.

The Borderline Patient in Treatment

For a DSM-IV diagnosis of borderline personality disorder, an individual needs to demonstrate five or more of nine criteria. In DBT, it is found helpful to organize these nine criteria into five areas in which the individual may be dysregulated: *affect* (affective instability; difficulty with anger), *relationships* (frantic efforts to avoid abandonment; unstable, intense relationships), *sense of self* (unstable sense of self; feelings of emptiness), *behavior* (impulsive behaviors; suicidal behaviors), and *cognition* (paranoia, dissociation, and hallucinations). Each of these not only bring misery to the patient but also can seriously impact the therapeutic relationship.

Three of the most stressful occurrences faced by mental health clinicians are suicide attempts by patients, suicide threats by patients, and anger expressed toward the therapist. Patients who meet criteria for BPD are the most likely to engage in a constellation of all three of these behaviors. Dialectical behavior therapy requires that all therapists doing any part of this treatment work as part of a team that provides support, guidance, and continuing education.

Dialectical Behavior Therapy: An Overview

This treatment, developed by Marsha Linehan at the University of Washington,[1] evolved over almost twenty years of work with chronically suicidal women. (Because most persons diagnosed with BPD are women, we will use the feminine pronoun throughout. We believe DBT is also relevant for men, but all empirical data on effectiveness are with women only.) DBT is rooted firmly in the principles and practices of behavior therapy and cognitive therapy, including a strong emphasis on systematic ongoing assessment and data collection during treatment; clearly defined target behaviors; a therapist-patient relationship that emphasizes collaboration, orienting the patient to the treatment, and education of the patient; and the use of standard cognitive and behavioral treatment strategies. But DBT also has a number of distinctive characteristics that have emerged partly in response to working with this patient population. One such characteristic is an emphasis on dialectics. The most fundamental dialectic with this population, and perhaps in therapy generally (and even life generally), is the need for both acceptance and change. For the therapist, this means finding a way to fully accept the patient as she currently is, while at the same time persistently and insistently pushing for change. It also means fostering an attitude of acceptance toward current reality on the part of the patient, while at the same time helping her to develop the motivation and ability to change herself and her life. This dialectic is addressed in DBT by the integration of behavior therapy with Zen principles and practice, Rogerian strategies, and other acceptance-oriented approaches.

Evidence of Effectiveness of DBT

In the only randomized controlled study of a psychosocial treatment for BPD patients published to date, DBT had significantly greater effects than "treatment as usual" in the community on frequency and medical severity of self-injury, frequency and duration of hospitalizations, treatment dropout rates, experience and expression of anger, and social role functioning. These effects endured over a six- and twelve-month follow-up period.[2] Recently we completed another treatment outcome study of DBT compared with "treatment as usual" in a V.A. clinic, treating twenty women veterans who met criteria for BPD.[3] After six months of treatment, both groups were significantly less depressed (though still quite depressed), and met fewer BPD criteria, but only the DBT patients also had significant reductions in suicidal ideation, hopelessness, anger, dissociation, and ambivalence over expression of emotions, as well as significantly improved health habits. It appears that this treatment can be conducted effectively at another site by a different research therapy team, and thus can be disseminated.

Theoretical Foundation of DBT

Two bodies of theory provide the foundation for DBT: (1) a biosocial theory of BPD, which helps the therapist to understand the patient's behaviors, and to know both how she needs to change and what she needs to learn; and (2) the core treatment principles, drawn from behavior therapy, Zen, and dialectics, which inform the therapist in how to help bring about those changes.

A Biosocial Theory of BPD

In developing a theory of the etiology and maintenance of BPD, Linehan was mindful of several requirements: (1) that it be compatible with current empirical data; (2) that it be practical, guiding the therapist in what to do when interacting with the patient; and (3) that it engender in the therapist an attitude of effective compassion that will help him or her to stick with the patient through difficult times. The core of the biosocial theory is that BPD results from a series of transactions over time of a person factor, namely a dysfunction of the emotion regulation system, with an environment factor, referred to as the "invalidating environment." The individual who displays extreme emotional reactions will tend to elicit invalidation of her experiences and behavior from others who have difficulty understanding their degree of intensity. The experience of being persistently invalidated, in turn, tends to increase emotional dysregulation and decrease learning of emotion regulation skills.

Emotion Dysregulation. Emotional regulation difficulties can occur because of a combination of two factors: an inherent emotional vulnerability and difficulty in modulating emotions. If the individual had little emotional vulnerability, or had emotional vulnerability but also good skills at modulating emotions, she would not behave in the ways that lead to this diagnosis.

Emotional vulnerability may, in part, be biologically determined as temperament. The emotionally vulnerable person has low thresholds, rapid emotional reactions, and high-level reactions. High levels of emotion, in turn, dysregulate cognitive processing, as they do for everyone. Unfortunately, most borderline patients spend much of their time in a state of high arousal and thus cognitively dysregulated. Emotional vulnerability also usually entails a slow return to baseline levels, which contributes to a high sensitivity to the next emotional stimulus.

Difficulty in modulating emotions is also a challenge for the borderline patient. Basic research has found several tasks to be important for emotion modulation, including the ability to re-orient attention, to inhibit mood-dependent action, to change physiological arousal, to experience emotions without escalating or blunting them, and to organize one's behavior in the service of external, non-mood-dependent goals. These are all skilled behaviors that can, to a large degree, be learned. They are skills that most borderline patients, for whatever reason, have not learned. An important aspect of the treatment, therefore, is teaching skills.

The Invalidating Environment. The primary characteristic of an invalidating environment is that private experiences (emotions and thoughts), as well as overt behaviors, "are often taken as invalid responses to events; are punished, trivialized, dismissed, or disregarded; and/or are attributed to socially unacceptable characteristics."[4] In addition, although emotional communication may be ignored or met by punishment, high-level escalation may result in attention, meeting of demands, and other types of reinforcement. Finally, an invalidating environment may oversimplify the ease of meeting life's goals and problem-solving. Certain behaviors of the emotionally vulnerable "difficult" child's behavior may elicit these types of responses from the environment. Some possible consequences of pervasive invalidation include difficulties in accurately labeling emotions, in effectively regulating emotions, and in trusting one's own experiences as valid. By oversimplifying problem-solving, such an environment does not teach problem-solving, graduated goals, or distress tolerance, but instead teaches perfectionistic standards, and self-punishment as a strategy to try to change one's behavior. Finally, reinforcement of only escalated emotional displays teaches the individual to oscillate between emotional inhibition and extreme emotional behavior.

This model is presented as not only a model of etiology, but also a model of maintenance of BPD behaviors and current transactions. Therapists need to be aware of the likelihood that they will have a tendency to respond to the patient in invalidating ways. In keeping with the emphasis that the model places on invalidation as a causal influence, validation is one of the two core sets of DBT strategies. Much of the behavior of the patient is invalid from many perspectives. All behavior can be valid from some perspectives, however. The therapist needs to make a conscious effort to locate and acknowledge the island of validity in the possible sea of invalidity of the patient's behavior (a dialectical approach) so that the patient, feeling understood and accepted, is able to move toward more skillful behavior.

Core Treatment Principles Underlying DBT

The three areas of knowledge from which DBT draws most of its treatment principles are behavior therapy, Zen, and dialectical philosophy.

Behavior Therapy. By principles of behavior therapy, we primarily mean principles of learning. DBT assumes that many maladaptive behaviors, both overt and private (thoughts, feelings) are learned, and therefore can, in principle, be replaced by new learning. Three primary ways in which organisms learn are through (1) modeling, which involves learning through observation of others; (2) operant conditioning, which refers to learning an association between a behavior and its consequences; and (3) respondent conditioning, which involves learning about an association between two stimuli. All three processes are central to understanding and changing maladaptive behavior.

When consequences follow a behavior and result in a subsequent increase or decrease in that behavior, these are the *operant (instrumental) conditioning* processes of reinforcement and punishment, respectively. When previously reinforced behavior is no longer reinforced, the behavior will decrease, a process called extinction. These principles are widely known and frequently employed systematically by parents, teachers, and others, but often are not considered by therapists in relation to patient behaviors and therapist-patient interactions. Therapists need to avoid unwittingly reinforcing maladaptive behaviors by, for example, providing greater attention to patients when they engage in this behavior than when they do not, or punishing or failing to reinforce fledgling efforts toward more adaptive behavior because they still fall so far short of the mark. Therapists also need constantly to be looking for opportunities, moment-to-moment, to deliberately and contingently provide interpersonal and other consequences to the patient's behavior.

In *respondent (classical) conditioning,* two stimuli become associated, so that the natural response to one becomes a learned response to the other. For example, if a person is raped in a dark alley, being near a dark alley may subsequently provoke a full-force fear response. Positive but maladaptive associations may also be learned in this way, such as an association between the sight or feel of a knife used previously in self-injuring and emotional relief.

Before trying to change a behavior, it is essential first to fully understand what variables currently are maintaining it. This understanding is arrived at through a *behavioral analysis,* which is a very detailed, step-by-step analysis of the sequence of the antecedents of the behavior, the behavior itself, and its consequences. We will describe later in more detail how this is done in a clinical context.

Zen. The introduction of principles from Zen practice into DBT came about largely because of the strong need for these patients to develop an attitude of greater acceptance toward a reality that is often painful. Other spiritual traditions also provide very valuable teachings on issues related to acceptance, but Zen in particular has developed methods for this. Some of the most important Zen principles and practices central to DBT are the importance of being mindful to the current moment, seeing reality without delusion, accepting reality without judgment, letting go of attachments that cause suffering, and finding the middle way. Zen is also characterized by the humanistic assumption that all individuals have an inherent capacity for enlightenment and truth, referred to in DBT as "wise mind."

Dialectics. Dialectics refers to a process of synthesis of opposing elements, ideas, or events, the thesis and the antithesis. Individuals with

BPD usually are very non-dialectical in their thinking and behavior, exhibiting extreme polarized beliefs and actions. Modeling and directly teaching more balanced, synthesized, and dialectical patterns of thinking and behavior is an overarching target of everything that transpires in DBT. In addition, a dialectical world view pervades the treatment. In dialectical philosophy, reality is viewed as whole and interrelated and at the same time as bipolar and oppositional, as in the opposing forces of subatomic particles. Reality is in continuous change as its components transact with one another. This world view is consistent with the transactional, systemic nature of the biosocial theory, and with a view of the patient and therapist as being in a dialectical relationship, transacting in ways that will inevitably lead to changes in both. Dialectical philosophy also is applied in the balance of treatment strategies that are heavily change-oriented with others that are heavily acceptance-oriented, as we will discuss in detail later. Balancing treatment does not mean watering down strong oppositions, but frequently the firm embracing of both, and rapid movement from one type of strategy to another. The quality of mindfulness in the therapist is essential for this speed and flow, and the therapist needs to develop this himself or herself by deliberately practicing mindfulness.[5] Finally, dialectical philosophy informs the treatment goals and skills taught in DBT, including the change-oriented goals of improving emotion regulation and interpersonal relationship effectiveness, and the more acceptance-oriented goals of learning mindfulness and the ability to tolerate distress. Patients need to learn to accept as much as they need to change. Learning to accept is, of course, a change in itself.

Structure of Treatment

Before discussing treatment strategies we will describe the different components of DBT, how it organizes and prioritizes the many problems typical of BPD patients, and how treatment is viewed as moving through stages as the patient's behavior becomes more controlled.

Modes of Treatment and Their Functions

In standard outpatient DBT, treatment includes four primary modes: individual therapy, skills training group, telephone consultation, and the therapists' consultation meeting. Other treatment modes may be better suited to other settings, such as inpatient or day treatment, but it is crucial that the modes used address the necessary functions of the comprehensive treatment. These functions are: (1) enhancing the patient's skills, (2) motivating the patient, (3) improving skills generalization, and (4) enhancing the therapist's skills and motivation.

Individual Therapy. All modes of DBT revolve around individual therapy, typically one hour per week. The individual therapist, as primary therapist in the treatment team, functions to motivate the patient, which in behavioral terms means to address the factors that interfere with the patient's use of skilled behavior, such as unhelpful contingencies, inhibiting emotions, and maladaptive thoughts and beliefs. The individual therapist may also teach skills in session, but the primary role is to help the patient deal with the numerous crises that inevitably arise from week to week. At the beginning of therapy, the therapist uses a number of specific strategies to get the patient to commit to specific targets for change. Throughout treatment, the individual therapist focuses the session on the change agenda, while also providing as much dependability, nurturance, and care as possible through validation of the patient's pain and the difficulty of the effort involved.

Skills Training. Skills training most often occurs in a group of six to eight patients with two skills trainers. The group typically meets weekly for 90 to 150 minutes. The training is heavily didactic, following a manual,[6] with the focus on skills instruction, strengthening, and generalization. The three modules of skills training—interpersonal effectiveness, emotion regulation, and distress tolerance skills—are all based around a core of mindfulness skills, taught between each of the others. Each module takes approximately eight weeks to complete, so that the entire curriculum can be taught in six months, although it is recommended that most patients go through the entire series twice to maximize learning. Each group session includes both a review of homework assigned the previous week and presentation of new material. Because of the emotional sensitivity of the patients, "process" discussions are discouraged. The relationship between skills trainers and group members is primarily that of teacher and student. Outside of skills training, their only contact is a phone call if the patient cannot come to the group, or in order to obtain the homework assignment. In spite of these limitations, the relationship is often one of warmth and attachment.

Telephone Consultation. In DBT, the individual therapist is available for telephone consultation with the patient for three purposes: (1) to help the patient use skills instead of engaging in parasuicidal or other maladaptive behaviors; (2) to coach the patients to generalize skills use in their everyday lives; and (3) to repair any perceived rifts in the therapeutic relationship between sessions.

Telephone consultations are *not* therapy by phone; rather, they are more like the time-outs that coaches call during the game. Patients are oriented to this important difference: that the consultation is usually limited to coaching on skills use or other more directive activity and is a brief interaction. Calls must be made *before* a maladaptive behavior has occurred. In addition, therapists must be clear about their own personal limits concerning phone calls—for example, "not after 10 P.M.," or "I may have to call you back if you get me at a bad time."

For calls related to suicide crisis behaviors, the target is risk assessment and safety, followed by coaching in the use of behavioral skills relevant to the current situation. For calls for help with skills or how to cope with a current problem until the next session, good questions to remember are: "What skills have you tried so far? What else do you think might work?" These questions keep the call on track, focused on the target of workable, patient-generated solutions. Finally, when the patient calls for relationship repair, the target is a decrease in the patient's sense of alienation or distance from the therapist, while not reinforcing dysfunctional behaviors at the same time.

Therapists' Consultation Meeting. The fourth major mode of DBT is the weekly consultation meeting. The consultation team strives to apply DBT in solving problems that come up in treatment, and encourages each clinician to observe his or her own personal limits with each patient and in each context. Members of the consultation team involved with the same patients do not say "treat my patient in this way," but instead consult with the patient on how to interact with the clinician. In this way they avoid the polarization so common in treatment teams of borderline patients where often some clinicians are seen as naive or too nurturing, while others are seen as either punitive or too rigid. In the DBT consultation team, although debate sometimes becomes heated, commitment to a dialectical philosophy allows conflict to produce synthesis, and relationships among clinicians to evolve and strengthen as they learn from and support one another's efforts to be both compassionate and effective.

Stages of Treatment and Targets

The overarching goal of DBT is to help the patient to create for herself a life worth living. This process has been conceptualized as proceeding through four stages, each with its own objectives and targets. The severely dysregulated or parasuicidal borderline patient is viewed as being in stage one, the goal of which is to move from severe behavioral dyscontrol to behavioral control. Stage two DBT has the objective of helping the patient move from "quiet desperation" to "ordinary happiness and unhappiness." Decreasing symptoms of post-traumatic stress and increasing emotional experiencing are targeted. A patient is said to be in stage three when she is able to outline her own objectives, such as resolving marital or family problems, problems at work or school, or problems in reaching an important life goal. Stage three proceeds into stage four when the objective becomes increasing the capacity for joy. Here, the patient defines her life as basically good, yet still feels that something is missing, such as more sense of meaning, a sense of contributing, or more opportunity for self-expression.

Pretreatment. Before treatment can begin, certain agreements between the therapist and patient must take place. Primary among these is agreement about the need to work on decreasing any suicidal or self-injurious behaviors. Until this agreement is reached, the patient remains in pretreatment, that is, this agreement remains the focus. The therapist uses various strategies to highlight the patient's need for change and to gain her commitment to target these behaviors. In addition, the patient is required to commit to attending individual therapy and skills training, to abide by any other clinic or research conditions, and to pay agreed-upon fees. In a collaborative spirit, the therapist also states agreement to standard ethical, professional behavior and to providing telephone consultation and needed therapy backup.

Stage One. Stage one DBT is the empirically validated and most unique part of the treatment, and the only stage we discuss in depth here. The targets for change are, in order of importance, suicidal and self-harm behaviors, behaviors that interfere with therapy, behaviors that interfere with the quality of life, and the need for improving skills.

Suicidal and self-harm behaviors include suicide crisis behaviors, suicide (or homicide) threats, parasuicidal urges and acts, suicide-related beliefs, expectancies, affects, and ideation. Suicide crisis behaviors and threats are never ignored. The therapist's response depends on several factors, including the assessed likelihood of suicide, the function of the behavior, the assessed skill level of the patient, and the reinforcement contingencies involved. DBT is not a suicide prevention program. Instead of resorting again and again to containment and hospitalization to "save" patients, DBT therapists must have some willingness to take risks in working with borderline patients. DBT is biased toward coaching the patient to stay out of the hospital, and emphasizing how behaviors that lead to hospitalization, and hospitalization itself, do not move her closer to her own goals. The therapist, as coach, stays near the patient in crisis to motivate and encourage her, while helping her generate more skillful solutions to her problems. However, hospitalization may be appropriate in circumscribed circumstances (for example: high suicide risk, psychosis).

The patient is asked to record parasuicidal acts and urges and suicidal ideation, including frequency and intensity, on a diary card which she brings to therapy. By parasuicide, we mean any deliberate, acute self-injury resulting in tissue damage or risk of death, regardless of intent. If a parasuicidal act has occurred, it is always discussed in the individual session, by means of a thorough chain analysis of events, actions, thoughts, and emotions leading up to and immediately following the act. Woven together with the chain analysis is a thorough solution analysis, where the patient and therapist generate ideas of more skillful behaviors she might have engaged in, and how to make them more likely to occur in the future. Also attended to, and challenged, are the patient's beliefs or expectations about suicide, such as a belief that if her cat dies she can no longer go on living, or that when she reaches 30, the age at which her mother died, she will be overwhelmed with the desire to die.

Therapy-interfering behavior is the second highest priority in this stage of treatment. It includes any behavior by the patient, such as non-attendance, not collaborating with the therapist, medication non-compliance, or continually overstepping the therapist's stated limits, that could threaten the progress of therapy or contribute to therapist burnout. Borderline patients often evince many such behaviors. The therapist orients the patient to what is expected of her, and to the therapist's own limits about such issues as phone calls, missed appointments, and in-session behaviors. The therapist points out how non-collaborating behaviors such as not doing homework or repeatedly changing topics during a session interfere with goals, and then targets these behaviors if they occur, using behavioral analysis, solution analysis, and commitment strategies. Therapists may also engage in therapy-interfering behaviors, such as being either too oriented to change or too oriented to acceptance and thus failing to balance the treatment, being late for appointments, being distracted or sleepy during sessions, not returning phone calls, being disrespectful of the patient, and so forth. The borderline patient tends to be vigilant about every aspect of the therapist's conduct toward her, and the therapist needs to be alert to, and willing to acknowledge, how his or her own behavior can interfere with the therapy. The consultation team can be especially helpful in identifying therapy-interfering behaviors of both therapist and patient.

Quality of life–interfering behaviors, while not life-threatening, interfere with the goal of establishing a life worth living. They constitute the third most important target of stage one DBT. Borderline patients may have many such behaviors, including substance abuse, bingeing/purging, unsafe sexual behaviors, shoplifting, homelessness, not having any activities or social contacts beyond therapy, and so on. Quality of life–interfering behaviors to be targeted are agreed upon early in treatment and noted on the diary card. Should these occur in a given week, behavioral analysis of them is conducted as a third priority. It is important to note that, despite the severity of some of these behaviors, therapy-interfering behaviors are given a higher priority because, if unattended, there soon may be no therapy.

Increasing behavioral skills of mindfulness, emotion regulation, interpersonal effectiveness, and distress tolerance is the fourth most important target of stage one individual DBT, but has a higher priority in the skills training group. In order to move from severe behavioral dyscontrol to behavioral control, successful generalization of skillful behavior in all relevant contexts is necessary. The mood dependency of borderline patients' behaviors can make skills acquisition difficult in individual therapy, hence the separate skills training group. In individual therapy, the objective is to help the patient integrate skills into her daily life.

Stage Two. Arrival at stage two is in itself an achievement, as patients have not only eliminated severe behavioral problems, but have begun to implement skillful behavior in nearly all aspects of their lives. Yet troubling behavior patterns often remain, including those related to unresolved traumatic life events such as sexual abuse, emotional trauma, neglect, significant losses, persistent rejections, and the effects on career and relationships of repeated past hospitalizations. In stage two DBT, the goal is acceptance of the fact of the trauma, loss, or abuse. The target is to decrease the self-invalidation associated with the trauma, including feeling somehow responsible for the abuse or loss, feeling ashamed for one's response to the abuse, or minimizing the severity of the trauma. In addition, the therapist assists the patient to evaluate herself non-judgmentally and appropriately and to increase her self-respect. As this stage of therapy draws to a close, it is important that the therapist reinforces self-respect by the patient that is independent of the therapist. This does not mean that the patient is not related to or does not depend on others, but that she is able to do so without invalidating herself. Perhaps the most important point about the concept of stages is to avoid the common, frequently tragic, mistake of focusing on past trauma with a patient who still has very poor emotion regulation and distress tolerance skills, which often leads to more suicidal and other problematic behavior.

Secondary Behavioral Targets. DBT also targets several other behavior patterns common in BPD patients that may be functionally related to the primary targets. One goal is to increase emotion regulation skills and decrease emotional reactivity. The goal is to help the patient move from intense rage to manageable anger, from paralyzing fear or panic to reasonable fear, from prostrate sadness to ambulatory sadness, and so forth. Two other secondary targets are directly related to emotion regulation. One is to increase emotional experiencing, encouraging the patient to feel her emotions rather than avoid or inhibit them. The other is to increase accurate identification and communication of emotions. The patient is taught about the body sensations, action urges, and after-effects associated with emotions.

Another important secondary target is increasing self-validation and decreasing self-invalidation, which can quickly deteriorate into self-hate and suicidal behaviors. Also targeted is any pattern of behavior which is crisis-generating. The goal is to increase realistic decision making, no small task when the ability to problem-solve is impacted by mood and by lack of modeling. Yet another secondary behavior pattern is a passive problem-solving style or "active-passivity" (active in getting others to solve the problem), which may result both from a biological predisposition and from learned helplessness. The goal is to teach the patient active problem-solving and how to structure her environment to help her control her own behavior.

DBT Strategies

Confronted with the enormous amount of change that a borderline patient must accomplish to attain a life worth living, and the patient's high level of distress, a therapist may focus relentlessly on change strategies, targeting the patient's thoughts, interpersonal behaviors, motives, abnormal biology, emotional reactivity, and intensity. This approach, however, runs the risk of recapitulating the invalidating environment and often contributes either to the patient feeling misunderstood and angry or to increased self-invalidation, perfectionistic standards, and hopelessness. Either way, little behavioral change is likely to occur. Alternatively, the therapist may focus primarily on validating the patient's pain, and on helping the patient to accept her problems, including parasuicide, frequent hospitalization, and interpersonal chaos. Once again, the invalidating environment is recreated, as the patient's experience that her life is intolerable as it is, and desperately needs to change, is not addressed. In DBT, change and acceptance strategies are woven together, integrated throughout the treatment, always in an effort to achieve a dialectical balance.

A therapist doing DBT therefore strives to balance the use of both acceptance strategies and change strategies. Balance involves movement between polarities as much as it does finding a middle way. DBT strategies are identified on four levels, each representing a particular acceptance/change dialectic. In *core strategies,* the key dialectic is between validation (acceptance) and problem-solving (change). In *communication style strategies,* it is between a reciprocal style (acceptance) and an irreverent one (change). In *case management strategies,* it is between intervening in the environment for the patient (acceptance) and being a consultant to the patient (change). The case is also managed in a dialectical manner through the therapists' consultation meetings. In addition, there is an overarching set of strategies that, because they use the conflict of the polarity to achieve synthesis, are termed *dialectical strategies.*

Dialectical Strategies

The most fundamental dialectical strategy is *balancing* all the other treatment strategies, as the needs of patient and situation constantly shift. Another is *entering the paradox,* where, much as in a Zen koan, the therapist simply highlights the constant paradoxes of life without attempting to explain them, instead modeling and teaching "both this and that," rather than "this or that." Another dialectical strategy is the use of *metaphor.* When collaboration has broken down, when the patient is feeling hopeless, or in many other situations, teaching, persuading, and making a point through metaphor often can be far more powerful than direct or literal communication. Borderline patients in particular seem to respond well to metaphor, and a helpful metaphor may be revisited in a variety of ways over the course of treatment. In the *devil's advocate* strategy, the patient's statement or commitment is strengthened by the therapist producing arguments for the opposing point of view, a strategy akin to some paradoxical interventions. The dialectical strategy of *extending* borrows a concept from the martial art aikido. The partner's blow is not opposed, but rather flowed with and pulled beyond its intended target. For example, the patient's statement: "If I don't get X . . . I may as well kill myself" might be met with: "This is very serious. How can we talk about X, when your life is on the line? Perhaps we should think about hospitalization." The *wise mind* strategy refers to the belief, and communication to the patient, that each person has inherent wisdom, knowledge of what is best for her in each situation, and can learn to attend to this once emotional dysregulation is controlled. *Making lemonade out of lemons* is a dialectical strategy of making the best of a difficult situation, always remembering that to make lemonade one will also need sugar (validation). In *allowing natural change,* the therapist accepts the fact that nature and the patient's world are constantly changing, and therefore makes no special effort to shield the patient from change in the treatment parameters or the environment. In *dialectical assessment,* the therapist continuously seeks to understand the patient in a situational context, constantly asking: "What is left out?"

Core Strategies: Validation and Problem-Solving

Validation. This involves communicating to the patient that her responses make sense in the current context. The therapist actively accepts the patient as she is; does not discount, pathologize, trivialize, or interpret the patient's response; but instead searches for what is valid, true, and relevant, amplifies it if necessary, and then reflects it back to the patient. Cognitive distortion is a common consequence of emotional dysregulation, and borderline patients are frequently quite dysregulated. Validation strategies involve looking for the nugget of gold (what is valid) in the bucket of sand (what may not be valid). Attention to the gold does not preclude attention to the sand, but it is in finding the gold that the validation takes place.

In DBT, validation is considered necessary for change. It creates the context for change, balances change strategies, and teaches self-validation. How much validation is needed will vary across different patients and, within patients, will vary across stage of therapy, topics addressed, and the stress level in the patient's current situation. Typically, early in therapy, when addressing very painful issues and when the stress level is especially high, the need for validation is likely to be higher. Over time, patients are taught and encouraged to trust their own responses and to validate themselves.

Linehan describes six levels of validation strategies.[7] First is simple, unbiased listening. Being actively attended to without judgment usually is experienced as validating. In level two validation, the therapist accurately reflects back to the patient what he or she is hearing, without any attempt at interpretation. Often the therapist's accurate reflection to the patient provides an opening for a level three validation, accurate reading of emotions. A therapist who is good at reading the complex emotional cues of very dysregulated patients is skillful indeed, and most patients appreciate this skill. In level four validation, the therapist communicates to the patient that her response is reasonable given her biology or learning history. For example, the therapist might say, "It is understandable that you would be frightened when you saw a strange man on your doorstep, given that you have been raped." The risk of validating a patient only on the basis of her past learning is that the therapist may highlight for the patient how different she is from "normal" people as a result of her life experience. More validating, usually, is validation in terms of present circumstances (level five), such as, "It is understandable that you were frightened by a strange man on your doorstep when you were home alone." Finding a kernel of truth in the patient's reaction, and amplifying it in this way, can be very effective.

The highest level of validation described in DBT is called radical genuineness. This level involves the therapist being awake in the moment to the moment, and it is expressed through therapist behavior which is natural and genuine rather than role-defined and "professional." Borderline patients in particular may chafe under role-defined therapist limits, which they often perceive as arbitrary, insincere, unpredictable, or parental. When a therapist is radically genuine, he or she communicates implicitly that the patient is not fragile, but can tolerate being spoken to by the therapist as he or she would speak to a friend or family member who is distressed or behaving maladaptively.

This level of validation is employed when the therapist tells the patient, "When you repeatedly come late to session, I feel my motivation to work decrease. I don't want that to happen so you've got to keep me motivated, so I can motivate you!" Thus, radical genuineness need not necessarily be soothing to the patient, but it does validate the patient's inherent capability.

Problem-Solving. Effective problem-solving is most likely to occur in a context of validation, which may elevate mood and hence improve problem-solving capability. The therapist and patient must first understand the target behavior (problem) as specifically as possible, and accept that it is indeed a problem. The primary strategy used to understand the problem is behavior analysis, described below. Once the problem is fully described, insight and didactic strategies are used to help the patient accept and better understand the problem and what may influence it. The therapist then helps the patient to change using solution analysis strategies, orienting the patient to their role in potential solutions and eliciting the patient's commitment to the solution. Throughout, problem behaviors are viewed as resulting from various combinations of skills deficits, unhelpful contingencies, faulty cognitions, and inhibiting emotions. Solutions typically involve changes in one or more of these four areas (see "Problem-Solving Procedures" below).

Behavior analysis. Problem-solving needs to begin with a definition and thorough assessment of the problem at hand. The goal of a behavioral analysis is to uncover a sequential rendering of the preceding vulnerabilities, prompting events, interpretations, feelings, urges, and observable behaviors that came before, and followed, a specifically defined problem behavior. For example, the diary card indicates, or the patient says, "I've been depressed all week." After checking to make sure there have been no suicidal behaviors (which would take priority), the DBT therapist wants to know in detail what the patient means by "depressed," how intense it was day by day, what might have prompted it, what she said to herself about the event or feeling, what she did then, and what occurred after that. At first, patients unused to examining their thoughts and feelings in this way may answer with some variant of "I don't know" or "I've been depressed all my life." The therapist probes further about the patient's mood, beginning with asking again when it began. Now the patient says, "I started feeling bad when my husband said he was fed up with me. I didn't get out of bed all day. I just got up today because I had to come see you." The problem is now more defined: there is a prompting event, what the patient's husband said, and a series of problem behaviors, beginning with staying in bed. The therapist continues to search for the missing links from the events before, during, and after the behavior, to understand the antecedents and consequences. The more links in the chain, the more possible solutions there are. For example, what happened when she stayed in bed all day? Eventually, her husband brought her meals on a tray and apologized. By then, the patient felt ashamed and hopeless and could not face going to work.

This exhaustive chain analysis of all the factors occurring before, during, and after the problem behavior may seem tedious at first for the therapist not trained in behavior therapy but, after experience, is likely to be viewed as indispensable. The patient not used to this therapy model may also want to avoid behavior analysis, which exposes her to her own painful emotions and maladaptive behaviors. The therapist encourages the patient, stays on track, validates the patient's pain, difficulty, or frustration, and continues to ask, "What happened next?" Acting as a detective, the therapist makes no assumptions, but adopts an almost naive style. At the beginning of therapy, the therapist will conduct behavioral analyses of the most significant past suicide attempts or other high-priority targets. But as therapy progresses, the therapist will each week be choosing one or more prioritized problems from the previous week, as indicated on the diary card. Each link in the chain may suggest one or more solutions, which will require some change in the patient's behavior or the environment.

Problem-Solving Procedures

Once a behavior-in-situation has been analyzed and understood, and possible solutions evaluated by the therapist and patient, implementing those solutions may require some combination of four sets of behavior therapy procedures: skills training, contingency management, cognitive modification, and exposure. If the patient simply does not know how to behave more skillfully, skills training is indicated. If, however, the patient knows what to do, but is punished or not reinforced for doing so, or is reinforced for doing otherwise, contingency management is called for. If skilled behavior is impeded by the patient's beliefs, attitudes, and thoughts, cognitive modification procedures may be helpful. If the patient is unable to act more skillfully because of strong emotional reactions, exposure procedures that allow those reactions to habituate may be useful.

Skills Training Procedures. These can teach new skills and also facilitate the use of learned, but unused skills. Skills acquired need to be strengthened and to generalize across situations. The individual therapist and skills trainers may help the patient acquire skills by direct instruction, by modeling, such as by thinking out loud in front of the patient or by self-disclosing his or her own use of skilled behaviors, and particularly through role play and behavior rehearsal. Fledgling skills then need to be strengthened by further in-session behavior rehearsals and imaginal practice, as well as *in vivo* practice. Any small movements toward more skilled behavior on the patient's part need to be noticed and promptly reinforced by the therapist, even though this means reinforcing still unskilled behavior (shaping). Skills are also strengthened by direct feedback and coaching from the therapist, conveyed in a non-judgmental manner focused on performance rather than inferred motives. Borderline patients are particularly sensitive to critical feedback, yet this often needs to be given, so it is best surrounded by positive feedback. Skills generalization is enhanced by *in vivo* behavior rehearsal assignments and also by between-session telephone consultation. Other skills generalization procedures might include having the patient tape-record the therapy session for later review, which provides repetition, may lead to new insights, and provides for learning occurring in the home context. Changing the environment to one that reinforces skilled behavior may also be necessary. Examples of this are having the patient make public commitments, or having the therapist meet with a couple or family.

Contingency Management Procedures. If unhelpful reinforcement contingencies are a problem, the therapist tries to arrange for target-relevant adaptive behaviors to be reinforced, and for target-relevant maladaptive behaviors to be extinguished through lack of reinforcement or, when this does not work, the use of punishment. The primary reinforcer used by the DBT therapist is his or her behavior in relationship with the patient. The therapist observes and consciously directs, in a contingent manner, his or her warmth versus coolness, closeness versus distance, approval versus disapproval, and other dimensions of the therapist's behavior in the relationship. Some may question whether this is a "manipulative" therapeutic relationship. In fact, our natural responses in all relationships function as consequences that do influence others' behavior. The main difference here is the intended beneficiary of the use of contingencies (usually the patient), and their more deliberate application. For the therapeutic relationship to be used contingently, it must be highly valued by the patient. The DBT therapist works hard to establish a strong therapeutic relationship, to "get money in the bank" in order to have it to spend, by developing an attachment between therapist and patient that is mutual and genuine.

The therapist also attends to contingencies outside the therapeutic relationship that may need to change. Suggesting to patients that their maladaptive behavior may be maintained by reinforcement can be experienced as invalidating. "Are you saying that I injure myself in order to get into the hospital?" the patient may respond. It is helpful to discuss with patients how reinforcement works regardless of intent or awareness, and that even unintended consequences influence behavior.

Reinforcement and punishment are defined by their effects on behavior, which can only be determined by experience with a particular patient and behavior. Although praise is a reinforcer for most people, some borderline patients feel embarrassed, fear raised expectations, or for some other reason find praise aversive. The therapist then would need to expose the patient to praise, and make it reinforcing by repeatedly pairing it with a reinforcer (respondent conditioning). For most patients, therapist relationship behaviors that are reinforcing include the expression of approval, interest, concern, and care, liking or admiring the patient, reassurance regarding the dependability of the relationship, direct validation, being responsive to the patient's requests, and increasing attention from, or contact with, the therapist. Therapists need to take care that they do not engage in these behaviors immediately following some maladaptive behavior of the patient, even though it may be their natural urge to do so.

Withholding, or arranging for the non-occurrence of, reinforcers that previously followed a behavior may gradually extinguish it, but behaviors on an extinction schedule typically show a "burst" in responding before they decrease. If the therapist then backs down and provides a reinforcer, he or she will now have reinforced an increased intensity of the behavior. Battles should therefore be picked wisely, so to speak, and targets for extinction guided by the hierarchy of targets. It is also essential to help the patient find another response that will meet with reinforcement, and to soothe and validate the patient regarding the emotional effects of being on an extinction schedule.

Punishment should be used with great care in behavior therapy, because it can lead to strong emotional reactions that interfere with learning, strengthen a self-invalidating style, and fail to teach specific adaptive behavior. Nonetheless, it is sometimes necessary or helpful, usually when very high priority behavior is still occurring and is reinforced primarily by consequences that are not under the therapist's control, so that extinction cannot be used. Examples are the affect regulation that frequently accompanies self-injury, and inpatient psychiatric admissions that may reinforce such behavior for some patients. The most common punishers in DBT are the therapist's disapproval, confrontation, or reduction in the therapist's availability. With emotionally sensitive individuals, disapproval needs to be mild in order to be most effective. Care must be taken to punish specific behaviors rather than the person, and to observe the distinction between punishment and punitiveness. Support from the consultation team helps a therapist to avoid expressing vindictive or hostile feelings under the guise of being therapeutic. Other punishment procedures used in DBT include overcorrection (doing the reverse behavior or undoing the effects of the behavior and going beyond that), taking a "vacation from therapy" in which access to the DBT individual therapist is made contingent on some commitment or behavior change, and, as a last resort, termination of therapy. Although a strong commitment to therapy is required of both patient and therapist, just as in a marriage, it is also the case that not all marriages work out and not all therapies do either. This rare event in DBT generally can be avoided by appropriate attention to the "observing limits" procedures, to which we now turn.

Observing limits procedures. Contingency management procedures are applied in DBT not only to behaviors that interfere with the patient's life, but also to those that interfere with the therapist's life. Therapists strive to be aware of their own limits and take responsibility for being clear with the patient about these limits and the consequences for moving beyond them. This is a somewhat different concept from "setting limits," which typically is viewed as something for the good of the patient, to help her "establish boundaries," rather than for the good of the therapist. DBT takes a dialectical stance, viewing boundaries as essentially context-driven and relational. A patient's distressed call in the middle of the night may be unacceptable to me, whereas such a call from my best friend may not be. This is because my personal limits are different in each situation, not because the act of calling is in itself pathological. People often need what others are not willing to give. Rather than feeling guilty for attending to their own needs instead of just the good of the patient, DBT therapists must observe their own limits in order to prevent the burnout and dropout from treatment that otherwise are likely. The extent and content of these limits are not defined by DBT, but are those that are natural to this therapist, with this patient, at this time, and in this situation. Since there are no rules to fall back on, the therapist needs to be self-aware, receptive to feedback from the consultation team, and assertive with the patient. Limits are often not known until they are closely approached. Common areas where therapists need to observe and discuss their limits with patients are frequency or utility of telephone calls, suicidal behavior, aggressive behavior, and sporadic attendance or other non-engagement in the treatment. We have found that when one's own limits are clearly delineated and described as something about oneself rather than about patient pathology or what is best for the patient, and when the behaviors that cross these limits are clearly specified in a non-judgmental way, many battles over how the patient "should" behave can be resolved or avoided.

Cognitive Modification Procedures. DBT differs from cognitive therapy in placing a less central emphasis on cognition. Instead, thoughts, beliefs, assumptions, and expectations are seen in DBT as just one category of behaviors that influence, and are reciprocally influenced by, transactions with emotional processes, overt behavior, and environmental factors. DBT also differs from cognitive therapy in its emphasis on first validating the wisdom in the patient's cognitions. This helps decrease the likelihood that the patient will interpret the cognitive model as "It's all in your head" or "It's your own fault; just change your attitude," which they typically have heard incessantly. In general, however, all of the standard cognitive therapy procedures are consistent with, and used in, DBT. The therapist stays alert for distortions of cognitive content and style. Cognitive content refers to negative automatic thoughts and maladaptive beliefs, attitudes, or schemas, frequently concerning the self as worthless, defective, unlovable, and vulnerable, and others as excessively admired, despised, or feared. Problems of cognitive style in BPD include dichotomous thinking (splitting) and dysfunctional allocation of attention (ruminating, dissociating, and so forth). The therapist tries to help patients change these contents and styles by (1) teaching self-observation through mindfulness practice and written assignments; (2) identifying maladaptive cognitions, for instance when conducting a behavioral analysis, and by pointing to non-dialectical thinking; (3) generating alternative, more adaptive cognitive content and style in session and for homework assignments; and (4) developing guidelines for when patients should trust versus suspect their own interpretations, since self-validation is often also a goal. The concept of "wise mind" can be useful here. To the extent that emotions are high, trust cognition less.

DBT recognizes a special case of cognitive modification, namely, *contingency clarification procedures*. It is extremely important that the patient understand the contingencies that currently operate in her life, including in the therapeutic relationship, and see how her behaviors are influenced by them. It is particularly helpful with borderline patients to have very clear rules, which the patient nonetheless may have difficulty learning or following. Consistent use of contingencies and clear communication are the best response to this.

Exposure Procedures. One of the greatest successes of behavior therapy has been the treatment of many anxiety disorders. The core of these treatments involves repeated exposure to the anxiety-provoking stimulus or situation, while assuring that the normal escape or avoidance response does not occur. This basic approach is extended in DBT to other emotions such as guilt, shame, and anger. When these emotions are problematic in themselves, lead to dysfunctional avoidance behavior, inhibit the use of skills, or are associated with PTSD symptoms, exposure procedures may be useful. During stage two of treatment, when maladaptive behaviors are under control, more structured protocols for PTSD may be developed, but typically, exposure and response prevention are done more informally. Space does not permit a detailed description here, but the primary steps are (1) to orient the patient, often using a story or metaphor that teaches the basic phenomenon of habituation; (2) to provide non-reinforced exposure, meaning exposure that does not meet with an outcome that could reinforce the emotional response; (3) to block action and expressive tendencies associated with the problem emotion, especially behavioral or cognitive avoidance; and (4) to enhance the patient's control over exposure as much as possible, for example by graduating intensity, since it is easier to tolerate aversive events when one experiences one's self as having some control.

Most of the change strategies used in DBT (and some of the acceptance strategies) can be viewed as involving emotional exposure. This occurs when scrutinizing the patient's recent behavior and experience in a behavioral analysis; in skills training, such as practicing behaviors in interpersonal situations that generate discomfort; in contingency strategies, by exposure to the therapist's disapproval or approval that may set off feelings of shame or fear, anger, or pride; and in mindfulness practice, where the object may be to observe, in a non-judgmental manner, the ebb and flow of one's thoughts or feelings. A thorough understanding of the importance of exposure for changes in emotional behavior can therefore help the therapist to take advantage of the innumerable opportunities that present themselves during all aspects of therapy sessions to work directly on the patient's emotional reactions, using the principle of graduated exposure.

Stylistic Strategies

The therapist's style of communication is used strategically in DBT. When the therapist is effectively reciprocal, that is, responsive, engaged, self-disclosing, and genuine, he or she is employing strategies that communicate acceptance to the patient. At other times a therapist may want to get a patient's attention, prompt her to reconsider a favorite assumption, or help her to look at her behavior with new eyes. Irreverent communication strategies are especially helpful in helping patients to change perspective in the moment, often through the unexpected comment, directness, humor, or all three.

Reciprocal Communication. This style is the norm in DBT. The therapist takes the patient's agenda seriously, and responds in a relevant way to the content of her communications and to her questions. The style is generally warm and empathic. One form of reciprocal communication is self-disclosure. Two types of self-disclosure are used in DBT: self-involving self-disclosure and personal self-disclosure. The first type involves the therapist disclosing his or her reactions to the patient's behavior. When the therapist says, "I'm thrilled to hear how skillful you were in that tough situation with your landlord," self-disclosure can be a powerful reinforcer. Similarly, when the therapist discloses his or her reaction to the patient crossing stated limits, this serves as a contingency clarifier or punisher. The therapist tries to make clear the effects of the patient's behavior on others. This is feedback that others may not give effectively because of fear of the patient's reaction (devastation and/or anger). Self-disclosure of reactions to limit crossing are very important, as many borderline patients previously have been terminated by therapists, often without realizing what they had done until it was too late.

Personal self-disclosure is used for modeling. The therapist discloses professional information including training and experience in working with suicidal patients. He or she also discloses personal information about age, marital status, and so on, according to comfort level. More important, however, the DBT therapist discloses to the patient his or her own experience with problems in living, for the purpose of modeling coping skills, including both successes and failures. The problems in living of borderline patients are often far different from those of their therapists. However, it is often possible to find some common ground, such as being a woman in a sexist society, having lived on a very limited income, being a shy person, or some other shared experience. Therapists should be careful about disclosing current serious problems to patients, or in any way blurring the line between who is the therapist and who is the patient.

Irreverent Communication. This refers to a style that balances reciprocal communication. It does not meet the patient where he or she is. The therapist may reframe something the patient has just said in an unorthodox way. For example, the patient says, "I'm tired of being a polite little mental patient." The therapist responds, "What are you tired of, being polite, or being a mental patient?" Used well, such a communication gets the patient's attention and swiftly refocuses the session. Another type of irreverent strategy is to use a very direct, concrete, and candid approach. The DBT therapist does not treat the patient as fragile, but matter-of-factly discusses relevant issues including suicidal behaviors, ideation, and threats. It is not that the therapist is unemotional, but that the communication style used cuts across the grain of the patient's intensity, treating weighty matters both lightly and with seriousness. A therapist might also use a confrontational tone irreverently, for example: "You didn't for a minute think I'd believe that, did you?" Use of this tone depends on a strong alliance. Another irreverent strategy is calling the patient's bluff, which is also the dialectical strategy of extending. For example, a patient who hates skills training but is very attached to her individual therapist says, "I'm quitting group." The therapist, not missing a beat, says, "Dropping out of therapy, eh?" The therapist is then careful to provide a net. After a moment he or she says, "Let's talk about how you can feel more comfortable in group." Whenever the therapist adopts the opposite level of intensity to that of the patient, such as being relaxed when the patient is intense, or playful when the patient is balky or silent, irreverent communication strategies are being used. These strategies pick up the pace, move the patient from where she might be stuck, and often provide moments of humor. Judicious use of irreverent strategies always involves being sensitive to its potential for straining the therapeutic relationship, and should be surrounded by validation, especially genuineness.

262 Clive J. Robins and Cedar R. Koons

Case Management Strategies

Borderline patients often have come to adopt a passive problem-solving style. They may get others mobilized to help them in crisis, but when they are unable to care for themselves effectively, they lose confidence and self-respect. DBT strongly emphasizes teaching and coaching the patient in how to manage her own environment, be it her psychiatrist, parole officer, academic dean, landlord, or lover, rather than intervening in the environment on the patient's behalf, except in very limited circumstances where such intervention is deemed necessary.

Consultation-to-the-Patient. This strategy emphasizes the conviction that the patient can learn the skills she needs to manage her environment in most circumstances. The strategy has three main objectives: (1) to teach patients the essential skills to manage their own lives, (2) to demonstrate respect for the patients' abilities and foster their self-respect, and (3) to decrease "splitting" among persons in the patient's network. Whatever short-term losses might occur as a result of initial lack of expertise or experience will be far outweighed by the long-term gains of developing effective self-care skills. In the long run, it is more helpful to teach a person to fish than to give her a fish.

The DBT therapist generally does not consult with anyone outside the DBT team about the patient without her being present. General information about the treatment program is given, including the philosophy of treatment and the individual or program limits. Many professionals are used to calling a borderline patient's therapist to get guidance on how to respond to the patient in a crisis. When this occurs, the DBT therapist tries to get as much information about what is going on as the professional will give and provides any necessary information the patient cannot give, or confirms or corrects any information given. Following this, the therapist tells the professionals, be they police, rescue squads, emergency room personnel, inpatient treating clinicians, or housing supervisors, "Follow your usual procedures." The therapist then asks to speak with the patient and coaches the patient on how best to interact or cope with the situation.

Environmental Intervention. Clearly there are times when the approach described above is not ethical, feasible, or effective. When the patient currently is unable or unwilling to act on her own, no matter how well coached, and the outcome is so important that the short-term gain is worth the loss in learning, the therapist should intervene. For example, in some circumstances, unless the therapist intervenes, the patient might die, lose her public assistance or access to health care, or be committed involuntarily to a state hospital when it is not in her best interest. In addition, the therapist may be required to intervene more with a minor patient. Finally, DBT recognizes that there are times when intervening is the humane thing to do and will cause no harm.

When appropriate, the therapist may provide information about the patient to others independently of the patient, such as when she is unconscious. It is crucial that only needed information be exchanged, to protect confidentiality and communicate respect for the patient. The therapist also may act as an advocate for the patient in situations where it is absolutely necessary, for example, helping her get evaluated for PTSD by the V.A. Rating Board for a rape which occurred while she was in the military. Some bureaucracies will not respond to a patient's requests, no matter how skillful, without a professional's recommendation. Finally, the therapist may, at times, enter the patient's environment, for instance by going to get the patient when her car breaks down on the way to therapy. This would be the humane thing to do and would be unlikely to cause harm, since it is not likely that car problems would be reinforced. It is important for the therapist to observe his or her own limits whenever the issue of entering the patient's environment appears, and to recognize the difference between *in vivo* coaching or support and taking on the patient's responsibilities.

Concluding Remarks on the Therapeutic Relationship in DBT

In writing this brief chapter, we struggled with how to provide an overview of DBT comprehensive enough to adequately represent it, while also discussing DBT's approach to the therapeutic relationship. In closing, we highlight some of the ways in which DBT's approach to the therapeutic relationship is most evident or receives particular emphasis.

Theoretical Foundation

In DBT, an important function of theory is to help the therapist understand and deal with the effects of common BPD behaviors on therapists. The biosocial theory is intended to influence therapists' attitudes. Its concept of the invalidating environment leads naturally to the emphasis on validation strategies in the treatment, and the overarching position of dialectics leads to a therapeutic relationship that pays attention to dialectics, balance, and rapid movement back and forth on the teeter-totter that the therapist is on with the patient.

Treatment Targets

Problematic interactions in the therapeutic relationship are directly targeted for change in DBT. These include a variety of therapy-interfering behaviors of both therapist and patient, which are a priority second only to life-threatening and self-injurious behaviors. The secondary targets of DBT, such as self-invalidation by the patient and emotion dysregulation, frequently show up in session in response to interactions between patient and therapist. These interactions are analyzed collaboratively and modified when possible. Finally, DBT pays attention particularly to in-session behavior, probably to a far greater extent than behavior therapies in general.

Modes of Treatment

Each mode of therapy has its own set of parameters for the therapeutic relationship. Relatively unique to DBT is the use of planned telephone or other consultation availability between sessions, which tends to generate a very different type of therapeutic relationship than is prescribed in some other treatments. DBT also emphasizes another therapeutic relationship, that between the therapist and the consultation team, who provide the support and guidance that is so helpful in this work.

Treatment Strategies

Every strategy suggests some form of therapeutic relationship, but we highlight several. The dialectical strategy of *allowing natural change* to occur is very different from emphasizing the need for structure and consistency in the treatment of borderline patients. At the level of core validation strategies, a good therapeutic relationship is seen in DBT as having healing qualities of its own for many patients, even though usually not sufficient for the goal of a life well worth living. The emphasis on validation itself, and particularly the use of cheerleading strategies, also sets DBT apart from some other treatments. Finally, the position of radical genuineness—largely being one's natural, rather than role-defined, self—leads to a very different type of therapeutic relationship than a more formal, reserved, or superior stance.

Many of the core behavioral strategies also suggest aspects of the therapeutic relationship as central and sometimes different from other approaches. These include the therapist as detective, conducting behavioral analyses; therapist as model; therapist as teacher; therapist as reinforcer/punisher; and therapist as exposure stimulus, as when the patient is exposed to closeness or other adaptive feelings or behaviors that she usually avoids.

At the level of stylistic strategies, the therapist quite deliberately varies his or her interpersonal style. Reciprocal and irreverent styles are poles apart both in the therapist's behavior and in their impact on the therapeutic relationship.

Characteristics of the Therapist

DBT, done well, requires the ability to behave and relate in a number of often highly contrasting ways. Since most of us tend to have our strengths toward one end of most dimensions, all DBT therapists have to be aware of the polar oppositions that they also need to strengthen in their repertoire. The primary dimension on which DBT therapists strive to maintain dialectical balance is the dialectic of acceptance and change. An excessive orientation toward either is therapy-interfering behavior, yet strength in both may require development by the therapist, with the help of the consultation team. Other variants of this acceptance/change dialectic are nurturing and taking care of the patient on the one hand, and a benevolent demandingness of the patient on the other; a compassionate flexibility regarding treatment parameters on one hand, and a non-moving centeredness about treatment principles on the other.

In closing, we note that our description of DBT includes a great many elements, and it is not clear empirically which are important. In fact, although DBT is the only psychosocial treatment to date shown to have efficacy, the database demonstrating this is still small. Our greatest hope is that, on the basis of research, DBT will continually evolve, and that it and other treatments will be found to be effective in helping change the lives of those we describe as having borderline personality disorder.

Notes

1. Linehan MM. 1993. *Cognitive-Behavioral Treatment of Borderline Personality Disorder*. New York: Guilford Press; Linehan MM. 1987. "Dialectical Behavior Therapy: A Cognitive-Behavioral Approach to

Parasuicide." *Journal of Personality Disorders,* 1:328–333; Linehan MM, Armstrong HE, Suarez A, Allmon D, Heard HL. 1991. "Cognitive-Behavioral Treatment of Chronically Parasuicidal Borderline Patients." *Archives of General Psychiatry,* 48:1060–1064; Linehan MM, Tutek DA, Heard HL, and Armstrong HE. 1994. "Interpersonal Outcome of Cognitive Behavioral Treatment for Chronically Suicidal Borderline Patients." *American Journal of Psychiatry,* 151:1771–1776.

2. Linehan MM, Heard HL, and Armstrong HE. 1993. "Naturalistic Follow-up of a Behavioral Treatment for Chronically Parasuicidal Borderline Patients." *Archives of General Psychiatry,* 50:971–974.

3. Koons CR and Robins CJ. 1998. *Efficacy of Dialectical Behavior Therapy with Borderline Women Veterans: A Randomized Controlled Trial.* Manuscript in preparation, Durham V.A. Medical Center.

4. Linehan MM and Kehrer CA. 1993. "Borderline Personality Disorder." In DH Barlow (Ed.), *Clinical Handbook of Psychological Disorders,* 2nd ed. New York: Guilford Press, pp. 346–441.

5. Lynch RE and Robins CJ. 1997. "Treatment of Borderline Personality Disorder Using Dialectical Behavior Therapy." *Journal of the California Alliance for the Mentally Ill,* 8(1):47–49.

6. Linehan MM. 1993. *Skills Training Manual for Treating Borderline Personality Disorder.* New York: Guilford Press.

7. Linehan MM. 1997. "Validation and Psychotherapy." In A. Bohart and L. Greenberg (Eds.), *Empathy Reconsidered: New Directions in Theory, Research, and Practice.* Washington, D.C.: American Psychological Association, pp. 353–392.

11 Treating Chronically Traumatized People: Known Approaches and New Approaches

Emily Newman

Our understanding of the effects of interpersonal violence has grown enormously in the past fifteen years. We know that sexual and physical assault in childhood and adulthood results in a range of psychological difficulties, and we have explanatory models to guide case formulation and treatment planning with patients who have experienced these traumatic events. Clinicians in the field have developed considerable expertise in treating victims of different types of interpersonal trauma, such as rape and childhood sexual abuse. Our society's most severely traumatized people, however, generally lack access to traditional psychotherapeutic services and often do not receive effective treatment. Experiences of chronic interpersonal victimization are often also compounded by racism, poverty, and ongoing community violence. This constellation of past and present traumatic stressors can make accessing and using psychotherapy more difficult. The purpose of this chapter is to address how to make trauma-focused treatment relevant and available to these chronically traumatized people.

Several case examples will serve to illustrate what I mean by the term "chronically traumatized." Valerie is a 39-year-old African-American woman who grew up in the inner city. She was subjected to sadistic physical abuse by her mother; for example, her mother would punish her by making her kneel on grains of rice for hours if she had misbehaved. Valerie's mother's boyfriend began having sexual intercourse with her when she was 8 years old, and continued to do so until his death when she was 18. When Valerie told her mother about the abuse, she was punished. Valerie left home when she was 15, and began using crack cocaine and working as a prostitute. During this period she was sexually assaulted twice, once by a group of men. In addition, her three children were removed from her custody. Bill is a 23-year-old Latino man who was raised in a violent home by parents who abused drugs and alcohol. He was sexually abused from ages 4 to 7 by a neighbor who ran a child pornography ring. The neighbor gave Bill hallucinogenic drugs, sodomized him, and forced him to perform sexual acts with other children while he photographed them. Bill went on in adolescence to deal cocaine, and witnessed several deaths by shooting on the streets. Sam is a 21-year-old man of mixed-race ethnicity who was sexually and physically abused in childhood by his mother, who was later institutionalized with a diagnosis of schizophrenia. Sam was often physically attacked as a teenager because of his appearance; he cross-dressed in women's clothes. At age 20 Sam was badly beaten in a mugging, and required facial surgery. Sandra is a 22-year-old Caucasian woman who grew up in a strictly religious family. She was sexually abused by her father, a minister, and by her two older brothers throughout her childhood. She ran away from home at age 15 and worked as a prostitute. At age 17 she married a man who later stabbed and almost killed her. She had been pregnant at the time, and delivered a stillborn girl one month after the assault. These cases of repetitive, unremitting violence and abuse throughout childhood and adulthood illustrate the type of chronically traumatized person for whom the following discussion is most relevant.

Background

There is now a large volume of epidemiological data which documents the prevalence of posttraumatic stress disorder (PTSD) in populations that have experienced sexual or physical violence, including rape,[1] domestic violence,[2] and childhood physical and sexual abuse.[3] We also know that repeated episodes of violence add to the cumulative severity of PTSD.[4] In addition to PTSD, researchers have described the prevalence of many comorbid diagnoses in this population, including mood disorders, other anxiety disorders, eating and dissociative disorders, somatization disorders, personality disorders, and substance abuse disorders.[5]

Some theoreticians would argue that well-defined DSM-IV diagnoses are only one aspect of these patients' problems. The effects of early and repeated abuse and neglect, particularly at the hands of caretaker adults, can result in basic problems with self-image and self-esteem, affect regulation and tolerance, and abilities to relate to other human beings. This pattern of difficulty has been described as "complex PTSD"[6] or "Disorders of Extreme Stress Not Otherwise Specified" (DESNOS).[7] As an alternative to looking at particular diagnostic categories, some authors have conceptualized the difficulties that chronically traumatized people have as deficits in self capacities.[8]

All of the conceptualizations described above are useful in informing the treatment of chronically traumatized patients. The simplest way I have found to organize my own thinking about these cases, however, is to define five basic "problem areas" common in chronically traumatized people; being mindful of these issues helps to guide me in making treatment choices. The basic areas of concern, as I see them, are as follows: first, there is the difficulty traumatized patients have in the areas of trust, power, and control; second, traumatized patients have trouble feeling an internal sense of safety and self-efficacy; third, traumatized patients struggle with the issue of shame; fourth, they are unable to understand the concept of self-care; and finally, difficulties in these areas often lead to reenactments in therapy and repeated revictimization in the world. Recognizing the universality of these basic difficulties helps to define the goals of therapy with chronically traumatized people. They are: to help patients learn to trust appropriately, to empower them to exercise control in their own lives and over their own internal experience, and to decrease their shame and increase their self-esteem and self-care capacities. Being mindful of these goals in the context of managing reenactments in therapy will lead to increasing safety and reducing revictimization in patients' lives.

In the following sections I will outline the genesis of chronically traumatized patients' difficulties in each area, the basic treatment strategy to address the problems, and some ways to modify the structure and content of traditional dynamic psychotherapy to best operationalize these treatment principles.

The Effects of Trauma and an Approach to Treatment: Specific Focus Areas

Trust, Power, Control

Abused children experience unpredictability and violence at the hands of caretaking adults, whom they need for stability and comfort. Powerful adults who are supposed to be unquestionably trustworthy are in fact just the opposite. Oftentimes these parents or other adults say to the child, "trust me, I won't hurt you," when in fact they are intruding upon and hurting the child for their own ends. The effects of this form of violation are so profoundly damaging that they cannot be overstated. We cannot assume any given level of basic trust for individuals who have experienced chronic abuse, because they have no basis on which to assume people are trustworthy. Traumatized people are least likely to trust authority figures, because they have an expectation that people with power will intentionally misuse it. They have no reason to believe the words of those who try to convince them of their trustworthiness since they have been lied to before.

Adults who were abused in childhood lack the ability to feel a sense of control over their environment. This is because their early home environment was, in fact, frequently and unpredictably disrupted by violence. For example, children who are abused by a substance-using adult see that person behave one way when sober, and a completely different way when drunk or high. Perpetrators of sexual abuse often use the element of surprise to maintain control over victims; victims of childhood sexual abuse are often assaulted at night, when they are asleep. Traumatized children are intruded upon, and they are unable to control the things that are done to them. Therefore, they are unable to master some of the basic developmental tasks of childhood, including gaining a sense of autonomy and control over their bodies and their actions, and understanding the effects of their actions on others, and vice versa. Traumatized children cannot master these developmental tasks because their autonomy is not respected, and in some cases is systematically undermined. To complicate matters, some of these children are told that they ask for the abuse, or that they are somehow seductive. Many are told specifically by the perpetrators that if they tell anyone about the abuse, they or someone they love will be hurt or killed. Judith Herman has written about the systematic taking away of control in domestic situations that parallels the techniques used in political torture.[9] Techniques common to both situations include making arbitrary rules and enforcing them arbitrarily, intruding upon basic bodily functions, and isolating the victim from potential sources of help and support. It is easy to see how children raised in such an environment of terror can be conditioned to believe that they are incapable of controlling anything in their lives.

As traumatized children grow up, their adult experiences often reinforce their conviction that keeping themselves safe from other people is beyond their control. Repetitive traumatic experiences will lead them to one of two conclusions: either trust no one, and be alone, or trust everyone unquestioningly in a wish to compensate for past disappointments. Either way, these adults will not be able to evaluate accurately the trustworthiness of another person, and may end up either isolated, or in violent or abusive relationships. Sandra, for example, demonstrated her lack of ability to evaluate trustworthiness in her search for a roommate. She had stated that it was important to her to be in a safe, sober living environment. Visiting an apartment that was advertised as "clean and sober," she noticed that her potential roommate had bottles of liquor in his room. Despite the evidence that this indicated lack of sobriety in the house, Sandra had not thought to use this information in making her decision about moving in. Until she focused attention on it in therapy, she had unquestioningly trusted this roommate and assumed safety. It had simply not occurred to her that she could use new information to assess safety and trustworthiness. Valerie, on the other hand, decided that she couldn't trust anyone, and that the best way to stay safe was to be alone; for several years after she was raped, she did not have a conversation with a single person outside of her family.

The inability to assess trustworthiness means that chronically traumatized people have an extremely difficult time accessing psychotherapy or other mental health services. In order to seek psychotherapy, a person takes a lot of risks. She meets with an unknown doctor or other professional, an authority figure, who sets the rules for the encounter. She is on unfamiliar turf. She is asked to sit in a closed room with a stranger, unwitnessed, one-on-one, and answer questions about herself. The power differential is huge—unstated but obvious. In the eyes of the traumatized person, this situation is terrifying, unpredictable, and potentially abusive.

The inherent difficulties in the one-on-one psychotherapy relationship are well recognized in recent writing about the psychotherapy of traumatized people.[10] In general, the strategy is to make the therapy

interaction trust-enhancing and empowering rather than retrauma-
tizing. In order to do this effectively and safely, we first need to recognize that the traumatized patient approaches therapy, as he approaches life, with two compelling and contradictory wishes. These
wishes come out of the reality that the traumatized person in fact has
no internal sense of control and no ability to trust himself or evaluate
whether the therapist is trustworthy. Therefore, he both wants to remain safe by staying completely in control, which entails not trusting
the therapist at all, and he also wishes to relinquish this exhausting
task and be cared for and rescued by someone idealized and benevolent. Neither of these approaches is really safe or ultimately
growth-enhancing for the patient. Instead, the therapist's task is to
empower the patient to feel self-efficacious, teach him how to assess
his level of trust in the therapy relationship, and then help him maintain a reasonable degree of control during therapy.

The therapist can demonstrate her commitment to working safely
with her patient in the first session. To help decrease anxiety about the
initial encounter, the therapist should maximize the predictable and
minimize the unexpected. Therefore, in arranging an initial meeting,
the therapist can describe what she looks like and specify exactly where
and for how long the first meeting will be. She should also be as specific
as possible about explaining what she is going to do in the initial session. She can explain why she is asking the questions she is asking, so
the patient will understand that there are reasons for the questions, and
that she is not asking out of her own arbitrary or prurient interest. She
can also offer the patient choices whenever possible (for example, offering a choice of two different chairs to sit in). Reinforcing the patient's own sense of agency and competence in decision making in this
way is a therapeutic action in itself. The therapist can also tell the patient that she will help him identify and monitor his own level of trust in
her as she goes along. She can demonstrate this by encouraging the patient to think about and choose how much of his history he feels comfortable sharing in the first session. The therapist also needs to show
the patient that he will not have too much power in the therapy setting.
She should explain the rules of the clinic and the reasons for them—for
example, expectations for coming to appointments sober, the limits of
confidentiality—and she should introduce a treatment contract, explaining the expectations for both patient and therapist.

I will return to the topic of how to structure therapy with chronically traumatized people later in this chapter. Before I do, though, I

would like to highlight some difficulties that differentiate therapy with chronically traumatized patients from other types of therapy, right from the outset. The first problem is one of access. Many of the most severely traumatized people are never going to make it to the initial encounter simply because of their impairment in trust and lack of a sense of internal control. The traditional psychotherapy model requires a lot of the patient: locating the resource, calling for an appointment, coming to an evaluation on time, returning for scheduled appointments. This series of steps is inherently insurmountable for some traumatized patients. In addition, therapists are usually located in psychiatric departments or mental health clinics; we hope that traumatized patients will find us there. Unfortunately, the most severely traumatized patients often do not seek out the help of therapists. They may be more likely to turn to primary care doctors in public clinics or to family planning or other community clinics. They may come to emergency rooms or be hospitalized after being acutely assaulted. They may seek help in substance abuse programs. They may be in prison or involved in child protective services. They may be in homeless shelters or on the streets. Or they may be isolated at home, not able to seek help at all. How can we work to make our treatment more accessible and relevant to these patients' needs? One way to do this is to be a known resource to others who may have contact with traumatized patients and can facilitate connection, for example primary care and other physicians, emergency room staff, the police, and the courts. Having drop-in times can make us more available to patients when they are ready.

A second problem is that of social unfamiliarity. Differences in ethnicity, sexual orientation, or socioeconomic status between chronically traumatized patients and potential providers can pose additional barriers to accessing and using psychotherapy. When white providers treat ethnic minority patients, or when heterosexual providers treat gay or lesbian patients, the perceived power differential is reinforced, and this can be a barrier either to seeking therapy, or to developing trust in the therapeutic relationship. One obvious solution to this problem is to have therapists of color and of differing sexual orientations on staff in clinics and institutions that serve chronically traumatized patients. The issue of addressing personal differences between therapist and patient in psychotherapy is too complex to be addressed in this chapter; as a general rule, however, if there are obvious differences in ethnicity or sexual orientation between the therapist and the chronically traumatized patient, the therapist must take the lead in addressing the issue directly and openly in the therapy. This demonstrates to patients a commitment to reducing secrecy and shame in the therapy. For example, Valerie was initially reluctant to describe her family life to her first therapist, who was white. When her therapist asked Valerie if she had feelings about the differences in their ethnic backgrounds, Valerie said that she didn't want to say anything about her family because the case worker who had made the decision to remove her children had been white, and she didn't trust the therapist not to do the same. The therapist acknowledged how difficult this association must be and stated her wish and commitment to helping Valerie as best she could. She showed a copy of the child abuse reporting laws to Valerie and explained the reason for the law. She and Valerie agreed that they shared a concern about her children, and that together they would continue to talk about how things were going at home so that they could identify ways Valerie could get help when she felt overwhelmed. Issues of ethnicity can be complex, however, as Valerie's experience with her second therapist illustrates. Valerie initially said she expected that her new therapist, an African-American woman, could understand her better since she was a "sister"—but during the therapy the obvious differences in their professional and socioeconomic statuses became a source of shame for Valerie. Again, her therapist acknowledged the real differences between them, and expressed a respectful interest in understanding Valerie's unique experience and feelings.

A third problem with doing psychotherapy with chronically traumatized patients is that, in their hierarchy of needs, other tasks may come before the traditional tasks of therapy (that is, understanding intrapsychic processes and analyzing relationship patterns using the transference). This reality necessitates role flexibility for the therapist. Because basic environmental safety and stability are prerequisites to discussing interpersonal issues or trauma material, we may need to begin treatment acting more as case managers than as traditional psychotherapists, helping our patients find housing, apply for disability, or locate sources for legal assistance or vocational training. Assisting patients with their immediate practical needs also enhances our trustworthiness. We may also need to step out of the role of therapist to act as crisis counselor: for chronically traumatized, urban poor patients, acute crisis can be an ongoing state. Crisis management may involve helping our patient locate a shelter after she is assaulted, or helping her make a safety plan if she is in an acute domestic violence situation. The content of therapy sessions may be dictated by these case management or crisis intervention needs rather than by a focus on transference issues, discussion of past trauma, or even coping skills. As always, case management and crisis intervention can also be carried out with an eye toward empowering the patient and helping her feel in control. For example, if the therapist needs to help the patient locate a shelter, she can sit with the patient in her office, give her the numbers for shelters, and support her while she makes the phone calls. If the patient is anxious about making the calls, the therapist can spend time helping her prepare a written list of questions to ask, and then role-play asking the questions before she makes the actual calls.

Sam's case illustrates the need for open access and extensive case management in treating chronically traumatized patients. Sam was referred to psychotherapy after the hospital surgeon who did his post-assault facial surgery recognized his symptoms of panic and agoraphobia. Sam was too terrified to leave his house to come to an intake appointment. Instead of insisting on this step as a prerequisite to treatment, Sam's therapist talked to him on the phone, normalizing his anxiety and his symptoms, and telling Sam that he could come in any time he was ready. The therapist discussed ways he could help Sam with his hospital bills, and helped him fill out disability application forms over the phone. After six months of intermittent phone contact, Sam was able to come to the clinic, but only at unscheduled times; during these visits, time would be spent practicing relaxation exercises and deep breathing. After a year of disabling panic Sam was able to try an anti-anxiety medication, and eventually he was able to come to regularly scheduled appointments with a continued focus on helping him evaluate safety in his environment and practicing stress-management and relaxation techniques.

Internal Safety and Self-Efficacy

In addition to feeling as if the external world is beyond their control, chronically traumatized patients feel that their internal experience is out of control and unsafe. Flashbacks and intrusive memories are an example of this difficulty. We often take it for granted that our patients conceptualize time and place the same way we do—that time is linear and place is a concrete reality. For chronically traumatized patients, however, time and place are not experienced as consistent and reliable. During flashbacks, for example, the past is not remembered but re-experienced: the present is actually lost, and the past takes over. By the same token, the security of place is not immutable. A flashback can erase images of current location and transport the patient back to the surroundings where the trauma occurred. Worst of all, flashbacks can occur at unexpected moments, triggered by stimuli that may be out of awareness. Some patients feel so terrified of this loss of control that they become agoraphobic in an effort to avoid flashback triggers. During flashbacks, patients will no longer be in the room mentally, emotionally, or even physically, in their perception. For example, when Valerie first revealed her history of rape, she was visibly transformed. She began to shake, and described seeing around her the interior of the car where she was assaulted and feeling the physical sensations of the assault in her body.

Flashbacks are powerful draws into the past, and patients need a lot of preparation to manage them before delving into traumatic memories. A common mistake therapists make is to encourage patients to talk about the details of their traumatic experiences before they are adequately prepared to manage flashbacks or other symptoms that may arise. The danger of doing this is that, in the absence of alternative self-regulatory and grounding skills, patients will use whatever means they can to reduce painful affect and obliterate distressing memories, including alcohol, drugs, or self-harming behaviors. A more effective strategy is to teach patients grounding skills before discussing past traumas. For example, in the beginning of her therapy, Sandra's therapist encouraged her to buy calendars and clocks to put in all the rooms of her apartment to remind herself that she is in the present, and safe; to write out grounding "scripts" to read aloud during flashbacks; and to carry a small stone in her pocket to touch when she feels her body slipping out of the present. Sandra's mastery of these grounding skills was what allowed her to manage the inevitable flashbacks successfully. She was able to increase her level of control over her internal experience by having a repertory of skills, and eventually felt able to describe traumatic events to her therapist without becoming overwhelmed.

Dissociation is another common symptom that leads to feeling a lack of control over internal experience. Because dissociation is such an immediate defense for some traumatized people, time and place can be lost or warped almost automatically, often without their full realization. Patients who come in for weekly sessions may not remember specifically how they spent their time between sessions. I am not referring to patients with dissociative identity disorder who at times act completely out of awareness. For many chronically traumatized patients, time is more like a vague haze. If they stop and focus on a particular memory of an incident, a person, or a date, they can sometimes, but not always, form clearer outlines around time and events. This vagueness can make therapy difficult and confusing, because patients often do not come in with a clear narrative about what has happened that week, and cannot remember what thoughts or feelings they have experienced. Journals and homework are therefore useful tools in trauma therapy. If a particular discussion in therapy is helpful or illuminating, it is useful for patients to write it down; what they may not be able to record in memory they will have on paper, in their own words and their own handwriting.

Oftentimes memory problems and dissociation are a source of shame and embarrassment. Therapists can normalize these experiences by educating patients about why dissociation happens and how it functioned to protect them in the past. Dissociation is in fact an ingenious defense that children use to protect themselves from painful and violent experiences; it is problematic for adults, however, because functioning effectively in the world depends on being alert, focused, and in control of internal experience.

Chronically traumatized people feel internally unsafe and ineffective in other ways as well. Patients often feel overwhelmed by any emotions, either negative or positive, and can only manage the feelings by turning to substance use, bingeing or purging, or other self-harming behavior. This pattern of affective overload and maladaptive self-regulation clearly overlaps with the diagnostic criteria for borderline personality disorder.

Judith Herman and others have described a staged model of trauma treatment that focuses first on achieving current external and internal safety and basic self-care, and only then on discussing traumatic material.[11] Psychoeducation about the effects of trauma, teaching coping skills like relaxation and deep breathing, and helping with concrete problem-solving are ways to help patients achieve internal safety and self-efficacy. Simply "letting out the trauma" is generally not a helpful intervention as an end in itself. Focusing exclusively on either current functioning or disclosure alone is probably not the most useful approach. Rather, the therapist needs to recognize the purpose and timing of both interventions, and the need for balance. Having the patient disclose her past trauma without ways to calm herself down or a cognitive framework to understand where her reactions are coming from is not productive. On the other hand, focusing only on current safety and not allowing any discussion of past trauma tends to send the message that the traumatic experience is shameful and intolerable. I have found it most helpful to include some disclosure of traumatic experiences combined with managing symptoms in the present.

Shame

The origins of shame in chronically traumatized people are threefold. First, there is shame about abusive things that they themselves have done; second, there is shame about pleasurable feelings they may have had during experiences of abuse. Finally, the type of shame most resistant to change is an internal sense of "badness" that for traumatized people has often become a core belief about the self.

I will first address the concrete causes of shame. Therapists naturally feel empathic with the pain patients have suffered. Often, however, therapists minimize the complexity and multidimensionality of the victim's experience. Children form their self-identity through internalization of others, particularly parents or other caregivers. Therefore, the abused child will necessarily internalize aspects of the perpetrator in some form. We like to see victims as pure and defenseless, possessed of moral authority because of their experience. We do not like to think that they may also have fantasies or urges to be perpetrators themselves, or that they may actually act on these urges against others. The fact is that these feelings exist almost universally in traumatized people, and our ignoring them confirms our patients' belief that they are "unspeakably" bad, and heightens their feelings of intense and terrible shame.

I have been frequently surprised to hear from my traumatized patients what actions they have perpetrated against others, usually when they were children. At the age of seven, Sandra forced a five-year-old girl to insert a tampon in her anus. (She was demonstrating to the neighborhood children what sex was.) Valerie used to masturbate while looking at her one-year-old niece's exposed genitals. Bill talked about knowing instinctively which young boys he saw on the street could potentially be targets for abuse. (Bill was never a perpetrator of abuse and was quite troubled by his thoughts.) It is essential to elicit the history of perpetration or the fantasies of it because these are often potent "dirty secrets" that are the sources of unrelenting shame, feelings of inner badness, and an unwelcome sense of being no different from the abuser. Therapists can elicit this history by universalizing and destigmatizing the phenomenon: for example, by saying, "Children who are abused are overstimulated in an inappropriate way. Their nervous systems and their sexual arousal systems are rewired in ways they did not wish for. Sometimes this comes out in sexual thoughts or actions that may be disturbing. Has this happened to you?" Obviously if a patient is actively involved in perpetration, therapists need to follow the usual protocol for mandated reporting, and make the cessation of this acting out the focus of treatment; if patients do not express remorse for the things they have done to others in the past, the main task of therapy is to help them own responsibility for their actions. If former victims report fantasies or acts in childhood, however, and if they are remorseful and concerned about what effects their actions may have had on others, therapists can, while not minimizing their actions, point out to them that it is exactly their sense of responsibility for their actions that differentiates them from their perpetrators.

Another very difficult but essential question to ask is whether victims enjoyed any aspect of their abuse. Bill loved his abuser and looked forward to seeing him because he paid attention to Bill, and taught him "fun games" that felt good. Valerie started seeking out her perpetrator for physical comfort as a teenager. A recent group I led had eight participants; every single one described sexual pleasure at some time during their abuse, and two had been orgasmic. Hearing that this had been the case for all of them was a tremendous relief for the entire group. They had all thought they were "perverted" and "deserved what they got," even "asked for it" because of their partial enjoyment. Sandra imagined her father's face when she was masturbating or having sex with her boyfriend. She was repulsed by this and cried every time she had sex. It can help patients to explain theories about neurological and hormonal effects of sexual abuse. When children are sexually stimulated they will experience physiological pleasure, and this response can be conditioned and generalized. The body can respond independently of the mind's thoughts or emotions. Clearly abuse influences the development of sexuality, including the content of fantasy. The effects of abuse on sexuality are powerful, but they are not immutable. What can be conditioned into a brain and body can also be conditioned out; cognitive-behavioral techniques are an effective tool to use in this work.[12] With practice, Sandra was able to replace images of her father with other pictures of her choosing during sex.

The core sense of shame is the most difficult to change in traumatized patients. I have rarely heard patients describe a shift in this basic sense during individual therapy. However, participants in group therapy sometimes do demonstrate movement in their beliefs about themselves. This can happen more readily in the group for several reasons. First, hearing others express what they have thought or done and feeling compassion for others may allow the patient to forgive herself for her own acts. Hearing from others who have experienced chronic trauma is also more powerful than hearing about it from a therapist, who has likely not really "been there." For example, Sandra stated in her group that she felt like "nothing but a whore, a slut, I'm only good for sex." There were two other women in the group who had also worked as prostitutes. Sandra was able to hear from them, more than from the therapist, that they knew her to be a good person who had been forced to survive in whatever way she could. For the first time, she was able to acknowledge this; in individual therapy she had always immediately dismissed the idea that her experiences were anyone's fault but her own. Sandra's self-esteem also increased in the group because she was able to take on roles other than that of the patient—for example, she could act as teacher, supporter, adviser, or expert to other group members when the time came for them to tell their stories.

Self-Care

Because victims of chronic abuse and violence have such low self-esteem, they often have no understanding of the concept of self-care. In fact, the message they received while growing up was often that they were not worth caring for. Most chronic trauma survivors cannot remember having been sick as children; this is likely because the adults in their lives often did not notice that they were ill, or viewed their illness as an imposition. Valerie, for example, described having broken her arm after falling from a tree; she hid the injury from her mother because she feared punishment (which in fact was her mother's eventual response). Because these victims never experienced care, they do not know how to care for themselves as adults. This lack of self-care ranges from not eating properly to not seeking medical care for illnesses.

The lack of basic self-care also relates to chronically traumatized patients' beliefs about their physical selves. Victims are intensely ashamed of and confused about their own bodies. Some fear and imagine that horrible damage has been done to them. Sandra had been to the gynecologist more than fifty times because she was convinced she was infected "down there." She had an image of a "foreign body, maybe a splinter" lodged permanently in her vagina, causing "green and black pus" to build up. (She had never actually had an infection.) Others think there must have been something intrinsically wrong with them to have been chosen for abuse. Bill thought he was chosen because he was a big kid, "easier to stick a dick into." This belief led to self-hatred and shame about his large, muscular frame. He had not gone to a doctor in many years because he was afraid that during the examination someone would discover that he didn't have "a virgin anus." He was also convinced that someday he would develop fecal incontinence.

Traumatized patients may have rational knowledge of anatomy and physiology, but when they picture their own bodies, they sometimes describe bizarre ideas of what they imagine is inside their organs or flowing in their veins. This can lead to multiple medical visits and unnecessary treatments. For some patients, their relentless pursuit of physical confirmation that something is wrong with their body can lead to more drastic interventions, including unnecessary surgery. However, it is more often the case that patients' ideas about their bodies will cause them to avoid physicians and physical exams altogether. Valerie said that she "knew" there was something wrong with her genitals, and she was too embarrassed for a gynecologist to see it and be "disgusted." She had not had an internal exam for more than forty years.

A gynecological exam is obviously a difficult experience for anyone who has been sexually intruded upon, because it can be such a direct somatic trigger. However, these patients are entitled to and need basic medical care. Self-care must begin with the body, and we as therapists can help our patients obtain proper care. Individually, we can explore with our patients what they imagine is going on inside their bodies and what they fear is wrong with them, as well as what they anticipate an encounter with a physician will be like. Groups may again be the most useful therapeutic medium to address self-care issues. In the groups I have led, members often share names of physicians who are sensitive to their concerns, and exchange tips on how they have managed exams successfully (by bringing a friend, by practicing grounding techniques before going to the appointment, by meeting with the doctor several times before the exam and expressing their concerns directly, and so forth).

Reenactments and Revictimization

Reenactment in psychotherapy is universal with traumatized patients. Much of the recent literature on posttraumatic therapy focuses on management of the inevitable, intense transferences and counter-transferences that arise in the course of individual trauma therapy. Most of these problematic interactions can be understood as reenactments of some aspect of the trauma experience. In this section, I will first outline the current theoretical understanding of why reenactments occur in therapy and then describe some strategies for managing them. I will then discuss the related issue of revictimization. While reenactment in therapy is problematic and difficult, revictimization in the world is dangerous and damaging, and should be the primary focus in all trauma treatment.

The ease with which therapists can become involved in reenactments with trauma patients is easily understood if we first imagine the experience of a child who is traumatized. Normally, a developing child experiments with different roles and feelings in the safe realms of play and fantasy. The traumatized child, in contrast, is made to actualize and act out extreme roles that are both frightening and over-stimulating. Experimentation is foreclosed, and, what is more subtle, less exciting roles are abandoned or never discovered. As a result, the person who has been chronically traumatized has a very limited cast of characters in her internal world, and can imagine very few roles that others can take in the external world. These roles, though limited, are very compelling and powerful. The list most trauma therapists cite includes the roles of helpless victim and sadistic abuser, the bystander who knows yet does nothing, and the idealized rescuer. This cast of characters is so powerfully written into the script that it is almost impossible for a survivor of chronic trauma to imagine herself or other human beings taking on any other role. It is also almost impossible for the patient and the therapist to resist the pull to reenact these roles in the therapy interaction.

Some examples will help illustrate the various types of reenactments that occur. Sandra had been talking in therapy about her fruitless attempts to find a job. Her therapist, feeling anxious about Sandra's financial troubles, spent time at home looking through job classifieds, and made up a list of phone numbers. Giving the list to

Sandra was an acting out of the therapist's desire to rescue and care for her. It was also a reenactment: Sandra felt that her mother had never taught her how to take care of herself, and was both rageful about this and believed herself helpless to change it. Her therapist's action short-circuited Sandra's rage at her mother and also reinforced her feeling that she was incompetent to find a job on her own.

Valerie would sometimes slip in references during therapy to dangerous things that were happening in her home environment. For example, she once mentioned in passing that her sister liked to have parties. With each passing session she would make a reference to her sister and what she was doing: drinking a little too much, not coming home till late, losing her temper with her kids. Her therapist completely missed the meaning of these communications; what it turned out to be was that Valerie was concerned about the safety of her sister's children. As her therapist listened to these stories, but did nothing, she had been in the role of the uncaring and unhelpful bystander.

Bill liked to describe graphically violent scenes that he had seen in movies. He often did so in the context of saying how proud he was that he was "getting out more." He described the scenes in a humorous way, often laughing at the violence, so it took a while for his therapist to realize that he was victimizing her with the gory details of these movies. He also liked to describe his sexual activities and then scan his therapist's face for her reaction. This was likely a reenactment of what he was forced to do as a child: he was intruded upon sexually and was watched and photographed.

Clinically, we know that reenactment is happening when we feel an uncomfortable emotion or physical sensation: titillation, repulsion, nausea, exhaustion, boredom, or confusion. John Wilson calls this phenomenon "empathic strain" and describes it as something that occurs when the therapist's empathic stance is disrupted by feelings of disequilibrium and dysphoria.[13] The experience of empathic strain leads to two major types of countertransference reactions on the part of the therapist: avoidance and overinvolvement. These types of reactions correspond to taking on attributes of different figures in the patient's internal world. Which type of reaction is activated is as dependent on the susceptibilities of the therapist as it is on characteristics of the patients and their trauma experiences. If empathic strain is not recognized, actions that reflect countertransference reactions, such as extending session time, adding extra sessions, or canceling sessions, may be clues that a reenactment is happening.

In the case of Sandra's job list, her therapist's vulnerability to reenacting the role of the rescuer, an "overinvolved" stance, came partly from her sense of responsibility as a therapist, and partly from her investment in seeing herself as caring and nurturing. The clue that this was not a useful interaction was that she felt resentful and mildly embarrassed by what she had done, since she did not as a rule give things to patients without their requesting them. Valerie's therapist was eventually able to understand the meaning of Valerie's communications by recognizing that she was confused and irritated by Valerie's seemingly irrelevant discussions about her sister. She was able to ask Valerie directly about what she was missing in their conversations. When Valerie told her, she asked that they problem-solve together. Valerie decided to act to protect her sister's children herself by calling Child Protective Services from her therapist's office. Bill's therapist realized that his stories were a form of reenactment because she identified some voyeuristic excitement as well as repulsion while he was talking. She began to look forward to hearing his stories, while at the same time feeling violated and intruded upon. This feeling correlated directly with how Bill felt as a child being sexually victimized by his neighbor. Her vulnerability lay in her desire to prove to Bill that she was "tough," and that she could handle anything he brought in. As they talked about this process in the therapy, Bill was able to realize that he "talked tough" often because he felt that his sexuality and his ability to tolerate and perpetrate violence were his only worthwhile qualities.

One way to stay vigilant about reenactment is to remind ourselves and our patients of our treatment contract. The purpose of the contract is for the therapist and the patient to decide together on specific goals for therapy, and outline clearly the boundaries of the treatment relationship and the expectations from both parties. For example, a patient's goal in therapy might be to work on finding a safe way to get income; a second goal may be to understand why he has had difficulty keeping a job. Expectations for the therapist should also be clear in the contract. This should include a review of the therapist's schedule, when he or she can be reached, and how to access emergency backup. Expectations for patients include the responsibility of informing the therapist if they are not coming to an appointment and using emergency services if they need to. The meaning of confidentiality and its limits should be reviewed. The patient should also hear an explanation of what therapy is: for example, that he will talk honestly about what is going on with him, the therapist will listen and provide some guidance in how to make things better, and they will work together to improve his understanding of his feelings and his symptoms. That includes talking about interactions in the therapy and how they can be examined to further help the patient manage his life.

If therapist or patient acts out of bounds of the treatment contract, the chances are it is a reenactment. In the cases described above, the therapist's setting limits on what they did in the therapy was what helped end the reenactment. The next step was talking directly about the interaction with the patient to see if the reenactment could be used to understand something new about her. It can also be useful to explain the concept of reenactment to patients explicitly. We do not need to be afraid of exposing our techniques; the more psycho-education about trauma dynamics we share, the better. If patients know what reenactment is and why it happens, then the interaction can be named, and patient and therapist can then work together to try to understand its meaning.

Managing reenactments can be tricky. Setting limits, for example, is one of the most useful ways to manage reenactments, but it can also backfire. First, the therapist should be sure that, in fact, the limit is not an expression of his or her own unprocessed hostility. Even if the limit is a necessary intervention, the patient will likely see the limit as punitive and random. This is because, in the experience of the traumatized person, rules are arbitrary and sadistic. It is therefore useful to help the patient anticipate that he is likely to see the limit that way, and to state directly that what you are interested in is not punishment, but negotiating safety in the therapy. You do need to be honest about the fact that the negotiation has limits; after all, you are in a more powerful position as the therapist.

A different but related problem is our belief that we as therapists can and should provide compensation for our patients' suffering. It is this attitude that often leads us to overextend in "doing for" traumatized patients and reenacting the "rescuer" role. In fact, however, it is disempowering to communicate to a traumatized patient that she needs special, extra treatment. It reinforces the idea of being different, permanently stigmatized, altered. A discussion about this wish will likely be more fruitful than enacting the wish for compensation. People whose lives have been destroyed by abuse and violence do deserve compensation. Unfortunately, it is rare that they get it. No one can ever compensate for the loss of the healthier lives they might have had without the abuse. We cannot make up for this in therapy; it is only something that we can acknowledge and mourn together with our patients.

How is reenactment different from traditional psychoanalytic views of transference and countertransference? In traditional psychotherapy we often try to enhance the transference, or wait until the transference has deepened so that we can explore its meaning with our patients. In working with chronically traumatized people, however, this strategy is unnecessary, and may be counterproductive. This is because the traumatic transference is intense, unmodulated, and instantaneous. The therapist does not need to wait or work to heighten it, because it is present immediately, and it feels confusing and unmanageable to patients. This traumatic transference/countertransference can easily become a non-productive reenactment. Therefore it is less useful to wait to see how the transference develops than to try early on to give patients a framework to make sense of their feelings. We can educate our patients by talking openly about the process of therapy, and sharing our understanding of why people who have been traumatized have such intense feelings in therapy. This normalizing and educating process can never start too early in therapy.

Reenactments are unavoidable in individual trauma therapy because of the intensity of the one-on-one therapy interaction. It is difficult but possible to manage these reenactments in a way that can transform them from repetitions to opportunities for learning and growth. We need to be vigilant and to notice reenactments quickly, so that we can bring ourselves out of the loop of history and gain new perspective. There are some patients, however, for whom the pull to reenactment is stronger than their ability to process the therapy interaction productively. For many chronically traumatized people, managing the relearning in a one-on-one environment is too charged a task. The dyadic structure itself can be so affectively overwhelming that it becomes impossible to effectively assimilate new knowledge. Instead, the therapy becomes an unbreakable, repetitive cycle of reenactment and unintentional retraumatization.

Valerie's experience with individual therapy is a good example of the type of difficulty that may arise. In her first contact with her therapist on the phone, before they had actually met, Valerie became tearful and sobbed, "I need a mother." Despite rigorous boundary-setting and attempted definition of achievable goals, Valerie consistently felt overwhelmed in therapy sessions. She would become disorganized and dissociative around almost any subject matter. Valerie connected her difficulty in therapy to the fact that her mother had publicly humiliated her when she first disclosed her experiences of abuse. She feared humiliation from her therapist, and at the same time wished intensely for her therapist to "take care of things" for her. Despite recognizing this connection and discussing it with her therapist, Valerie often purposely missed sessions because it felt "too intense." She also described feeling so angry in sessions that she would want to destroy things in the office, and related her fear of getting "out of control" to her missing appointments. Outside of therapy, however, Valerie was able to attend a job training program, set appropriate limits with her boyfriend, who had relapsed on drugs, and care for her four children. The structure of individual therapy in itself was problematic for her, so much so that she needed to avoid it.

Because individual therapy is so inherently loaded for some patients, group therapy is a valuable alternative or auxiliary treatment modality. Group therapy may even be a preferable structure for treatment because it emphasizes sharing skills and coping strategies. In addition, it equalizes the power differential because advice and teaching come from both peers and professionals. Reenactments can also happen in groups, but they are usually less intense and more quickly recognized. This is because the roles are shared among two therapists and many group members, and thus there are more people able to identify and process reenactments early.

Individual therapy can also feel unmanageable if it is not defined by clear goals and bounded by a known end-date. Many clinicians in the trauma field assume lengthy, even unending therapy and do not work with patients to define specific treatment goals. Most argue that, with enough time, the traumatic reenactments that happen in therapy can be understood and reworked, and new ways of functioning will develop. In my experience, however, the prospect of limitless, unending treatment is often more overwhelming than helpful to the patient. Knowing that therapy will be limited to a defined period of time makes the work more manageable. One way to do this is to pre-set a specific number of sessions or an end-date, and enumerate specific issues to target. Therapy "blocks" can be done non-continuously, with breaks between treatment periods. This maintains the long-term relationship without overwhelming the patient.

Long-term, continuous individual trauma therapy can be exhausting and demoralizing for the therapist; the intermittent therapy model can therefore be helpful for therapists as well. Group therapy is another way to modulate the difficulties of trauma therapy. In a group structure, the burden of support and reflection is shared by the entire group and by two group therapists. Group therapy is therefore often a more manageable option for both patient and therapist.

Although we can make structural modifications in trauma therapy, therapists are still at risk for experiencing vicarious traumatization and burnout.[14] Does our work have to be so depleting? Part of the problem may be the expectations we place on ourselves to restructure the damaged selves of traumatized patients. As therapists, we have to accept the limits of what we can do for patients. It is possible to teach patients tools to change their way of being in the world; it is not always possible to change their internal world entirely.

I will turn now to the issue of revictimization, which is related to reenactment in that familiar patterns of interpersonal interactions are repeated. Issues of revictimization are critical to address in trauma treatment because our patients are at constant risk of experiencing repeated assaults and incidents of interpersonal violence. Oftentimes issues of risk for revictimization are overlooked by clinicians. It is not a common practice, for example, when gathering a clinical history to ask patients routinely about their current level of safety, particularly in domestic relationships and living situations. Clinicians who are used to talking with patients about events that happened in the past have a difficult time adjusting to the idea that their patient may currently be experiencing violence, and therapists may feel unskilled at helping patients manage acute crises.

The reason that trauma patients are at increased risk for revictimization is that they often do not understand the concept of safety. Patients who have been traumatized from childhood may never have experienced a safe environment or had a non-violent relationship. Imagine the child who grows up in a chronically chaotic and violent home. Although he may learn to recognize warning signs that a violent event is going to happen (for example, that his parent is intoxicated or yelling), he is powerless to stop the violence and is unable to protect himself, or his mother or siblings, from harm. Chronically traumatized patients may live in a constant state of hyperarousal and hypervigilance, but they are not able to imagine being efficacious in protecting themselves from imminent danger.

This state of felt helplessness in the face of danger leads some traumatized patients to simply stop noticing dangerous clues, or stop interpreting them as warning signs. For example, Sandra described in group therapy a first date she had had with a man she met at a bus stop. Sandra at first said only that he "seemed nice, and like he respected me." When group members asked her more about him, she remembered that he said he had just been released from prison. She also described his behavior on the date; he had walked several steps ahead of her the entire time, and he had not made eye contact with her once during their date. Until she got feedback from group members that they were concerned about this man's potential dangerousness, it had not occurred to Sandra that she could evaluate his safety herself. She was not able on her own to interpret clues about his history or behavior as red flags or warning signs about potential future dangerousness.

Chronic dissociation is another way that traumatized people are at risk for further victimization. When people walk around in a numbed state of consciousness, they will be less alert to cues in the environment. This lack of alertness also puts people at risk for accidents. I have often heard people in therapy describe driving on the highway in a "fog," and it is possible that some car accidents come about as a result of dissociation.

Another way in which traumatized patients can put themselves at increased risk for revictimization is that they often feel they are magically "untouchable" and "protected." For people who suffered uncontrollable violence at the hands of others, the idea of having an almost magical power to protect themselves is a compensatory wish that is, unfortunately, not true. This false feeling of safety is often balanced by a conviction that something bad will definitely happen, but at a controlled, future date. Sam, for example, was convinced that he was going to be attacked at some time in the future and that it "had to happen" on his 35th birthday. Therefore, he decided that he could safely walk out on the streets at any time of day or night because nothing would happen to him until that time. These superstitious schemas are ways to control and manage the terror of unpredictable violence by inventing a structure to expect and contain it. Unfortunately the world is not constructed in this way, and the feeling of intermittent safety is false and may actually increase risk for revictimization.

Another reason why traumatized patients sometimes put themselves at risk is that they may feel an almost addiction-level attraction to danger. The "fight-or-flight" response to terror is a biological, neurohormonal response. Fear induces an adrenaline rush, and this "high" can probably be as biologically addictive as an external drug-induced high. Patients do often talk about enjoying the familiar feeling they get from danger, and worry that life feels too gray and uninteresting without it. Bill, for example, had a difficult time imagining what could be enjoyable in his life after he stopped dealing drugs and was no longer exposed to danger on the streets. He finally decided that being a fireman was an alternative profession that he could enjoy. Although this crisis-intervention job was in some ways a reenactment of feeling chronically endangered, it was a more healthy, safer variant of this condition than drug-dealing. For Bill, no other type of job was an option. His biological self could not tolerate adrenaline-deficit any more than his psychological self could tolerate the absence of risk. For patients who are unable to find healthier alternatives, this addiction to danger may lead them to seek out criminal or other high-risk activities.

A more simple reason for revictimization is lack of appropriate social skills teaching. Sandra, who had worked as a prostitute from the ages of 15 to 18, stated: "I never know what clothes to wear. My first impulse is to put on something really sexy to get attention, even though I don't really want that attention." Sandra was actually unable to assess the appropriateness of her dress. She had always been taught that she was only a sexual object, and she had received social reinforcement only for representing herself in that guise. Her goal in therapy was to learn how to wear different clothes and dress more in a way that would reflect to the world a different persona. She worked on this by finding a reliable female friend whom she could ask about the outfits she chose to wear to double-check their appropriateness.

There is an even more intractable issue to address when trying to help our patients avoid revictimization: namely, their lack of belief that they are worthy of safety. Lacking the ability to value themselves, they cannot value their own safety. It is this lack of self-valuing, along with shame and the absence of self-care, that makes the treatment of traumatized people so difficult and painful. It is only through new experiences that our chronically traumatized patients will be able to develop an alternative self-view. It is only through feeling they are valued by others, that others see them as deserving of self-care and of self-respect, that they will learn to value themselves. The bottom-line task of both individual and group therapy is to help chronically traumatized patients finally experience this valuing and care.

Notes

1. Mary P. Koss and Mary R. Harvey, *The Rape Victim* (Newbury Park: Sage Publications, 1991), pp. 77–80.
2. Beth M. Houskamp and David W. Foy, "The Assessment of Post-traumatic Stress Disorder in Battered Women," *Journal of Interpersonal Violence,* 6 (1991): 367–375.
3. David Finkelhor, "Early and Long-term Effects of Child Sexual Abuse: An Update," *Professional Psychology: Research and Practice,* 21 (1990): 325–330.
4. Victoria M. Follette, Melissa A. Polusny, Anne E. Bechtle, and Amy E. Naugle, "Cumulative Trauma: The Impact of Child Sexual Abuse, Adult Sexual Assault, and Spouse Abuse," *Journal of Traumatic Stress,* 9 (1996): 25–36.
5. Susan D. Solomon and Jonathon R. T. Davidson, "Trauma: Prevalence, Impairment, Service Use, and Cost," *Journal of Clinical Psychiatry,* 58 (1997): 5–11.
6. Judith L. Herman, "Complex PTSD: A Syndrome in Survivors of Prolonged and Repeated Trauma," *Journal of Traumatic Stress,* 5 (1992): 377–391.
7. David Pelcovitz, Bessel van der Kolk, Susan Roth, Francine Mandel, Sandra Kaplan, and Patricia Resick, "Development of a Criteria Set and a Structured Interview for Disorders of Extreme Stress (SIDES)," *Journal of Traumatic Stress,* 10 (1997): 3–16.
8. John N. Briere, *Child Abuse Trauma: Theory and Treatment of the Lasting Effects* (Newbury Park: Sage Publications, 1992).
9. Judith L. Herman, *Trauma and Recovery* (New York: Basic Books, 1992).
10. I. Lisa McCann and Laurie Anne Pearlman, *Psychological Trauma and the Adult Survivor: Theory, Therapy, and Transformation* (New York: Brunner/Mazel, 1990).
11. Leslie Lebowitz, Mary R. Harvey, and Judith L. Herman, "A Stage-By-Dimension Model of Recovery from Sexual Trauma," *Journal of Interpersonal Violence,* 8 (1993): 378–391.
12. Barbara Olasov Rothbaum and Edna B. Foa, "Cognitive-Behavioral Therapy for Posttraumatic Stress Disorder," in Bessel A. van der Kolk, Alexander C. McFarlane, and Lars Weisaeth (Eds.), *Traumatic Stress: The Effects of Overwhelming Experience on Mind, Body, and Society* (New York: Guilford Press, 1996), pp. 491–509.
13. John P. Wilson and Jacob D. Lindy, "Empathic Strain and Countertransference," in *Countertransference in the Treatment of PTSD* (New York: Guilford Press, 1994), pp. 5–30.
14. Laurie Anne Pearlman and Karen W. Saakvitne, *Trauma and the Therapist: Countertransference and Vicarious Traumatization in Psychotherapy with Incest Survivors* (New York: Norton, 1995).

12 Our Psychoanalytic Legacy: The Relevance of Psychoanalysis to Psychotherapy

Alfred Margulies

When Freud was told that his upcoming visit to the New World was receiving enthusiastic support, he replied, the story goes, that the Americans must not understand him; they did not realize that he was bringing them the Plague. Like it or not, his ideas were contagious—and dangerous to the status quo. His ideas, he knew, would unsettle civilization. Freud's comment took an implicitly epidemiological and Darwinian view of how ideas actually get propagated. And Freud was right: his ideas would be both embraced and then resisted, but they would surely catch hold and spread. Pessimist that he was, Freud also knew that he would always be misunderstood, that the sharpness of his ideas would be blunted, their wildness domesticated.

Decades later W. H. Auden would write in the poem "In Memory of Sigmund Freud": "To us he is no more a person / now but a whole climate of opinion." Recently the literary scholar Harold Bloom (1994) ranked Freud with James Joyce, Proust, and Kafka as the four most influential authors of the twentieth century. Freud is among the ten most cited writers in the humanities, along with Shakespeare, Aristotle, and the Bible (Pinker, 1994, p. 23); *Life* magazine (Fall 1997) puts Freud sixteenth on the list of the most important people of the millennium. Plague, indeed.

Practicing almost a century after the birth of psychoanalysis, I too have caught the Freudian spirit, which continues to evolve as a body of ideas and an organized movement, both shaping and shaped by our American culture. As part of our climate, Freud is inseparable from the whole array of psychotherapies that have seen him either as an inspiration or as a big mistake. He is, inescapably, in our cultural genes. The history of ideas, then, is not a serene ivory-tower affair, but a fierce Darwinian struggle for hearts and minds. The field of psychotherapy, too, is evolutionary, though not necessarily progressive. Sadly, history does not lead inevitably toward a state of grace and truth.

To delineate the relevance of psychoanalysis to psychotherapy, then, one must consider not only the evolution of the history of psychotherapy but the contemporary climate that has now settled over our field, one that fosters the survival of some conceptions and the suppression of others. Under the name of progress, the most subtle aspects of being a person in psychological trouble are now being steam-rolled by a gathering bureaucratic industry, flattened by a mind-numbingly simplistic approach. By its very efficiency, by its ruthless control of how much time a clinician is allotted to listen to his or her patients, managed care ensures its own perpetuation of what is sanctioned and what can be done. And so the managed care mind becomes de facto a powerful and implicit philosophical approach to human suffering that limits the terms of discourse and debate. Why, I wonder, has "progress" become so problematic?

Moreover, how can we distinguish real progress from mere change? Pursuing the notion of the Darwinian struggle of ideas—and introducing Dawkins's concept of the "meme"—Daniel Dennett, philosopher of mind, writes (1991, p. 205): "According to the normal view, the following are virtually tautological: Idea X was believed by people because X was deemed true. People approved of X because people found X to be beautiful. What requires special explanation are the cases in which, in spite of the truth or beauty of an idea, it is not accepted, or in spite of its ugliness or falsehood, it is." Dennett is tracking the fragile signs of progress in Science and Art: proof and aesthetic criteria, truth and beauty. Here is Richard Dawkins (1989, p. 192): "Just as genes propagate themselves in the gene pool by leaping from body to body via sperms or eggs, so memes propagate themselves in the meme pool by leaping from brain to brain . . . If a scientist hears or reads about a good idea, he passes it on to his colleagues and students. He mentions it in his articles and his lectures. If the idea catches on, it can be said to propagate itself, spreading from brain to brain."[1] On the Internet, an ideal carrier of memes, lives this definition (S. Cook, 1997): "Any idea, phrase, thought . . . can be viewed as a meme; those that spread, that have implicit in their paradigm the ability and need to spread, are the most 'evolutionarily' successful. Memes compete with one another in a Darwinian struggle for replication; spreading quickly or eliminating competitors help a meme to survive."

Such an epidemiological model of ideas helps us approximate an understanding of the cultural domination of systems of thought. American English, for example, is rapidly becoming *the* world language, so much so that both France and Japan have passed laws meant to inoculate their languages from American infection. English, of course, is not inherently superior to French, but wins out because of American dominance in commerce and communications (for example, movies and the Internet) and thus its appeal to the young. And with this domination comes an increasing momentum that suppresses and eventually precludes its competitors (to capture the greatest market share, software had better be in English). My point is that the history of ideas is not one necessarily of progress but rather of the domination of paradigms. One person's good idea is another's plague.

Science, of course, does tend to have a progressive quality—digital cameras are getting better every month. But it is erroneous to equate academic change with this model of technological progression. Academic knowledge ("acada-memia"?) often *seems* progressive toward truth, but for reasons that can obscure the ruthless, competitive selective processes that nurture which ideas are allowed to flourish, which get grant support, tenure, and so forth. Memes then can look like "truth" that has evolved, but actually they reflect the Darwinian cultural environment which selects out some ideas and destroys others. In psychiatry, for example, how we treat psychiatric illness—how we can even conceptualize illness—is reflective of cultural battles to establish "truth." Diagnosis, then, reflects societal norms and power structures. The history of the American Psychiatric Association's *Diagnostic and Statistical Manual* is replete with such examples—for instance, the pathologizing of homosexuality, which it took a cultural and political movement to rectify. In sum, the evolution of ideas is not a movement toward a pinnacle of perfection but rather reflects a pitiless selection. Selection merely is—and all of us have stakes in influencing it.

A Short History of Psychiatric Ideas

When I was a resident in the 1970s, I initially avoided psychoanalysis because I thought it was too narrow relative to the larger field of psychiatry. Psychiatry was different then, more intellectually expansive and encompassing of widely diverse theoretical positions. My map and field guide was Leston Havens's (1973) remarkable overview and synthesis of the state of psychiatry, *Approaches to the Mind*. Back then Havens attempted to describe contemporary psychiatry in a broad theoretical context of methods and data. That is, he delineated four schools of psychiatry that together were comprehensive in their coverage of theory and practice.

The older schools of objective-descriptive psychiatry and psychoanalysis were well established and familiar. The objective-descriptive (or medical model) school has as its domain the delineation of disease states in a logical and systematic sequence: a database of symptoms and signs is gathered to describe a syndrome which then implies a differential diagnosis, which now directs further data collection, which will then lead to a final diagnosis, which will imply treatment options, course, and prognosis. In this view, pathology is within the objective space of the body. The psychoanalytic school explored the hidden territory of the unconscious, which revealed itself through free association, particularly as expressed within the development of a transference neurosis. In the light of reason, aided by the analyst's interpretations, the neurosis would resolve through a steady working through of its myriad manifestations. In this view, pathology exists within the psychic space of the structures of mind.

The "newer" schools of psychiatry developed in reaction to the older schools' notions of locus of disease and their implicit conceptions of humanity (Havens, 1973; Margulies and Havens, 1981). The interpersonal school emphasizes not only the social context of experience, but a social essence to the human psyche—there is no such thing as an independent self (Sullivan, 1953, 1954; Havens, 1976). What makes us sane or crazy is other people! In this view pathology exists not quite within a person, but in the social space between and encompassing an interpersonal embeddedness. Interpersonal method follows suit in aiming to explore and reduce the projected miscommunications (parataxic distortions) induced by threats to the interpersonal regulation of self-esteem.

The existential approach stresses the individual's singular and unrepeatable existence; the emphasis is not so much on pathology but on the question of Being itself, that is, our attempt to make meaning out of the life that we are dealt (Ellenberger, 1958; May, 1958, 1969). We are all thrown by chance and fate into our life situation, and with this we face—and avoid—terrible and a priori truths like our indeterminate yet certain death and our burden of freedom and choice. "Pathology," in this view, reflects a larger way of being-in-the-world, with its own unique space subtly colored by meaning, choices, and world view. Following the existential-phenomenological interest in lived experience, existential method can be described as a radical empathy, an attempt to enter into and share the experience of the other (Havens, 1973, 1974; Margulies, 1989).

Together these schools were not only comprehensive, but to my mind exhaustive of possibilities. That is, Havens's work was itself a theory of theories about the mind. I pored over his description of psychiatry: extraordinarily elegant in its conception, it has served as a scaffolding for all of my subsequent education within my profession. However, something nagged at me—I felt that somehow Havens was off the mark. Something was not right in his schema of schemas.

Though conceptually accurate in describing the realm of working methods, Havens seemed off in delineating the actual *weighting* of various schools. That is, though his description was exhaustive of the theoretical landscape—the schools were like broad continents—some of the schools were much more populated while others seemed like terra incognita, the New World. Perhaps I was limited in my Boston provincialism, but I did not see the newer schools represented within mainstream literature. Psychoanalysis and objective-descriptive psychiatry were clearly the main schools; existential psychiatry seemed marginal at best; interpersonal psychiatry was a persona non grata. In other words, Havens had described theoretical territory not yet fully settled by American psychiatry. Havens, of course, was aware of this, and his work was designed to introduce the newer schools to us (and in part to counter the hegemony of organized psychoanalysis). Nevertheless, I now realize that his mapping of the world of psychiatry was less a map of the existing terrain than the map of an ideal or a possibility—it is the map of a hope for our field. Moreover, I see now that Havens was describing not the real world of everyday clinical practice, but rather his own extraordinary understanding of psychiatry. In a sense he was describing himself: his own capaciousness of mind, and his unparalleled virtuosity and range as a clinician.

In the ensuing twenty-five years, remarkable changes occurred in the field of mental health. Similar to the collapse of the Soviet Union, these historical changes caught us all by surprise. Objective-descriptive psychiatry, which has been gathering momentum in a general trend to re-biologize and medicalize psychiatry, was given the final Darwinian advantage by managed care. The descriptive approach, concretized in the *Diagnostic and Statistical Manual,* has become the dominant model of our field, and in its very success, it has pushed out other approaches or reduced them to marginal economic niches (just as organized psychoanalysis once did to competing models within American medical academia). And so the plurality of psychiatry that Havens envisioned—and wished—has been largely lost. Who now picks up the frayed and broken thread of his vision? Here another historical surprise emerges.

I submit that in Havens's attempt to portray the psychiatry of the early 1970s, he ended up instead describing psychoanalysis in the 1990s! Like an old colonial empire of ideas, psychiatry has contracted (as psychoanalysis once did), and now psychoanalysis has expanded to fill the intellectual territory, absorbing the two newer schools of existential and interpersonal psychiatry in the process. This is to say, twenty-five years ago Havens predicted the intellectual future, not of psychiatry, but of contemporary psychoanalysis.

Havens's 1970s description of "psychoanalysis" would now be redescribed as the "classical" school, or the ego psychological position (here Charles Brenner [1973, 1982] has been perhaps the most articulate and influential writer). Many of the concerns of Havens's existential school have entered psychoanalysis through self psychology, which emerged with Heinz Kohut (1977, 1984) as a major force in the 1980s, nearly splitting organized psychoanalysis. The emphases of self psychology are existential in their essence, having to do with the nature of self, values and ideals, and the way in which an individual establishes meaning. As in the existential-phenomenological approach, the centrality of empathic attunement is the hallmark of this school, that is, the struggle to listen and engage from within the patient's perspective, to remain "experience near" (versus more theoretically abstract) in the clinical discourse. Self psychology, of course, has other agendas, including the developmental line of narcissism, the nature of selfobjects, descriptions of previously poorly understood transference phenomena, and so on. But my point here is that self psychology laid the ground for a more thoroughgoing discussion of larger existential themes that had been neglected within psychoanalysis.

The interpersonal school has perhaps been the most obvious appropriation of contemporary psychoanalysis. Indeed, within a few short years psychoanalysis has moved from a preoccupation with intrapsychic phenomena to a current absorption with the relational and intersubjective (for example, Greenberg and Mitchell, 1983; Mitchell, 1988; Renik, 1993). The 1990s will be remembered as a time when psychoanalysis delved deeply into the reciprocal molding of transference and countertransference, the relational field, intersubjectivity, the postmodern critique of knowing, and the reevaluation of such fundamentals as analytic neutrality, the frame of treatment, and the nature of insight itself. Though once marginal, Havens's "newer schools of psychiatry" are now robust within psychoanalysis; ironically, the "classical" psychoanalytic position (which at Havens's writing was *the* psychoanalytic school of psychiatry) is now the almost obligatory straw man.[2]

Finally, we should give at least passing notice to how much psychoanalysis has become enriched through its larger cultural context, that is, the intellectual movements of our time (including, for example, literary criticism, hermeneutics, and the postmodern debate about knowledge); the social upheavals (including the women's movement, gay rights, and the empowering of minority voices); and the broadening and pragmatic influence of a host of different psychotherapeutic and biological approaches. To return to my initial thesis, the history of psychotherapy is evolutionary, and sometimes, though not necessarily, progressive. What then are the enduring psychoanalytic conceptions? And, what is less certain, which ones will weather this new century?

The Psychoanalytic Legacy

On September 13, 1997, this description appeared on the front page of the *New York Times*: "[Princess] Diana—at once frail and beautiful, flawed and grand—a perfect transference symbol . . ." What would Auden have thought of this? What a surprising absorption of psychoanalytic technical language! Let's just gaze at this for a moment. As a profound reinterpretation of our human nature, psychoanalysis became assimilated into our Western philosophical tradition and our everyday lexicon. A short list of psychoanalytic cultural memes would include the unconscious, the meaning of dreams, Freudian slips, transference, the agencies of the mind (id, ego, super-ego), the Oedipal complex, and so on. More complexly, psychoanalysis has changed our conception of who we are, leveling us down with universal, unconscious dark forces: we are, none of us, "normal."

The early radicalness of psychoanalysis, its subversive questioning of accepted wisdom about human nature, pushed the directional flow of its concepts, its vector of influence, toward a larger cultural absorption. Over time and with a too easy acceptance, psychoanalysis then became a culturally conservative force itself. As part of the medical establishment and so as an "expert" arbiter of health and disease, psychoanalysis lost its questioning edge; it maintained the status quo; and it often lagged behind crucial social changes and redefinitions (like the women's movement and gay rights). Now, as psychoanalysis is supplanted in the health care industry and thus from the cultural mainstream, it is becoming radicalized once again, and, I submit, is re-finding its distinctive role as a disturber of reductionistic understandings of human motivation. The restless, questioning psychoanalytic attitude becomes a voice needing to be heard: Who are we, and who are we becoming? The vector of influence changes once again.

In my attempt to delineate now what will be the enduring legacy of psychoanalysis, I am pulled to the most basic and defining aspects of our work. My wish is to cut across the different subschools of psychoanalysis and to extract essences that are generally agreed upon. Some of these essences no longer belong solely to psychoanalysis, but have been appropriated by other schools of psychotherapy. No doubt all of these foundational conceptions will continue to evolve in the twenty-first century.

As professionals, we tend first to absorb larger perspectives, attitudes, and points of view—what I would here call "fuzzy memes"—rather than precise concepts. Many of us, for example, identify broadly with a "school" or influential figure long before we have anything like an articulated understanding. We feel ourselves to be Semradian, or Kleinian, or existentialists, or Lacanian, or intersubjectivists, or various combinations and permutations from the extensive menu of perspectives. Theories, then, are grasped first in an imprecise, mutated way, but tend to embody an attitude and a general approach. Only over time do we refine (sometimes) our patchwork structure of ideas to make them more coherent. Like the schools themselves, each of the concepts that I will explore in this section are also points of view, ways of thinking about our work; collectively they characterize a vision.

I'll begin by defining psychoanalytic treatment as a sustained dialogue over time with its goal of increased awareness—and so psychological freedom—all through the medium of an intense immersion in and exploration of the relationship itself. With this general definition in mind, let me now sketch out a short list of ten foundational and evolving psychoanalytic concepts. Taken together, these ideas constitute the psychoanalytic vision that makes possible the definition I have just given.

1. The Psychoanalytic Conception of a Dynamic Unconscious

How astonishing the idea of the unconscious must have been to Freud and Breuer! For doctors to approach the forbidden areas of sexuality and aggression was risky both professionally and personally; there was no sanctioning context. Freud apologized for the odd sound of his case histories; he was venturing into uncharted territory hitherto left to literature and the arts. The whole technical procedure of psychoanalysis was initially designed to reveal the unconscious: the fundamental rule of free association, aided by the introspectiveness induced by the analytic couch, revealed the contours of a dynamic (versus static) unconscious with its play of forces in conflict and its symbolic, associative inner structure. Over time the conception of an unconscious alive with sexuality and aggression has become incorporated into our everyday talk, losing its power to surprise us. Nevertheless, a true, personal apprehension of our unconscious processes (as in psychoanalytic treatment) will startle us still. There are wild and often unwanted forces below the surface of our experience that drive us, constrain us, and that we seldom glimpse head on.

Perhaps more surprising is that the conception of the unconscious is to this day hotly debated in academic circles. And yet the scientific evidence for the existence of unconscious processes is overwhelming. In an astute and sweeping review of the scientific literature, Westen (1999, p. 1094) concludes: "Taken together, the studies . . . lead to a single conclusion: Freud was right in his most central hypothesis, that much of mental life, including thought, feeling, and emotion, is unconscious. The findings of these studies are so robust, and taken from so many unrelated areas of psychological research, that the hypothesis of the existence and importance of unconscious processes is probably as close as any hypothesis in the history of psychology to being able to claim the status of fact." On the basis of these studies, Westen suggests that we refine our notion of *the* unconscious to a more accurate and operational conception of "unconscious processes" underlying affect, motivation, memory, and cognition.

From the perspective of clinical theory (versus Westen's review of the scientific literature), I would assert that each subschool of psychoanalysis has evolved its own conception of unconscious processes that is consistent with its larger vision and assumptions about human nature. We can now speak of the varieties of the unconscious. Most familiar to us is the classical version of the unconscious, which subsumes the structural agencies of the id with its sexual and aggressive drives, aspects of the ego with its defenses, and parts of the superego and its internalizations. In reaction to classical ego psychology, Lacan (1977) famously remarked: "The unconscious is structured like a language." The Lacanian unconscious then is understood in terms of the architecture of language and its complexly interconnected signifiers, which are linked in larger structures, like "rings of a necklace that is a ring in another necklace made of rings" (p. 153). By way of further contrast, a relational or intersubjective unconscious is seen as a co-production of minds engaging each other and belonging at once to both, an unconscious that occurs within the interpersonal field between two (or more) people. The contemporary fascination with "enactments" in the analytic relationship highlights the inevitable and necessary engagement in action and out of awareness of the unconscious processes of both patient and analyst. One contemporary writer (Renik, 1993), for example, has asserted that until such mutual unconscious enactments occur, treatment has not been and cannot be deeply engaged. Self psychology, in keeping with its notions of a supraordinate conception of self, even changed its metaphorical descriptions of the unconscious, suggesting that there can be vertical splits in the psyche that cut through the horizontal layerings of the classical structures of id, ego, and superego.[3]

I am here emphasizing the attempt to operationalize and synthesize competing notions of the unconscious; in clinical practice these abstract ideas allow new observations. Self psychology, for example, has explored novel transference patterns that had only been dimly apprehended before the notions of selfobject or the self's needs for the other to contextualize, maintain, and define itself. New ideas require new metaphors—yet we should be wary of being enthralled by these images. In keeping with its primary assumptions about the unconscious, each school will also have different notions of defense and adaptation, in particular, which aspects of experience most threaten awareness. Kleinians emphasize hostility; Kohutians emphasize hazards to the cohesiveness of self; Mahlerians emphasize separation. In parallel, such basic notions as transference, resistance, repetition compulsion, and character—all of which assume the existence of unconscious processes—are adapted to fit each school's distinctive conceptions of what the unconscious is. Each school will in addition have its own approach to dreams, Freud's "royal road to the unconscious." Nowadays, not only are the roads to the unconscious different for each school, but to some extent, so is the royal city of the unconscious itself.

While distinctive in their differences, the various psychoanalytic schools' versions of the unconscious all have at heart the hidden dimensions of thought, memory, feelings, and motivational forces, that is, the notion of psychological "depth."[4] Psychoanalytic depth, then, captures the multiple layering of mind in experience and memory, and so comes with an inherently complex and tangled notion of structure, causality, and psychological time. Moreover—as this brief survey only hints at—we can speak not only of the depth of individual psyches, but of theoretical depth: The competing voices of the various subschools of psychoanalysis each capture a facet of a mind-boggling unconscious complexity, and together they reflect the inexhaustible profundity of experience itself.

2. The Centrality of Talking and the Symbolic Function

That staid and good doctor Joseph Breuer must have been amused and taken aback when his patient Anna O described their work together as "the talking cure." The surprise of the unconscious went hand in hand with the discovery of the impact of talking. This observation—a medical cure through talking—may seem obvious, but if we gaze at it, it, too, is an astounding and simple fact: It is a distinctive essence of human nature that talking—in and of itself and anterior to all of our theorizing—can be healing. Central to psychoanalysis from the start, talking remains foundational for all psychotherapies. Just why this is the case is the subject of continual debate among the different schools of psychotherapy, each emphasizing different aspects of the talking relationship. So easy to take for granted, talking gets to the heart of human existence, and, sadly, is in danger of getting lost in psychiatric training and in clinical practice. What an irony it is in an age of managed care that it takes a national consumer magazine to study and doc-

ument just how high consumer satisfaction is with *verbal* psychotherapy, and, moreover, that this satisfaction is dose-related (*Consumer
Reports*, 1995; Seligman, 1995).

Talking, of course, is not "simply talking." Talking gets to the
heart of our human nature: we are symbolizers; we crave meaning; we
are bathed in language and thus culture from the moment—and even
before—we are born. And we are in constant dialogue with ourselves
and others as a fundamental feature of our very being-in-the-world.
Talking implicates the symbolic function of mind with its associative
processes and metaphoric structure; the entwined complexity of language, intentionality, will, and knowing; the structure of cognition,
perception, and apprehending the world; our immersion in a social
and cultural matrix. All of these are implicated in everyday talking.
Simple and complex at the same time, talking, then, grounds other essential features of psychoanalysis that we should now tease out. In
talking about talking, for example, we are also talking about
intersubjectivity and relationship.

3. The Relationship as the Medium of Increased Awareness

It is essential and defining for psychoanalysis that *insight emerges
through the relationship—not as a by-product, but through an awareness of the relationship itself*. The relationship is continually probed
and called into question as part of the ongoing, relentless psychoanalytic attempt to understand. Once again, it is hard to be amazed in
retrospect, but Freud's recognition of the clinical centrality of transference became a monumental discovery—it reshaped all subsequent
understandings and remains to this day the distinguishing hallmark of
psychoanalysis (Gill, 1982).

Freud initially underestimated the power of the clinical relationship;
"transference"—the patient's translation of prior relational experience into the analytic one—was for Freud a resistance, an obstacle, to
the rule of free association (that is, saying whatever comes to mind, no
matter how distasteful, embarrassing, or difficult). Patients would not
continue their charge because they had feelings about their doctor
which they did not understand and could not suppress. It was Freud's
characteristic genius to realize that this transference obstacle contained
a great hidden truth and opportunity. By making transference the cor-
nerstone of the clinical investigation, the whole psychoanalytic enterprise moved closer to immediate experience, the here and now. What is
realest of all are the feelings right in the consulting room and so in the

relationship between two people: love and hate, desire and frustration, the clash and encounter of character and style. Whatever doubts we may have about the unreliability of memory, the reporting of events, and the reconstruction of history, the relationship itself with all of its complexity is incontrovertible; it exists here in the moment between us. Of the enduring psychoanalytic concepts that I have included in my top ten list, most have been appropriated by other schools. Though Jungians are, for example, deeply into unconscious phenomena and talking, transference as the medium to awareness is not the central tenet of treatment. *To the extent that a psychotherapy focuses on the relationship as the vehicle to self-awareness, it is psychoanalytic.*

Though the relationship remains central to psychoanalysis as the road to awareness, to many contemporary analysts the classical focus on transference had become too lopsided. Nowadays there is an increasing emphasis on the complexity of the transference-counter-transference interaction, that is, the analyst's contribution to the unfolding of the relationship itself. As a participant observer the analyst cannot rest in a protective stance of scientific detachment: the relationship is a co-creation, an intersubjective phenomenon.

Finally, I can here only hint at the impact of object relations theory on traditional psychoanalytic understanding—the field has moved from a reductionist reading of drive theory toward an appreciation of the overarching and fundamental need for relationship (Greenberg and Mitchell, 1983). Libido, then, aims not for drive discharge per se, but toward human connection. With this, our understanding of the unconscious becomes more complex and enriched; our inner world is populated, as it were, by the powerful internalized presence of those who have most mattered to us. The complexity of the "repetition compulsion," then, further unfolds: We continually recreate fundamental relationships as we (re-)encounter the world.

4. The Centrality of Affective Life

In listening to another, the sheer mass of associative complexity can be overwhelming; a beacon through the unconscious for the psychoanalytic clinician is affective reality. Affect is the thread that weaves through and holds together our psychological associative structure, and affect is uncannily resonant across the interpersonal gap of inevitable differences. It is the extraordinary variations on the basic themes of human affective life—particularly love and hate—that ground experience, empathy, and so analytic engagement. Emotion, that most subjective aspect of experience, becomes—in its very singularity—the shared grounding of existence: I feel, therefore I am.

When one thinks of a dream as strange and confusing, for example, it is the contents of the dream that we disown as unreal, its images and plot that seem particularly bizarre, disorienting, and other-worldly. In contrast, dream feelings seem to be pure colors, realer than real; one's heart beats faster in anxiety, hatred, sexual arousal, or joy. We own dream feelings because they seem to own us. In psychotherapy, then, reality is the reality of our feelings, and it is the unique history and evolution of personal feelings that one attempts to understand as a therapist. Rather than the more abstract notion of "drives," affects are our clinical guideposts. The analytic clinician listens to where the affect is—and where it isn't, that is, the negative space of listening. Listening to another's expression of feelings, one becomes aware of where feelings become painful, problematic, and defended against. Moreover, the power of feelings gives empathic resonance a special validity as a mode of apprehending the inner life of another: We don't just listen to the associative threads of another's experience, we resonate on a deep-feeling level, one that is non-verbal and out of immediate awareness.

Perhaps the most profoundly human emotion is that of desire, which enlivens and drives us and is the source of so much suffering: Desire is never satisfied; it perpetually renews itself; it insists; it is our fate. The subtlety of the oedipal configuration, for example, goes beyond the familiar notion of a triangular relationship among parents and child—the "oedipal" denotes at heart an experience of the frustrating incompleteness of desire. And with this incompleteness comes urgency and, often, grief—that is, the oedipal is about love lost or love that can never be. Indeed, frustrated desire is part of the oedipal structure built into life and so into every psychoanalysis itself.

5. Insight and Awareness as an Essential Goal

From the moment it became "the talking cure," psychoanalysis foregrounded verbal insight. The patient attempts to speak the unspeakable, to put words to the ineffable, to capture that which is necessarily hidden and so not fully conscious. The analyst's words are crafted to crystallize the meaning of the unconscious through "interpretation"; in the spirit of enlightenment, the truth shall set you free. It became specific and essential to the definition of psychoanalysis to focus on insight and awareness.

As the nature of objective truth has been challenged, the notion of insight has evolved to a broader emphasis on awareness (not all awareness is conscious or verbalizable) and the creation of personal meaning. The psychoanalytic goal, then, is not so much after truth or objective reality per se, but toward meaning, that is, how we construct significance out of the intricacies of personal experience. Moreover, it is recognized that many of the healing aspects of analysis can never be made fully aware (for example, transmuting internalizations, corrective emotional experiences, transference cures, selfobject functions—all aspects of the curative role of relationship).[5] Nevertheless, the analytic ideal lies with heightened awareness of one's internal life—including and especially its relational aspects—and the meaning that one constructs.

6. Freedom of Mind as an Ideal—for Both Patient and Analyst

Freud's fundamental rule of free association—to say whatever comes to mind, no matter how difficult, embarrassing, offensive, or trivial it may seem—embodies another ideal, never fully realized, of psychological freedom. Despite the paradoxical aspect of the fundamental rule (a dictum to be free!), it captures a unique relational ideal: "Here in this relationship we have a chance to create a freedom of feeling and expression that does not exist in the everyday world. We will try to suspend judgment." Many psychoanalysts never state the rule directly: free association is paradoxical, non-intellectual, and cannot be met so directly; free association is a state of mind, a goal, a way of being. Like Zen, free associative practice is not linear and logical, but rather a suspension of a certain busyness of thinking and attention. Unlike Zen, the experience is toward increasing engagement of intense affects. I am reminded of the phenomenological attitude of openness and of Keats's "negative capability," an attempt to suspend an "irritable reaching after fact & reason" (Margulies, 1984). The analyst's resonating awareness, or "evenly hovering attention," requires a parallel freedom, an attitude captured famously in Bion's injunction to listen without memory or desire. Of course the ideal of free association teaches us that we are by our very nature both free and not free: We are up against, we confront, our elusive, unconscious existence. Perhaps more than any other result, a successful psychoanalysis catalyzes a steady progress toward a liberation of mind—one feels freed up.

7. The Role of Human Development and Temporality

That childhood experience influences adult experience is a mainstay of psychoanalysis and of common wisdom, despite continual academic debates over nature versus nurture. Clearly genetics, neurobiology, and experience come together in a complexly woven interaction that is now the most exciting uncharted region remaining in science. By its nature and design, the psychoanalytic method will privilege the experiential aspects of growth and development. Psychoanalysis assumes that people have a historical arc of meaning, a trajectory to their existence that begins even before their birth with the history of their parents and their parents' parents.

The various theoretical descriptions of childhood capture each psychoanalytic subschool's mythic narrative of development (the Freudian little Oedipus, the Kleinian devouring infant, the Lacanian mirror gazer, the Winnicottian child-mother, and so on). And, as with cultural myths, these condensed narrative templates are both untrue and yet deeply true in their symbolic sedimentation of universal aspects of meaning. Perhaps these systems are best understood as post hoc constructions based on adult memory and experience and caught through the lens of necessarily narrow and thus incomplete theoretical perspectives. In recent years there has been an explosion of psychoanalytic research based on infant and childhood observation that has challenged and revised our models of development and so opened new possibilities of observing and understanding (for example, Stern, 1985). Nevertheless, in contemporary psychoanalysis there has been an overall de-emphasis on attempting to reconstruct the past per se and a renewed appreciation of the narrative imperative to meaning making: We are always reconstructing and retranscribing memory and experience; we are always rewriting ourselves.[6] One's personal sense of historical trajectory reflects the extraordinary, non-linear complexity of human temporality: Early history (development) is played out in present-day experience, and present experience reconstructs and reinterprets the past. In contemporary psychoanalysis it is well recognized that memories are reconstructions of our past—and, as Freud recognized, they are, at best, memories of memories. Always these memories are being worked and reworked; there is no final significance upon which we can rest. Transference itself then is predictable and yet unstable; it is the ever-changing retranslation of prior experience into repetitive, complex patterns of reactions to the analyst, patterns that define one's style and character in the here and now. Indeed, it is the relative instability of transference that offers the possibility of change within a new relationship.

8. Psychological Causality

It is central to psychoanalysis that not only does childhood relational experience have a causal impact on development and subsequent experience, but that meaning making and insight are as powerful as neurotransmitters. This assertion will seem self-evident and trivial to many readers (at all levels meaning and neurological structure must surely come together as complementary aspects of mind-brain), and yet its essence remains fiercely debated at all levels within academic psychiatry. More subtle are the intertwined recursive aspects of experience and meaning: Experience changes understanding, which then changes experience in a perpetual spiral of ratcheting change. This spiral is the rationale itself for "insight" and awareness: Insight has a causal impact on experience, meaning, and significance; insight is psychologically (and so presumably biologically) mutative. The causal impact of language and meaning—the transformative force implied in insight—delivers psychology into biology. This now brings us to psychoanalytic method, which I will here only gloss.

9. Method and Process as an Approach to Mind

Freud launched more than a series of theories—he came up with a distinctive method to approach the mind. Some of the essential features I have already touched on: free association, the analysis of defense and resistance (and so a focus on character structure and therefore long-term adaptation); the centrality of transference and (these days) countertransference as the vehicle to interpretative activity on the road to insight, increasing awareness and freedom of mind. The compelling experience of psychoanalysis is found in the unfolding of the relationship itself—psychoanalysis is at heart not an intellectual experience but a gripping emotional one between two people struggling to understand.

Given the voluminous literature, a review here of psychoanalytic technique would be at best superficial. But I have other reasons for keeping this section on technique limited: Technique is the most disputed area within the contemporary literature of psychoanalysis, and the intense arguments often reflect the narcissism of small differences.

Moreover, technique changes. What was classical becomes passé; what is considered modern becomes, looking back, merely surfing the trends. Over the past century, psychoanalysis has moved from an "Id psychology" with its focus on revealing unconscious drives and fantasies, to "Ego psychology" with its downplay of the id and an emphasis on ego defenses and adaptations, to an interest in empathy and the development of the self, to a contemporary interest with the relational and intersubjectivity. Nevertheless, one could argue (and I would agree) that clinical psychoanalysis has improved with our century of experience and experimentation; we have moved as clinicians to a more embracing view that must weigh all of these approaches. That is, in addition to controversy, we also have more points of view and more clinical tools to draw upon. While psychiatry has contracted its perspective toward the rapid resolution of symptoms within an "objective descriptive" managed care framework, the scope and methods of psychoanalysis have acquired a rich pluralism.

Data and method go hand in hand: One cannot observe the constellation of stars in the glare of noon, and one cannot seriously explore human experience without having the space and time for regular and deep immersion. Implicit in the psychoanalytic approach are such well-known—and criticized—elements as frequency (often) and duration (long). These elements are neither sacrosanct nor definitive for the psychoanalytic process, and must be adapted to each clinical situation. Nevertheless, they reflect a temporal essence of experience that cannot be compressed or streamlined beyond certain broad limits, despite external demands for efficiency. Grieving, by way of analogy, can be suppressed, but it cannot be speeded up; grieving has its own insistent pace and arc no matter how insightful and aware a person may be. Furthermore, such basic and mundane elements as frequency of sessions, length of treatment, and fees are collectively part of an implied contract of clinicians with their patients and society.

10. The "Social Contract" of Psychoanalysis

Central to any consideration of foundational concepts within psychoanalysis is the nature of the "therapeutic frame," that is, the way the treatment situation is structured in its most concrete and pragmatic aspects, including fees, frequency, duration, confidentiality, and the neutrality of the analyst. Like the frame of a house, the treatment frame is foundational, and when in place it is usually invisible. The frame creates a safe environment for both participants to sustain a deep immersion in the relationship, providing a certain security and freedom which are fundamental to the process. And, as in a democratic society, what seems natural and ordinary is the freedom that we take for granted; only when the frame is called into question do we realize how crucial it really is. For example, though fees meet the personal needs of the therapist, the negotiation of fees itself reflects the fundamental freedom of a contractual agreement, which by its nature dampens the power aspects inherent in any relationship (particularly those that mobilize intense childlike feelings). Both parties are free agents—you can fire your therapist at will. Similarly, in pursuit of freedom of mind the therapeutic relationship by its very nature presupposes and demands privacy.

Initially the "neutrality" of the analyst was recommended as an attitude of non-interference, of not weighing in on any one side of a conflict or an agency of mind. At its heart, then, neutrality reflects the therapist's ongoing struggle to withhold certain judgments and action, a struggle that can only be an ideal. Clearly, though, the clinician can hide behind "neutrality" as a way of distancing, denying, or not getting involved in the relationship. Reflecting the contemporary interest in intersubjectivity and interpersonal reciprocal molding, the nature and meaning of the therapist's neutrality is the subject of hot debate; many consider neutrality a theoretical fiction, and undesirable at that. How, then, do we rethink neutrality? Are we trying to capture a kind of respect? The importance of an attitude of respectful neutrality—an implicit social contract of abstinence on the part of the therapist—keeps the patient's interests as top priority, and paradoxically most comes forward when it is abandoned. Perhaps boundary violations are the most dramatic and awful examples. Less obvious is the gradual cultural erosion of the expectation of the therapist's neutrality. All aspects of the frame—the ability to contract freely, privacy and confidentiality, the priority of the patient's interests and the neutrality of the therapist (which we have always taken for granted)—are under direct threat by larger changes in our society. To the extent that these frame issues are challenged, so too is the nature of our work, and, I would argue, the very nature of our collective conception of who we are and want to be.[7]

What Will Endure?

This chapter has provided an opportunity to reflect on the sweep of our field, to gaze at who we are, where we have been, and where we are going. It now gives me an opportunity to predict what will become of us. Somewhere the Talmud gives wise advice to a would-be prognosticator: If you would predict what will happen in the future, be careful that you don't also say when. Reflecting on developments to come in the twenty-first century gives me, I think, some latitude. Here are my predictions:

The larger context for psychotherapy will itself continue to change dramatically, as psychiatry increasingly becomes a neurological subspecialty. Physicians will simply not be paid by managed care to do long-term psychotherapy, and so the teaching of psychotherapy to psychiatric residents will mostly be lost except as short-term and behavioral medicine adaptations. With this change, academic psychiatry, medical schools, and hospital settings will become largely irrelevant to in-depth learning and doing psychotherapy—even for non-physicians. Psychotherapy training, then, will take place in postgraduate years, primarily through free-standing organizations which will spring up to fill this niche. For psychoanalytic institutes to survive, psychotherapy will be introduced as the core of psychoanalytic training. So far, institutes have only slowly adapted to this reality.

Moreover, psychoanalysis will redefine itself in terms of clinical theory and practice. The traditional separations between psychoanalysis and psychodynamic psychotherapy will be blurred and then will disappear: long-term, individual, insight-oriented psychotherapy will become virtually synonymous with clinical psychoanalysis. Psychoanalysis then will be seen as occurring on a continuum of intensity of use of the therapeutic relationship to enhance awareness. There will, then, be a new de facto definition: The hallmark for psychoanalytic therapies will be relational intensity, with an emphasis on examination of the relationship itself as an avenue to awareness. Psychoanalytic technique will develop around skills needed to titrate an optimal level of intensity of the relationship that necessarily goes with the growth of awareness. Old markers like frequency of sessions will be subsumed under the idea of "intensification."[8] Other markers will disappear over time: Will the psychoanalytic couch itself become a relic as relational approaches dominate? (This would of course entail gains and losses: the couch pushes to a certain dreamy introspectiveness that can be eclipsed by an emphasis on the interpersonal field.) The absorption to psychoanalysis of the techniques and attitudes of different schools of psychotherapy will continue, leading to a broad interpenetration of theory and practice. This will lead to a blunting of the precision and power of more narrow approaches, but also to a more comprehensive, eclectic, and pluralistic view. There will be a more fluid and easy melding of psychoanalytic attitudes with medications, behavioral and cognitive techniques, and combinations with family and couples therapies.

Conclusion: The Psychoanalytic Vision

The best evocations of psychoanalytic experience are not in our professional literature at all, but in works of art that we recognize as immediate, resonant, and deep. James Joyce's *Ulysses* comes to mind, as does Proust's *In Search of Lost Time* and, certainly, almost anything by Shakespeare. It is not so much that these writers pick up familiar psychoanalytic themes—that is inescapable and even, on occasion, interesting. Rather, it is that these works are astonishingly resonant and irreducible, surprising and yet, somehow, inevitable. And, like psychoanalysis itself, they approach the unfolding of meaning within the impossible richness of an individual's experience, at once both unique and universal. Most important, these works absorb the reader into the flow of unfolding insight—and, in so doing, they capture one of the most elusive features of existence. This process itself of continually arriving at meanings that will not settle themselves is what I experience as the essence of "psychoanalytic."

A contemporary novel that comes close to the *feel* of the psychoanalytic process is D. M. Thomas's *The White Hotel*. Not that Thomas had all of his facts right about Freud or analysis, but the very structure of his novel induces something like a psychoanalytic experience in the reader. And Thomas did this by creating from the beginning a haze of unknowing that gradually clears as we gain more information, more experience, and more context. The reader is thrust into different perspectives over time, views that amplify and sharpen one another, repeating with slight variations and so creating an ever-widening context. The beginning of Thomas's novel—composed of obscure dreams and poems—only achieves its haunting meaning at the end with the death of one person caught within a tragic historical moment. The novel forces a circular unfolding of meaning in which the parts illuminate the whole, which then re-contextualizes and illuminates the parts. And from this process of folding back on itself there emerges a resonant depth that one experiences as the Real.

Psychoanalysis, by its very nature, is anti-reductionist, subversive of simple or even straightforward formulations. Any psychoanalytic treatment will defy a re-telling: it will be unrepeatable and singular in its details. Psychoanalytic clinical accounts come up against the sheer complexity of a human life and another person's attempt to understand it. Moreover, psychoanalytic experience, by its very nature, has a certain wildness to it, a surprising element, an unknown quality, that is only vaguely related to something statistical in that a certain patterning of experience emerges over time. The glory of psychoanalysis *is* this very complexity, resonance, and depth that make it so hard to describe, much less explain. Rather than reduce this complexity to an "as if scientific" discourse, we should look at it and describe it on its very own terms.

One hundred years after *The Interpretation of Dreams*, the psychoanalytic vision is now absorbing and embracing the perspectives of the other major schools of psychiatry. This still-evolving vision now encompasses the complex and conflicting meanings of our biological givenness, our unconscious nature, our interpersonal matrix, and the anxiety of our existential situation of awareness, freedom, and choice. It is not really a surprise that Harold Bloom in his *Western Canon* (1994) links Freud with Joyce, Proust, and Kafka as the four most influential writers of the twentieth century. These authors profoundly affected our Western culture and so shaped our understanding of humanity. Their ideas, though, no longer belong to them, but have mutated and evolved. The psychoanalytic vision now outstrips Freud's thinking, but like Proust, Joyce, and Kafka, Freud passed on to us his memes. Finally, as the economics of our time threaten to level down our clinical work to a breathtakingly mindless, thoughtless, and mechanized approach to humanity, the irony is that the human and intellectual aspects of our larger field are as engaging and promising as ever. And here psychoanalysis in its expanding vision embraces Havens's wish for a pluralistic approach to human understanding.

Notes

1. Of course, my now writing about the meme is doing just that: The meme as a concept is a meme! (I'm intellectually sneezing on you.) The limits of Darwinism have become part of a furious exchange in academia, and I am not endorsing Dawkins's or Dennett's overall positions or politics. See

Gould's critique (6/12/97; 6/26/97) and his weighing in on an infectious—versus a Darwinian—model of the sociology of ideas.

2. The biological domain, too, is now receiving intense interest among psychoanalysts, and not only for pragmatic reasons (that is, the concomitant uses of psychopharmacology) but for the broader theoretical and heuristic goals of integrating contemporary models of brain, mind, and the organization of experience. For example, Edelman's (1989, 1992) work on Neural Darwinism has been central to Modell's (1990) explorations of "retranscription" in the continual reworking of memory and experience. Vaughan (1997) has written an appealing popular account of a contemporary integration of biology, cognitive science, child development, and psychoanalytic theory.

3. I have become convinced that much of what we mean by the unconscious is that which can only emerge over time and with a retrospective gaze at our behavior, that is, a temporal or process definition of unconscious (Margulies, forthcoming). This would be in keeping with Freud's notion of *Nachträglichkeit* or "deferred action" (see also Laplanche and Pontilis, 1973, and Modell, 1990).

4. The Lacanian conception of "depth" has a twist to it: The unconscious is often "surface" but is simply, irresistibly, missed, like Poe's "The Purloined Letter" in which a crucial document is cleverly hidden away in the most obvious place (Miller, 1991). We are then saturated (I am now using a different metaphor) with the unconscious all of the time.

5. Of course, there are aspects of self that necessarily should remain to oneself, and are not to be violated or intruded upon.

6. The Freudian notion of *Nachträglichkeit* (see above), which deals with the continual revision of memory and the instability of meaning, here seems strikingly contemporary and postmodern.

7. Here organized psychoanalysis has played—and will, necessarily, continue to play—a key role in defending the ideals of the psychotherapeutic frame through influencing legal and legislative processes.

8. Havens (personal communication) feels that it is precisely this focus on intensity that can be problematic in psychoanalysis, not only for the patient, but for the clinician as well. Not all therapeutic work is best thought of along such a continuum. I would largely agree; my emphasis would remain on the optimal level that is helpful. Surely there are other helpful approaches that downplay such intensity.

References

Bloom, H. (1994). *The Western Canon: The Books and School of the Ages.* New York: Riverhead Books.

Brenner, C. (1973). *An Elementary Textbook of Psychoanalysis,* revised edition. New York: International Universities Press.

Brenner, C. (1982). *The Mind in Conflict.* New York: International Universities Press.

Consumer Reports. (1995). Mental health: Does therapy help? November 1995, pp. 734–739.

Cook, S. (1997). *Inf(l)ections: Cyberspace & Critical Theory.* Internet address: *http://dynaweb.stg.brown.edu/projects/hypertext/landow/cpace/ infotech/cook/screamingmeme.html.* Viewed Sept 6, 1997.

Dawkins, R. (1989). *The Selfish Gene.* Oxford: Oxford University Press.

Dennett, D. C. (1991). *Consciousness Explained.* Boston: Little, Brown.

Edelman, G. M. (1989). *The Remembered Present: A Biological Theory of Consciousness.* New York: Basic Books.

Edelman, G. M. (1992). *Bright Air, Brilliant Fire: On the Matter of Mind.* New York: Basic Books.

Ellenberger, H. F. (1958). A clinical introduction to psychiatric phenomenology and existential analysis. In R. May, E. Angel, and H. F. Ellenberger (Eds.), *Existence.* New York: Simon and Schuster.

Freud, S., and Breuer, J. (1893). Studies on hysteria. *Standard Edition* 2. New York: Norton, 1955.

Freud, S. (1900). The interpretation of dreams. *Standard Edition* 4, 5. New York: Norton, 1953.

Freud, S. (1912). Recommendations to physicians practicing psycho-analysis. *Standard Edition* 12: 109–120. New York: Norton, 1958.

Freud, S. (1915). The unconscious. *Standard Edition* 14: 161–208. New York: Norton, 1957.

Freud, S. (1923). The ego and the id. *Standard Edition* 19: 1–66. New York: Norton, 1961.

Gill, M. (1982). *Analysis of Transference,* vol. 1. New York: International Universities Press.

Gould, S. J. (6/12/97). Darwinian fundamentalism. *The New York Review of Books,* 44: 34–37.

Gould, S. J. (6/26/97). Evolution: The pleasures of pluralism. *The New York Review of Books,* 44.

Greenberg, J., and Mitchell, S. (1983). *Object Relations in Psychoanalytic Theory.* Cambridge, Mass.: Harvard University Press.

Havens, L. L. (1973). *Approaches to the Mind: Movement of the Psychiatric Schools from Sects toward Science.* Boston: Little, Brown.

Havens, L. L. (1974). The existential use of the self. *American Journal of Psychiatry,* 131: 1–10.

Havens, L. L. (1976). *Participant Observation.* New York: Jason Aronson.

Hoffman, I. Z. (1991). Discussion: Toward a social-constructivist view of the psychoanalytic situation. *Psychoanalytic Dialogues,* 1: 74–105.

Kohut, H. (1977). *The Restoration of the Self.* New York: International Universities Press.

Kohut, H. (1984). *How Does Analysis Cure?* Chicago: University of Chicago Press.

Lacan, J. (1977). *Ecrits: A Selection.* (A. Sheridan, Trans.) New York: W. W. Norton.

Laplanche, J., and Pontalis, J.-B. (1973). *The Language of Psycho–Analysis.* (D. Nicholson–Smith, Trans.) New York: W. W. Norton.

Margulies, A. (1989). *The Empathic Imagination.* New York: Norton.

Margulies, A. (In progress.) *The Infinite Conversation.*

Margulies, A., and Havens, L. (1981). The initial encounter: What to do first? *American Journal of Psychiatry,* 138: 421–428.

May, R. (1958). Contributions of existential psychotherapy. In R. May, E. Angel, and H. F. Ellenberger (Eds.), *Existence.* New York: Simon and Schuster.

May, R. (1969). The emergence of existential psychology. In R. May (Ed.), *Existential Psychology.* New York: Random House.

May, R., Angel, E., and Ellenberger, H. F., Eds. (1958). *Existence.* New York: Simon and Schuster.

Miller, J.-A. (1991). *The Seminar of Jacques Lacan: Book II, The Ego in Freud's Theory and in the Technique of Psychoanalysis, 1954–1955.* (S. Tomaselli, Trans.) New York: Norton.

Mitchell, S. A. (1988). *Relational Concepts in Psychoanalysis.* Cambridge, Mass.: Harvard University Press.

Modell, A. (1990). *Other Times, Other Realities: Toward a Theory of Psychoanalytic Treatment.* Cambridge, Mass.: Harvard University Press.

Pinker, S. (1994). *The Language Instinct.* New York: HarperPerennial.

Renik, O. (1993). Countertransference enactment and the psychoanalytic process. In *Psychic Structure and Psychic Change: Essays in Honor of Robert S. Wallerstein, M.D.,* ed. M. J. Horowitz, O. F. Kernberg, and E. M. Weinshel. Madison: International Universities Press, pp. 137–160.

Seligman, M. E. (1995). The effectiveness of psychotherapy: The *Consumer Reports* Study. *American Psychologist,* 50: 965–974.

Stern, D. (1985). *The Interpersonal World of the Infant.* New York: Basic Books.

Sullivan, H. S. (1953). *The Interpersonal Theory of Psychiatry.* New York: Norton.

Sullivan, H. S. (1954). *The Psychiatric Interview.* New York: Norton.

Vaughan, S. C. (1997). *The Talking Cure: The Science Behind Psychotherapy.* New York: Grosset/Putnam.

Westen, D. (1999). The scientific status of unconscious processes: Is Freud really dead? *Journal of the American Psychoanalytic Association,* 47: 1061–1106.

Epilogue

Leston Havens

In the foregoing chapters, Margulies has referred to a "real" element in the patient and in relationships, Robins and Koons to a "radical genuineness," Griswold to the need for "authentic interventions." Plank finds a person in the patient when everything seems to conspire against it. Gustafson wants us to find a person amidst the great human dilemmas. What is this person in the patient? We take for granted that every physical disorder will be seen against a baseline of normal, healthy findings. The bulk of such findings in even the sickest patients are in fact normal, so the person, the host, the underlying healthy physiology, is clearly recognized. How are we to recognize *psychological* health and strength, particularly in the face of manifest and serious disorders?

Winnicott wrote of "spontaneous gestures" that he thought were indicative of "true self."[1] These emerged, he suggested, when mothers could be with their children and still leave the children alone. Then the child was able to be itself. Kohut wrote of selfhood developing when "mirrored" and "idealized,"[2] when the individual felt that his or her deepest interests were over and over reflected back and reinforced by a respected person. Rogers thought the same problem required an "unconditional positive regard."[3] But how are we to recognize spontaneous gestures, true self, and selfhood?

Therapists speak of knowing when there is "someone home."

Asked for details, they describe their own feelings in the presence of the patients, or the emergence of liveliness and assertiveness in the patient. More impressive is evidence of reflectiveness and self-possession, pointing, for example, to what is "one's own," a cherished desire, value, or ambition.[4] Still others depend on what Bowen called self-differentiation.[5] The central test is the patient's ability to withstand social pressures, especially from the family of birth, so that the patient doesn't feel reduced or unnatural. Many patients, going back to their families of birth, experience being twisted out of shape, by old demands felt anew.

A further test is the use of empathic statements,[6] that is, remarks that put before the patients what they may feel or want. We have encountered many examples of this in the preceding chapters. But such statements are inevitably approximations of what the other experiences, so that what comes spontaneously back from the patient *tests* the accuracy of the empathic remarks, and encourages fresh attempts to get closer to where the other is. Thus we can begin to sense what the patients experience and may want to make their own.

These are beginnings. But the issue remains a pressing one. Without truly effective measures, the recognition of disease must be guesswork because concepts of disease remain without dependable limits. It is also true that lacking such measures we cannot know if we have recognized the person in the patient, and therefore cannot know if our relationship is with the person or with the disease, which may undermine our work as well as the patient. So many patients are referred to as bipolar or borderline or schizophrenic, as if that's all they were.

Meanwhile, we search for the person in the patient because that person is our ally in the work to be done. We begin to recognize that person by his or her interests, talents, ambitions, values, and common humanness. This last we do not so much identify as identify with— the capacities to love and hate, fear and hope, join and separate, the infinite variations on the common human ground. It is our sympathy with and confidence in this person that underpins our support of the work, just as the surgeon decides that the patient's strength of heart and lungs is what makes possible the surgery. Many times the therapist, like the surgeon, must take responsibility for the outcome because a despairing patient cannot believe there is a different future to be gained. Therapists carry the hope in such alliances until the patient sees what may result. Hence the alliance is a kind of believing in and hoping for, by workers who sense the real person in the patient.

An earlier generation will protest that this is suggestion, long a forbidden activity, taking the work away from the central task of exploration. Yet it is not suggestion so much as *recognition,* by the sensible acknowledgment of the person whom the therapist may in fact have found.

The goal of this relationship, then, is not only the excavation of the past. It is as much the construction of a future, a future that can be believed in. This involves the identification not only of syndromes and complexes but also of interests and values, of the person in the patient. As a result, therapists have someone to ally with. What is more, by the construction of the patient's future, therapists gain new elements in their own futures, for what the patient accomplishes becomes in some measure part of the history of the therapist. All of us who have long done this work can look back at those happy times when the patient's gain has also been, in part, our own. Thereby an extraordinary joy enters the work, for both parties, through this making of lives. Can there be better work to do in the world?

Notes

1. Winnicott, D. W. *The Maturational Processes and the Facilitating Environment.* New York: International Universities Press, 1965.
2. Kohut, H. *The Restoration of the Self.* New York: International Universities Press, 1977.
3. Rogers, C. *On Becoming a Person.* Boston: Houghton Mifflin, 1961.
4. Mann, D. *A Simple Theory of the Self.* New York: Norton, 1994.
5. Bowen, M. *Family Therapy in Clinical Practice.* New York: Aronson, 1978.
6. Havens, L. *Making Contact.* Cambridge, Mass.: Harvard University Press, 1986.

Acknowledgments
Name Index
Subject Index

Acknowledgments

This book was completed during a period of great turmoil in American health care. It is fitting to acknowledge a number of people who, behind the scenes, made the clinical work possible for me over the past six years: Ray Brien, Chris Doyle, Marge Cohan, Eileen Myers, Doug Spoehr, Tom Romeo, Rob Cella, Ruth Blodgett, and Dave Phelps. Without their daily backing, it would be impossible to carry out our clinical mission of delivering care to all the people in the community who need it. Second, I would like to thank Paul Appelbaum, chairman of my department at the University of Massachusetts Medical School, for his consistent support and encouragement. I am also indebted to my many teachers and colleagues at the Cambridge Hospital, Austen Riggs Center, and McLean Hospital where I have been privileged to learn and practice psychiatry. I am especially appreciative of the day-to-day "curbside" (and more formal) consults with the excellent psychiatrists and clinicians in our Joint Venture who discuss their cases with me, and who, through this process, greatly extend my understanding. I thank my patients for allowing me to share in their important struggles and for teaching me on a regular basis. Alyce Kaplan deserves special thanks for her teamwork as an RNCS and also for her thoughtful review and helpful comments on the Introduction and Chapter 2. Special thanks also go to Denise Rose and Mary Litano for strategic moments of support in the preparation of the manuscript. We are most appreciative of the work of Elizabeth Knoll, Mary Ellen Geer, and Kirsten Giebutowski at Harvard University Press, who have represented the highest levels of professional excellence and cordiality. The authors themselves have made extraordinary contributions to the care of their patients and to our understanding of the essential elements of psychotherapy. I have been especially fortunate to work with Les Havens over the years: his mentoring, intelligence, and friendship are treasured. Finally, I would like to thank Susan, Emily, and Becky for their sense of humor and playful support during the writing and editing of this book. They are the source that kept the river flowing.

Alex N. Sabo
Richmond, Massachusetts

The most rewarding part of my almost half a century at Harvard has been the medical students, residents, and staff that I have known at the Massachusetts Mental Health Center and for the last twenty years at the Cambridge Hospital. John O'Brien, the astonishing leader of the Cambridge Hospital, deserves special mention. They all have been the teachers of my continuing education, supplying the viewpoints, observations, and often the books of this priceless experience. Happily, some are among the authors of these chapters. I also want to thank Susan Miller-Havens for her steady encouragement of this enterprise, and Alex Sabo for his leaderly comradeship.

Leston Havens
Cambridge, Massachusetts

Name Index

Adler, Gerald, 165–167, 168, 169, 174
Alexander, F., 218, 225
Allen, T. F. H., 231, 232
Anderson, Sherwood, 215
Angel, E., 296
Auden, W. H., 292
Auerbach, Red, 63

Balint, Michael, 218, 219
Bateson, G., 222
Beck, Aaron, 221
Beck, J. C., 136, 137
Beck, J. S., 221
Bergson, H., 215, 233
Binstock, W. A., 216, 218
Binswanger, L., 216, 229
Bion, W. R., 173, 306
Blake, William, 11, 166
Bloom, Harold, 292, 313
Bollas, Christopher, 184, 200
Boszormenyi-Nagy, Ivan, 90
Bowen, M., 318
Bowlby, John, 169, 171, 175
Brenner, Charles, 297
Breuer, Joseph, 214, 218, 222, 302
Brown, Margaret Wise, 84
Buie, Daniel, 132, 165–167, 168, 169, 174

Cassirer, Ernest, 154, 203
Cirillo. S., 218, 219, 230
Coles, Robert, 183
Cook, S., 294

Davanloo, H., 216
Dawkins, Richard, 293
Dennett, Daniel, 293
De Shazer, S., 218

Ellenberger, H. F., 296
Epston, D., 221
Erickson, Milton H., 218
Erikson, Erik, 229

Fisch, R., 218
Frank, Jerome, 39
Freire, P., 223, 224
French, T. M., 218, 225
Freud, Anna, 183
Freud, Sigmund, 28, 30, 65, 168, 214, 216, 217, 218, 222, 229, 292–293, 300, 303

Gill, Merton, 303
Greenberg, J., 298, 304
Griswold, Todd, 67, 317

Subject Index

Abuse: borderline personality disorder and, 167, 174–175; therapist as witness, 213; working with, 213. *See also* Chronic trauma; Trauma
Acceptance, 18–19
Achilles, 169
Active-passivity, 249
Adrenocorticotropic hormone (ACTH), 170
Affective originality, 200
Affective reality: psychoanalysis and, 304–305
Aggressiveness: emergency psychotherapy and, 133–134; practical, 158–159
Agoraphobia, 276
Aikido, 251
Alcoholics Anonymous, 105
Alcoholism, 221
Ambivalence: in suicidal patients, 133
American pragmatism, 215
Anger, 68; family violence and, 97; in psychiatric emergencies, 129; psychosis and, 151–152; borderline disorder and, 165–166, 172–175, 177–178; in valued relationships, 175
Angry All the Time (Potter-Efron), 103
Antisocial behavior: poverty and, 81; underlying logic of, 221

Anxiety: as appropriate and healthful, 70; brief psychotherapy on, 216; exposure procedures and, 259
Approaches to the Mind (Havens), 295
Assumptions: avoiding in borderline therapy, 176–177
Attachment figures, 171
Autism: psychosis and, 152, 159–160
Automatic disobedience, 154
Automatic obedience, 153–154, 160–161
Autonomy: psychosis and, 155–156
"Awakenings," 161–162
Awareness: in psychoanalysis, 305–306

Basilar artery migraine, 217–218
Batterers. *See* Group therapy for violent men; Violent men
Behavioral physiology, 169–170
Behavioral skills training: in dialectical behavior therapy, 240, 244, 254–255
Behavior analysis: in dialectical behavior therapy, 242, 253–254
Behaviorism, 221–224
Behavior therapy: in dialectical behavior therapy, 238, 241–242; exposure procedures and, 259
Biosocial theory, 239–241, 263–264
Bipolar disorder, 48, 175

Media: contemporary poverty and, 75–76
Medical exams: the chronically trauma-
tized and, 281
Medication: changing knowledge about,
34–35; dilemmas with, 42–46;
polypharmacy, 47–48. *See also*
Psychopharmacology;
Psychopharmacotherapy
Megalomania, 221
Memes, 293–294
Memory: chronic trauma and, 275–277;
nonlinear complexity of, 307
Metaphor: dream as, 229; dialectical
behavior therapy and, 250–251
Middle class life, 82–83
Migraines: brief psychotherapy and, 217–
218
Modeling, 241
Monomania, 27
Morphine, 169–170
Motivation: psychopharmacology and,
44–46; women in poverty and, 84–85

Naloxone, 170
Narcotics Anonymous, 105
Need to please, 24–25
Neutrality: in psychoanalysis, 310
Non-suaveness, 151. *See also* Suaveness
Not knowing, 21, 34–36
Nurses. *See* Clinical nurse specialists

Objective-descriptive psychiatry, 295, 297
Object relations theory, 304
Obsessions, 221
Obsessive-compulsive disorder, 56, 57
Odor, 188
Oedipal configurations, 305
Operant conditioning, 241–242
Opiate receptors, 170
Optimal disillusionments, 166
Outpatient therapy: emergency service
clinicians and, 138–141
Overcorrection, 257
Overdoses: emergency psychotherapy and,
128, 143–144
Oxytocin, 57–58, 170

Panic disorder, 56
Paradoxes: entering, 250
Paranoia: emergency psychotherapy and,
142–143

Parasuicidal behavior: dialectical behavior
therapy on, 247
Parent-child relationship: child affective
originality and, 200, 207n13
Passivity: psychotic patients and, 158–159
Perfectionism: borderline personality dis-
order and, 241
Personal self-disclosure, 260–261
Physical abuse: borderline personality dis-
order and, 167; therapist as witness,
213
"Physician-extender" strategies, 7–8
Placebo effects, 6
Pleasing, need to be, 24–25
Poetry: psychosis and, 154
Polarization, 212
Political torture, 270–271
Polypharmacy, 47–48
Positron emission tomography (PET), 57
Post-traumatic stress disorder (PTSD):
complex, 167, 269; brief psychotherapy
and, case study example, 219–220;
exposure procedures and, 259; chronic
trauma and, 268, 269
Poverty: in housing projects, case study
setting, 71–72; welfare system and, 72,
77–78; conditions and characteristics of,
74–75; media images and, 75–76; psychological impact of, 75–78; isolation
and, 76–77; defenses and adaptations
to, 78–83; antisocial behavior and, 81;
comparisons with middle-class life, 82–
83. *See also* Women in poverty
Power and Control Wheel, 102
Pragmatism, 215
Praise: in dialectical behavior therapy, 256
Preoccupations, 27–28
Primary care physicians: working with
psychopharmacologists, 53–54
Problem saturation, 223–224
Problem-solving: borderline personality
disorder and, 241, 249; in dialectical
behavior therapy, 253, 254–260
Progress: notions of, 293–294
Projection, 26; poverty and, 79–80;
avoiding in borderline therapy, 176–177
Projective identification, 164–165
Prostitution, 75
Provocative self-destructiveness, 143–144
Prozac, 43–44
Psychiatric disorders: underlying logic of,
221

Psychiatric emergency services, 121. *See also* Emergency psychotherapy

Psychiatry: managed care industry and, 6–9; clinical nurse specialists and, 7–10, 52–53; psychopharmacology and, 56; schools of, 295–296; contemporary trends in, 297–298

Psychoanalysis: psychotherapy and, 213, 311; Freud and, 292; defined, 295, 300; contemporary trends in, 297–298; pluralism in, 297–298, 313; cultural legacy of, 298–299; radicalness of, 299; principal conceptions in, 299–310; the dynamic unconscious and, 300–302; depth, 302; talking and, 302–303; symbolic function of mind and, 303; therapeutic relationship and, 303–304, 308; affective reality and, 304–305; insight and awareness in, 305–306; freedom of mind and, 306; human development and temporality in, 307–308; transference instability and, 307–308; psychological causality and, 308; technique and, 308–309; fees and, 309, 310; frequency and duration of, 309; social contract of, 309–310; neutrality in, 310; future of, 311–312; evocations in literature, 312; nature of, 312–313

Psychoanalytic depth, 302

Psychological abuse, 213

Psychological analgesics, 18–19, 38–39

Psychological causality, 308

Psychological freedom, 30, 306

Psychological health, 317–318

Psychopharmacologists: psychotherapists and, 51–52; clinical nurse specialists and, 52–53; primary care physician and, 53–54

Psychopharmacology: dialectic between knowing and not knowing, 34–36; therapeutic relationship and, 36–42, 58; externalization and, 38–39; record keeping and, 42; treatment options and, 42–44; dilemmas in, 42–48; patient motivation and, 44–46; psychotherapy and, 45–47, 48–51; split treatment model, 46–47, 48, 49–50, 51–52, 54–56; polypharmacy issues, 47–48; recent history of, 56; problems in, 56–57; medical technology developments and, 57; future of, 57–58; brief psychotherapy and, 221

Psychopharmacotherapy: therapeutic relationship and, 5–6; managed care industry and, 6; psychosis and, 154, 155, 161–162

Psychosis/Psychotic patients: therapeutic relationship and, 67–68, 150–151, 154–162; emergency psychotherapy and, 129–130; meanings of term, 149–150; social stigmatization and, 150, 155; non-suaveness and, 151; vulnerability and openness of, 151, 152; rage and, 151–152, 158–159; rigidity and, 151–152; autism and, 152, 159–160; schizoid states and, 152; social relationships and, 152; loss of meaning and, 153; command automatism and, 153–154, 160–161; loss of control and, 153–154; medications and, 154, 155, 161–162; poetry and, 154; providing sympathetic concern for, 154; validating sensitivity of, 154–155; interventions for, 154–161; assisting autonomy and self-consciousness in, 155–156; assisting suaveness in, 156–158; long-term goals for, 156–161; confidence and, 158; leaning against fury or passivity in, 158–159; self-respect and, 160; work situations and, 160–161; mania and, 161; personal entitlement and, 161; personal interest and, 161; "awakenings" in, 161–162

Psychotherapists: tensions and dilemmas in psychological work, 29–33; suicidal behavior of patients and, 30; providing support without constriction, 30–32; responsibility and, 32; working with psychopharmacologists, 51–52; attitudes and capacities required of, 63–64; self-disclosure and, 65; recognizing the person in the patient, 68–70, 317–319; recognizing and acknowledging dilemmas, 69; anxiety in the therapeutic relationship and, 70; flexibility and, 73–74; treatment of women in poverty, 83–90; issues in group therapy for violent men, 107–110, 112; support networks and, 191–192; integrative experiences and, 206–207n9; as witnesses, 213; dialectics and, 243. *See also* Dialectical behavior therapists; Emergency service clinicians

Psychotherapy: pluralistic approach to, 1,